CAMBRIDGE COMPANIONS TO LITERATURE

The Cambridge Companion to Greek Tragedy
edited by P. E. Easterling

The Cambridge Companion to Old English Literature
edited by Malcolm Godden and Michael Lapidge

The Cambridge Companion to Medieval Romance
edited by Roberta L. Kreuger

The Cambridge Companion to Medieval English Theatre
edited by Richard Beadle

The Cambridge Companion to English Renaissance Drama
edited by A. R. Braunmuller and Michael Hattaway

The Cambridge Companion to Renaissance Humanism
edited by Jill Kraye

The Cambridge Companion to English Poetry, Donne to Marvell
edited by Thomas N. Corns

The Cambridge Companion to English Literature, 1500–1600
edited by Arthur F. Kinney

The Cambridge Companion to English Literature, 1650–1740
edited by Steven N. Zwicker

The Cambridge Companion to Writing of the English Revolution
edited by N. H. Keeble

The Cambridge Companion to English Restoration Theatre
edited by Deborah C. Payne Fisk

The Cambridge Companion to British Romanticism
edited by Stuart Curran

The Cambridge Companion to Eighteenth-Century Poetry
edited by John Sitter

The Cambridge Companion to the Eighteenth-Century Novel
edited by John Richetti

The Cambridge Companion to Victorian Poetry
edited by Joseph Bristow

The Cambridge Companion to the Victorian Novel
edited by Deirdre David

The Cambridge Companion to American Realism and Naturalism
edited by Donald Pizer

The Cambridge Companion to Nineteenth-Century American Women's Writing
edited by Dale M. Bauer and Philip Gould

The Cambridge Companion to the Classic Russian Novel
edited by Malcolm V. Jones and Robin Feuer Miller

The Cambridge Companion to the French Novel: from 1800 to the present
edited by Timothy Unwin

The Cambridge Companion to Modernism
edited by Michael Levenson

The Cambridge Companion to Australian Literature
edited by Elizabeth Webby

The Cambridge Companion to American Women Playwrights
edited by Brenda Murphy

The Cambridge Companion to Modern British Women Playwrights
edited by Elaine Aston and Janelle Reinelt

The Cambridge Companion to Virgil
edited by Charles Martindale

The Cambridge Companion to Ovid
edited by Philip Hardie

The Cambridge Companion to Dante
edited by Rachel Jacoff

The Cambridge Companion to Goethe
edited by Lesley Sharpe

The Cambridge Companion to Proust
edited by Richard Bales

The Cambridge Companion to Thomas Mann
edited by Ritchie Robertson

The Cambridge Companion to Chekhov
edited by Vera Gottlieb and Paul Allain

The Cambridge Companion to Ibsen
edited by James McFarlane

The Cambridge Companion to Brecht
edited by Peter Thomson and Glendyr Sacks

The Cambridge Chaucer Companion
edited by Piero Boitani and Jill Mann

The Cambridge Companion to Shakespeare
edited by Margareta de Grazia and Stanley Wells

The Cambridge Companion to Shakespeare on Film
edited by Russell Jackson

The Cambridge Companion to Shakespeare Comedy
edited by Alexander Leggatt

CAMBRIDGE COMPANIONS TO CULTURE

THE CAMBRIDGE
COMPANION TO
GOETHE

EDITED BY
LESLEY SHARPE

CAMBRIDGE
UNIVERSITY PRESS

CAMBRIDGE UNIVERSITY PRESS
Cambridge, New York, Melbourne, Madrid, Cape Town, Singapore, São Paulo

Cambridge University Press
The Edinburgh Building, Cambridge CB2 2RU, UK

Published in the United States of America by Cambridge University Press, New York

www.cambridge.org
Information on this title: www.cambridge.org/9780521662116

First published 2002

A catalogue record for this publication is available from the British Library

Library of Congress Cataloguing in Publication data

The Cambridge companion to Goethe / edited by Lesley Sharpe.
p. cm.
Includes bibliographical references and index.
ISBN 0-521-66211-7 – ISBN 0-521-66560-4 (pbk.)
1. Goethe, Johann Wolfgang von, 1749-1832 – Criticism and
interpretation – Handbooks, manuals, etc. I. Sharpe, Lesley.
PT2168 .C36 2002
831′.6 – dc21   2001043654

ISBN-13 978-0-521-66211-6 hardback
ISBN-10 0-521-66211-7 hardback

ISBN-13 978-0-521-66560-5 paperback
ISBN-10 0-521-66560-4 paperback

Transferred to digital printing 2006

CONTENTS

CONTENTS

CONTRIBUTORS

PROFESSOR THOMAS P. SAINE, University of California, Irvine

PROFESSOR NICHOLAS SAUL, University of Liverpool

DR JOHN R. WILLIAMS, University of St Andrews (rtd)

PROFESSOR DAVID V. PUGH, Queen's University, Canada

PROFESSOR JANE K. BROWN, University of Washington, Seattle

PROFESSOR T. J. REED, The Queen's College, Oxford

PROFESSOR LESLEY SHARPE, University of Bristol

PROFESSOR MARTIN SWALES, University College London

PROFESSOR DENNIS F. MAHONEY, University of Vermont

DR DANIEL STEUER, University of Sussex

PROFESSOR BARBARA BECKER-CANTARINO, Ohio State University

PROFESSOR BEATE ALLERT, Purdue University

PROFESSOR W. DANIEL WILSON, University of California, Berkeley

PROFESSOR H. B. NISBET, Sidney Sussex College, Cambridge

PROFESSOR GERHART HOFFMEISTER, University of California, Santa Barbara

ACKNOWLEDGEMENTS

To the distinguished contributors to this volume I owe a sincere debt of thanks for their prompt work, flexibility and commitment to this project. My thanks go also to the School of Modern Languages at the University of Exeter for allowing me a grant to cover editorial assistance, and to Lizzie Catling for providing that assistance so conscientiously. Thanks also to James Baughan for his excellent work on the index.

ABBREVIATIONS

In order to make this volume accessible to those with no German, quotations in the main text have been given in English; unless otherwise indicated, translations are the chapter authors' own. Where Goethe quotations are not included for the sake of their literary qualities, they are usually given in translation only but with a reference to one of the standard editions (listed below) so that the original can easily be found. Translations are not given in the short section in Chapter Three on Goethe's poetic metres because the discussion presupposes some knowledge of German. The guide to further reading includes titles in English and German.

EDITIONS OF GOETHE'S WORKS AND LETTERS:

FA   *Johann Wolfgang Goethe. Sämtliche Werke. Briefe, Tagebücher und Gespräche.* Ed. by Hendrik Birus and others. Two divisions, 40 vols. Frankfurt am Main: Deutscher Klassiker Verlag, 1987–99.

HA   *Goethes Werke. Hamburger Ausgabe.* Ed. by Erich Trunz. 14 vols. Hamburg: Wegner, 1948. (This edition has been revised and reprinted numerous times, and it is sometimes necessary to specify which impression is referred to, e.g. HA⁴.)

HAB   *Goethes Briefe. Hamburger Ausgabe.* Ed. by Karl Robert Mandelkow. 4 vols. Hamburg: Wegner, 1965–67.

LA   *Goethe. Die Schriften zur Naturwissenschaft. Vollständige mit Erläuterungen versehene Ausgabe im Auftrage der Deutschen Akademie der Naturforscher. Leopoldina.* Begun by Lothar Wolf and Wilhelm Troll. Ed. by Dorothea Kuhn and Wolf von Engelhardt. Two divisions, 28– vols. Weimar: Böhlau, 1947–.

MA   *Johann Wolfgang Goethe. Sämtliche Werke nach Epochen seines Schaffens.* Münchner Ausgabe. Ed. by Karl Richter in collaboration with Herbert G. Göpfert and others. 21 vols. in 30. Munich: Hanser, 1985–99.

WA   *Goethes Werke. Herausgegeben im Auftrag der Großherzogin Sophie von Sachsen.* Four divisions, 143 vols. Weimar: Böhlau, 1887–1919.

OTHER FREQUENTLY CITED WORKS:

Boyle   Nicholas Boyle. *Goethe. The Poet and the Age.* Vol I: *The Poetry of Desire*; Vol. II: *Revolution and Renunciation 1790–1803.* Oxford: Oxford University Press, 1991, 2000.

Eckermann Johann Peter Eckermann's collection of conversations, *Gespräche mit Goethe in den letzten Jahren seines Lebens.* As this work exists in numerous editions, quotations are identified by the date of the conversation; a volume number has been indicated only in the case of Eckermann III, as it begins a new sequence.

Gespräche *Goethes Gespräche. Eine Sammlung zeitgenößischer Berichte aus seinem Umgang auf Grund der Ausgabe und des Nachlasses von Flodoard Freiherrn von Biedermann, ergänzt und hg. von Wolfgang Herwig.* 5 vols. Zurich and Stuttgart: Artemis, 1965–87.

Grumach *Goethe. Begegnungen und Gespräche.* Ed. by Ernst Grumach and Renate Grumach. Berlin: de Gruyter, 1965–.

Handbuch *Goethe-Handbuch.* Ed. by Bernd Witte and others. 4 vols. Stuttgart: Metzler, 1996–98.

NA   *Schillers Werke. Nationalausgabe.* Ed. by Julius Petersen and others, 42 vols. Weimar: Böhlau, 1943–.

1749   Johann Wolfgang Goethe born in Frankfurt am Main on 28
         August to prosperous patrician parents.

1750   Birth of Goethe's sister Cornelia.

1765–8   Goethe studies law at the University of Leipzig.

1768–70 Falls ill and returns to Frankfurt.

1770–1   Studies law at the University of Strasbourg. Meets Herder,
         who interests him in folksong. Reads Shakespeare, Ossian,
         Pindar and Homer. Friendship with J. M. R. Lenz. Romance
         with Friederike Brion.

1771–4   Work as a lawyer. First version of *Götz von Berlichingen*
         written in 1771 after Goethe's return to Frankfurt. In Spring
         1772 sent by his father to gain experience of the Imperial
         Court (Reichskammergericht) in Wetzlar. Falls in love with
         Charlotte Buff, who is already engaged. Returns to Frankfurt
         in September 1772.

1773   Publication of revised *Götz von Berlichingen*. Marriage of
         Cornelia.

1774   Publication of *Die Leiden des jungen Werthers* (The Sorrows
         of Young Werther).

1775   Engagement to Lili Schönemann (broken off later that year).
         Journey to Switzerland. In November arrives in Weimar at

the invitation of Duke Carl August. Parts of *Faust* and *Egmont* are already written.

1775–86   Takes on ministerial duties in Weimar. Growing interest in the natural sciences; meets and begins intense platonic friendship with Charlotte von Stein; writes prose version of *Iphigenie auf Tauris*, *Wilhelm Meisters theatralische Sendung* (Wilhelm Meister's Theatrical Mission) and draft of *Torquato Tasso*.

1777   Death of sister Cornelia. Travels in the Harz.

1779   Travels in Switzerland.

1782   Ennobled by the Emperor Joseph II at Duke Carl August's request.

1786   (September) Frustrated by administrative burdens and by the relationship with Frau von Stein, Goethe escapes to Italy.

1786–8   In Italy. Lives in Rome, travelling to southern Italy and Sicily. Studies classical art, geology and botany. Completes *Egmont*, *Torquato Tasso* and some scenes of *Faust*.

1787   Blank verse version of *Iphigenie* published.

1788   On his return to Weimar begins liaison with Christiane Vulpius. *Egmont* published.

1789   Birth of son August (other children died in infancy).

1790   Publication of *Faust. Ein Fragment* and of *Torquato Tasso*; also first publication on the natural sciences, *Versuch die Metamorphose der Pflanzen zu erklären* (Essay Explaining the Metamorphosis of Plants). Second Italian journey, to Venice.

1791   Becomes Director of the Weimar Court Theatre. Publishes *Beiträge zur Optik* (Contributions to Optics).

1792   Required to accompany Duke Carl August in the invasion of France by imperial troops.

1793   Present at the siege of Mainz.

1794   Beginning of the friendship and correspondence between Goethe and Schiller (1759–1805) when Schiller invites Goethe to contribute to his journal *Die Horen*.

1794–1805   Joint work of Goethe and Schiller on ballads, theoretical essays on literature and *Xenien*. Collaboration in the Weimar Court Theatre.

1795   *Römische Elegien* (Roman Elegies) published.

1795–6   Publication of *Wilhelm Meisters Lehrjahre* (Wilhelm Meister's Apprenticeship).

1797   *Hermann und Dorothea* published. Goethe resumes work on *Faust*, with Schiller's encouragement. Travels in Switzerland.

1798–1800   Publication of Goethe's art history journal the *Propyläen* (Propylaea).

1805   Death of Schiller.

1806   Occupation of Weimar by French troops after the Battle of Jena; marriage to Christiane Vulpius.

1807   Death of Dowager Duchess Anna Amalia.

1808   Publication of *Faust I*. Meeting with Napoleon at Erfurt.

1809   Publication of *Die Wahlverwandtschaften* (The Elective Affinities) and *Pandora*. Start of work on his autobiography, *Dichtung und Wahrheit* (Poetry and Truth).

1810   Goethe's theory of light and colour incorporated into *Zur Farbenlehre* (Theory of Colour).

1811–14   First three parts of *Dichtung und Wahrheit* appear.

1816   Death of Christiane, 6 June 1816. Goethe begins art history journal *Über Kunst und Altertum* (On Art and Antiquity) (to 1832).

1816–18	Publication of *Italienische Reise* (Italian Journey).
1817	Ceases to be Director of Weimar Court Theatre.
1819	Publication of *West-Östlicher Divan* (West-Eastern Divan, written 1814–18), which included some poems by Marianne von Willemer, to whom Goethe had developed a romantic attachment.
1821	Publication of first version of *Wilhelm Meisters Wanderjahre* (Wilhelm Meister's Journeymanship).
1825–31	Completes *Faust*. Act III of the play published in 1827 under the title *Helena, klassisch-romantische Phantasmagorie. Zwischenspiel zu Faust* (Helena. A Classical-Romantic-Phantasmagoria. Interlude to *Faust*); part of Act I published in 1828.
1828	Death of Duke Carl August.
1829	New version of *Wilhelm Meisters Wanderjahre* published. First public performance of *Faust I*, in Brunswick.
1830	Death of Goethe's son August.
1831	*Faust II* completed.
1832	Death of Goethe on 22 March, in Weimar. *Faust II* published posthumously.
1833	Last part of *Dichtung und Wahrheit* published.

LESLEY SHARPE

Introduction

Johann Wolfgang Goethe (1749–1832) was the first German writer of un-questioned European stature. And no other writer of his stature has his range and diversity. Author at the age of twenty-five of the first German interna-tional bestseller, *Die Leiden des jungen Werther* (The Sorrows of Young Werther), his impact on the literary scene at home and beyond Germany's borders was immense. Throughout his long productive life (he finished the second part of *Faust* only months before his death in 1832) he continued to surprise his contemporaries with the freshness and unexpected new departure of each work. He was a supreme lyric poet who also produced masterpieces in the genres of drama, prose fiction and verse epic. He was a serious natural scientist, an art critic and art historian as well as a painter, a chronicler of his own life and times, a theatre director and actor, a Privy Councillor and administrator. He conducted a vast international correspondence and was acquainted and had dealings with many of the prominent political players of the time. His collected works, the amount known about his life, the amount written about it and about his works are all huge. While this volume can-not begin to do justice to its subject, it aims to give the reader approaching Goethe for the first time some sense of the character of his work, some im-pression of his achievement, and some awareness of and orientation in the critical debates that have raged and still rage over aspects of his work and status.

For Goethe's dominant position in the world of German letters no longer seems secure and self-evident. The year 1999 was the 250th anniversary of his birth on 28 August 1749 in Frankfurt am Main. The small town of Weimar, where he spent much of his adult life, was European City of Culture for the year. The huge number of newspaper articles that marked the anniversary in Germany indicated the complexity of his position and its history in the cultural life of that country. Like most great canonical authors of world literature he is little read in his homeland, though his words are quoted often unawares by his countrymen in their everyday speech. It is significant that several journalists supplied chronologies to accompany their articles, no longer confident that such basic facts would be known to their readers. Many articles alluded to the diverse and often negative opinions expressed about him in his lifetime, particularly towards its end, by gifted and not so gifted contemporaries who criticized not only his literary work as unapproachable but also his sexual morality, his political conservatism, his Olympian aloofness, his blindness to new writers of talent. The Goethe jubilee of 1999 saw a revival of complaints that, far from being the Sage of Weimar, Goethe was unprincipled, callous, an exploiter of those closest to him, an emotional cripple – in other words, anything but a role model for the new millennium. Yet at the same time the very abundance of articles also bespeaks the huge fascination still exerted by his writing and personality, the sense one has, now as in his day, of being confronted with extraordinary intellectual and poetic gifts, gifts that issued in works that still convey with astonishing perception the experience of men and women in a modern world.

That Goethe today provokes such a variety of responses in Germany, and among them so much personal criticism, is not just a reaction to the admiration shown the nation's greatest writer in the past or to the tedium of school lessons or to the postmodern scepticism about the value traditionally attached to certain texts (though such factors doubtless play their part). It is also the product of the peculiar position occupied by Goethe in the German cultural tradition. For it was Goethe's fate to become a national icon, to embody the nation's cultural aspirations, and thus reception of his work has always reflected the vicissitudes of German national identity. He lived his entire life in a Germany that did not exist as a political entity, a nation state, and would not become one until 1871. The Holy Roman Empire into which he was born was made up of over three hundred states, ranging from the large to the tiny. After the abolition of the Empire by Napoleon in 1806 and the settlement of the Congress of Vienna in 1815 the patchwork of states was rationalized and simplified but it remained a patchwork, over which Prussia would eventually attain hegemony. In this situation of political fragmentation a sense of cultural identity and tradition assumed political significance as a unifying factor. Those who in the middle decades of the nineteenth century promoted political unification and liberalization were often those who invoked Germany's literary heritage, in particular Goethe and Schiller, as the figureheads of the *Kulturnation*. If self-cultivation (*Bildung*) was the goal of the educated German, Goethe was the paradigm of that process and study of him and his works the means to achieve it.

Goethe had been internationally famous and an object of admiration, indeed veneration, for many since he burst onto the literary scene in the 1770s. He enjoyed extraordinary literary authority throughout his life and towards its end was increasingly seen as the embodiment of wisdom. His prestige and dominance called forth dissenting voices, however, even in his own lifetime, for example the writers of a younger generation in the 1820s, such as the liberal critic Ludwig Börne, who saw him as a servant of princes. Moreover, to many Germans Goethe was a dubious figure as both a pagan and a man of many love affairs. He was not a writer for the people in the way that his friend and ally Schiller, whose work seemed to contain clear statements of liberal and national sentiment, was held to be. Yet Goethe's status grew in the nineteenth century, both as a writer and as an exemplary figure. He became an ideal human being, 'the genuine and proper embodiment of German art' (Herman Grimm). By the time unification came in 1871 Goethe was even linked with Frederick the Great or with Bismarck as one of the founders of the (now Prussian-led) German nation, in a skilful blending of the political and cultural aspirations of the prosperous middle classes. His universalism and cosmopolitanism, it was claimed, had helped the Germans rise above local patriotism and find their identity in the new nation state. Faust's land reclamation project in the second part of *Faust* was even read as enshrining a vision of colonial expansion. The pursuit of the cult of Goethe in the later decades of the nineteenth century also gave rise to much serious Goethe scholarship and the publication of a great amount of material documenting aspects of his life and work, but the nationalist strain could often be heard through it.

The year 1918 brought the collapse of Imperial Germany. The symbolic importance of Goethe was redefined, however, when the first German republic was founded in Weimar. Its leading politicians invoked 'the spirit of the great philosophers and poets' as an inspiration for a nation recovering from military defeat and in need of a tradition to hold on to (a tradition, arguably, that tapped into existing bourgeois cultural traditions at a time of threat from proletarian uprisings). Fifteen years later that republic had been swept away. Goethe's cosmopolitan outlook, amongst other things, made him less exploitable than some writers by the leaders of the Third Reich. After 1945 Goethe enjoyed a renaissance of popularity in both East and West Germany. In the East great efforts were made by the new socialist state to boost its legitimacy by laying claim to the classical tradition (Weimar itself was in the GDR) and trying to blend it with the official doctrine of Socialist Realism. The West was glad to turn to him as representative of the German humanist tradition that had been so devastatingly submerged during the Third Reich. In the wake of 1968, however, a new generation looked with suspicion on those who had survived that regime, rejecting their parents' cultural norms and questioning their past. The elevation of the Goethe of the humanist tradition in the Adenauer years seemed more like a way of obscuring the guilt of those who had consented to the Nazi regime. As part of this critical reassessment Goethe's preeminence was challenged and he too was subjected to *Ideologiekritik* as a cultural elitist, political conservative, servant of princes, perpetuator of his own myth.

The shock was in some ways salutary. Present generations of German pupils and students grow up largely in ignorance of Goethe's work. A recent survey of students of German literature at Cologne University found that some believed Schiller to be a play by Goethe. Yet the fascination still exerted by this writer is strong and scholarship has continued to flourish. And while ignorance that would have shocked Germans who grew up in the 1950s is indeed widespread, the liveliness of response by critics and commentators to the recent 250th anniversary is also testimony to the possibility of a rediscovery of Goethe. As one journalist wrote, Goethe's work is a territory much charted and yet unknown, and he went on to express his delight in discovering the youthful intensity of Goethe's poetry of the 1820s, written when the poet was in his 70s. Two major critical editions were completed in the anniversary year, the Munich edition published by C. H. Beck and the Frankfurt edition published by the Deutscher Klassiker Verlag. Both offer significant new research set out in critical apparatuses that are accessibly written. The new version of the *Goethe-Handbuch* (1996–8) shares this freshness, accessibility and attractive presentation. Nicholas Boyle's two volumes of biography (1990–9), published in English and German and covering the years up to 1803, combine cutting-edge scholarship with an enthralling introduction to Goethe's intellectual world as well as to his life and work.

English-speaking readers of Goethe are mostly unaware of the cultural and political baggage loaded onto the writer and the man. Goethe is preserved as a canonical writer on many university German courses but has disappeared from others, many of which have shifted their focus from the eighteenth and nineteenth to the twentieth century. For many students Goethe must appear a daunting monolith, a writer of works so numerous, so varied and (in some cases) so long that it is hard to find a way in. This volume is designed to ease such problems for it aims, like all the Cambridge Companions, to provide an overview of the subject and to combine information with critical evaluation in a sophisticated and yet approachable manner. All contributors have an eye to the European as well as to the specifically German context. Though they have been sparing with the traditional apparatus of scholarship, their essays bring readers up to date with the fruits of recent as well as older scholarship, while the guide to further reading suggests routes to further study.

The volume begins with two chapters designed to give orientation to those new to the subject. The first is an introduction to the world in which Goethe lived, showing how the momentous political changes in Europe impinged on the small state of Saxe-Weimar-Eisenach. The second gives a survey of Goethe's whole career as a writer from the point of view of his self-understanding as well as from the changing perspective of literary history. Readers can then progress to discussion of individual genres and works. These include writings (for example, his autobiographical writings and essays on art history) that are often mined for quotations but less often considered within the context of their particular genres. There are chapters also on his wider activities and concerns (natural science, work in the state government, directorship of the Weimar Theatre, views on religion and philosophy). Readers will be struck by the extent to which different areas of activity fructify each other. It is a cliché of Goethe criticism to refer to his comment that his works were all 'fragments of a great confession'. The implication of these words is not just that Goethe was in some ways a confessional writer but also that the various fragments ask to be understood in relation to each other as part of a lifetime's quest to see, to know, to understand and to express the world of our experience. That Goethe could attempt to see the world whole in the way that the contributors to this volume repeatedly highlight was the product of his remarkable range of talents and powers of expression – qualities that helped him to point the way to his contemporaries and gave him his extraordinary authority but also set him apart from them. Yet though he was in many ways out of step with his times (he did not write for the literary market; he opposed the French Revolution; he was deeply suspicious of Romanticism; he battled against Newtonian optics) he showed to the end of his life an extraordinary receptivity to and critical awareness of the currents of thinking, literary trends and social and political developments of his day.

Two chapters appraising Goethe's political standpoint and his perception and literary presentation of gender relations remind us that Goethe did live in a world far removed from our own and give us a salutary warning against assuming that he shared the attitudes of our own age. Balanced against this awareness is the surprising accessibility of much of Goethe's work: the immediacy of many of the lyrics, the passion of Werther, the moral and marital dilemmas of Die Wahlverwandtschaften (The Elective Affinities), the small-town concerns and yet larger humanity of Hermann und Dorothea. The contemporary reader will be struck by Goethe's modernity: by his experiments with new literary forms and his consciousness of textuality, by his awareness of the problems (literary, moral, philosophical) of living in a post-Christian world, by his understanding of humanity's complex relationship with the natural environment, by his fascination with cultural diversity. Perhaps more important still is the power of his language, the freshness of lines of poetry that achieve apparently effortless perfection.

I

THOMAS P. SAINE

The world Goethe lived in: Germany and Europe, 1750–1830

Goethe occupied a position that often placed him closer to historical events than he might have liked and forced him to come to terms with them, not only personally, but above all for the sake of Duke Carl August (1757–1828) and the small German state of Saxe-Weimar-Eisenach that Goethe served throughout his adult life. Thus Goethe was not just a man of letters, but also a man of affairs; he was acquainted with, met – not least through his regular sojourns at the Bohemian spas – or had dealings with an impressive number of the leading players of his age ranging from Prussian kings and statesmen to Napoleon Bonaparte, Czar Alexander I of Russia and Prince Metternich, the architect of Restoration Europe. To his companion Johann Peter Eckermann he said in 1824:

> I had the great advantage of being born at a time that was ripe for earth-shaking events which continued throughout my long life, so that I witnessed the Seven Years' War, then the separation of the American colonies from Britain, the French Revolution, and finally the whole Napoleonic era down to the defeat of the hero and what followed after him. As a result I have attained completely different insights and conclusions than will ever be possible for people who are born now and have to acquaint themselves with all those important happenings out of books which they don't understand.   (Eckermann, 25 February 1824)

This was perhaps a rather improbable life-outcome for someone born on 28 August 1749 in Frankfurt am Main, one of the few still somewhat flourishing imperial free cities of the Holy Roman Empire of the German Nation. It was a day and age in which practically everyone remained in his station in a traditional society in which place, the rights and privileges of rank, precedence and titles, social hierarchy, customs and rules were still all-important. By rights Goethe too should have remained in his station, for whoever gave up his rightful position voluntarily had to be able to make a new life for himself. Goethe was born to privilege, connections and wealth (unlike so many of the striving intellectuals of his day); he enjoyed strong family support and a liberal education (not only in the law); but he was so bored and depressed at the prospect of spending the rest of his life in Frankfurt that in late 1775 he accepted an invitation from the young Carl August, who had just begun his reign, to visit Weimar and soon became the most necessary member of his government. One can hardly imagine a more dramatic change of venue than this. Saxe-Weimar-Eisenach was not even a unitary state, but rather two separate territories consisting of scraps of Thuringia totalling some 750 square miles, held by Carl August as fiefs of the Holy Roman Empire. In 1775 they had a total population of approximately 100,000 and were desperately poor, underdeveloped and still suffering from the effects of the Seven Years' War. Weimar itself had stagnated for decades. Its 6000 inhabitants, few of whom (even among the aristocrats) possessed any considerable tangible wealth, were largely dependent on a court which itself was financially challenged. Goethe was attracted mainly by two things: a culturally active circle around the dowager duchess Anna Amalia, who had ruled as regent for some fifteen years and laid the basis for Weimar's rise to the status of a German Athens; and his genuine affection and friendship for the young duke, eight years his junior, whom he somewhat idealistically hoped to be able to mould into a model German ruler.

There was not really any 'Germany' to speak of in Goethe's day; there were only the territorial entities which made up the Holy Roman Empire, whose boundaries moreover, never coincided with those of the German-speaking world. The Holy Roman Empire had hardly flourished since the High Middle Ages, and since the Reformation it had lurched from crisis to crisis. The Treaties of Westphalia (1648), which formed the constitutional basis for relations both between members of the Empire and with foreign states until its final disintegration in 1806, had ended the Thirty Years' War and thus produced a certain inflexible status quo, but at a substantial political price that finally came due in the eighteenth century. From 1750 on the Empire was in a state of terminal exhaustion, owing to the growing rivalry between Prussia and Austria for hegemony within it and to pressures and interference resulting from the relations and entanglements of members of the Empire with outside powers (especially France, Poland, and Russia).

The Empire consisted of three kinds of entity: states (both secular and ecclesiastical) ranging in size from almost microscopic to rather large; imperial free cities (*Reichsstädte*); and imperial free knights (*Reichsritter*). They all had representation (but hardly equal weight) in the Imperial Diet (*Reichstag*), which met at Regensburg from the end of the Thirty Years' War until the end of the Empire. The office of Emperor was elective rather than hereditary, although with only one exception it had remained with the Austrian Habsburgs since the fifteenth century. The leading princes of the Empire were the electors (*Kurfürsten*), ranging in number at various times from seven to nine, but as of 1792 comprising the rulers of Saxony, Hanover, Brandenburg (Prussia), the Rhenish Palatinate, Bohemia (with the title of king rather than elector), Mainz, Trier and Cologne. The three last were archbishops at the head of ecclesiastical states, who usually came from distinguished aristocratic families and often ruled over other ecclesiastical territories as well. These territorial rulers were followed in rank by a profusion of dukes, margraves, landgraves, bishops and abbots. The Treaties of Westphalia had loosened the bonds between the Empire and the territorial rulers and allowed them to become practically independent, so that they could even enter into their own treaties and relations with foreign powers (they were, however, prohibited from waging war against the Empire, which did not keep them from waging war against Austria from time to time); but they did not possess full sovereignty, as strictly speaking they were vassals of the Emperor. They also were subject in varying degrees to the limiting powers of their territorial Estates, who generally had the right to grant or withhold taxes; the development of absolutism in the German territories was the history of the struggles of rulers to gain the upper hand over their Estates. Hundreds of imperial free knights (mostly sprinkled through the territories of the south and southwest) had generally small holdings bestowed directly by the Emperor, and by the eighteenth century they were mostly an anachronism. Needless to say, the neighbours of small ecclesiastical states, imperial knights, and imperial free cities looked upon such enclaves with some envy as possible objects of annexation.

The imperial free cities such as Frankfurt, Nuremberg or Augsburg, unlike territorial cities or residences (*Residenzstädte*) such as Berlin, Leipzig or Mainz, were subject only to the Emperor and enjoyed special privileges; although they usually controlled a certain amount of territory, they were for the most part islands of otherness increasingly under pressure from the states which surrounded them. They were generally in decline throughout our period and some were not much more than glorified villages. While they were proud of their tradition of self-governance and liked to regard themselves as 'republics', so that some resisted being 'revolutionized' when occupied by French forces early in the revolutionary period on the grounds that they already had a republican form of government, they were hardly bastions of liberal thinking or democratic government. One would look in vain for representatives of a 'bourgeoisie' in Marx's sense in German cities of this period; when rights were claimed and defended it was most often not liberal or abstract 'human rights' that were in question, but the traditional rights of corporations, guilds and social classes. The free cities were controlled by town councils whose members were drawn from the patrician families and

8

the guilds. Anything that was out of the ordinary or would have upset the status quo was inherently suspect, even when life in the city or its economy would have been improved as a result. Citizenship was strictly controlled, as were the number and occupations of the non-citizens who were allowed to reside there, and thus the population of the free cities was mostly stagnant, while many territorial cities and *Residenzstädte* grew significantly in the eighteenth century.

The Treaties of Westphalia had ended the conflict between the three major confessions (Roman Catholic, Lutheran and Calvinist) by allowing each to remain unchallenged where it already dominated, but that had not really resolved the religious problem in the Empire. For one thing it meant members of other religious groups or sects (particularly the Jews) still had no enforceable rights to freedom of religion and were reduced to relying on rulers who were willing to 'tolerate' or protect them (often because they were economically useful). For another it meant that adherents of the dominant confession could strictly limit the rights of members of the other confessions: while it might, for example, no longer be respectable to expel Protestants from Catholic territories (although it still happened from time to time), one could forbid them to build churches or hold worship services, as in Cologne, where the Catholic citizens refused to welcome rich Protestant Netherlanders, or in Goethe's own Lutheran Frankfurt, where the Calvinists had to go outside the city to worship. Prussia, where Lutherans, Catholics and Calvinists were on an equal footing with regard to the state, was a notable example of religious toleration (largely for economic and political reasons). In general the Protestant areas of northern Germany were more 'modern', more enlightened, and economically and educationally more advanced than the Catholic areas in the south, including Austria (the suppression of the Jesuits in 1773 dealt an especially heavy blow to education in the Catholic regions). Up until the end of the Empire confessional suspicions and differences played a significant role in relations between members of the Empire; the Diet was even formally divided into a 'Corpus Catholicorum' and a 'Corpus Evangelicorum'. As tensions within the Empire increased in the second half of the eighteenth century, many of the smaller Catholic territories and the ecclesiastical states looked to Austria for support, while the smaller Protestant states increasingly found themselves looking to Prussia to protect them from Austrian and imperial pressure.

Before the French Revolution

Goethe's birth date falls between two major wars which led to dramatic changes in the balance of power and traditional diplomatic-military alignments in

Europe. The War of the Austrian Succession (1740–8) began when Frederick II of Prussia, later called the Great, invaded Silesia after the accession of Maria Theresia in Austria. Although Prussia had agreed to honour the so-called Pragmatic Sanction by which Charles VI, an Emperor with no sons, had sought to secure the succession of his daughter to all the Habsburg hereditary possessions (an exception to normal practice under the prevailing Salic Law excluding females from succession), Frederick went through the motions of presenting some rather far-fetched dynastic claims to justify the invasion. Basically, however, it was an opportunistic move which was feasible because Frederick could count on the support of France, which was also allied with the electors Augustus III of Saxony and Charles Albert of Bavaria against Austria. With French support Charles Albert became Emperor Charles VII; he died in 1745 after Bavaria had been defeated in the war, and Maria Theresia's husband, Francis Stephen, became Emperor as Francis I. The very messy and confusing war spread into Savoy and Italy as other sovereigns advanced their own claims on Habsburg territories. The war turned out to be much more challenging than Frederick had originally anticipated, but despite all Austrian attempts to retake the province, he remained in possession of Silesia at the conclusion of peace.

From 1748 on it was Maria Theresia's overriding ambition to rebuild Austrian power and secure alliance partners to help her regain Silesia. Whereas Austria had been allied with Britain and the United Provinces against France during the 1740–8 conflict, Maria Theresia's new chancellor, Anton Wenzel von Kaunitz, succeeded in gaining France as an ally against Prussia, a 'diplomatic revolution' which significantly affected European affairs up until the French Revolution; Austria also allied itself with Russia, thus threatening to encircle Prussia from east, south, and west. Prussia now allied itself with Britain, which needed to protect the electorate of Hanover against possible French attack – since from 1754 on it was already engaged in hostilities with France in America – and was in a position to pay Frederick substantial subsidies to keep his army in the field. Frederick launched a preemptive strike and occupied Saxony in 1756 to begin the Seven Years' War (1756–63); he won important victories against the French and against the Austrians in 1757, and against the Russians in 1758. Subsequent Russian victories in the east, however, and their occupation of East Prussia and Berlin put Frederick in a desperate situation from which he was ultimately rescued by a higher intervention: after the death of the Russian empress Elizabeth in 1762 her successor, Peter III, an admirer of Frederick, withdrew from the war. Peter, for his part, did not survive the year, being overthrown by his consort, who became Catherine II and showed herself friendly enough to Prussia to play it off against Austria to her own advantage throughout her reign. The conflict between Austria and Prussia was finally settled in the Treaty of Hubertusburg on 15 February 1763, which confirmed Prussia's possession of Silesia. The biggest loser in the conflict was France, which had to surrender most of its North American holdings to Britain in the Treaty of Paris (10 February 1763). All the continental participants in the conflict were thoroughly exhausted, militarily as well as financially, and needed an extended breathing space; the Seven Years' War left French finances on a descent into the abyss which, steepened by France's participation on the side of the colonists in the American revolutionary war, led finally to the convening of the Estates General in 1789 and the beginnings of the French Revolution.

The 1770s, when Goethe moved to Weimar and became a member of Carl August's Privy Council, saw renewed conflict between Prussia and Austria. Maria Theresia's son, Joseph II, who became Emperor in 1765 upon the death of his father, Francis I, now began to play a major role; Maria Theresia made him co-regent of the Habsburg dominions and then had to exert all her influence and that of chancellor Kaunitz to keep Joseph under control. When Elector Maximilian Joseph of Bavaria died in 1777 without an heir, Austria raised claims on portions of Bavaria and occupied them, while negotiating with Charles Theodore of the Palatinate, head of another branch of the Wittelsbach family who was in line to succeed Maximilian Joseph, to persuade him to accept Habsburg territory in southern Germany in exchange. Frederick was immediately alarmed by the prospect of Austrian expansion into Germany and organized opposition to the exchange; when Austria refused to evacuate Bavaria, he invaded Bohemia in July 1778, thus initiating the War of the Bavarian Succession. This time, however, the Austrian army gave a good account of itself and the war quickly turned into a stalemate and a struggle by both armies to get enough food to survive (thus the war came to be known also as the Potato War). The situation was finally resolved by French and Russian mediation in the Treaty of Teschen (1779) which provided for Austria to evacuate all of Bavaria except for an area east of the Inn River. The conflict served as another reminder to the smaller German states of the dangers of confrontations between Prussia and Austria. Saxe-Weimar-Eisenach, for example, was in a particularly ticklish situation. By geography it had to coexist with both Prussia (and Carl August was also a grand-nephew of Frederick) and Electoral Saxony (to which Carl August owed dynastic allegiance, especially since there were times when he had hopes of eventually becoming elector himself). In early 1779 Prussian generals in the neighbourhood, and finally Frederick himself, demanded that Carl August allow them to recruit in his territory; this put the Weimar government in an agonizing dilemma, since refusal would have led to Prussian reprisals, while acceding possibly would have led to Austrian demands for an equal opportunity to rob the territory of its finest young men. Fortunately the spring 1779 campaigning season never really got under way and Carl August's government got away with not responding. This was Goethe's first significant diplomatic crisis as a member of Carl August's Privy Council.[1]

After Maria Theresia's death in 1780 Kaunitz by himself was unable to restrain Joseph's ambitions. One of his projects which aroused considerable dismay precisely in Catholic circles was his attempt to realign diocesan boundaries so that bishops whose sees were outside the Habsburg territories would no longer have any authority in his realms. He also limited the authority of the pope in Habsburg lands and sought to reform the education of priests. This programme was a prime contributing factor in the conservative revolt in the Austrian Netherlands (roughly the area of modern Belgium) in the late 1780s and subsequently had to be scaled back drastically. Maria Theresia had abolished serfdom on the hereditary crown lands during her reign, substituting a system of monetary payments for the traditional obligatory services; Joseph sought to extend the programme to cover all the serfs in Bohemia, while revising the tax system to keep the magnates from escaping taxes by simply forcing the serfs/peasants to work harder and pay more. Joseph also irritated the Hungarian nobility by refusing to convene their Estates and by centralizing authority in the Hungarian chancery in Vienna, so that by the end of his reign the Hungarians were plotting with the Prussian government against him, and Carl August was being touted as a possible successor as king of Hungary. In the midst of all his reform projects Joseph was forced into a new war against the Turks in 1788 (because of the Austrian alliance with Russia), which threatened at first to end very badly and contributed directly to his death on 20 February 1790.

Of great significance for the further weakening of imperial bonds and sharpening of the opposition between Prussia and Austria was Joseph's reluctance, once he exercised sole power, to give up the project of obtaining Bavaria, or major parts thereof. In the early 1780s he began negotiating with Charles Theodore, who did not like Munich anyway, to exchange the Austrian Netherlands for Bavaria. In addition to the prospect of gaining Bavaria this was attractive to Joseph because the Netherlands were far from Vienna and difficult to govern, exposed to both French and Dutch pressures and, in spite of the wealth of the province, difficult to extract enough taxes from. The proposed exchange was appealing to Charles Theodore because he would step up in rank and become a king instead of a mere elector. Again Frederick brought pressure to bear, organizing a League of Princes (*Fürstenbund*) to 'stand up' for the Empire and oppose Joseph's attempts to subvert its constitution. The pact was sealed in July 1785, barely more than a year before Frederick's death in August 1786, and consisted of an agreement between Prussia, Hanover, and Electoral Saxony which contained secret articles providing for combined military action if the situation led to conflict. The lesser Protestant princes of northern Germany were invited to join the league, among them Carl August, who had been involved in the diplomacy, negotiations, and recruitment of possible members since the beginning of the matter in 1783. Unfortunately, Carl August had undertaken most of his organizing activities on the basis of his relationship with the crown prince (later Frederick William II, who was also his brother-in-law), who was acting more or less behind Frederick's back. Carl August's reason for expending so much effort in the matter had been his hope that the League of Princes could constitute a genuinely neutral 'Third Germany' not beholden to either Prussia or Austria and that the League could play a major role in reforming the institutions of the Empire.[2] Such was not, of course, Frederick's understanding of the purpose of the League, and after his accession to the throne Frederick William was not to be persuaded to try to reform the Empire either. Instead he eventually mounted a military demonstration in Silesia in the spring of 1790 (in which Carl August participated as a Prussian general, accompanied by Goethe), which could have led to a new war with Austria but in fact ended with a rapprochement in the Convention of Reichenbach (17 July 1790). Both sides (Leopold II was now Emperor) backed away from conflict, largely because there was already enough turmoil elsewhere in Europe.[3]

The French Revolution and the
revolutionary wars

When the French Estates General assembled in the spring of 1789 to deliberate on the nation's financial problems no one was thinking of a 'revolution'. When they turned themselves into a National Assembly which aspired to reform the French polity, solve the nation's financial problems, and write a constitution for the modern age, most educated Germans (including many enlightened aristocrats) watched with interest and sympathy. In general they regarded the French not as leading the way into a new age, but rather as catching up with them (the Germans, at least the Protestants, tended to believe that the Reformation had already done for Germany what the French were doing now).[4] Gradually, however, concern grew, at least among governments and monarchs. They had to be worried that the French people might abridge or even take away the rights of King Louis XVI, which would set an ugly precedent for kings and peoples elsewhere in Europe. The enthusiastic renunciation and abolition of feudal rights during the all-night session of the National Assembly on 4 August 1789 impacted not only on French nobility, but also on German princes who held seigniorial rights in French Alsace. Although the French were willing to negotiate compensation for their losses, the princes preferred to stand by their rights, and the issue eventually became one of the official grounds for the Empire to make war against the Revolution. Aristocrats had already begun to emigrate early on; after 1790 close to half the clergy refused to swear to uphold the Civil Constitution of the Clergy and began streaming out of the country as well. Many of these émigrés, who included the two brothers of Louis XVI and other princes of the blood, eventually settled in Rhenish territories (especially Koblenz and Mainz) and began both recruiting soldiers for an eventual return and lobbying German courts to intervene in France to restore Louis XVI to his former power. The king's flight to Varennes in June 1791 demonstrated the delicacy of his situation, and in August of that year Frederick William II and Leopold II seemed to give some support to the émigré cause with their Declaration of Pillnitz, in which they expressed concern about the way the French king was being treated. It was, had it been carefully read, on the whole not a terribly bellicose statement, but the émigrés made the most of it. In the meantime Prussia and Austria had also concluded a defensive alliance which bound each to aid the other in the event of an attack.

By this time war parties had formed on both sides. The Brissotin faction in the newly elected Legislative Assembly increasingly dominated French foreign policy in late 1791 and 1792 and pushed for stern action against Austria for tolerating the activities of the émigrés (it did not help that the queen, Marie Antoinette, was Austrian). The Brissotins hoped that a war would distract attention from internal problems and help secure the success of the Revolution, while royalists joined in the clamour for war in the hope that a French defeat would destroy the Revolution. The Austrian government was perhaps not as conciliatory as it might have been in responding to threatening French notes, but it is not probable that Leopold would actually have gone to war at that time. Unfortunately he died suddenly at the beginning of March 1792, leaving his young son to succeed him as Francis II. There was no longer anyone willing or able to cool off the situation, and the French declared war against Francis on 20 April 1792. A very unsuccessful French campaign against the Austrian Netherlands in the spring seemed to indicate that it would be relatively simple to defeat France and restore Louis XVI. The Prussians and Austrians planned a summer campaign that aimed to take them all the way to Paris; as it was being launched from Koblenz at the end of July their generalissimus, the Duke of Brunswick, published a ferocious manifesto threatening dire consequences if the French so much as touched a hair of their king's head. The manifesto, which has gone down in history as one of the most ill-fated documents of its kind, only rallied French resistance and contributed to the ultimate downfall of the king. Carl August commanded several cavalry regiments in the invading Prussian army and urgently requested that Goethe accompany him. Goethe at first shared the general optimism about the outcome, collecting letters of recommendation to be used when he got to Paris and taking requests for presents to bring back. By the end of the campaign, however, he was already voicing the apprehension that this might turn out to be another Thirty Years' War.[5] Both sides had massively misjudged the exertions that would be necessary to win the struggle.

It would be tedious to list all the coalitions and all the battles won and lost by both sides over the years between the campaign of 1792 and the battle of Waterloo in 1815 (by 1793 France was at war with practically all of Europe). Here we can only outline the course of events. In the campaign of 1792 the Prussians and Austrians slogged through miserable weather with an inadequate supply line as far as Valmy in the Champagne, where on 20 September they encountered French armies in superior positions and exchanged cannon fire for several hours without ever daring to mount an assault. After a week of negotiating with the French generals, they began their retreat to Germany. While the Germans were retreating, the French launched counter-attacks in Belgium and the Rhineland, with success in both theatres. They captured Mainz in October and even occupied Frankfurt until early December. While in Mainz they sought to raise the revolutionary consciousness of the populace, with the goal of persuading the inhabitants of Mainz and the other occupied areas on the left bank of the Rhine to organize themselves as a republic and petition to be annexed to the French Republic. This effort finally succeeded in March 1793, but by then Prussian and Austrian forces had retaken most of the left bank and were besieging the city, which surrendered at the end of July. During the campaigning season of 1793 the Prussians and Austrians, aided by contingents contributed by other German states to an imperial army, drove the French more or less back to their borders, but were unable to mount offensives which would have significantly advanced their war aims. After the capture of Mainz Frederick William II left the western front to oversee the takeover of the territory he had just gained in the second partition of Poland. From that point Prussian efforts in the west began to slacken and the Austrians were left to bear more and more of the burden. In late 1793 and early 1794 the Jacobin government in Paris, led by the Committee of Public Safety which was increasingly under the influence of Robespierre, organized a massive war effort that was to turn the tide on the German front.

In 1794 the French armies were back in Belgium and Holland and retook most of the left bank of the Rhine. From then on they even made regular forays beyond the Rhine.[6] A primary French objective throughout was to keep the war and their armies on foreign soil so as to make the enemy suffer the immense costs. Meanwhile, the Prussians had begun to negotiate their way out of the war in order to concentrate on their new acquisitions in Poland. The French were happy enough to drive a wedge between Prussia and Austria, which they had been trying to do ever since the fruitless negotiations in the aftermath of Valmy. In the Treaty of Basel (April 1795) Prussia recognized the legitimacy of the French government, agreed (in a secret article) to French annexations in the Rhineland to be determined in a future peace treaty, with Prussia receiving compensation on the right bank of the Rhine, and withdrew from hostilities into neutrality. Furthermore, the French agreed to allow most of northern Germany to become neutral under Prussian sponsorship. This freed their armies to focus on southern Germany and the remaining enemy, Austria.[7]

While Austria was not entirely alone in its struggle over the next years, being allied at various times with Britain and Russia, it received no support in the German and Italian theatres until the arrival of Russian forces under Marshal Alexander Suvorov in 1799 (who, after initial successes in Italy, was forced to retreat in Switzerland and was recalled to Russia). The French armies did not win all the battles, but once Napoleon had taken firm charge of the armies, the Austrians were doomed to eventual defeat (which, perhaps to their credit, they were never willing to accept as final). In the spring of 1797 Napoleon crossed the Alps from Italy and drove within eighty miles of Vienna. At this point the two sides decided to negotiate and signed the Treaty of Campo Formio, in which Austria agreed (as had Prussia in 1795) to eventual French annexations in the Rhineland (the losing rulers to be compensated through the secularization of ecclesiastical territories – this was the first time that secularization had been agreed upon in principle). Within a year, however, hostilities had begun again, this time ending with a decisive French victory at Hohenlinden (near Munich) on 3 December 1800 and the Treaty of Lunéville (February, 1801). The Treaty of Lunéville contained harsher terms than the Treaty of Campo Formio. Because Francis II refused to negotiate with the French on behalf of the Empire, the Diet had to appoint a delegation to propose a territorial settlement (that is, to decide what would happen to the rest of the Empire after the French had taken their piece up to the Rhine). The report presented by this Imperial Deputation was accepted by the Diet and proclaimed as law by the Emperor on 27 April 1803; it represented 'one of the greatest territorial rearrangements in all of European history'.[8] All but six of the imperial cities were absorbed by the territories surrounding them. All but three of the ecclesiastical states were secularized (the boundaries of Mainz were drastically redrawn) and added to other states. The greatest territorial winners were Prussia, Bavaria, Baden and Württemberg. As of April 1803 the Empire still continued in existence, but in drastically altered form (with Francis II proclaiming himself Francis I, Emperor of the Habsburg dominions, in August 1804 just in case). The Austrians went to war again, however, with the result that Napoleon occupied Vienna and decisively defeated Russian and Austrian forces at Austerlitz (in Bohemia) on 2 December 1805. This defeat did lead directly to the end of the Empire: on 12 July 1806 Napoleon established the Confederation of the Rhine, initially an association of sixteen Rhenish and southern states which, allied with France, was intended to be a buffer between France and its enemies in the east. By signing the charter of the Confederation these Napoleonic allies seceded from the Empire, thus leading Francis II to abdicate the imperial crown on 6 August and content himself with being only Francis I of Austria.

Prussia's days of neutrality were now numbered. It had refused to take sides in 1805, despite pressure from both sides to commit itself. After Austerlitz French pressure on Prussia was increased; despite signing a treaty with France in February 1806, Prussia mobilized some of its forces during the summer. Hostilities began after Prussian troops moved into Saxony and Thuringia in September, when it was clear it would have to face France alone.[9] On 14 October Prussian and French armies met at Jena and Auerstedt, within earshot of Goethe – Carl August was again serving in the Prussian army and the Duke of Brunswick was again the commander-in-chief – and the Prussians suffered a humiliating defeat, fully exposing the extent of the decline of both state and army since the days of Frederick II. Frederick William III (who had succeeded in 1797) and the court left Berlin and headed in the direction of East Prussia; the remaining Prussian and allied Russian forces were no match for Napoleon's armies. After gaining a victory against the Russians at Friedland on 14 June 1807 Napoleon negotiated an alliance with Russia and forced Frederick William to accept the Treaty of Tilsit (9 July). Prussia had to submit to French occupations until payment of 120 million francs in indemnities; it lost its lands west of the Elbe, which became part of the newly created Kingdom of Westphalia to be ruled by Napoleon's brother Jerome, and most of the Polish territory gained in the partitions of 1793 and 1795 was incorporated into a newly created Duchy of Warsaw. Prussia had to join the continental system blockade of Britain, and the Confederation of the Rhine was enlarged by twenty-three members, including Saxony and Carl August's Saxe-Weimar-Eisenach. Carl August was quite fortunate to avoid being dethroned by Napoleon at this point: he was especially suspect because he had fought again on the Prussian side, unlike the other minor Thuringian princes. He was rewarded by having a French ambassador to the Thuringian states stationed in Weimar to watch over him.

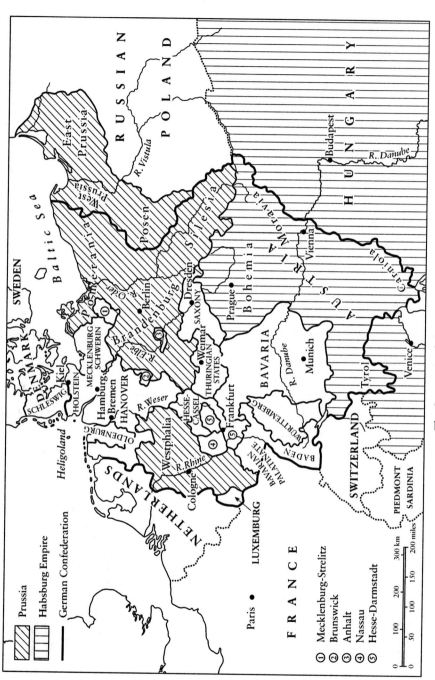

The German Confederation in 1815

Prussia

Habsburg Empire

German Confederation

① Mecklenburg-Strelitz
② Brunswick
③ Anhalt
④ Nassau
⑤ Hesse-Darmstadt

RUSSIAN POLAND

HUNGARY

Budapest

R. Danube

East Prussia

R. Vistula

West Prussia

Posen

Silesia

AUSTRIA MORAVIA

Carniola

SWEDEN

Baltic Sea

Pomerania

R. Oder

Berlin

Brandenburg

Dresden

SAXONY

Prague

Bohemia

Vienna

DENMARK

SCHLESWIG

HOLSTEIN

Kiel

Heligoland

MECKLENBURG SCHWERIN

Hamburg

Bremen

HANOVER

OLDENBURG

R. Elbe

Weimar

THURINGIAN STATES

BAVARIA

R. Danube

Munich

Tyrol

Venice

R. Weser

Westphalia

HESSE-CASSEL

Frankfurt

WÜRTTEMBERG

BADEN

NETHERLANDS

R. Rhine

Cologne

BAVARIAN PALATINATE

SWITZERLAND

PIEDMONT

SARDINIA

FRANCE

Paris

LUXEMBURG

0   100   200   300 km
0   50   100   150   200 miles

All of central and eastern Europe was now for a while at peace with France (while Britain and Spain continued to cause Napoleon severe problems). After Tilsit the leading Prussian reformers, first Karl Freiherr vom Stein and then Karl August von Hardenberg, sought (with only partial success) to reform and strengthen the Prussian state and military in the face of considerable inertia and resistance to new ideas. Of course the Russian alliance and the general peace did not last – Napoleon was probably incapable of functioning in a world that was truly at peace – and in late spring of 1812 he set out to subdue Russia with his grand army of 600,000 men, including 180,000 Austrians and Germans from all the allied states. Instead of being able to bring the Russian armies to decisive battle, Napoleon marched all the way to Moscow and then had to march back again. When he got out of Russia in December 1812, the grand army had shrunk to fewer than 50,000 men.[10] Napoleon raced back to Paris ahead of the news to begin raising new forces (passing through Weimar incognito he conveyed greetings to Goethe through his resident ambassador) while Prussia and Russia allied against him. With his new army he enjoyed some initial successes in Germany in 1813, winning victories at Lützen and Bautzen in May, without being able to end the conflict. At this point Austria finally joined the allies. Napoleon won another victory at Dresden at the end of August, but after a three-day battle at Leipzig, which began on 16 October and became known as the Battle of the Nations, he was forced to extricate himself and withdraw across the Rhine. In 1814 the allies were able to invade France again, for the first time since 1792; they took Paris in March, restored the Bourbon monarchy under Louis XVIII (the older of the two brothers of Louis XVI who had been émigrés in the 1790s), and packed Napoleon off into exile on the island of Elba. Carl August, who had been put in command of allied forces in Belgium, succeeded this time, unlike in 1792, in marching to Paris as one of the victorious commanders. An all-European conference to settle the affairs of the continent was convened in Vienna in the autumn.

Post-Napoleonic Germany and Europe

The Congress of Vienna met from September 1814 to June 1815 (inconvenienced by Napoleon's escape from Elba in March and the necessity of re-conquering him at Waterloo on 18 June, just days after the conclusion of the Congress). The major allied powers, Britain, Prussia, Russia and Austria, were in charge of the Congress, although eventually France, too, was allowed to participate in the deliberations (in actuality, Austria and Metternich played the predominant role). Czar Alexander I and King Frederick William III stayed throughout the Congress, and lavish entertaining filled the interstices between fits of progress in the negotiations. Many of the lesser German rulers also attended, and all had to have representatives there, as their future status hung in the balance. Carl August, both his lands and his personal finances in dire straits from a decade of occupation and war, had to borrow money in order to go with his negotiators (Goethe was invited but refused to accompany him to Vienna). While he paid his retainers reasonable *per diem* allowances, he spent very little on himself, relying on free entertainments and standing invitations at the tables of close friends.[11] France was stripped of all territorial gains. No one thought seriously of restoring the former ecclesiastical territories, and restoring the Holy Roman Empire was out of the question. While the former Rhine confederates initially had to worry whether they would be allowed to continue on their thrones, Saxony was the main loser: its king, Frederick August, had deserted the allies in the spring of 1813 to return to Napoleon's side and had even been captured at the Battle of Leipzig. Prussia went to Vienna hoping to dethrone Frederick August and annex all of Saxony, but in the end had to settle for something less than half of Saxony, a large serving of formerly ecclesiastical Westphalian and Rhenish territory, and pieces of Thuringia. Bavaria was enlarged somewhat and became the second-largest German state in the former Empire. Hanover was reconstituted (Napoleon had dismembered it and given much of it to the Kingdom of Westphalia), enlarged, and elevated to a monarchy. Austria received more Italian territory and also expanded somewhat to the west by gaining the former ecclesiastical territory of Salzburg. Carl August profited from his Prussian and Russian connections (although much less than he had originally hoped) to round off and just about double the size of Saxe-Weimar-Eisenach's territory, making it the largest state in Thuringia, and was transformed into a grand duke. A Polish state (Congress Poland) was reconstituted out of most of the Napoleonic Duchy of Warsaw, now to be a kingdom controlled by the Russian czar. Belgium was joined with the United Provinces in a monarchy under the House of Orange (but only until the 1830 revolutions). Study of the post-1815 map of Germany is instructive: it shows a handful of large states surrounding or closely encroaching on a number of very much smaller states in the centre, north and east, while only two or three of the medium-sized states (above all Baden and Württemberg) seem to have any breathing space at all.

Proponents of a unified German state, or even of a closely-knit federation, were disappointed. The Congress created instead a loose confederation of thirty-nine states. While the members of the Confederation were represented in a diet, the diet had few deliberative powers and the voting rules ensured deadlock whenever unanimity could not be reached. Important issues such as guarantees of the rights of citizens, lowering of tariff barriers, promotion of trade and improvement of infrastructures were left for the future. One of the most important sections of the confederation document was Article 13, which promised that each state in the Confederation would introduce a constitution (a *landständische Verfassung*). In September of 1815, back in Paris after Waterloo, the major powers agreed to join in a Holy Alliance to reintroduce strict Christian and monarchical principles of government, and to monitor and supervise political activity throughout Europe to guarantee conformity with those principles. The Restoration – the Metternich era – had begun. It was the repressive nature of the Holy Alliance oversight – exercised principally by Metternich with eager Prussian and Russian assistance – and the failure of many of the German states to follow through on the constitutional promise in Article 13 which were to lead to growing political unrest and an outburst of revolutionary activity in many parts of Germany following the French July Revolution of 1830. Saxe-Weimar-Eisenach, where Carl August had promptly instituted a relatively liberal constitution guaranteeing freedom of the press in 1816, quickly became a target of the reactionary overseers during the years 1816–20, but attained something of the status of a model for liberal and nationalist thinkers of the period and escaped the convulsions of the 1830s.

NOTES

1 See Hans Tümmler's essays 'Goethes politische Tätigkeit 1778–1790' and 'Goethes politisches Gutachten aus dem Jahre 1779', in *Goethe in Staat und Politik. Gesammelte Aufsätze* (Cologne and Graz: Böhlau, 1964); also Tümmler, *Carl August von Weimar, Goethes Freund. Eine vorwiegend politische Biographie* (Stuttgart: Klett-Cotta, 1978).

2 See Tümmler, *Carl August von Weimar*, pp. 47–92; also Ulrich Crämer, *Carl August von Weimar und der Deutsche Fürstenbund 1783–1790* (Wiesbaden: Hardt und Hauck, 1961) and the recent book by Volker Ebersbach, *Carl August von Sachsen-Weimar-Eisenach: Goethes Herzog und Freund* (Cologne, Weimar and Vienna: Böhlau, 1998), pp. 139–49.

3 On the final decades of the Empire see Karl Otmar von Aretin, *Das alte Reich: 1648–1806*, vol. III: *Das Reich und der österreichisch-preußische Dualismus (1745–1806)* (Stuttgart: Klett-Cotta, 1997); and John Gagliardo's *Reich and Nation: The Holy Roman Empire as Idea and Reality, 1763–1806* (Bloomington and London: Indiana University Press, 1980).

4 See especially the first chapter of my *Black Bread – White Bread: German Intellectuals and the French Revolution* (Columbia, SC: Camden House, 1988); also my article, 'A Peculiar View of the French Revolution: The Revolution as German Reformation', in John A. McCarthy and Albert A. Kipa, eds., *Aufnahme – Weitergabe: Literarische Impulse um Lessing und Goethe. Festschrift für Heinz Moenkemeyer zum 68. Geburtstag* (Hamburg: Buske, 1982), pp. 233–61.

5 On the campaign of *1792* see *Black Bread – White Bread*, ch. 3. See also my article on *Campagne in Frankreich 1792* in *Handbuch* III, pp. 369–85.

6 On French military activities in the Rhineland see especially T. C. W. Blanning, *The French Revolution in Germany. Occupation and Resistance in the Rhineland, 1792–1802* (Oxford and New York: Oxford University Press, 1983). On the revolutionary wars see in addition Blanning, *The Origins of the French Revolutionary Wars* (London and New York: Longman, 1986) and *The French Revolutionary Wars 1787–1802* (London and New York: Arnold, 1996).

7 See James J. Sheehan, *German History, 1770–1866* (Oxford and New York: Clarendon Press, 1989), p. 224.

8 Ibid., p. 243.

9 Ibid., pp. 233–5.

10 Numbers according to Sheehan, *German History*, pp. 312–13. Other accounts differ.

11 See Tümmler, *Carl August von Weimar*, pp. 243–57.

2

NICHOLAS SAUL

Goethe the writer and literary history

Even aged sixteen Goethe strove for authority. He may not have achieved the sublime degree of *autoritas* he envisaged as a Leipzig fresher in 1765 – that of a German university professor.[1] But among his peers he quickly acquired unparalleled poetic authority. After the publication of his first major innovative works, the Shakespearean patriotic drama *Götz von Berlichingen* (1773) and the Rousseauesque sentimental novel *Die Leiden des jungen Werther* (The Sorrows of Young Werther, 1774), Goethe was lionized. In his *Pandaemonium Germanicum* (c. 1775) Jakob Michael Reinhold Lenz portrayed Goethe atop the German Pantheon, surrounded by adoring critics whom he must shake off like flies. Johann Caspar Lavater's *Physiognomische Fragmente* (Physiognomical fragments, 1775–8) presented Goethe for page after page as a divine poetic genius. This poetic charisma remained undiminished as generations and literary paradigms passed. Twenty years on, in *Über die ästhetische Erziehung des Menschen* (On the Aesthetic Education of Humanity, 1795), Friedrich Schiller painted Goethe's portrait as the model classical poet. Such admiration also stretched across literary ideologies. In 1798 the leading early German Romantic Friedrich Schlegel asserted that Goethe's classical novel *Wilhelm Meisters Lehrjahre* (Wilhelm Meister's Apprenticeship, 1795–6) represented one of the age's three fundamental tendencies).[2] August Wilhelm Schlegel lauded Goethe in a wittily punning eponymous sonnet as master, leader, friend and divine messenger, and Friedrich von Hardenberg (Novalis), Romanticism's leading poet and novelist, suggested Goethe was 'the true steward of the poetic spirit on earth'[3] – pope of poetry. The late Romantic Zacharias Werner claimed their farewell in 1808 – Goethe had laid hands on Werner's head – to have been a rite of initiation into the highest mysteries of literature (see his letter to Goethe, 15 April 1808).[4] Heinrich Heine, who straddled late Romanticism and the Young German group of political and social critics, passed fitting comment on this secularized hagiographic tradition in his bittersweet memoir *Die romantische Schule* (The Romantic School, 1832). Meeting Goethe in 1824, he becomes humorously convinced that the stately seventy-five-year-old is indeed a god – Jupiter – and casts around involuntarily for the emblem of Jovial power, the eagle with lightning in its beak.[5]

Until recently, modern scholars tended to follow this tradition. Not all went as far as a radical Bremen pastor, Julius Burggraf. He made light of Goethe's repeated vehement rejection of Christianity and in 1913 published one of the most surprising hagiographic monuments to Goethe, the *Goethe-predigten* (Sermons on Goethe). Goethe is, however, perhaps the only German writer whose unquestioned authority is such as to inspire an unbroken tradition of scholarly monographs with the frankly self-legitimating, monolithic title *Goethe*.[6] The scholarly elevation of his status initiated by Friedrich Schlegel was taken still further by Hermann August Korff. His *Geist der Goethezeit* (Spirit of the Goethean age, 1923–52) promotes Goethe as the representative figure of an entire epoch, roughly from 1770 to 1832. Since then, the term 'Goethezeit' has become a basic element of the Germanist's vocabulary. T. J. Reed continues Korff's variant of the tradition to this day when he argues Goethe to be not just the centre of the epoch and inaugurator of its greatness, but also the centre of German literary history, the vantage point from which the still unfolding story of German literature can and should be written.[7]

Recently, however, the image of Goethe as norm-giving authority of his own epoch and German literary history has been questioned. Heinz Schlaffer has argued that Goethe's works, far from offering an unambiguously authoritative message, in fact possess a characteristically dualistic mode of intended reception. Read one way, *Wilhelm Meisters Lehrjahre* (for example) confirms the consensual view of educated Germans, that life is but the smooth unfolding of personality towards the holy grail of *Bildung*. Read another way, it subversively presents individuals and society as manipulated by secret groupings for economic and political ends.[8] Hartmut Böhme saw a similarly ambiguous relationship with contemporary authority and orthodoxy in Goethe's natural scientific discourse,[9] and Nicholas Boyle has exploited this trend to form an interpretation of man and epoch totally counter to received wisdom: 'There never was such a thing as the "Age of Goethe"' (Boyle I, 5). Goethe engaged with his age, but only in so far as he was opposed to virtually all its institutions and intellectual currents. He is at best the poet of a paradoxical 'marginal centrality' (100) – in his time but not of it, an authority maybe, but one misunderstood by his time, and by those of later generations who followed its perspective.

We have already moved far from Goethe's own ambition for writerly authority, a concept which, as we have seen, has repeatedly been appropriated and reinterpreted. What, then, against this background, *was* Goethe's conception of the writer and the writer's authority? I shall seek to reconstruct Goethe's self-understanding as a writer in the context of the literary culture of the epochs through which he lived, in order to determine the measure of his authority, willed and unwilled, over his peers. I argue that Goethe's writerly self-understanding passes through four chief phases of development. In the first phase, corresponding to the *Sturm und Drang* (Storm and Stress) epoch before his move to Weimar, Goethe responds to an epochal crisis of meaning by adapting the theory of genius to himself and his project. This makes him into an unwilling, and subversive, representative of his bourgeois generation, and indeed of modernity. The second phase, corresponding to the first Weimar decade, 1775–86, finds Goethe in deep isolation from bourgeois and courtly readerships and moving away from the broad aesthetic trend of popular writing. He struggles to formulate a classical aesthetic which will both purify his intrinsic subjectivism and mediate it with the objective world, but is uncertain both of his direction and his mission. The third phase corresponds to high Weimar Classicism, 1786–1805. The Italian journey makes possible a new sense of poetic mission. He jettisons most administrative duties and renews his ambition to write for a wider, homogeneous German public. It is the purpose of his new writing alliance with Schiller to create that as yet non-existent public. Alienated from the still dominant Enlightenment and Storm and Stress mode of his peers, he now engages in publicistic and poetological controversy, and seeks with the full weight of his authority to exert normative influence over the development of German literature in the critical phase of post-Revolutionary change – notably in his relationships with Romantics. The epoch following Schiller's death, 1805–32, marks the final phase. Goethe is once more disillusioned by and alienated from German poets and public alike. He writes autobiography instead of patriotic songs during the Wars of Liberation 1806–15. He is attacked for lack of patriotism by the Romantics and for political indifference by the Young Germans. He develops a sense of identity and community beyond his immediate culture and epoch, forming literary friendships with select fellow spirits of world literature both contemporary and past, from Occident and Orient. Now aimed at future readerships, his writing takes on a testamentary, but no less authoritative form.

Autonomy of person was perhaps Goethe's primal need. The need for autonomy, the regulation of one's life by internal rather than external authority, was early provoked in Goethe's personality. The autobiography *Dichtung und Wahrheit* (Poetry and Truth) records how his eccentric and dictatorial father composed a life plan for his son strongly resembling his own path (HA IX, 31–3) – it included, for example, an Italian journey. Other pillars of received, external authority – religion and nation – crumbled during the poet's adolescence. His acceptance of orthodox Christian doctrine gave way to alternative, pantheistic leanings. The Seven Years' War confirmed the nation's fragmentation and prevented identification with 'Germany'. At Leipzig in 1765–7, he sought to follow Professor of Poetry Christian Fürchtegott Gellert's sentimentalist ethics, but once Gellert seemed to have been discredited, Goethe acknowledged the disappearance of all authority from his life (HA IX, 294–6). A vacuum of meaning emerged – and a correlated yearning for it. Engagement with this, as a poet, was to determine the course of his career. For that vacuum, in these circumstances, could, as he recognized, be filled only in some sense by creativity within. Hence the sixty-year-old Goethe records the classic formulation of his youthful poetics: that he must look into himself and his own experience for poetic content and meaning, in order to write a new literature explaining both self *and* world, so that his works are but 'fragments of one great confession' (HA IX, 283–4). In Leipzig Goethe had already acquired an interest in the classical motif germane to this predicament: Pygmalion, the artist who, confronted with the absence of his desired object, creates a substitute from his own resources (WA I, vol. XXXVII, 39–41). But it was only after the encounter at Strasbourg in 1770 with Johann Gottfried Herder, the leading mind of the burgeoning literary revolt of the Storm and Stress movement, that the implications of Goethe's poetic project became evident and he found a terminology with which to describe it. For 'Genie' (genius) is the key concept of the Storm and Stress, and Goethe soon came to apply it to himself (HAB I, 44), with surprising results.

Rules were the motto of German poetics in the first two thirds of the eighteenth century. Johann Christoph Gottsched insisted that the purpose of literature was moral improvement, that this message was properly addressed to the intellect, and that literary method was the imitation of nature according to classical models derived from Aristotle. Now Johann Jakob Bodmer and Johann Jakob Breitinger had already focused attention on the imagination, and Gellert and Gotthold Ephraim Lessing had demanded increased emotionality and introduced new forms, themes and subjects. But Herder and his fellow members of the Storm and Stress instigated a far more radical departure. Inspired by a new philosophical pantheism, they rejected intellectualism and abstraction. Both nature and art participated in divine creativity. But that creativity could not be captured in a rule-bound system of thought. It was felt or intuited, in the heart or the imagination. Its organ was not thought, but expression in language or other sensual media. Art must still imitate nature (and culture), but as *natura naturans*, not *natura naturata*. The artist creates by analogy to divine creation, but only the untrammelled authentic artist: the *genius*. Herder summed this up in his pathbreaking essay on Shakespeare (1773) as the model genius who – given the affinity of English and German culture – could inspire a German literary renaissance. Shakespeare is not, as classicist authorities thought, the author of monstrous, rule-infringing dramas unfit to be included in the Sophoclean tradition. Shakespeare's drama *is* authentic tragedy, but only as *modern* tragedy. Born in different historical and cultural conditions, Shakespeare flouts the received system of rules, and boldly recreates tragedy to suit. Thus Shakespeare, like Sophocles, is a 'mortal gifted with divine power'.[10] Whilst the genius may, then, be subject to the flow of history and indeed cultural circumstance (as everything is for Herder), he is, as an artist, subject to nothing else: he is his own, ultimate authority.

All this Goethe took in, and it can readily be seen how far Herder's conceptual framework explained his own condition. His own prose hymn to Shakespeare (HA XII, 224–7) echoes Herder's formulations, and his essay on German architecture (HA XII, 7–15) discovers a local German genius in Erwin von Steinbach, author of Strasbourg cathedral. It is clear that Goethe understood Herder's implicit call for a new German genius to regenerate German literature as applying to himself, and that *Götz von Berlichingen*, with its Shakespearean treatment of national themes, is the result. But another of Goethe's early works reveals more. At the close of the Steinbach essay Goethe had reflected on the possibility of a genius appearing in his own decadent age. Such a genius would mediate between gods and men. The allusion is to the love demon Eros, who performs this function in Plato's *Symposium*. But Goethe here compares the mediatory function of genius with an altogether more earthly figure: Prometheus (HA XII, 15). As his own free-verse hymn 'Prometheus' (1774) reveals, this figure exerted a powerful and characteristic fascination on Goethe in this phase of his writerly self-understanding.

Perhaps the most self-centred text of German literary history, it scorns the highest divinity, Jupiter, and eulogizes human creativity. Although the text is cast as a dialogue, Jupiter never answers, so that the sole load-bearing communicative structure is Prometheus' voice, which inexorably, in defiant solitary greatness, acquires monumental stature. The rebellious titan (who stole the divine spark from Olympus) belittles the god's pitiably abstract majesty. Jupiter may decapitate mountain peaks as a boy beheads thistles, yet he cannot destroy Prometheus' slight dwelling. He is silent when petitioned, cold to suffering. Yet even he is subject to time and fate. What Prometheus has achieved is thus the product of his passionate heart and heroism alone. Like some existentialist hero, like Goethe's own Faust, Prometheus, far from quailing at the realization that the gods are forever absent, says 'yes' to this mode of existence. For he has power over it, he can (blasphemously, of course) form people in his image – to *live*, in the transitive sense of creating their own meaning amid theological absurdity. This mode of existence, then, is perhaps the ultimate affirmation of self, and the ultimate self-image of the Storm and Stress genius. Absolute autonomy is attained, even to the extent of destroying the self's higher origin, and the self – radicalizing the early Pygmalion poem – is presented at the close of the poem as its *own* creation. There is something quintessentially modern about this aspect of the young Goethe. Literary modernism arises around the end of the eighteenth century,[11] and one of its key features is the rise of the subject to autonomy and authority after cultural secularization. The young Goethe's experience of the need to create himself – through his own writing – makes him into *the* pioneer and emblem of modern writing. From this, no doubt, derives Goethe's extraordinary status amongst both contemporaries and scholars of his work as the representative writer of an entire epoch.[12]

It is on works such as 'Prometheus' that Goethe's charisma among his peers as the focus of national literary renewal was founded. To an extent he cultivated his status. After the huge success of *Götz* and *Werther* he made an ostentatious journey of the geniuses in May 1774 with the brothers Stolberg, dressed like Werther and (untypically) displaying the boorishness expected of those who follow only their own norms. Yet Goethe's self-understanding as a writer even then was far more self-conscious, complex and troubled than this suggests. He reflected critically on the concept of mastery. In the dithyrambic odes of the Greek Pindar he found a model of the lyric creative genius and a certain moment of self-recognition. Writing to his 'brother' Herder (10 July 1772; HAB I, 131–4) Goethe memorably images the poet who has mastered the surges of unruly genius after Pindar as a charioteer mightily submitting four unbroken horses to his will, and this image dominates the ebullient 'An Schwager Kronos' (To Coachman Cronus, 1774). But this does not mean that Goethe saw himself as having mastered that genius. In the Pindar letter the triumphant charioteer image is counterbalanced by its equal and oppo-site image: that of the poet's fragile boat on the trackless uncertain waves (HAB I, 131). More publicly, Goethe relativizes the assertiveness of his titanic hymn in others which comment on its hubris. 'Ganymed' (Ganymede, 1774) blankly contradicts 'Prometheus': the god above the clouds actually does de-scend upon a mortal to enjoy a homoerotic embrace. 'Wandrers Sturmlied' (Wayfarer's storm song, 1774) subtly satirises the pretence of the Storm and Stress genius to which its title alludes. It seems straightforward. A poet on his symbolic journey over the mountains through the storm celebrates genius. Thanks to its inner warmth he transcends the earthly elements. He vener-ates Dionysus, Apollo and Jupiter as its divine protectors. As he reaches his physical goal, he also attains his spiritual goal in a celebration of Pindar (with the charioteer image). Yet Goethe also skilfully suggests a less sublime counter-current. As the poet suffers the effects of mountain weather, a careful reading shows him becoming possessed by the thought of creature comforts. His wings of genius become strangely woolly. He longs to join a peasant by the fire. The Jupiter protective of genius becomes 'Jupiter Pluvius', rain god. The tumbling rhythms of the hymn stagger ever more wearily. This remarkable poem, then, deflates the pretensions of Storm and Stress by confronting its rhetoric of creativity with the elemental fact of everyday mud. From this perspective it also becomes clear that the emphatic assertorial quality of 'Prometheus' suggests an inner dialectic. But all this also typifies Goethe's writing strategy and self-understanding as a precocious authority in the newly emergent German republic of letters. For where does this leave the concept of genius? Goethe accepts and assumes the position of authority. But he also, simultaneously, questions it, in complex, dialectical statements.

It is from this perspective that Goethe's decision to serve the Duke of Saxe-Weimar from late 1775 makes sense. For Goethe's pre-Weimar texts, whilst widely read, did not find the right readers. Werther, for example, is another Storm and Stress titan – the titan of sentimentality. In that Werther experiences life primarily through the sentimentalizing lens of literature (Homer, the Bible, Ossian, Rousseau, Goldsmith, Klopstock), *Die Leiden des jungen Werther* actually treats the problem of life as literature. Literature increasingly dominates as compensation for unlived life, so that Werther's narcissistic commitment to feeling turns inward, tragically to consume him. As the novel's astonishing resonance proves, Werther was nothing less than the mirror-image of German public consciousness. Contemporary readers recognized their image but missed the concomitant critique. They sympathized with the protest at the limitations placed by feudal Germany on middle-class ambitions, and so misread the text as an apology of suicide. Allegedly some followed Werther's example. More pried into the life of those who had inspired the fictive figures. (Henceforth Goethe travelled incognito.) All this seemed to Goethe to repeat precisely the error *Werther* warned against. His role as critic of public consciousness became lost in the success of his role as its portrayer. Worse, it was confused with an unwanted role as public consciousness incarnate. From this time dates another fundamental (and pioneering) feature of Goethe's self-consciousness as a writer: his contempt for the German middle-class reading public, with which he henceforth played a game of hide-and-seek.[13] In any case, there was no executive power in the public sphere, and in fragmented Germany public opinion could neither help nor hinder anyone (HA IX, 535, 593–6). This conclusion, no doubt, influenced Goethe's decision in November 1775 to abandon the trip to Italy his father had so long planned, reject the middle-class readership for an aristocratic one, and rethink the project of German literary renewal from the place his bourgeois father dreaded, a court.

In Weimar Goethe was to discover that there was no alternative to the middle-class reader, but to do so he had to revise his notion of authorship. In aesthetic terms, the writing of his first Weimar decade, 1775–86, is dominated by the search for an alternative to the ambiguously qualified subjectivism of the Storm and Stress epoch. He slowly moved towards the foundation of a German classicism. This is evidenced in part by new enthusiasm for non-poetic vocations. The worldly role of court tutor, diplomat and minister, renewed interest in developing his artistic talent, and earnest pursuit of natural scientific knowledge all reflect a will to new engagement with the external and the objective on their own terms, yet without negating the cultivation of the subjective which is his prime motivation. All this might seem to entail writer's block. In fact, Goethe never stopped writing. Weimar, with the witty and philosophically deep Enlightenment writer Christoph Martin Wieland long ensconced, was already a 'Musenhof' (court of muses), and Goethe invited fellow Storm and Stress writers Friedrich Leopold Stolberg, Lenz, Kaufmann, Klinger, Leisewitz and Herder. (Thanks to their inability to share his new tendency, all, save Herder, were promptly disinvited.) He thus functioned as a court poet, offering admittedly slight occasional lyrics, *Singspiele*, and like poetic amusements for the narrow aristocratic circle, and ran the amateur court theatre. He never abandoned high literary ambition, and carefully reserved time from his official existence for that purpose (HAB I, 303). But Goethe found it impossible to complete major poetic works in this environment. Big projects begun before Weimar – *Faust* (1770–3) and *Egmont* (1774) – were repeatedly taken up and dropped again. Big projects begun in Weimar – *Iphigenie auf Tauris* (Iphigenia in Tauris, 1779), *Wilhelm Meisters theatralische Sendung* (Wilhelm Meister's Theatrical Mission, 1777), *Torquato Tasso* (1780) – were either not completed to his satisfaction and shelved, or remained fragments. The main reason, as his confessional ode 'Harzreise im Winter' (Winter journey in the Harz, 1777) demonstrates, was that Goethe was never sure of his direction, poetic or existential. A transformation of Goethe's lone ascent of the Brocken peak in the Harz mountains, it reveals him engaged in self-dialogue and seeking a sign to confirm his chosen path. Again Jupiter features, as the poet figures his auto-therapeutic song hopefully in the image of the Jovial eagle seeking prey – an augury of the future. But the text is dominated by the labyrinth image. Each human being, he reflects, has a God-given fate. Some follow the obvious path of fortune. Others leave the path without trace. He begs Jupiter, now addressed as god of love, for guidance, and finds it – not within, but in the inspiring sight of the vast mountain. Sublime and inscrutable, it nevertheless feeds the surrounding land with the rivers springing from its flanks. Henceforth he trusts to love, rejects Wertherian inwardness, and turns to externality.

In fact, this decade's representative work is neither courtly nor bourgeois, but private. Its keynote, as Goethe strives for classicism, is purity. In the internal sphere that purity is the deeply unWertherian, self-fulfilling yet self-less love for Charlotte von Stein, wife of a Weimar court official, to which 'Harzreise im Winter' probably alludes. To the discipline of this austere love Goethe willingly submitted for ten years. A lyric to 'Lida' exemplifies this. 'Warum gabst du uns die tiefen Blicke' (Why the gift of this profound gaze, 1776) explores the riddle of their fated bond. Other mortals pass their lives in untroubled self-ignorance. Yet these lovers recognise a deep affinity which seems to extend into the measureless past and future. In that utopian other time her calming influence and moral authority is balsam for his restless soul and purification for his sensuality. But since they are in reality separated, they must renounce happiness, and struggle to understand why. However, as Platonic memory reaffirms the higher truth of their bond, the poem ends on a note of comfort. A little later Goethe, taking up his favourite metaphor of life as sea voyage, refers to Frau von Stein's love as keeping his (evidently shipwrecked) person afloat, like a cork life-jacket (letter to Knebel, 3 February 1782; HAB I, 381). But its author deemed even this act of objective self-renunciation unpublishable. It appeared only in 1848.

Other work of this epoch translates the yearned-for purity into a privatized and psychologized version of the courtly sphere. *Iphigenie* abstracts from the bourgeois emotionality of *Werther* or the historical tumult of *Götz* and translates the austere Platonic love of Frau von Stein into a redemptive social ethos. *Torquato Tasso*, finished in 1789, distils Goethe's writerly crisis of a decade. The Weimar 'Musenhof' figures as the cultural idyll of Renaissance Ferrara. The moody poetic genius Tasso and the cool diplomat Antonio together incorporate Goethe's double life. Princess Leonore is Tasso's unattainable muse, Duke Alfons his indulgent patron. Unable to live as a free writer, Tasso receives a living in return for sacrificing ownership of his work to the Duke. Like Goethe, he feels accepted and understood by this select readership (HA V, 85). His work's strength derives from his being both of the court's worldly business and simultaneously distant – as the Princess is both beloved muse and untouchable royal person. But a conflict with Antonio tragically reveals this precarious harmony to be an illusion. They compete in mutual misrecognition. Upset, Tasso draws his sword on Antonio and embraces the Princess, so guaranteeing banishment. Yet *Tasso* is not just a poet's tragedy. Ferrara is no cultural utopia. The elite readership is too small and limited for Tasso's works to have their (deeply needed, HA V, 144) effect. The court grasps Tasso's meaning no better than the middle classes that of *Werther*. He rightly yearns for the papal glory of Rome and exchange with other great poets. Ferrara, then, is too provincial to hold him. The broken metaphor of his last speeches reveals the extent of Tasso's suffering. Antonio is both the rock on which his wave is dashed and (recalling once more the motif of life as sea voyage) a rock which wrecks his vessel, but also the rock to which he must cling. Reduced to the existential minimum of his malfunctioning poetic voice, Tasso needs a new environment *and* audience. This is Goethe's tactful yet withering judgement on the first ten Weimar years of his writerly career.

Of course these works are already in some sense the product of the renewal that Goethe portrays himself in *Tasso* as seeking. The journey to Italy of 1786–8, willy-nilly fulfilling his father's plan, generated the precarious synthesis of this first phase of Weimar Classicism. Goethe's deep self-consciousness had always compelled him, if not to introspection, then to constant self-review. His letters speak often of him shedding his skin like a snake or of events which make an 'epoch' in his life.[14] Italy was part of this constant, if retarded process of self-reinvention. Allegedly begun on his thirty-seventh birthday, the journey was planned as a rebirth. The encounter with Italian art and nature was conducted in the name of primordial objectivity (*Italienische Reise*, 17 September 1786; HA XI, 45): Goethe discovered the 'Urpflanze' ('primal plant'), studied the body and (neo)classical architecture, absorbed the proto-classicist aesthetics of Karl Philipp Moritz. Thus Goethe felt transformed into a whole man and a whole poet – especially by Rome (letter to Carl August, 2 September 1786, HAB II, 10). This spiritual and poetic self-reinvention went hand-in-hand with a transformation of his public image. Complete or collected editions of his works were for Goethe always troubling confrontations with his past self. When the Berlin bookseller Himburg's pirated collection of his writings in three volumes appeared in Berlin in 1775–6, he denounced them to Frau von Stein as 'old shed snake skins stretched over the white paper' (14 May 1779; WA IV, vol. IV, 37). The first authorized edition of *Goethes Schriften* (Leipzig: Göschen, 1787–90) was his response. Of eight volumes, four were allegedly complete when he left for Italy, and he struggled throughout his sabbatical with the rest. Goethe records how this 'Summa Summarum' (summation of his achievement, HAB II, 104) forces a recapitulation of his previous way of thinking and writing which benefits his progress. It will close one epoch of his writing career and open another (to Carl August, 11 August 1787; HAB II, 63). Thus the shelved works are at last published – as exhibitions of what Goethe has become during the first Weimar decade, if not what he is about to be. *Werther* had its passionate style smoothed and de-personalised, and acquired a more censorious narrator. Back home *Faust* was resurrected, and through three key additions – the pact scene, 'Hexenküche' (Witch's Kitchen) and 'Wald und Höhle' (Forest and Cavern) – gained enough narrative coherence and elevation of heroic character to make it publishable. All this conformed to the severe, formulaic aesthetic with which Goethe returned from Italy, and which is encapsulated in the essay 'Einfache Nachahmung der Natur, Manier, Stil' (Simple imitation of nature, manner, style, 1789; HA XII, 30–4), which is as far from Storm and Stress genius as can be imagined. Simple imitation, whilst not inconsiderable, is but the earliest degree of aesthetic achievement; it connotes an active and thorough, if only external, rendering of the object. Manner mixes this inevitably unsatisfying aesthetic experience with subjectivity; it expresses the object in the language of the subject. Style, the highest possible degree of aesthetic attainment, transcends this dualism; it is rigorously mimetic of the object, but presupposes a subjectivity so highly developed as to capture the object's inner essence, and this is expressed in a universal language.

The public, however, was not ready for Goethe's *Schriften*. Goethe complained that they were unpopular (to the publisher Göschen, 4 July 1791, HAB II, 141), fantasized about concentrating on natural scientific writing, and despaired of ever again publishing collected works. Nor was Goethe ready for Germany. Germany was prosaic (HAB II, 128) and formless (HA XIII, 102). His Weimar circle tired of the never-ending stream of nostalgia for Italy and greeted with incomprehension his new views on the homology of nature and art and the paradigmatic relation of art and society in classical antiquity (HA XIII, 102). But the *Schriften* mark only the retrospective end of the first classical decade, and Goethe was about to embark on another 'new career' (HAB II, 128): high classicism, from 1786 to 1805. This was marked in his personal life by the break from Charlotte von Stein in 1789 and the 'naive' enjoyment of pure sensuality in his natural marriage with Christiane Vulpius. In his literary life the impulse came from the unexpected quarter of the writer Friedrich Schiller, hitherto known for his passionate tragedies. By now a professed follower of the critical philosopher Kant, Schiller could not share Goethe's conviction that objective experience of Jovial nature should be the guiding light of human life. However, Schiller displayed a surprising sensitivity to Goethe's position. They detected common, complementary interests beneath their differences (HA X, 540–1) – one emphasizing the ideal of *nature*, the other the *ideal* of nature. Above all, both Schiller (motivated by Kantian aesthetics) and Goethe (moved by his experience of Italian sensual objectivity) shared a vision of human fulfilment as the poised harmony of mind and body. Both now saw aesthetic experience as the way to promote that harmony. In 1794, as Herder (who favoured a moralizing view of art) became alienated, they formed the strategic alliance with the purpose of propagating that shared vision, which was to dominate German letters until Schiller's death.

The organ of this alliance was Schiller's new literary journal *Die Horen* (The Horae, 1795–7). It propagated aesthetic experience as *the* medium in which conflicts – of mind and body, individual and state – can be resolved, and sought to create a genuine literary community of interest for the first time in Germany. It therefore served Goethe's most deeply felt need as a writer. Having failed to find either a bourgeois or a courtly audience, he now co-operated with Schiller to create a new readership. Hence the sensual *Römische Elegien* (Roman Elegies, written 1790, published 1795), which mark the true beginning of Goethe's post-Italian 'newer manner' (HAB II, 63), stand programmatically in the same issue as Schiller's letters *Über die ästhetische Erziehung der Menschen* – the one leading the reader through sensuality to form, the other leading through abstraction to sensuality.

This project had several aspects. For Goethe, the encounter with Schiller was one of those rare occasions when he felt himself understood and realized that he too could learn something. For example, Schiller's conceptually precise characterization of him as a model naive and/or classical poet helped Goethe make sense of his transformation from a problematic youthful genius to a mature poet with a grasp of his own limitations. Once again, this experience was a poetic rebirth (January 1798; HAB II, 323). As he had hitherto done only with Herder, Goethe passed his nascent poetic projects, notably *Faust* and *Wilhelm Meisters Lehrjahre*, to Schiller, and granted him something like the right of tacit co-authorship. Schiller played a large part too in the re-founded Weimar theatre, of which Goethe was director. They also entered publicistic debate. Both were clear that they needed to form readers and writers (to Schiller, 8–19 October 1794; HAB II, 187). They sought alliances with writers of approved tendency: the temperate August Wilhelm Schlegel but not his extremist brother Friedrich, nor the voluptuous Jean Paul (see Goethe's letter to Schiller, 2 June 1796; HAB II, 226–7). When *Die Horen* was mocked, they countered with a jointly written set of monitory epigrammatic couplets, the *Xenien*. Prescriptive writings were the positive side of this. Both were influenced by Kant's notion of the artist from §46 of the *Critique of Judgement* (1790) as the genius, an elemental natural force whose spontaneous creativity, however, also, uniquely, sets objective aesthetic norms for others. Thus they produced separately and jointly sets of literary norms on epic and dramatic poesy and dilettantism, and Goethe wrote models of modern classic genres: epics such as *Hermann und Dorothea* and *Märchen* (Fairytale). But the profoundest didactic effort of Goethe's Schillerian rebirth, and the work which made his name again, was his model novel *Wilhelm Meisters Lehrjahre*.

The reincarnation of his stillborn attempt to reach a middle-class audience in the early Weimar years, *Wilhelm Meisters theatralische Sendung*, the *Lehrjahre* reject aesthetic mission and teach *Bildung* as practical philan-thropy. Unfortunately, the enigmatically tragic artist-figure Mignon seems to suggest exactly the opposite. In Friedrich Schlegel's mind such ambigu-ity generated a famous creative misunderstanding. To him, and irrespective of its utilitarian message, *Wilhelm Meisters Lehrjahre* seemed a novel in which art was reflected upon with sovereign irony *in* art, and so finally emerged as a kind of meta-hero of the text. As such, Schlegel felt he had dis-covered a paradigmatic expression of the Romantic aesthetic. With this in mind he clearly wished to appropriate Goethe to Romanticism. Goethe and the *Lehrjahre* were systematically lionized, notably in the Schlegels' journal *Athenaeum* (1798–1800). This brilliant campaign re-established Goethe as *the* literary authority. Almost every major novel (or novel-like text) by the early Romantics, from Wilhelm Heinrich Wackenroder's *Herzensergie-ßungen eines kunstliebenden Klosterbruders* (Outpourings of an art-loving friar, 1796) to Hardenberg's *Heinrich von Ofterdingen* (1801) follows and re-aestheticizes Goethe's paradigm of the *Bildungsroman*. Romantic 'Symphilosophie' and 'Sympoesie' (shared authorship) also follow Goethe's and Schiller's example, and Goethe at last became a kind of literary police au-thority or censor. When Hardenberg and Friedrich Wilhelm Joseph Schelling differed over the former's *Die Christenheit oder Europa* (Christendom, or Europe, 1799), a utopian design for post-Revolutionary peace which in-vokes a reborn papacy and Society of Jesus, Goethe was asked whether this and Schelling's coarse riposte *Epikurisch Glaubensbekenntnis Heinz Wider-porstens* (Heinz Widerporst's Epicurean confession of faith, 1799) might be published. They were not. With both Schiller and the Romantics (if not the Enlightenment writers) under his spell, the years around 1800 mark the high point of Goethe's literary authority during his lifetime.

For a time Goethe sought to co-operate with the early Romantics. Finally, however, he rejected Romantic adulation (HAB II, 349–50), and condemn-ed 'das klosterbrudrisirende...Unwesen' ('artyfriarifying...monstrosity'; WA I, vol. XLVIII, 122). Even if he sympathised with its pantheistic and critical tendencies, Romanticism represented positions he had overcome or always rejected: inwardness, abstraction, one-dimensional nationalism, religious tendency, mysticism, aestheticism, graveyard melancholy. The early Romantics soon distanced themselves from him. Hardenberg rejected *Wilhelm Meister* as a 'gospel of economics'.[15] Friedrich Schlegel left the coun-try and moved towards a position identifying art with Roman Catholic de-votion which opposed Goethe's conviction of art's autonomy. When Schiller died on 9 May 1805, the gap in Goethe's creative life was so painful that he seemed to need a substitute. In 1808 he seriously entertained the possi-bility of promoting the Catholicizing Romantic dramatist Friedrich Ludwig

Zacharias Werner into that role (HAB III, 62–8). Something similar happened with a figure on the fringes of Romanticism, Heinrich von Kleist (HAB III, 53, 64). Both were invited to Weimar or to send their work, it was performed without success, and they were then dismissed for their mystical, untheatrical, tasteless or disharmonious productions. Goethe continued to produce enjoyably vitriolic anti-Romantic aphorisms until his death.

With Schiller's death, alienation from the now dominant Romantics, and Germany's collapse in 1806–7 before the invading Revolutionary armies, Goethe felt more keenly than ever at odds with his time. Schiller seems shortly before his death to have suggested a further edition of collected works. Intended as definitive (WA IV, vol. XIX, 13), *Goethes Werke* (13 vols, Tübingen: Cotta, 1806–10) provoked another attack of self-doubt. This inaugurates the last, long phase of Goethe's writerly self-understanding. Again he sheds his literary skin in a crisis. There is, first, the need to preserve the substance of his lifelong project for better times; this is intensified by the traumatic encounter with French troops at home (Goethe to Zelter, 22 June 1808; HAB III, 75). *Faust I*, now complete in all respects, is perhaps this edition's main achievement. Second, as a personal encounter with Napoleon himself in September 1808 revealed – the great man focused almost entirely on *Werther* (HA X, 545–6) – Goethe saw again how far public opinion still distorted his achievement. Only his youthful works seemed to interest the Germans. Having read so much, they were insensitive to new forms, and had no sympathy for his new writing (HAB III, 226). Yet he never lost his thirst for public success, even if he had to wait twenty years for it (HAB III, 173). Third, worse, was his oeuvre's strangeness to himself and his *own* relative indifference to it (WA IV, 19, 323). The result, apart from *Goethes Werke*, was a sustained burst of highly complex autobiographical writing over the next two decades. It was certainly designed to serve one traditional end of such discourse, intimate self-insight. With Schiller's death Goethe was reduced to self-dialogue. But the autobiography is never merely introspective. Self-insight, he insists (HA IX, 9), emerges not from unmediated introspection, but from analysis of the subject in dialogue with his objective contexts. The horizon of Goethe's autobiography encompasses both the life-story *and* a totalizing interpretation of the epoch.

Thus *Dichtung und Wahrheit* (1811–14, 1833) exemplifies Goethe's alienation on several levels. The very fact of it being autobiography runs counter to the tendency of the age. The Germans, passionately resisting Napoleon, now cultivated reckless nationalism for the first time. Virtually all major writers (Theodor Körner, Arndt, Hoffmann von Fallersleben, Werner, Clemens Brentano) turned to forms of collective aesthetic experience (notably folksong and tragedy) which strengthened the emergent sense of national identity at the expense of the classical sense of autonomous individuality and generated an image of France as the hated other. Against this noisy and uncompromising literary background, autobiographical writing seemed a complacent self-indulgence, a manifestation of the sovereign Jovial arrogance of which Goethe was often accused. In fact, *Dichtung und Wahrheit* subtly advocates Goethe's resistance to contemporary German nationalism. His accounts of the effect on his young personality of the French occupation of Frankfurt am Main and the investiture of Charles I as Holy Roman Emperor at Frankfurt in 1757 both defend the cosmopolitan humanity of the French and satirize the archaic Holy Roman Empire at a time when such opinions were almost unsayable.[16] *Dichtung und Wahrheit* was also designed to fill the gaps in his canon of writings and manipulate readers' understanding of their meaning from the perspective of his own self-development. *Die Leiden des jungen Werther*, despite having been rewritten for *Goethe's Schriften*, is explained yet again as medicine for the sickness of the Storm and Stress. Autobiography takes up over a fifth of the forty volumes in the final definitive self-edition,[17] without, however, a single mention of Weimar.

As the Napoleonic wars subsided and the German Confederation (1815–66) was founded, the conservative German public of the *Biedermeier* epoch, whilst it lost the taste for collective affirmations of national identity, also rediscovered its liking for mass-produced trivial literature. Not just Goethe, but all the authors of the great Classical-Romantic age were reduced to obscurity as absent gods of high culture. The great Herderian project of a German culture unified through its high literature, which Goethe and Schiller had sought to realize on the model of classical Greece, had stalled. Throughout his career, Goethe expressed his writerly isolation through the yearning for a 'Gemeinschaft der Heiligen' (community of the blessed).[18] *Die Wahlverwandtschaften* (Elective affinities, 1809) was written as a circular to friends, not the German public, that mere caricature of the ideal Greek *demos*. The only defence against public opinion were the ability to wait and faith in the work's assertion of its value (HAB III, 117). The *Farbenlehre* (Theory of colour, 1810) contains anticipatory retaliation against unsympathetic readers, in the form of a polemic against uncritical reliance on received authority (HA XIV, 50, 56), and vainly anathematizes Newton. Goethe continued to write. But he now sought his band of kindred spirits beyond German borders in time, space and language.

He found it first with the *West-östliche Divan* (West-eastern divan, 1819, HA II, 7–120). Still another poetic rebirth, this lyric cycle reawakens Goethe's youthful Orientalism and integrates the Oriental world into the horizon of his maturity. Goethe's project for literary renewal had, like Herder's, always been more than nationalist. Their common interest in folksong as vehicle of national culture was always subsumed under the cosmopolitan cultural relativism which derived from their humanism and anthropological interest. In the fourteenth-century Persian court poet Hafiz Goethe recognized a peer. The *Divan* is an intercultural dialogue of the living and the dead in the meta-historical dimension inhabited by Goethe's community of the blessed. As such, many of its confessional lyrics, echoing Storm and Stress genius, verge self-consciously on the hubristic. Goethe's lyric persona openly identifies with the master-poet Hafiz. Steeped in the spiritual tradition of his culture, he asserts his authority ('Beiname' (Appellation), 20–21). Only those who have transcended their mono-cultural provenance and assimilated three thousand years of culture have right of admittance into this circle – 'Wer franzoset oder britet' (Whoever frenchi- or britannifies, 49). They proclaim their superior status as god-given ('Timur spricht' (Timur speaks), 50) and the poet is in a sense as great as the emperor ('Komm, Liebchen, komm!' (Come, beloved, come!), 68). Goethe's *Divan* commentary (HA II, 126–267) is equally provocative. Its defence of Oriental poets' practice of serving a despot (178) recalls *Tasso*. Elsewhere he praises the Oriental custom of selecting a poet-king at court, with analogous status and powers to the real king (151). It is no coincidence that the *Divan* serves among other things as a monument to Goethe's own golden age of 1786–1805, figured as the Oriental 'Zeit der Barmekiden' (Age of the Barmecides, an enlightened Persian ruling elite, 7): an ideal of cultural achievement which may one day, somewhere, under like conditions, come again (147).

For this latter project, the utopian renewal of a lost idyll, his ultimate compensatory expression of post-classical renunciation, Goethe finally arrived at the concept of *Weltliteratur* (world literature). The image of the genius never quite disappears from Goethe's writing (the Pindaric charioteer recurs in *Faust II* as Knabe Lenker; HA III, 172–7). But now the frank assertion of still lively, overweening genius is silenced as Goethe, once more a pioneer, formulates the broadest possible category under which his own activity might be understood. In the epoch of the nation-state's triumph and apogee of colonialism, he asserts that the age of national literature is past and that of world literature come (to Eckermann, 31 January 1827). World literature is a thoroughly decentred, and in this sense anti-authoritative idea.[19] Conceiving of ancient and modern, high and low, European and non-European literatures as the highest expression of relative cultural identities, it posits dialogue between characteristic works of national literatures as the apt mode of communication between national cultures. This benefits both sides, through mutual understanding, criticism and tolerance. *Weltliteratur* has no overarching standpoint or master narrative: it does not envisage the formation of a supranational literature or canon, nor does it posit a particular literature or work as unconditionally normative (even though Goethe never abandons classical Greece as a provisional maximum of cultural achievement). This, perhaps Goethe's most striking thought out of season, has become a foundation-stone of today's post-colonial intercultural theory.[20]

For the rest of his writerly existence Goethe lived this concept. At once present and absent in Germany, he read foreign literature in phenomenal quantity: Scott, Byron, Cooper, Manzoni, the British, American and French reviews, and much more. His house became the stopping-point for cultured foreign travellers; he corresponded with promising non-Germans. The same policy governs his last writing phase. The cultivation of memory, as Goethe recalls his deep sense of a modernity out of control and incapable of self-knowledge (HAB IV, 146–7), is its common term. Goethe thus allows Eckermann to function as Boswell to his Johnson. He assiduously completes still-outstanding projects, the autobiography, *Wilhelm Meisters Wanderjahre* (Wilhelm Meister's Journeymanship, 1829), and *Faust II* (1832), and determines their position in the final definitive version of his works. Sensitive about the reception of *Faust II*, Goethe had the package sealed for posthumous publication. His late works thus have a testamentary quality, in that they assimilate the significant tendencies of the epoch and subject them to higher critique for posterity's sake, without presupposing the understanding of his contemporaries. The *Wanderjahre* thus expand Meister's story to include a critique of technologized mass civilization. *Faust II* expands his story to cover three thousand years of cultural history and almost everything significant about the nineteenth century, from paper money and mechanistic natural science to ecology and colonialism. Yet neither of these monumental works imposes an authorial line on the reader. The *Wanderjahre* narrator is ostentatiously incapable of integrating his material into a coherent whole, so that the reader must justify his own interpretation. Thickly hedged with distancing devices, *Faust II* offers the same challenge. Only those can understand these works who can understand them. The last word on Goethe's self-understanding in this sense, as a writer, must therefore belong to him. A late essay, 'Ein Wort für junge Dichter' (Some advice for young poets), defines as master one who directs our work and following whose principles we achieve our artistic goal. Goethe thus insists he was master of no one. If forced to characterize his significance for Germans and German poets, he would call himself their liberator (WA I, vol. XLII/2, 106). Echoing the terms of his youthful poetics, Goethe argues only that the poet must work out of himself. He gives them no norm (108); that they must do themselves. Thus Goethe in his self-understanding finally emerges as paradoxical authority who is none. It is perhaps just this real, yet intangible and fundamentally dialectical quality which has made him available for appropriation to lesser causes since his death. But it is also this which makes the real Goethe into the authority modernity deserves.[21]

NOTES

1 See his letter to his sister Cornelia, 13 October 1765 (HAB I, 13).
2 Athenäums-Fragment no. 216, in Friedrich Schlegel, *Kritische Friedrich-Schlegel-Ausgabe*, ed. Ernst Behler, Hans Eichner, and Jean-Jacques Anstett, 35 vols. (Paderborn, Munich, Vienna and Zurich: Schöningh, 1958–), II, pp. 198–9.
3 *Novalis. Schriften*, ed. Paul Kluckhohn, Richard Samuel and others, 6 vols. (Stuttgart, Berlin, Cologne, and Mainz: Kohlhammer, 1960–), II, p. 466.
4 In *Briefe des Dichters Friedrich Ludwig Zacharias Werner*, ed. Oswald Floeck, 2 vols. (Munich: Georg Müller, 1914), II, p. 124.
5 Heinrich Heine, *Die romantische Schule* (Munich: Goldmann, 1964), pp. 51–2.
6 Authors of works called *Goethe* from 1877 to the present include Herman Grimm, Richard Meyer, Albert Bielschowsky, Georg Brandes, Friedrich Gundolf, Georg Simmel, Benedetto Croce, Eugen Kühnemann, Friedrich Muckermann, Philip Witkop, Paul Altenberg, Joseph-François Angelloz, Emil Staiger, Peter Boerner, T. J. Reed and Dorothea Hölscher-Lohmeyer.
7 *The Classical Centre: Goethe and Weimar 1775–1832* (London: Croom Helm, 1980), esp. pp. 11–19, 255–8. See too Reed's *Nobody's Master. Goethe and the Authority of the Writer. With a Reflection on Anti-literary Theory* (Oxford: Oxford University Press, 1990).
8 'Exoterik und Esoterik in Goethes Romanen', *Goethe-Jahrbuch* 95 (1978), 212–26.
9 'Lebendige Natur – Wissenschaftskritik, Naturforschung und hermetische Allegorik bei Goethe', *Deutsche Vierteljahrsschrift* 60 (1986), 249–72.
10 *Sturm und Drang. Kritische Schriften*, ed. Erich Löwenthal (Heidelberg: Lambert Schneider, 1972), p. 566.
11 See Silvio Vietta, *Die literarische Moderne. Eine problemgeschichtliche Darstellung der deutschsprachigen Literatur von Hölderlin bis Thomas Bernhard* (Stuttgart: Metzler, 1992), pp. 21–33.
12 Compare David E. Wellbery, *The Specular Moment. Goethe's Early Lyric and the Beginnings of Romanticism* (Stanford, CA: Stanford University Press, 1996), esp. pp. 1–83, 120–83.
13 As he later said to Reinhard (22 June 1808; HAB III, 79).
14 See the letters to Frau von Stein, 9 October 1781; HAB I, 370–1 and to Langer, 29 April 1770; HAB I, 107.
15 *Novalis. Schriften*, III, 647.
16 See Klaus-Detlef Müller, *Autobiographie und Roman. Studien zur literarischen Autobiographie der Goethezeit* (Tübingen: Niemeyer, 1976), pp. 242–332.
17 *Goethes Werke. Vollständige Ausgabe letzter Hand*, 40 vols. (Stuttgart: Cotta, 1827–1830), vols. XXIV–XXXII.
18 See letters to Herder, 10 July 1772; HAB I, 133; to Zelter, 18 June 1831; WA IV, 48, 241.
19 See Fritz Strich, *Goethe und die Weltliteratur* (Berne: Francke, 1946); and Hendrik Birus, 'Am Schnittpunkt von Komparatistik und Germanistik. Die Idee der

Weltliteratur heute', in Hendrik Birus (ed.), *Germanistik und Komparatistik* (Stuttgart and Weimar: Metzler, 1995), pp. 439–57.

20 Homi K. Bhabha, *The Location of Culture* (London: Routledge, 1994), pp. 11–12.

21 On the concept of modern authority as requiring transparency and legitimacy see Richard Sennett, *Authority* (New York: Knopf, 1980).

3

JOHN R. WILLIAMS

Goethe the poet

Approaching Goethe's poetry

If we associate hexameter with Homer and Virgil, distichs[1] with the Latin elegiac and satirical poets, *terza rima, ottava rima*, and the sonnet with Dante and the Italian Renaissance poets, the sonnet and iambic pentameter with Shakespeare, the alexandrine with Victor Hugo and even Baudelaire, there is no particular poetic form we can immediately associate with Goethe; he wrote in all these forms and many, many more. Indeed, Goethe's supreme gift is that of convincing the reader that his chosen lyrical form, and no other, is the appropriate one for the expression of a particular poetic statement. His historical situation at a vibrant stage in the development of German language and literature, a time when the culture was becoming self-consciously German and yet was also highly receptive to foreign influences, his position at the threshold of European Romanticism, which he did much to shape and further, determined the scope and variety of his eclectic lyrical output – allied with an outstanding gift of poetic articulation, a quasi-magical command of language that suggests, no doubt misleadingly, that he was someone to whom poetic expression came as easily and as naturally as eating or breathing. Poetic language and expression informs and characterizes the whole range of Goethe's writing, quite particularly his verse dramas, but also much of his prose fiction, his private correspondence, and even some of his scientific work, the results of which were frequently expressed in lyrical form, in verse epigrams, or in longer didactic poems.

The sheer quantity and variety of Goethe's lyrical output poses the question of how his poetry is in practice to be critically approached or anthologized. Most modern anthologies, and many critical studies of his poems, are chronologically structured – allowing for the problem that many of his poems cannot be dated with certainty, and that he often revised individual poems, sometimes drastically, for publication. A persuasive case can also be made for reading his poems (and more especially the earlier poems) in their original form, as far as this can be established, with their often eccentric and highly expressive spelling and punctuation;[2] but this is not easy in practice, since even in standard critical editions editors have nearly always cautiously or 'diplomatically' modernized the text.

Goethe's own arrangement of his poems was strictly non-chronological; indeed, he expressly and deliberately set out to deter any biographical or genetic approach by grouping them according to theme, form, or genre. But his own groupings of his poems, and his ordering of individual poems within those groups, were also complicated by the publication history of the major collections of his verse during his lifetime.[3] Goethe's own rubrics survived into the Weimarer Ausgabe and thence, with certain editorial additions, corrections, and modifications, into some modern critical editions of his works: the Jubiläums-Ausgabe, the Artemis Gedenkausgabe, and the Berliner Ausgabe.[4] His ordering of the poems is instructive, even when he is not writing in formal lyrical cycles or genres, and his sequences should be noted and respected, even if they are not used as the basis for study. They are arranged in a non-chronological but thematically coherent order; the sequence may at times appear whimsical, but it is often based on principles of comparison and contrast, on a contrapuntal or dialectical progression, with some poems appearing to contradict, but more usually complementing or balancing previous or following ones.

Any arrangement of Goethe's poems will slant or even skew them in one way or another by imposing a structure or profile on his lyrical oeuvre. It is generally, though not universally, accepted that his poems show a broad chronological profile corresponding to the personal and cultural experiences, the literary, philosophical, and scientific preoccupations of a long life; and with all the caveats against reading the poems as biography, or reading the biography into the poems, many critics and editors substitute for Goethe's own rubrics and sequences an apparently more illuminating chronological arrangement, with certain departures determined by generic or thematic grouping. The recent Münchner Ausgabe (MA) prints the poems in chronological order, grouped throughout the edition among the collected works – which is instructive, but scarcely practical for the student.[5] The Frankfurter Ausgabe collects the poems into two volumes (with the *West-östliche Divan* in a third volume) in a compromise that combines a chronological order with the historical sequence of Goethe's own collections of his poems, whether in manuscript or published form; at the cost of some repetition, this is an illuminating and practical arrangement. Both the Münchner Ausgabe and the Frankfurter Ausgabe scrupulously print the early versions of the poems – though even here the texts have been discreetly modernized. Erich Trunz's selection and arrangement of the poems in Volume 1 of the Hamburger

Ausgabe (with the *Divan* in Volume II), and its separate imprints, has been influential; for all the serious scholarly reservations about that edition,[6] it is widely accessible and familiar – but it is only an anthology. The recent *Goethe-Handbuch* has also chosen to deal with the poems on a broadly chronological basis, structured on the phases of Goethe's creative career. This is, in the first instance, the approach adopted here.

Goethe's lyric poetry: an overview

Goethe's earliest recorded poem, a New Year's greeting to his maternal (Textor) grandparents written in alexandrines at the age of seven, is almost certainly not his own unaided work. Otherwise, the 'Poetische Gedanken über die Höllenfahrt Jesu Christi' (Poetic Thoughts on Jesus Christ's Descent into Hell), some occasional poems, and some very quaint verses in French and English are the only very early poems to have survived his drastic burning of his juvenile writings in Leipzig in October 1767, and again in Frankfurt shortly before he left for Strasbourg in 1770. Goethe's career as a serious lyric poet is usually dated from the poems he wrote in Leipzig during his early student days, which were collected in manuscript form into three albums: the collection *Annette* of 1767, the three odes to his friend Behrisch from the same year, and an album of songs entitled *Lieder mit Melodien* (Songs with Melodies), published in 1769 (dated 1770) without Goethe's name as *Neue Lieder* (New Songs).

The *Annette* poems are very much in the style of the prevailing lyrical fashion in francophile Leipzig, a style to which Goethe made strenuous efforts to adapt his more homespun German literary instincts. It is the idiom commonly (and often disparagingly) labelled 'Anacreontic' or 'Leipzig Rococo', heavily indebted, not so much to the classical Anacreon, but to eighteenth-century rococo poets such as Hagedorn, Gleim, Gerstenberg, Wieland, Weiße and Zachariae. One poem is in fact addressed to 'Herrn Professor Zachariae'; others are adapted from Italian or French sources, one explicitly 'aus dem Französischen des Herrn v. Voltaire' (from the French of M. de Voltaire); one is an elegy on the death of Behrisch's brother, expressing in a sentimental idiom some mildly subversive political rhetoric on the tyranny of princes. For the most part, however, these poems (some, in the manner of Gerstenberg, partly in prose) strive for an effect of sophisticated wit and elegance. They revolve around seduction strategies and roguish erotic adventures in arcadian settings between lovers with neoclassical names, aided or frustrated by a rococo Cupid or Amor. The *Neue Lieder* continue the 'Anacreontic' idiom, addressing the themes of transience, *carpe diem* (the Horatian injunction to seize the present moment), erotic fulfilment or frustration in an allegorizing and often wryly sententious manner. The three odes to Behrisch are written under the very different influence of the lofty and declamatory rhetoric of Klopstock's classicizing odes. In short and dense unrhymed quatrains, Goethe voices a passionate empathy for his wronged friend in a laconic expression of disgust concentrated into images of a tree attacked by loathsome insects and of swamps infested with snakes and toads.

Goethe quickly shed the poetic idiom of Leipzig Rococo under the influence of the stimuli to which he was exposed during the brief but intense period of scarcely seventeen months in Strasbourg. Under Herder's tutelage, his new models were Homer, Pindar, Shakespeare, Klopstock and Ossian, the culture of the Reformation, the expressiveness of the German language in the robust vitality of the Lutheran Bible, and the native tradition of folksong: a host of enthusiasms came together to free Goethe's lyrical expression. The songs, ballads and odes, the burlesque sketches in prose and verse that pour from his pen in the Strasbourg and subsequent Frankfurt years are characterized by a youthful exuberance and energy and by an intensely personal idiom. The detached and facetious manner of the Leipzig verse gives way to serious emotional enthusiasm; poetry is not presented as entertainment, as an ironic game of wit and affected sophistication, but as a visceral response to love as a life-enhancing force, to nature as a dynamic organism, creative or destructive, idyllic or sinister. The creative genius of humanity is presented in a series of larger-than-life mythical and symbolic figures who project the role of the charismatic hero, the prophet, the genius, the pilgrim, the creator. A new freedom of expression, of strophic and metrical form, a joyful experimentation with the expressive power of language, mark Goethe's emergence as an original lyric poet.

The exuberance and energy of Goethe's youthful lyric poetry are evident in the ecstatic shouts of 'Maifest' (May Festival; later 'Mailied', May Song), or in the headlong rhythmic gallop of 'Mir schlug das Herz' (My heart was pounding; later 'Willkommen und Abschied', Greeting and Parting); but we should bear in mind that not all the poems from this phase are so spectacularly energetic or rhapsodic. Even among the so-called 'Sesenheim' songs there are more subdued and reflective poems ('Ein zärtlich jugendlicher Kummer', A tender youthful sense of sorrow), and even some whose imagery appears to cling to rococo allegories ('Kleine Blumen, kleine Blätter', Small flowers, small leaves). Goethe's lyrical experimentation and his exploration of the possibilities of expressive language are most strikingly evident in the Storm and Stress odes that rehearse a whole spectrum of existential stances: the rhapsodic frenzy of the inspired poet of 'Wandrers Sturmlied' (Wayfarer's

Song to the Storm) who merges comically and bathetically with the figure of the bedraggled traveller struggling along muddy roads in atrocious weather; the majestic progress of the prophet Mahomet in the image of the river bearing its tributaries to the ocean; the impatient arrogance of 'An Schwager Kronos' (To Coachman Cronus), in which life is a headlong coach journey that ends rattling through the gates of hell; the defiant challenge to divine authority of Prometheus – which is immediately qualified and complemented by the ecstatic submission of Ganymede. The 'Harzreise im Winter' (Winter Journey to the Harz), written in 1777 but related to the earlier odes in style and theme and situated among them by Goethe, is an obscure but powerful meditation on human fortune, structured around a mysterious quest for revelation on the summit of the haunted mountain, and peppered with specific references to Goethe's own journey to the Brocken in November and December that year. Fractured and jumbled syntax stretches the limits of coherent expression in 'Wandrers Sturmlied' and 'An Schwager Kronos' – though, as we shall note below, these poems are by no means incoherent in structure. Hymnic invocations, repetitions, parallelisms, inverted genitive constructions ('Deiner ewigen Wärme / Heilig Gefühl', the sacred touch of your eternal warmth), striking compounds and bold verbal juxtapositions tumble out in lines of free but emphatic rhythms that owe much to Klopstock's lofty style and to a fruitful misunderstanding of Pindar's metres, but which also display the linguistic exuberance of a young poet testing his expressive powers.

The poems to Lili Schönemann that conclude the creative phase from 1770 to 1775 tend to reflect what we know about Goethe's brief and fraught five months of betrothal – of which more than two were spent on a journey (or flight) to Switzerland. The uneasy conflict of uncertain feelings, the irksome social obligations imposed by the relationship, and wider existential questions of destiny and personal freedom, find their expression in the tensions of 'An Belinden' (To Belinda) and 'Lilis Park' (Lili's Park). The emotional ambivalences of this period are symbolically expressed in 'Auf dem See' (On the Lake) and 'Im Herbst 1775' (Autumn 1775; later 'Herbstgefühl', Autumn Mood). 'Auf dem See' exploits the grandiose Alpine scenery to articulate the succession of three contrasting states of mind: the dynamic exuberance of the first stanza is interrupted by four lines of introspective recollection, giving way to a more subdued progress in which the renewed forward perspective is qualified by a subtly reflective dimension suggested by the imagery of maturing fruit mirrored in the surface of the lake. 'Herbstgefühl' is a more intense meditation on maturity, a myopic brooding on the swelling and ripening of grapes on the vine expressed in direct second-person verb forms, densely concentrated syntax, elaborately inverted genitive constructions, and emphatic alliterations.

The year 1775 does not mark as decisive or radical a turning point in Goethe's poetic development as it did in his biographical career. 'Seefahrt' (The Voyage) and 'Harzreise im Winter', written respectively in 1776 and 1777, continue the series of Frankfurt odes, and even some of the poems to Lili Schönemann were written in Weimar during the winter of 1775/6. More strikingly, the uneasy tensions and ambivalent feelings of these poems continue, if anything in a more intense and introverted form, into much of the poetry addressed to Lida (Frau von Stein) during the first decade in Weimar. This early Weimar period of 1775–86 is often perceived as one of the less productive phases of Goethe's literary career, a time when he was finding his way into a new situation, increasingly burdened with official duties or occupied with relatively trivial court entertainments, a time when so many major works (*Faust, Egmont, Tasso, Iphigenie, Wilhelm Meister*) were projected or started, but not finished. It is true that Goethe worked only sporadically and desultorily on these major projects; but the first decade in Weimar was productive of some of his most celebrated lyric poetry. The ballads 'Der Fischer', 'Erlkönig', and 'Der Sänger' (The Angler; The Alder King; and The Minstrel) were written during this decade, as were the poems exploring (in a more reflective and controlled style than the Frankfurt odes) a range of ethical and existential questions on human autonomy and responsibility, on the relationship between individual human life and fate, between mortals and gods, humans and animals, us and the world we inhabit: 'Gesang der Geister über den Wassern', 'Grenzen der Menschheit', 'Das Göttliche' (Song of the Spirits over the Waters, Human Limitations, The Divine).

The early Weimar period produced a series of enthralling, if profoundly ambivalent, love poems to Lida, characterized by the urgent and obscure questioning of 'Warum gabst du uns die tiefen Blicke' (Why did you give us such profound perceptions), with its insistent repetitions and shifting perspectives. It produced the subdued and uncertain nocturnal poems 'Jägers Nachtlied' (Hunter's Night Song) and 'An den Mond' (To the Moon), poised between peace and restlessness, joy and grief, possession and loss, exploring the labyrinth of private feelings. It produced the two celebrated 'Wandrers Nachtlieder' (Night Songs of a Wayfarer), and Mignon's quintessential expression of yearning for a lost Italian idyll – which is also Goethe's own imaginative wish-fulfilment of escape to Italy. It produced the allegorical statement of the poet's mission, 'Zueignung' (Dedication), which since the Cotta edition of Goethe's works in 1815 has stood as the introduction, not simply to his collected poems, but to his whole literary oeuvre. It produced a host of occasional verse, of which the most substantial are the bustling, affectionate tribute to the stage manager of the Weimar amateur theatre, 'Auf Miedings Tod' (On the Death of Mieding), and the complex, soul-searching poem that is only ostensibly an official tribute on the occasion of Carl August's twenty-sixth birthday: 'Ilmenau'. 'Ilmenau' reviews much of Goethe's inner life during the early Weimar years (or as much as he cared to reveal in a poem). The introversion, uncertainty and ambivalence that characterize so much of the poetry of this period are expressed here in an intimately personal form; his relationship with Duke Carl August, his uneasy status as friend, counsellor and subject, his own uncertain destiny, his hopes, frustrations and failures as an artist – all these positions are rehearsed as the poet confronts his own ghostly *Doppelgänger* of a few years earlier in an encampment deep in the forests around Ilmenau. For all the upbeat mood of the final section, in which the Duke is urged to establish responsible government and a prosperous economy for his small state, the poem represents Goethe's own reckoning with himself at a critical stage in his life.

During his first Italian journey of 1786–8 Goethe wrote little lyric poetry. It is tempting to conclude that the spiritual and existential liberation of his Italian experience, which he so frequently and emphatically affirmed both during and after his journey, had also liberated him from the twilight musings and misty introversion of the early Weimar poetry. Indeed, he appears to confirm this in the opening lines of the seventh Roman Elegy, where he looks back from the vivid light and colours of the Italian scene to the time 'da mich ein graulicher Tag hinten im Norden umfing' (when in the north a drab dullness pervaded the sky), or in the fifteenth Elegy, where he recalls 'die Nebel des traurigen Nordens' (the mists of the gloomy north). We should bear in mind, however, that the Elegies were written not in Italy, but after his return to the 'gloomy north'; and though Goethe may have been lyrically inactive in Italy, no doubt distracted by his travels, his new experiences, his activities as a painter and student of art, and his growing interest in botany and anatomy, he was also busy with the preparation, revision, and completion of his major works for the publisher Göschen – including his collected lyric poems for the eighth volume.

The Roman Elegies are nevertheless the most direct and striking lyrical product of his Italian experience, a joyous cycle of poems that celebrate, not the labyrinthine and ambivalent emotions of platonic or unrequited love, but 'die Freuden des echten, nacketen Amors' (the joys of authentic, naked love, FA I, vol. I, 394). The scene is not the obscure crepuscular landscape of Thuringia, but Rome, 'ewige Roma', the eternal city past and present, with all its associations and precedents in mythology and literature: Zeus, Mars,

Venus, Amor, the 'heroische Zeit, da Götter and Göttinnen liebten' (the heroic age of gods' and goddesses' embraces), the 'triumvirate' of the Latin elegiac poets, and Ovid – with whom he identifies himself when describing his emotional farewell from Rome (FA I, vol. xv/1, 596–7). The Elegies uninhibitedly mix humour and passion, irony and erotic intensity, fun and dignity; and they come full circle as the poet finally reveals his compulsion to confide his liberating experience, not to the reeds as the servant of King Midas had done, but to the dignified cadences of hexameter and pentameter.

Even before his departure to Italy, Goethe had experimented with classical metres and genres, notably with distichs. But the Roman Elegies mark the serious preoccupation with classicizing forms that characterizes much of his poetic production during the decade or so of Weimar Classicism: epigrams, epistles, the elegies 'Alexis und Dora', 'Euphrosyne', and 'Amyntas', the 'Metamorphosis' poems, and the polemical *Xenien* he wrote with Schiller in 1795 and 1796. To be sure, he also wrote quasi-Romantic lyric poems during the 1790s; but he increasingly sought classical models to emulate, though not slavishly to imitate: the Latin elegiac poets Catullus, Propertius and Tibullus for the Roman Elegies, Horace for the Epistles, the satirists Martial and Juvenal for the Venetian Epigrams and the *Xenien*, the natural philosopher Lucretius for the 'Metamorphosis' poems, and Homer for the epics.

The French Revolution, which preoccupied, distracted, and thoroughly unsettled Goethe during the 1790s, and indeed well beyond that, was scarcely the ideal subject for lyric poetry. It is a common, and quite misleading, perception that during the Revolution and its aftermath Goethe withdrew into an Olympian classical isolation in Weimar, perversely turning a blind eye to the greatest political upheaval of his age. On the contrary, not only did he experience at first hand the effects of the Revolution at Valmy and at Mainz; he returned to it time and again in his literary work in his efforts, as he put it, 'through poetry to come to terms with this most terrible of all events, its causes and its consequences' (FA I, xxiv, 597). He does refer fleetingly to the Revolution in the second Roman Elegy ('wütende Gallier', furious Gauls), and there are some allusions in the Venetian Epigrams to 'Frankreichs traurig Geschick' (France's unhappy fate); but it was in his minor dramas and prose works and in the two hexameter epics he wrote in the 1790s, *Reineke Fuchs* and *Hermann und Dorothea*, that Goethe sought to come to terms with the Revolution, with its causes (which he acknowledged) and its effects (which he deplored).

Based closely on Gottsched's prose translation of a sixteenth-century Low German verse account of the ancient and popular tale of Reynard the Fox, Goethe's 'Homeric' version by no means confronts the French Revolution directly. *Reineke Fuchs* is, rather, an exposure of the abuse of power, of the corruption, greed, and venality of the ruling estates – royalty, nobility, and clergy – that in Goethe's negative and monocausal perception had precipitated the catastrophe of the Revolution. He preserves the late medieval political, religious and legal structures of the story, mixes in some parodic Homeric allusions, and exploits the animal allegory to reveal the bestiality of human nature. The fox fights his own corner, not with any moral weaponry, but with his own native gifts of wit and cunning, with a quick intelligence that combats mendacity, sophistry and hypocrisy with their own weapons and turns stupidity and cruelty against themselves. He is an ambivalent anti-hero, a deplorable character who elicits sympathy and even admiration, an unscrupulous survivor in the social and political jungle who satisfies his own appetites by confronting the double standards of a corrupt establishment and who outwits it by fair means or foul; cunning, subterfuge and even savagery are legitimate instruments of survival in corrupt and savage times. Goethe himself described the story as 'a profane secular Bible' (FA I, vol. XVII, 24); but it is likely that he was attracted to the subject for the opportunity to narrate an entertaining tale with a tongue-in-cheek epic dimension at least as much as for the purpose of delivering a didactic treatise on corrupt human nature and institutions.

Hermann und Dorothea is a more self-consciously quasi-Homeric epic, but one that owes as much to Johann Heinrich Voß's rural idyll *Luise* as it does to Homer. We hear of the Revolution itself only vicariously, in flashback: in the Magistrate's account in the sixth canto, or in Dorothea's account, in the final canto, of her former fiancé who left for Paris to fight for the new ideals, only to die as the Revolution devoured its own children. The story shows the fragile parochial idyll of a small village on the right bank of the Rhine during the revolutionary wars; the Revolution is perceived here in its effects rather than its causes, in the plight of the refugees uprooted by the aftermath of political instability that threatens the ordered, indeed complacent, quietism of the domestic idyll. It is neither a political polemic against the Revolution nor an unqualified celebration of apolitical quietism, but a sentimental anecdote that mixes pathos and irony, and sets real suffering against mildly philistine contentment. The epic hexameter, the nine cantos that take their titles from the nine Muses, the use of Homeric extended similes, repeated epithets and allusions, the unhurried pace of narrative and dialogue, the reiteration and retardation – all this gives ironic epic breadth to an incident that takes up no more than a single day. The mundane parochialism of the domestic milieu of the village is set against the desperate plight of the refugees, their preservation of human values and social structures, and the heroism of Dorothea in defending herself and her companions against rape; Dorothea's calm maturity and independence is set against the awkward diffidence of Hermann, who in spite of his name (the German form of Arminius, who led the Germanic resistance to the Roman Empire and destroyed Varus's legions in 9 AD) is an unlikely German hero. When he harnesses the dray-horses to the cart in the yard of his father's inn to go in search of Dorothea, there are parodic echoes of Achilles preparing to do battle with Hector; when the parson drives the fearful apothecary back to the village, he grasps the reins to control his 'foaming steeds'. The humour of this mock-heroic treatment, and the very real nature of the threat to the village idyll from the historical convulsions on its margins, save the story from domestic banality; similarly, the easy informality of Goethe's use of the hexameter and the ironic 'alienation effect' of discrete style and content preserve it from archaic pomposity.

Goethe's use of hexameter and the classical epic form did not survive the turn of the century; his experiment with an authentically Homeric subject, the *Achilleis*, did not progress beyond the first canto and was abandoned in 1799. During his classical years, however, he returned to a narrative form that recurs throughout his career: he and Schiller wrote, almost competitively, a series of ballads during the so-called 'ballad year' of 1797. The early ballads which Goethe had written under the influence of Herder's ideas on folksong, epic and oral poetry – 'Heidenröslein', 'Der König in Thule', 'Hoch auf dem alten Turme', 'Vor Gericht', 'Der untreue Knabe' (Rose on the Heath; The King of Thule; High on the Ancient Tower; Before the Court; The Faithless Lad) – set out to exploit the artless and primitive character of popular culture; in addition to his own experience of collecting folksongs in the Alsatian countryside (see FA I, vol. 1, 103–25) he had also drawn on early German printed sources and on published collections like Percy's *Reliques of Ancient English Poetry*. The early Weimar ballads – 'Erlkönig', 'Der Fischer', 'Der Sänger' (The Alder King; The Angler; The Minstrel) – while still drawing on popular motifs and folk superstition, are more sophisticated literary constructs. 'Erlkönig', for example, is a lyrically complex and highly structured ballad that is quite beyond its primitive model, Herder's translation of the Danish ballad of 'Erlkönigs Tochter' (Alder King's Daughter).

The ballads of 1797 not only display a sophisticated formal structure; they are also more extended, more sentointious and more didactic than the earlier ballads. If Goethe had sought in his Strasbourg and Frankfurt ballads to introduce the popular idiom into the literary canon, in the later ballads he and Schiller were both exploring the contemporary potential of the narrative genres and seeking to popularize their own literary and ethical values.

'Die Braut von Corinth' (The Bride of Corinth) and 'Der Gott und die Bajadere' (The God and the Bayadère) are historically and culturally specific accounts of the violation of humane values by religious and cultural bigotry, illustrated respectively in the story of a dead woman who returns from the grave to claim the fiancé denied to her in life, and that of the Hindu temple prostitute who is tempted, tested and ultimately redeemed by the god Shiva. Even 'Der Zauberlehrling' (The Sorcerer's Apprentice), for all its slapstick humour, points a moral; indeed, it has been read as a satire on the French Revolution or on the new technologies of the Industrial Revolution. Goethe returned to the ballad many times, and well after 1797. The sheer variety of theme and treatment defies categorization: bizarre or macabre incidents ('Hochzeitlied' (Wedding Song), 'Der Totentanz' (Dance of Death)), anecdote of individual heroism ('Johanna Sebus'), homely cautionary tales ('Der Schatzgräber' (The Treasure Seeker), 'Die wandelnde Glocke' (The Walking Bell)), biblical legend ('Legende'), folkloric tales ('Der getreue Eckart' (Faithful Eckart), 'Ballade'), or religious-existential allegory ('Paria' (Pariah)). For all their didacticism, Goethe's later ballads reveal his awareness of the genre as a public form of entertaining narrative.

In 'Das Sonett', one of the two sonnets he wrote around 1800, Goethe introduces a self-referential note that he had already used discreetly in the Roman Elegies: he talks about the sonnet within the sonnet as he addresses the dilemma of the poet faced with a contrived and alien form, with the imposition of a prescribed poetic structure. 'Das Sonett' expresses his unease with the constrictions of rigid formal patterns; 'Natur und Kunst' (Nature and Art) answers these reservations with an acknowledgement of poetry as craftsmanship, of the mastery that accepts the formal discipline within which the imagination can be shaped. He returned to the sonnet form in 1807/8, stimulated (or provoked) by the *Sonettenwut* (sonnet mania) of the Jena Romantics, and by the work of August Wilhelm Schlegel and Zacharias Werner on Romance poetic forms, to write a cycle of seventeen poems that chart a brief love affair between an older (and, we infer, distinguished) poet and his younger correspondent – the cycle is structured on a poetic dialogue, conducted in part through an exchange of letters.

The programmatic opening poem, 'Mächtiges Überraschen' (Powerful Intervention), suggests not only the eruption of 'daemonic' passion in its symbols of torrent, landslide and lake; it is also a poetological statement of the harmonizing of passion and control, freedom and discipline, within the confines of the sonnet. From the clash of water and rock emerges a state of balanced synthesis, symbolized in the reflection of stars in the calm surface of the lake and defined, in what is surely an allusive tribute to Dante's

Vita Nuova, as 'ein neues Leben' (a new life). In the hunt for biographical references, the 'heroine' of the sonnets has been identified with Minna Herzlieb, Bettina Brentano and Silvie von Ziegesar, young women who were personally close to Goethe at the time. Certainly, Sonnets VIII–X appear to draw on Goethe's correspondence with Bettina Brentano; the name Herzlieb (heart-love or heart-dear) is clearly alluded to in Sonnet X, and is also encoded as the solution to the charade of Sonnet XVII. But it is highly improbable that any one of the three was the object of the poet's erotic attention, any more than Beatrice was for Dante or Laura for Petrarch; and the elegant tributes to Dante in Sonnet I and to Petrarch in Sonnet XVI suggest that the impulse for this cycle was above all literary, that it represented Goethe's response to the challenge of a particular poetic form, that it was a self-conscious experiment with *Sonettenwut* rather than a direct brush with the 'Raserei der Liebe' (frenzy of love).

The playful irony of the sonnet cycle, the poetic flirtation of the lovers in dialogues and letters, the encoded charades, the figured exchanges of a latter-day Petrarch and Laura, the reflections on the writing of poetry within the poems – all this anticipates in many ways the more elaborate and exotic role-playing of the *West-östliche Divan* (West-eastern Divan), Goethe's imaginative flight to the East, his assumption of the persona of Hafiz and his exploration of the poetic landscape of his Persian sources. Inspired by his reading of Joseph von Hammer's translation of Hafiz, by his visits to his native Rhineland in 1814 and 1815, and by the intellectual and emotional stimuli of those journeys, Goethe poured out a flood of poems so diverse that they are only just held together by his Oriental fiction. To be sure, there is a structure in the *Divan*; it is divided, in the manner of Goethe's sources, into a series of books, and the books are themselves structured as four groups of three. Within this external structure, critics have struggled to discern a pattern of complementary contrast and mirroring, question and answer, parallel motifs and echoes; but the principal feature of the *Divan* is its very unpredictability, the threading of the most diverse material onto the axis of East and West.

The collection is by no means a pastiche of Persian poetry, for all that Goethe exploits all manner of Oriental reference. The figure of Timur (Tamberlaine) merges with that of Napoleon; the political unrest of the age of Hafiz is assimilated to the contemporary endgame of the continental wars and the Congress of Vienna; the lovers Hatem and Suleika play out the private emotional dialogue of Goethe and Marianne von Willemer – a literary partnership that informs much of the *Divan*, and particularly the 'Buch Suleika' (Book of Suleika); the poppies in the fields near Erfurt bloom like the roses of Shiraz ('Liebliches' (Vision of Loveliness)). Dialogues, aphorisms, riddles, proverbs and legends mingle with poems of intense exotic sensuality, of erotic mysticism, and emblematic *Dinggedichte* (poems dealing with a single concrete object); Marianne von Willemer's verses rub shoulders with Goethe's. Muslim and Christian, the Koran and the Bible, Persian and German, Mecca and Jerusalem, the Euphrates and the Rhine, are juxtaposed and assimilated. The *Divan* is, in an entirely positive sense, escapist poetry, an imaginative hejira into an exotic dimension of lyrical freedom where the poet's voice alone calls the tune, where the poet's hand can shape water into a perfect sphere, where 'Dichten ist ein Übermut' (poetry is just high spirits), and where the 'frische Quelle' (the fresh spring) of poetry, as the houri assures her poet, will continue to flow in paradise.

Goethe collected much of his later philosophical and existential poetry under the rubric 'Gott und Welt' (God and World). The group opens with 'Prooemion', a quasi-liturgical statement of a creative principle immanent in the world around us, and of which the world we perceive is a likeness or simile (*Gleichnis*). The acknowledgement of the world perceived by our senses as an emanation of divine creativity, of a world not mechanically constructed and directed by a God 'der nur von außen stieße' (who could guide only from without), but one in which God and world, God and nature are one, is a belief that informs Goethe's profound sense of awe and delight in the 'reichbegabte Welt' (richly gifted world). In the verses framing the two 'Metamorphosis' poems ('Parabase', 'Epirrhema' and 'Antepirrhema'), Goethe also expresses his sense of wonder at the integrity and harmony of the created world in a series of antithetical pairings that indicate his holistic vision: great and small, near and far, inner and outer, singularity and multiplicity, permanence and change. 'Antepirrhema' is a remarkable recasting of some lines Goethe had written in the early 1770s, in which Mephistopheles seeks to convey to the young student the infinite complexities of the human mind (*Faust*, lines 1922–7). Here the Devil's lines are modified into a metaphor of divine creativity that defines God not as the supreme architect or clockmaker, but as the master-weaver – not as the creator of a finished edifice or mechanism, but as a permanently active force in a continuum of creative renewal that presupposes a constant chain of formation and transformation, creation and re-creation, change and survival.

Three poems continue this dynamic of opposites in 'Gott und Welt'. 'Dauer im Wechsel' (Permanence in Change) is a meditation on the mutability and ephemerality of living organisms, derived from Goethe's reading of the work of the neurologist Johann Christian Reil, who had argued that the human body constantly and progressively changes and renews itself so that 'no atom remains of what we were eighty years before'; only the consciousness of the continuity of our personality ensures our identity (see FA I, vol. II, 1082–3). Goethe's elegiac statement of relentless mutability asserts this consciousness in terms of the artistic creativity that gives permanence to transient experience. 'Eins und Alles' (One and All) takes up this awareness of the mutability of creation, but in a less elegiac perception; it is an unequivocal affirmation of the creative principle addressed in 'Prooemion', of the Spinozan *hen kai pan* (one and all) invoked in the title 'Eins und Alles', of the perpetually re-creative flux of a world that constantly renews itself, of a mutability that is itself a condition of survival. Goethe's predilection for expressing himself in terms of counterpoint and paradox is further deployed in the companion poem 'Vermächtnis' (Testament), which opens with an apparent contradiction of the closing lines of 'Eins und Alles'. In fact, it is a reaffirmation of the survival of creation in and through perpetual change and regeneration, and of the laws that govern macrocosm and microcosm: to the Copernican solar system corresponds the Kantian moral conscience. This insight into the ordered coherence of existence is the intellectual inheritance that enables us to make sense of the present in the flux of time, to acknowledge the past and anticipate the future; it is also Goethe's own poetic testament in its celebration of the 'living treasures' of the cosmos and the 'richly gifted world' we perceive around us.

Goethe voiced his quasi-religious sense of wonder and delight in creation in more directly lyrical terms in poems like 'Schwebender Genius über der Erdkugel' (Genius poised above the Globe) and in the 'Zahme Xenien' (Gentle Satires) that address his scientific convictions: 'Keine Gluten, keine Meere', 'Das Leben wohnt in jedem Sterne', 'Wenn im Unendlichen dasselbe', 'Nachts, wann gute Geister schweifen'. The constant wheeling of the heavens, the alternation of day and night, the pulsations of the earth, the rise and fall of the barometer, the infinite complexity and the vast energies of the cosmic order, are subsumed under a vision of profound harmony and peace; what is above and what is beneath, the infinite blue of the sky and the colourful variety of the world around us, the landscape by day and the skyscape by night, are celebrated in terms of eloquent affirmation. But this sublimely affirmative vision is brutally qualified in the violent emotional spasm of the 'Trilogie der Leidenschaft' (Trilogy of Passion), in which the serene equilibrium of much of Goethe's late poetry is shattered.

A series of occasional poems to the young Ulrike von Levetzow, whom Goethe met in Karlsbad and Marienbad in 1821–3, gives little warning of the crisis; indeed, it has been seriously questioned whether the 'Marienbader

Elegie' is an accurate emotional record of Goethe's friendship with (or court-ship of) Ulrike.[7] Whatever the truth, the central Elegy is the most direct and unequivocal expression of inconsolable suffering. The desperate desolation of loss, the bitter invocation of the ambivalent figure of Pandora, the final visceral shout of despair – none of this suffering is resolved within the Elegy itself, nor in the prefatory poem 'An Werther' (To Werther), which was writ-ten after the Elegy, nor again in the concluding 'Aussöhnung' (Conciliation), which was written before the Elegy and has only a fortuitous bearing on it. In 'An Werther', not only is the affirmative delight in creation, voiced so eloquently in Goethe's later poems, questioned and even contradicted; but also the cathartic and therapeutic power of poetic expression, celebrated in Tasso's lines and affirmed by Goethe himself, appears to be powerless to relieve suffering. In the Marienbad Elegy poetry is able to articulate, but not to mitigate, the 'death' of separation.

It may be that the true coda or lyrical *Aussöhnung* of the Marienbad Elegy is not in the poem that actually concludes the trilogy, but in one Goethe wrote shortly afterwards: 'Der Bräutigam' (The Bridegroom). This enigmatic poem, about which Goethe made no recorded comment, begins and ends on the theme of separation, and perhaps also of death. It appears to express the reflections of an ageing man on a long-past betrothal, in which his earlier longing for admittance over the threshold of the bridal chamber has been sublimated into a longing for reunion beyond the threshold of death. What-ever the precise reference of this inscrutable poem might be, it resolves the elegiac sense of separation and loss in one of Goethe's most celebrated lyrical statements of affirmation: 'Wie es auch sei das Leben, es ist gut' (Whatever it may bring us, life is good).

The last of Goethe's lyrical cycles, the *Chinesisch-deutsche Jahres- und Tageszeiten* (Sino-German Seasons and Hours) of 1827, was stimulated by his reading of Chinese novels and poems, mostly in French and English trans-lations. As the title suggests, the cycle emulates the cultural exchanges of the *West-östliche Divan* – though Goethe's engagement with his cultural models is by no means as extensive, as lasting or as intensive as in the earlier col-lection. In these delicately brushed poems written from his 'garden house' by the Ilm, the Chinese motifs are discreetly and allusively integrated into a western landscape. The opening poem, like the 'Hegire' (Hejira) that opens the *Divan*, suggests an imaginative flight to an exotic culture, a Mandarin's escape from professional and political burdens into an idyllic scenery of park and garden. The specifically Chinese colouring lies in the visual delicacy of pictorial expression, in the finely drawn details of an essentially decora-tive and ornamental landscape as the cycle moves through the seasons from spring to autumn: flowers, peacocks, willow branches dancing on moonlit water, the painted roof of a house, the eremetical seclusion of the poet-sage, and his gift of laconic wisdom to his disciples.

The two 'Dornburg' poems of 1828 – 'Dem aufgehenden Vollmonde' (To the Full Moon Rising) and 'Früh, wenn Tal, Gebirg und Garten' (When garden, hill and valley early) – were clearly written as companion pieces, and are almost invariably, and rightly, printed together as a lyrical diptych. The one is nocturnal, the other diurnal; they have an almost identical metre, a similar external and internal structure, even a corresponding adverbial genitive construction at exactly the same place in the tenth line – 'Reiner Bahn' (in a pure path) and 'Reiner Brust' (with a pure heart); and yet they are strikingly different in mood and cadence. The nocturnal poem is structured in two-line syntactical units as an intimate dialogue between self and moon; the diurnal poem is based on sharp optical observation of forms and colours, moving in unbroken (though obscurely constructed) syntax from start to finish, in a series of subordinate clauses and dynamic verbal forms. Both poems characterize the best of Goethe's remarkable late landscape poetry: the gift of expressing in deceptively simple lyrical language, but with a complex subtlety of rhythm, sound, and syntax, a vision that accepts and affirms life and the world, though not without a degree of elegiac resignation, in an unforced synthesis of perception and emotion, of sharp observation and symbolic vision.

The alternative Goethe

Our received image of Goethe is more often than not – and not without reason – that of a poet whose characteristic lyrical expression is almost wholly positive, optimistic and life-affirming. We should also bear in mind that there is much of his poetry in which he expresses himself with anger, contempt, ribaldry and abuse. This is not the Goethe of the love poems, the nature poems and the existential poems, but the Goethe of the epigrams, invectives, satires and polemics – the savagery of which is, to be sure, consistent with these genres, but which at times betrays a bitterly mordant personal animus. Goethe could attack mercilessly those former friends and allies whom he came to despise, like Lavater, or those like Kotzebue and Werner with whom he had a close but often uneasy relationship.

Sulpiz Boisserée described his shocked reaction to Goethe in full polemical flow as he cursed a whole spectrum of contemporary fashions and institutions with bitter malice and mockery; it was, reported Boisserée, as if he had found himself on the Blocksberg (*Gespräche* III/2, 41). And in conversation with Johannes Falk, Goethe vented his spleen on the German public, anticipating with savage glee its reaction to his more extreme and provocative work, which he withheld from publication but which, he knew, would come to light one day (*Gespräche* IV, 90–3). The contents of his *Walpurgissack*, as he called it, included such ribald material as *Hanswursts Hochzeit* (Jack Pudding's Wedding) and its even more drastic unfinished sketches (*paralipomena*); the two priapic Roman Elegies; the unpublished Venetian Epigrams; 'Das Tagebuch' (The Diary) – for all its ironic morality; his Latin commentary to the *Carmina Priapeia* for Carl August; and the unpublished scenarios for the *Walpurgisnacht*.[8]

Goethe's early satirical sketches *Götter, Helden und Wieland* (Gods, Heroes and Wieland), *Pater Brey* (Father Porage) and *Satyros* (The Satyr) display his talent for sharp personal polemic, directed against the Weimar luminary Wieland (with whom he later developed warm personal relations) and the prophet of sensibility at the Darmstadt court, Franz Michael Leuchsenring (with whom he did not). But the one figure who suffered most frequently and grievously from his critical savagery was undoubtedly Friedrich Nicolai, the Berlin rationalist and critic who first fell foul of Goethe with his pompous reception of *Werther*, and who is mercilessly mocked in the hilarious and scatological poem describing Nicolai defecating on Werther's grave, 'Ein junger Mensch, ich weiß nicht wie' (Once a young man, I don't know how); in the many *Xenien* devoted to Nicolai's travelogues; and in the ludicrous figure of the *Proktophantasmist* (The Man with the Haunted Backside) in the 'Walpurgisnacht' in *Faust I*.

In the published and unpublished Venetian Epigrams, the *Xenien* and other invectives, Goethe returns time and again to attack Lavater, Nicolai and Kotzebue, Newton and the Newtonians, the Christian Church, the academic, political and literary establishment, egalitarianism, press freedom, philistinism and dilettantism. There are also more obscure targets: the pietist Christoph Kaufmann ('Als Gottes Spürhund'), Böttiger ('Den Gott der Pfuschereien'), Pustkuchen ('Pusten, grobes deutsches Wort!'), Juliane von Krüdener ('Junge Huren, alte Nonnen'), Luise Krafft ('Wenn schönes Mädchen sorgen will'), Wolfgang Menzel and Garlieb Merkel, whose name Goethe more than once rhymed with 'Ferkel' (piglet) – all these, and many more, fell foul of Goethe at his most peevish and savage. Goethe was capable of writing exquisite lyric poetry in the most eloquent and compelling language; he was also capable of expressing his most deeply held convictions (or prejudices) in the most coarse and brutal language. We should not lose sight of the irreverent, at times even malevolent, Goethe behind the received image of the serene lyric poet.

Goethe's lyrical forms[9]

The thematic range and variety of Goethe's lyric poetry is matched by the range and variety of his metrical and strophic forms. The analysis of a poet's use of metre and verse form is of course the analysis of only an aspect of his poetic articulation; but it is a crucial aspect. Other factors constitute the aural or 'musical' dimension in the reading of lyric poetry – rhythm, tempo, pitch, degree of emphasis, volume, inflection and tone of voice, even gesture; but these are variables supplied by the reader rather than by the poet. Metre and verse form (even free forms) are consciously and deliberately imposed by the poet as part of an expressive strategy – they are, as it were, the 'geprägte Form' (imprinted form) of the poems. It should be borne in mind, however, that there is no inherent or *a priori* mimetic significance in a given metre, any more than there is in a given sound or cluster of sounds. Rather the sense will always give the lead to sound or metre, while sound and metre will in turn reinforce and complement the sense with an aural or rhythmic dimension; this relation connects even modern lyric poetry with its historical origins in song and performance.

The symbiosis of form and meaning, or rhythm and sense, that characterizes Goethe's lyric poetry is nowhere better illustrated than in the first version of 'Auf dem See'. The opening anacrusis or 'upbeat' of the first-person pronoun, combined with the robustly emphatic verb ('Ĭch sāug an meiner Nabelschnur'), the equally emphatic twin stresses of the alliterative opening of the second line ('Nūn Nāhrung aus der Welt'), and the trochaic inversion of the third line ('Ĭst dĭe Nătūr') articulate the exuberant response to maternal nature, before the rhythm settles into a steady iambic beat in lines 5–8, alternating in a simple pattern of four and three stresses, of eight and six syllables respectively. The more reflective four lines at the centre of the poem change to trochaics, to four-stress lines rhyming in couplets; two feminine lines of eight syllables are followed by two masculine lines of seven that emphasize the resolve to turn away from memory to the here and now – reinforced by the twin stresses in line 12 ('Hīer aūch'). The final eight lines preserve the trochaic rhythm of the central section, but revert to the rhyme scheme of the first eight lines, while subtly varying both metre and cadence. They are consistently of three stresses, four feminine lines followed by four alternating feminine and masculine lines; but the steady alternation of *Hebung* and *Senkung* (stressed and unstressed syllables) is broken by the dactylic rhythms of the even lines 14, 16, 18 and 20. Strophically the poem is almost symmetrical (more obviously so in the printing of the second version), but metrically it has a subtle asymmetry that reinforces the dialectic of its development from extraverted exuberance through introspective recollection to a mood of buoyant expectancy: the dactylic rhythms reinforce the imagery of sunlight glittering on the waves, of soaring peaks, morning breeze and ripening fruit ('Tausend schwebende Sterne'; 'Rings die türmende Ferne'; 'Die beschattete Bucht'; 'Sich die reifende Frucht').

Goethe's metrical virtuosity can be illustrated by any number of examples. Compared with the subtle prosodic diversity of 'Auf dem See', the twin poems 'Meeres Stille' and 'Glückliche Fahrt' read like five-finger exercises in metrical mimesis. In the first poem, the oppressive stasis of the becalmed ship is conveyed in uniform trochees: 'Tiefe Stille herrscht im Wasser' (– ⌣ – ⌣ – ⌣ – ⌣). In the second, release and movement are expressed in restless dactylic rhythms – or, more technically speaking, in amphibrachs (⌣ – ⌣): 'Die Nebel zerreißen, / Der Himmel ist helle' (⌣ – ⌣ ⌣ – ⌣ / ⌣ – ⌣ ⌣ – ⌣). Lines 2, 4, 6 and 8 of 'Meeres Stille' are catalectic – that is, the final unstressed syllable is anticipated, but not realized: 'Glatte Fläche rings umher' (– ⌣ – ⌣ – ⌣ – (⌣)), as are lines 4 and 10 of 'Glückliche Fahrt': 'Das ängstliche Band' (⌣ – ⌣ ⌣ – (⌣)).

The short dipodic lines of 'Maifest', the enjambment that drives the syntax from line to line and stanza to stanza, the accumulation of brief phrases and clauses, and the repeated exclamations carry the pace of the poem as appropriately as the 'galloping' iambic rhythms of 'Willkommen und Abschied'. The urgent trochaic chanting of 'Warum gabst du uns die tiefen Blicke' is reinforced by the insistent accumulation of second-person verb forms. The simple folksong form of 'Der König in Thule' is, whether Goethe was aware or not, the archaic metre of the medieval epic poem *Das Nibelungenlied*. In the rippling amphibrachs of 'Unbeständigkeit', the restless dactyls of 'Rastlose Liebe' – here as elsewhere, poetic expression is reinforced and complemented by metrical and strophic patterns.

The quiet musing of 'Ein zärtlich jugendlicher Kummer' is articulated in flexible iambic 'madrigal verse', with lines varying from two to six stresses and a range of rhyme forms: alternating (abab), encapsulated (abba), in couplets (aabb), as monorhyme (aaa), and in the final line a single unrhymed *Waise*. The iambic pentameter of 'Der Bräutigam' is constantly varied by the enjambment that carries the syntax across two, or even three, lines of verse; lines are divided by caesura to contrive emphatic trochaic stress as the phrase restarts in the middle of the line ('welch erquicktes Leben': – ⌣ – ⌣ – ⌣; 'lohnend war's und gut': – ⌣ – ⌣ –); in the penultimate line, the metrical pattern is strikingly overridden by emphases that throw stress onto the first six syllables ('O sei auch mir dort auszuruhn bereitet'). The metrical structure of 'Über allen Gipfeln' is a subtle rocking rhythm, a dactylic pattern that is partly obscured by the arrangement of the lines and by the catalectic lines 2, 5, 6 and 7, where the final unrealized syllable is as integral to the metrical line as a rest is to a bar of music.

Although Goethe never adopted Klopstock's classicizing strophic ode forms (Alcaic, Sapphic and Asclepiadic), in which the metrical profile is prescribed not for a single line, but for a whole strophe, his early unrhymed poetry – the three odes to Behrisch – evidently owes much to Klopstock's free rhythms. The Storm and Stress odes (and the 'Harzreise im Winter') are similarly indebted to Klopstock; but they also appear to be based on a constructive misunderstanding of Pindar, whose strict metres were at that time perceived, and printed, as free rhythms. Goethe uses this apparent freedom to develop a rhythmic diction that is utterly flexible, but which preserves the deliberate cadences and formal syntax of classicizing hymnic or 'dithyrambic' poetry. 'Der Wandrer' is the most controlled imitation of classical idyllic verse; in his other odes, Goethe exploits metrical and strophic freedom to mimetic and expressive effect ('Prometheus', 'Mahomets Gesang', 'Ganymed'). Expression becomes delirious to the point of incoherence in 'An Schwager Kronos' or 'Wandrers Sturmlied'. Yet even at their most apparently chaotic, some of Goethe's odes display careful formal organization. The 'Sturmlied', for example, is structured on three sections, each one invoking three models or sources of inspiration: *Genius* (the spirit of poetic creativity), the Muses and the Graces; Bacchus, Apollo and Jupiter; Anacreon, Theocritus and Pindar. In addition, there is a distinct, if informal, triadic pattern in the strophic structure of the 'Sturmlied', based on the sequence of the classical ode. Goethe knew these structures perfectly well from his reading of Pindar and the Greek tragedians – and he was to return to them in the classicizing prosody of the third act of *Faust II*.[10] The thirteen stanzas of the 'Sturmlied' can be roughly structured as: strophe 1, antistrophe 1, strophe 2, antistrophe 2, strophe 3, antistrophe 3, epode; strophe, antistrophe, epode; strophe, antistrophe, epode. To be sure, the metrical profiles of strophe and antistrophe are here not identical, but they correspond in general shape. Moreover, the correspondences are reinforced by verbal repetitions and echoes, as in the following four examples of corresponding lines: 'Wen du nicht verlässest, Genius', 'Den du nicht verlässest, Genius'; 'Das ist Wasser, das ist Erde... Göttergleich', 'Über Wasser über Erde/Göttergleich'; 'Nicht am Ulmenbaum', 'Nicht im Pappelwald'; 'blumenglücklichen/Anakreon', 'Honiglallenden... Theokrit'. A similar though more straightforward triadic pattern can be discerned in 'Ganymed', where strophe and antistrophe (each followed by a *mesode*, a brief two-line interjection) articulate Ganymede's response to the surrounding springtime, and the epode his heavenward assumption.

Goethe later returned to a more serious engagement with classical prosody. He began writing in imitation of classical metres some time before his Italian journey; but it was after his return, and more especially during the decade or so of Weimar Classicism and his collaboration with Schiller, that he wrote the bulk of his classicizing poetry in continuous (epic) hexameter and in distichs or elegiac couplets (hexameter + pentameter). The idylls and elegies of Goethe's classical years are all written in distichs, as are the Venetian Epigrams and the satirical *Xenien* he wrote with Schiller. 'Die Metamorphose der Pflanzen' is also in elegiac couplets, but the 'Metamorphose der Tiere' is in continuous hexameter – the latter was evidently conceived as part of a planned, but unrealized, extended epic poem on the model of Lucretius's *De rerum natura*.[11] Otherwise, apart from the *Episteln* and some minor poems under the rubric 'Antiker Form sich nähernd', only the three epics *Reineke Fuchs*, *Hermann und Dorothea* and *Achilleis* are in epic hexameters.

The Roman Elegies represent the most relaxed and flexible examples of Goethe's classicizing metres. He observes the formal requirements of the distich in so far as his hexameters consistently end in dactyl + trochee ($- \smile \smile - \smile$); he rarely makes use of the spondee; he strictly observes the caesura in the pentameter, and always constructs the second hemistich of the pentameter as: $- \smile \smile - \smile \smile -$. He thus preserves the alternately rising and falling cadence of hexameter and pentameter, which is illustrated axiomatically in the fountain metaphor of Schiller's model couplet 'Das Distichon', but he uses the form in an imaginative and expressive way. In particular, he exploits the symmetry of the pentameter by mimicking the prosodic balance of the two half-lines with chiastic or antithetical statements: 'Wäre die Welt nicht die Welt, wäre denn Rom auch nicht Rom' (Elegy I, 14); 'Folgte Begierde dem Blick, folgte Genuß der Begier' (III, 8); 'Sehe mit fühlendem Aug, fühle mit sehender Hand' (v, 10); 'Wie sie des Tags mich erfreut, wie sie des Nachts mich beglückt' (xx, 22).

The Romance forms of *terza rima*, *ottava rima* and the sonnet are used occasionally by Goethe. He only used *terza rima* on two occasions in his whole work, in 'Schillers Reliquien' and in Faust's monologue in the opening scene of *Faust II* (lines 4679–727). It is a fixed and yet fluid form with a relentlessly recurrent rhyme scheme that drives the verse forward, binding each tercet to the previous and following one: *aba, bcb, cdc*, etc. Ottava rima (hendecasyllabic, in Goethe's poems occasionally decasyllabic, lines rhyming *abababcc*) is generally reserved by him for more solemn, elegiac or formal expression, notably in 'Zueignung' (and in the poem of that title that opens *Faust*), in the 'Epilog zu Schillers "Glocke"', in the 'Urworte. Orphisch', in some formal encomia, and in the mock-sententious poem 'Das Tagebuch'. The structure of the *ottava rima* stanza lends itself to discursive argument or narrative in the sestet, while the concluding couplet often serves as a resolution or summarizing statement in epigrammatic or sententious form, rather like the relationship between the octave and sestet in the Petrarchan sonnet, or between the three quatrains and the final couplet of the Shakespearian sonnet. The sonnet itself had been a major form for German Baroque poets, whose preferred metre was the alexandrine. The sonnet had been revived by Gottfried August Bürger, using mostly trochaic verse, and was furthered by his pupil August Wilhelm Schlegel who, with Zacharias Werner, provoked the 'sonnet mania' that impelled Goethe to write the cycle in which he uses the form with self-conscious irony. By that time, the alexandrine was perceived as alien, old-fashioned and stilted, and was no longer a serious verse form in German literature; Goethe used it in his very early work, and thereafter only for parodic effect. Both he and the Romantics wrote Petrarchan sonnets in hendecasyllabic lines – that is, effectively in iambic pentameter with feminine endings.

Goethe's ballads have a range of prosodic forms that matches the variety of their themes, from the simple song structures of the early ballads to the rhythmic virtuosity of 'Erlkönig' and the metrical sophistication of the 1797 ballads. The three most celebrated ballads of that year ('Die Braut von Corinth', 'Der Gott und die Bajadere', and 'Der Zauberlehrling') are distinguished by their use of a 'metrical refrain', as opposed to a refrain literally repeated; in 'Der Gott und die Bajadere', for example, the steady trochaic rhythm of eight narrative lines is followed by a refrain in three lines of dactylic (strictly speaking, amphibrachic) metre. 'Johanna Sebus', exceptionally, has a verbally, but not metrically, distinct refrain at the *beginning* of each section of verse.

The *West-östliche Divan* also has a huge prosodic range that can only be touched on here. The most frequent form is a trochaic line of four stresses, the so-called 'Spanish trochees', to which renewed attention had been drawn by August Wilhelm Schlegel's translations of Golden Age drama and poetry. Goethe had used this form in his very earliest poems in *Annette* and the *Neue Lieder*; he uses it frequently in his later poems, and in the *Divan* for a wide spectrum of lyrical expression: 'Hegire', 'Selige Sehnsucht', 'Gingo biloba', 'Vollmondnacht', and the dialogues of the 'Schenkenbuch'. But the *Divan* exploits a whole range of forms: the epigrammatic style of the 'Buch der Sprüche', the quasi-prosaic lines of 'Der Deutsche dankt', the dipodic dactyls of 'Phänomen' and 'Zwiespalt', the trochaic pentameter of 'Vermächtnis altpersischen Glaubens'. Even *Knittelvers*, the homespun and informal rhyming couplets used by Goethe for some of his early satires and dramas (notably for the *Urfaust*), is used, comically and most incongruously, in the 'Buch des Paradieses', where one of the houris of the Muslim paradise speaks in 'Knittelreimen' to honour a German guest. Goethe had never been too pedantic with rhyme, at least in his less formal verses; in the *Divan*, the rhymes are at times wilfully incongruous or negligent (unless we assume that Goethe's native accent had been intensified by his Rhineland journeys of 1814 and 1815): flötet/drommetet ('Zwiespalt'), Macht/Smaragd ('Bedenklich'), erhöhn/untergehn ('An Suleika'). But the celebrated 'phantom rhyme' of Morgenröte/Hatem (i.e. Goethe) in 'Locken, haltet mich gefangen' is unique.

Goethe made no great effort to imitate Persian poetic forms in the *Divan*, except to experiment occasionally and approximately with the repetitive verbal patterns of the *ghazal*, in which a word or phrase is repeated over and over again in a different syntactical context, as in the poems 'Da du nun Suleika heißt', 'Höchste Gunst', 'Ob der Koran von Ewigkeit sei', 'Sie haben uns wegen der Trunkenheit', 'Wo man mir Guts erzeigt'. By far his most imaginative adaptation of the *ghazal* form is 'In tausend Formen', which not only repeats at the end of alternate lines, but also reiterates a litany of compounds that play on the phonetic coincidence of the German *All* and the Muslim *Allah*: an ingenious and elegant signature of the east-western character of the *Divan*.

NOTES

1 Or elegiac couplets. See pages 59–64 for explanations of metres and their use.
2 See T. M. Holmes, 'Vicissitudes of the Text: Some Early Poems of Goethe on the Modern Page', *Oxford German Studies* 15 (1984), 77–94.
3 See the authoritative account by Regine Otto, 'Die Gedichtsammlungen in den autorisierten Ausgaben von Goethes Werken 1789-1827', in *Handbuch*, I, pp. 18–31.
4 For details of the Weimarer Ausgabe see List of abbreviations. Jubiläums-Ausgabe: *Goethes Sämtliche Werke*, ed. Eduard von der Hellen, 40 vols. (Stuttgart and Berlin: Cotta, 1902–19); Gedenkausgabe: *Johann Wolfgang von Goethe. Gedenkausgabe der Werke, Briefe und Gespräche*, ed. Ernst Beutler, 24 vols.+3 (Zürich: Artemis, 1948–71); Berliner Ausgabe: *Goethe. Poetische Werke. Kunsthistorische Schriften und Übersetzungen*, 22 vols. (Berlin and Weimar: Aufbau Verlag, 1960–78).
5 A useful chronological table of the composition and publication of Goethe's poems can be found in Berliner Ausgabe IV, 902–79.
6 See the strictures of T. M. Holmes in 'Vicissitudes of the Text', pp. 84–92; of Bernd Witte in *Handbuch*, I, pp. 77–8; and of Thomas P. Saine in his review of Deirdre Vincent's *Werther's Goethe and the Game of Literary Creativity*, *Goethe Yearbook. Publications of the Goethe Society of North America* 7 (1994), 247–9.
7 See Witte in *Handbuch* I, pp. 478–88.
8 These works can be found in Andreas Ammer (ed.), *Goethe. Erotische Gedichte* (Frankfurt am Main and Leipzig: Insel, 1991).

9 Since this brief discussion of lyric forms presupposes the ability to read German, no translations have been given here.

10 See Goethe's translation of the 'Fünfte Olympische Ode' (Fifth Olympian Ode), mistakenly attributed to Pindar, which is structured as strophe, antistrophe and epode (FA I, vol. XII, 141–2). Strophe and antistrophe have an identical (or near-identical) metrical pattern; the epode is metrically distinct. In the Helen episode of *Faust*, the strophic pattern is metrically much more symmetrical than in the 'Sturmlied' – see *Faust*, lines 8516–23, 8560–7, 8591–603; lines 8610–37; and lines 8697–753.

11 See H. B. Nisbet, 'Lucretius in Eighteenth-Century Germany. With a Commentary on Goethe's "Metamorphose der Tiere"', *Modern Language Review* 81 (1986), 97–115.

4

DAVID V. PUGH

Goethe the dramatist

Goethe left a rich and heterogeneous body of work in the dramatic genre. Besides the five major dramas (*Götz von Berlichingen*, *Egmont*, *Iphigenie auf Tauris*, *Torquato Tasso* and *Faust*), various completed works survive of differing style, length and quality, as well as a large number of fragments and sketches. But even if we isolate the major dramas, we are again struck by their diversity. To be sure, while *Faust* (which is treated separately in this volume) is unique and incommensurable, *Götz* and *Egmont* are both historical plays written in prose, while *Iphigenie* and *Tasso* are both written in blank verse. A closer examination will show, however, that each work has its own unique features. For Goethe each dramatic work represented a fresh challenge to discover the appropriate vehicle for his immediate needs. In view of this diversity I shall not confine myself here to the small canon of major works, as some other critics have done, but shall try instead to do justice to the breadth of Goethe's remarkable body of work in this genre.

It is a paradox of Goethe's career that by the time he was appointed Director of the Weimar Court Theatre in 1791 he had already written (with the vital exception of *Faust*) all the major dramas for which he is remembered. We thus cannot see the interdependence of writing and theatrical production that we find in the lives of Shakespeare, Molière or even Schiller. Another paradox concerns the tension between the impersonality of the dramatic genre and the essentially confessional nature of Goethe's genius, to which he attested in a famous remark in his autobiography, calling his works 'fragments of a great confession' (HA IX, 283). While it is difficult to identify common themes or tendencies running through Goethe's dramatic oeuvre, we can perhaps observe a distinctive feature of his major dramas that arises from this confessional function, namely, their tendency to be organized around a single dominant character who serves in part as a surrogate for its author, with further characters serving largely as ancillaries. This tendency (most marked in the case of *Egmont* and least in that of *Iphigenie*) might seem to militate against any high achievement on Goethe's part in the genre, with drama giving way to a kind of dramatic oratorio, in which a single character expresses the author's emotions to the accompaniment of a chorus. But, as will become clear, this focus on the central figure is counterbalanced by a dialectical play with the concepts of nature and culture, an antithesis rooted in the pastoral tradition but given new currency in the eighteenth century in the thought of Jean-Jacques Rousseau. Goethe's protagonists thus usually represent some facet of nature, and they have to contend with antagonists who stand for a quality of character (dissimulation, for example) or a social milieu (generally the court) which are presented as hostile to nature. Goethe varies this formula in each of the major plays, though not to the extent that it is ever completely submerged.

The two dramas that survive from Goethe's earliest creative period display a flair for dialogue and characterization, as well as an ability to breathe life into the rhymed alexandrines that were still the standard dramatic verse form at that time. *Die Laune des Verliebten* (The Lover's Spleen, 1767–8)[1] is the finest existing example of the one-act pastoral drama, a genre that Goethe encountered in Leipzig. But his play is more than a technical exercise, it is also a personal achievement. It follows the norm in contrasting a happy couple with an unhappy one; the plot guides the latter couple towards acceptance of the community's ethos of tolerance. But the figure of Eridon, the jealous lover, is powerfully drawn and prefigures such later misfits in Goethe's works as the lover in *Werther* or even Tasso. The action of *Die Mitschuldigen* (Partners in Guilt, 1768–9) takes place in an inn and hinges on the nocturnal theft of money from the room of Alceste, a noble guest. The culprit, Söller, is the innkeeper's son-in-law, a good-for-nothing who is descended from the stock figures of the *commedia dell'arte*. One of his two 'partners in guilt' is his wife Sophie, who also visits Alceste's room, for he is a former lover of hers. Though the visit ends innocently enough, Söller, hidden behind a curtain, is forced to hear his wife pouring out her contempt for him. The other partner is the innkeeper, who has entered the room wishing to read his guest's correspondence. These furtive comings and goings make for a successful comic plot, and, though the play has been criticized for mixing farce with a more moralistic kind of comedy, it is still impressive enough to make one wonder why Goethe's subsequent avoidance of comedy has not provoked as much discussion as has his avoidance of tragedy.

Goethe's major achievement as a dramatist before he went to Weimar, and also the work that established his fame in Germany, was *Götz von Berlichingen* (1773), a first version of which was written in 1771 soon after Goethe's return from Strasbourg, where he had come under the influence of Johann Gottfried Herder. The work, which is loosely based on the autobiography of an actual knight from the time of Luther, is the outcome of the meeting of these two extraordinary talents and represents a literary revolution. But it was a revolution that had been in the air for some time; Lessing had called for a Shakespearian German theatre as early as 1753, and prose translations of Shakespeare by C. M. Wieland and J. J. Eschenburg had been appearing since the 1760s.

The task was to be Shakespearian and authentically German at the same time. Goethe squares this circle by making the love of an inherited feudal freedom his hero's central character-trait. But this love reflects the author's quest for freedom of self-expression. In his speech *Zum Shakespeares Tag* (On Shakespeare's Day, 1771), Goethe described the dramatic unities of place, time and plot, which were required by neoclassical doctrine, as a prison. There is a symbolic identity between this structural prison and the tower of Heilbronn where Götz is confined in Act IV and dies in Act V. Götz's love of freedom and his resistance to artificial courtly ways are a symbolic parallel for Goethe's rejection of French style. The paradox is that, whereas Götz pursues the traditional life of his family and class, his author has to go outside Germany to find the dramatic means to express it.

Goethe breaches the neoclassical unities of time and place; the action lasts a number of years and is spread over many different places. Instead of the handful of characters customary both in neoclassical drama and in the domestic tragedy championed by Lessing, we have a cast of over thirty people and a stage that is often crowded with soldiers, peasants or gypsies. Gone are the heavy alexandrines, replaced by the prose of the Shakespeare translations. While the courtly characters speak a cultivated and sentimental prose similar to that of domestic tragedy, the common people speak a lively pastiche of south German dialect. Götz's invitation to an opposing commander to 'mich im Arsch lecken' (lick my arse: one of the most famous lines of German literature) is a calculated breach of the decorum that the public had long taken for granted.

In some ways *Götz von Berlichingen* resembles the oratorio-like structure that I outlined above. With his traits of courage and forthrightness, Götz is a positive figure throughout, and he is surrounded by a retinue consisting of his wife Elisabeth, his knight Lerse, his squire Georg and his ally Hanns von Selbitz, whose chief function is to sing Götz's praises. Although we might have reservations about a way of life in which feuding plays such a prominent part, the text does not really support such reservations. The arguments in favour of law and order are discredited by being given to Weislingen, Götz's faithless friend who has given up his knightly independence to serve the princes. Götz is not afflicted by self-doubt, he gets the better of the arguments on the stage, and he is resolute in the action scenes. When he gets involved in the Peasants' Revolt in Act V, it is only in the hope of limiting the violence, and so his final imprisonment seems unjust. Moreover, throughout the play his real opponent is Adelheid von Walldorf, a Goneril-like figure whose domination of her husband Weislingen and her use of sex to further her power are symptomatic of the social dislocation that destroys Götz and his patriarchal way of life.

But if the drama thus runs the risk of nostalgia and hero worship (both of them highly un-Shakespearian qualities), a more interesting reading is also possible. The key to this is the extraordinary symbolic resonance given to Götz's iron hand, which epitomizes not only his strength but also his weakness. As we are told in Act I, his hand was *shot* off in a battle, an indication that the knightly existence based on armour and castle walls is dying. Time is working against Götz, and it is notable that he ages in the latter parts of the play faster than anyone else. But the motif of the hand also fixes a symbolic role for Weislingen, a subtler poetic creation than the account thus far has suggested. On losing his real hand, Götz had hoped that Weislingen would henceforth be his right hand. Weislingen's fate is thus to 'depend' in the literal sense of to 'hang down' (German: *abhängen*). His tragedy is that even as a great lord he not only remains inwardly dependent on Götz but is also conscious of the fact; his war against Götz is motivated largely by self-hatred. Weislingen is thus an extraordinary study in vacillation and a figure reflecting much authorial self-searching. Weislingen breaks his betrothal to Götz's sister Marie as Goethe had deserted Friederike Brion and as he was later to desert Lili Schönemann. Moreover, Weislingen's decision to serve the princes anticipates Goethe's own later move to Weimar. If Götz represents vague aspirations towards personal freedom and a traditional German culture, Weislingen is the vehicle for his author's more intimate confessions.

Numerous fragments of uncompleted dramas survive from these years up to Goethe's move to Weimar in 1775. Such is their variety that it seems as if Goethe had taken a deliberate decision to use a different dramatic form each time. True, the projected dramas on *Caesar* and *Mahomet* are connected with Goethe's preoccupation with the Storm and Stress ideal of the great man and hence have a certain family resemblance, but the energies that flowed into them had evidently found more adequate expression in *Götz*, and so they did not progress beyond fragments.

The two acts of *Prometheus* (written 1773, published 1830) are a different matter. Goethe adopts here the free rhythms that had been pioneered by Klopstock, but in his hands they combine with odd diction and syntax to produce an unprecedentedly dense and harsh effect that is intended to approximate the Greek of Aeschylus and Pindar. Goethe also rewrites the myth. His Prometheus is not a Titan but a defiant son of Zeus who insists on creating a human realm on his own terms. With the help of Minerva he brings his statues to life, but by water and not by fire (an anticipation of the dispute of Thales and Anaxagoras in *Faust II*). Finally, we see Prometheus teaching his creatures how to cope with the earthly existence that he has given them. Goethe later interpreted the fragment, and the ode he extracted from it, in the context of the religious controversy associated with Spinoza.

A series of scintillating satirical sketches dating from between 1773 and 1775 bears witness to a talent that Goethe was later, regrettably, to restrain.[2] He designated *Jahrmarktsfest zu Plundersweilern* (Lumberville Fair) as a *Schönbartspiel*, a type of popular farce originating in the works of Hans Sachs, the shoemaker-poet of the sixteenth century. The structure here is given by the comings and goings of people at a fair, and the language is blunt and down-to-earth. We can see here the world experienced as a 'Raritätenkasten' (raree-show), in the manner in which, as Goethe had earlier argued, Shakespeare had presented it. The dialogues frame a play within a play, as two acts of a biblical drama that parody contemporary religious themes are performed on a stage at the fairground, and at the end a shadow show depicts the biblical story of the creation.

Religion remains a concern in *Pater Brey*, a lampoon on a pietistic cleric notorious for interfering in the romantic lives of young women, and to some extent this is true of the more substantial *Satyros* as well, for one of the satyr's first deeds is to throw the hermit's crucifix into a river. Though Goethe described this work as a *Fastnachtspiel* (lenten play), and though much of it is written in the German *Knittelvers* (rhymed doggerel), it also resembles a pastoral drama in its Greek setting, and in fact the plot outline is borrowed from such a play by the seventeenth-century poet Harsdörffer. The satyr of the title is an enigma. As Goethe wrote later, he was based on an actual person, but scholars have not been able to identify him. At times the satyr seems to be only a ruffian, at others a false prophet, mouthing nonsensical profundities to a gullible crowd and winning converts to a natural lifestyle which includes a diet of raw chestnuts. At yet other times, however, the satyr seems to possess a genuine poetic genius, and his defiance of conventional religion has been rightly linked to that of Faust and Prometheus.

Götter, Helden und Wieland (Gods, Heroes and Wieland) is a satire of a more urbane kind. It is written in prose in the Lucianic form of a dialogue of the dead, and it has a specific target, namely the *Singspiel* by Christoph Martin Wieland on the theme of Alcestis and Wieland's subsequent claim to have outdone the Euripidean original. In Goethe's dialogue, Wieland is summoned from his bed to account for himself in Hades before Euripides and his characters, and Goethe exploits the situation to good comic effect. He is protesting here at the older author's attempt to adapt the Greek tragic theme to a modern frame of reference. While in some passages Goethe is merely promoting crude Storm and Stress values, at others he manages, despite his genuine respect for Wieland, to show up the limits of the writers of the previous generation.

An adequate commentary on the dramatic texts that Goethe designed for setting to music would require a lengthy survey of the musical context. I shall thus merely mention two works dating from the pre-Weimar years.[3] The first versions are in the style of the German *Singspiel*, but Goethe substantially rewrote them both in Italy, deleting all traces of his Storm and Stress style and, by changing the prose to verse, making them more like librettos for Italian *opera buffa*. *Erwin und Elmire*, based on a ballad from Goldsmith's *The Vicar of Wakefield*, is of interest mainly for the critique of over-refinement in modern education in the opening dialogue (deleted in the second version) between Elmire and her mother. Similarly, Erwin is urged by Bernardo, an older man, to refrain from melancholy and self-torment and to grasp the happiness in which he cannot believe. Despite the slightness of the form, the themes here are related to those of more substantial works like *Götz* and *Tasso*. *Claudine von Villa Bella* alludes to the 'cloak and dagger' style of Spanish models, but, with the figures of the courtly Pedro and his brother, the vagabond Crugantino, the play is clearly structured around the antithesis of nature and culture, country and court, previously personified in the figures of Götz and Weislingen. Claudine may choose the respectable Pedro at the end, but the mutual attraction between her and Crugantino is a sign that the essential conflict is unresolved.

This survey of Goethe's pre-Weimar period concludes with his two prose plays in the style of the domestic tragedy championed in Germany by Gotthold Ephraim Lessing (1729–81). In *Miss Sara Sampson* (1757), Lessing had offered a sentimental version of this new genre, while in *Emilia Galotti* (1773) he explored more assertively the contrast of court and private life, producing a play of a more political character. Though Goethe avoids the theme of paternal authority, which is crucial for both Lessing and Schiller, his *Clavigo* (1774) and *Stella* (1775) follow Lessing's twin models in representing respectively public and private interpretations of the genre.

Clavigo, which Goethe wrote in a week, is a dramatization of an actual event from the life of the French dramatist Beaumarchais. The work disappointed the admirers of *Götz* because of its stylistic conservatism, but it is a well-constructed play that has had a successful stage career. What initially attracted Goethe to the story was Beaumarchais' tense account of his confrontation with the Spanish *littérateur* who had jilted his sister, and this part of the play (Act II) is transcribed almost verbatim from the French source. More significant is the portrait of the Spaniard Clavigo himself as a self-made man of letters, torn between his thirst for advancement at court and his loyalty to a fiancée who can offer him only domestic tranquillity. The analogy with Weislingen is evident, but here the protagonist's vacillation becomes the focus of the play. In Act III Clavigo persuades Marie to forgive him, and his eloquence leaves us in no doubt that, when he denounces the vanity of ambition, he is speaking sincerely. But in Act IV Clavigo's friend Carlos intervenes and induces him to overturn his decision. The force and artfulness of the dramatic dialogue here cannot be overstated. Clavigo emerges as a man who is not only indecisive but actually seems able to inhabit two contradictory mentalities at once. The final act, in which Beaumarchais and Clavigo fight over the coffin of Marie, is a melodramatic disappointment. Clavigo's dying words of reconciliation with Beaumarchais and his hope for reunion with Marie in the next world reflect the side of eighteenth-century sentimentality that is least compatible with modern taste.

Stella repeats the configuration of *Miss Sara Sampson* (and also *Götz*) in placing a man between two women. However, where Lessing had set his young heroine against a vicious rival who ends by murdering her, Goethe creates a different dilemma for his protagonist, Fernando, by making Stella and Cäcilie, the mistress and the wife, differ in age but not in their exalted moral character. Goethe alludes to Lessing by having his own play start in an inn, but from the second act on the action moves to Stella's manor house, a utopian realm where all worldly pressures are forgotten. The result is a play that is long on emotional outpourings but short on action and characterization. The ending, in which Fernando and the two women agree to exist in a *ménage à trois*, scandalized Goethe's public. Although attitudes to marriage have become a good deal more flexible since Goethe's time, the ending is still hard to accept, partly on the grounds of psychological implausibility, partly for the moral argument that the female figures, and perhaps the author too, seem oblivious to the contemptible nature of Fernando's actions. Recent critics have described the play as a male fantasy about female submissiveness, and it is hard to disagree with them. The tragic conclusion involving the double suicide of Stella and Fernando, which was added by Goethe for the work's first performance in Weimar in 1806, is arguably more convincing than the original one.

Though *Egmont* was not finished until 1787, much of it had been written before Goethe went to Weimar in 1775. He later concluded Part IV of his autobiography *Dichtung und Wahrheit* (Poetry and Truth), which ends with that departure, with a quotation from a speech by Egmont in Act II, and we can infer from this that the latter's character had been conceived largely in terms of Goethe's own emotional state at that time.

Like *Götz*, *Egmont* is a play about the sixteenth century, written in prose, but with a lyrical component in the form of two songs. As with *Götz*, Goethe uses the historical genre in part out of genuine interest in the period, but in part also as a way of exploring the situation of his own contemporaries. In each work, the dramatic situation precedes the outbreak of a conflict that was to have a lasting effect on the Europe of Goethe's time. Like Götz, Egmont is a nobleman and a defender of the traditional constitution against the new force of absolutism, but in both cases Goethe suggests a paradoxical unity of this conservative position with a sense of personal freedom that can be of value for the modern bourgeoisie. And, as in the earlier play, the fate of the noble characters is placed in a wider context by the inclusion of characters from the lower ranks of society.

But there are also major differences between the two plays. First, Goethe abandons the mass of short scenes that he had used in *Götz*, so giving the play a slower and more meditative character. Second, whereas Götz was merely the lord of Jaxthausen, Egmont is a representative of the Dutch people, not just in the political sense but also in that he is a figure of emotional identification for them. Formally, this makes possible the identity of hero and people that underlies the play's strange operatic conclusion complete with music and allegorical *tableau vivant*. This national element caused Goethe to lavish great care on the crowd scenes, for this crowd must be a worthy correlative to the protagonist. A third difference is that much of the play revolves around Egmont's romantic attachment to Klärchen, a woman of the burgher class. Liaisons of this kind had often been the subject of domestic tragedies, but these normally contrasted middle-class virtue with aristocratic vice. Here, however, the liaison is presented in a positive light. Klärchen's suicide is a free action, at once a decision not to survive her lover and a protest at the suppression of the freedom of the Netherlands.

The first act of *Egmont* is a good example of the oratorio-like structure. In the opening scenes we hear Egmont being discussed first by the people of Brussels, then by the Regent Margaret of Parma and her adviser, and thirdly by Klärchen and her mother. The opening of Act II returns to the citizens, but now their debates take a fierce turn. It seems that a riot must break out, when Egmont suddenly enters. Using his authority and his skill in adjusting his tone to each individual, he rapidly restores order, while at the same time hinting that he shares the citizens' dislike of Spanish rule. This *coup de théâtre* is followed by the most famous scene of the play. Egmont deals first with his correspondence; Goethe lets the political situation emerge from the letters, which a secretary summarizes, while simultaneously defining Egmont's character – a beguiling mixture of liberality and carelessness – through his treatment of each item of business. A more personal letter prompts Egmont to an impassioned defence of his way of life, a section that reaches its climax in the famous metaphor of 'die Sonnenpferde der Zeit' (time's sun-horses) and Egmont's comparison of himself to a sleepwalker. The scene ends with a political discussion with Oranien (William of Orange) culminating in Egmont's refusal to heed the warning that the Spanish king intends to suppress Dutch liberties and to put the two of them to death.

From here on, the play becomes more problematic, for Egmont's sole action is to walk unsuspectingly into the trap that the Duke of Alba sets for him. True, he performs well in the debate preceding his arrest, but in Act v his role is largely restricted to recovering his freedom from care as he awaits execution. Egmont's passivity can be attributed to the fact that Goethe is using him as vehicle for a private ideal, but the strain between this ideal and the play's political content nearly breaks the work apart. In Act II, Egmont speaks of his ambition to reach the zenith of his existence ('meines Wachstums Gipfel'). While it is unclear how we are to interpret this, it is certainly not a political or a national goal, more a personal hope for a life without worry. Egmont's means of achieving this ideal existence is to pay Klärchen a visit. The love scene in Act III, in which he surprises her by coming dressed in the robes of the Order of the Golden Fleece, comes perilously close to bathos, and Klärchen's dog-like devotion to him throughout is an annoyance to modern readers and spectators. As Schiller wondered, are we really supposed to admire Egmont for risking not just his life but the freedom of the Netherlands for simple pleasures like this?

In defence of the play, we can argue that its complexity, even where the work's unity is at risk, inspired Goethe to go beyond the achievement of *Götz von Berlichingen* and give the play a poetic range and resonance which mitigates all its shortcomings. As a representative of nature, what Egmont does is less important than what he is. He is a more mercurial figure than Götz. His dislike of council meetings and his love of horseriding are predictable, his glorying in the experience of battle is not. He also has a mystical streak from which he derives a rhetorical power that Götz lacks. Beyond this, the play avoids a simple antithesis of court and nature, for there are two representatives of culture here, the Duke of Alba (a surprisingly articulate spokesman for absolutism), but also Oranien, the leader who will later win Dutch independence. Though the final tableau evokes this future victory as inspired by Egmont's sacrifice, that victory could not be won without Oranien's arts of dissimulation. The political situation is thus intricate, and Egmont's involvement with it is also more complex than anything in *Götz*. The completed work remains an odd mixture of genres, but *Egmont* retains its classic status for its portrayal of a magnetic hero, for its splendid dialogue, and for its subtle interplay of public and private themes.

During his first decade in Weimar, Goethe's dramatic writing was inspired less by his earlier 'mania for dramatizing' (HA x, 58), and more by the needs of the Weimar *Liebhabertheater*, the amateur dramatic group in which Goethe, the Duke and other notables took part. Most of the work of this period indeed has the flavour of courtly amusement. The astonishing thing is that we also have the amateur theatre to thank for *Iphigenie auf Tauris*, one of Goethe's greatest works in any genre, and indeed one of the transcendent masterpieces of German literature. The prose version of the play, which survives, was performed by this group in 1779, with Goethe in the role of Orestes. The verse version was completed in Italy in 1787.

I shall first glance at three of the minor dramas of this decade, for there is some thematic continuity between them and *Iphigenie*. *Die Geschwister* (Brother and Sister, 1776) is a prose play in one act, written in the mode of the sentimental domestic tragedy but with the unusual theme of the love between siblings. Wilhelm and Marianne are not in fact brother and sister, but Marianne is unaware of this until the end, and her preference for her 'brother' over a suitor is certainly connected to the intense sibling relationship of the later play. The theme of healing arises here, for the dénouement enables Wilhelm to overcome the melancholia from which he has long suffered as a result of his selfish conduct towards women as a young man. Healing is again in the forefront in *Lila*, a courtly masque with song and dance dealing with the cure of a noblewoman from the derangement which has befallen her on hearing the false report of her husband's death. In the powerful monodrama *Proserpina*, finally, we can see a preparation for the portrayal of the themes of exile and of protest against the gods in *Iphigenie*.[4] (The latter theme also looks back to *Prometheus*.) The author's strong investment of emotion in these two female figures may be connected to the death of his beloved sister Cornelia in 1777.

In *Iphigenie auf Tauris* Goethe starts from the plot of the play by Euripides on the same subject: Iphigenia, the daughter of Agamemnon, has been rescued from sacrifice by Artemis (Diana) and transported to Tauris, where she has long served as a priestess to the barbarians. The plot concerns her rescue by Orestes, who, after murdering Clytemnestra, is told by the oracle to expiate his sin by stealing the Taurians' statue of Artemis. But where Euripides is concerned only with the success of the intrigue, Goethe transforms the material into a profound reflection on trust and responsibility. For his Iphigenie has qualms about the theft of the statue; despite her longing to return home, she is not prepared to repay the Taurians' hospitality to her with a shabby deed. There is also a religious theme, which hinges on an ambiguous oracle: when Apollo told Orest to restore his sister to Greece, did he mean Diana or Orest's sister? This motif is the occasion for an exploration of the relationship between the human and the divine. Such features give Goethe's play an inward and spiritual quality distinct from ancient or Shakespearian tragedy, and it is thus justifiable to speak of a new affinity between Goethe and the theatre of Racine.[5]

In portraying an individual's resistance to authority in the name of moral principle, *Iphigenie* is a work of the Enlightenment (comparable in this respect to Lessing's *Nathan der Weise* (Nathan the Wise, 1779) and Schiller's *Don Carlos* (1787)). The decisions by Orest (Act III) and Iphigenie (Act V) to risk everything by telling the truth anticipate Pamina's similar decision in Mozart's *Zauberflöte* (Magic Flute, 1791). *Iphigenie* is, however, superior as a dramatic work to all of these, and this has to do with its handling of plot, character and language. The poetry is a unique achievement, for Goethe creates a synthetic language that mimics the aphoristic compactness and the solemnity of Greek tragic verse without stretching the German beyond tolerable limits. We can also note the masterly use of stichomythia (dialogue in one-line exchanges) and the repetition of a few key words that serve to bind the work into a unity of sound and idea. Three examples are 'retten' (save), 'rein' (pure), and 'fremd' (alien).

In *Iphigenie*, Goethe achieves a balance between character and action that surpasses all his other plays. Iphigenie herself (contrary to the findings of older scholarship that glorified her as a statuesque ideal) undergoes violent changes during the course of the five acts. At the beginning, she is under the curse of the Tantalid family, for she radiates the gloom of which the 'band of bronze' around the forehead (line 331) is the metaphor. In part the curse is interpreted psychologically, in part ethically, for the play systematically contrasts openness with dissimulation. (In the dispute between Iphigenie and Pylades in Act IV over this issue, which resembles that between Egmont and Oranien, we can see the antithesis of nature and culture continuing to exert its influence.) But in part the curse is also a matter of religion, for Iphigenie attributes her fate to the gods' hatred for her family and (as the 'Song of the Fates' in Act IV suggests) for all of humankind as well.

When Iphigenie tells Thoas the terrible story of the Tantalids, this is not a piece of erudition required by the classical plot but rather an explanation for her refusal to marry him, while for the audience Iphigenie's narrative accounts for the grief that afflicts her. Similarly, Goethe transforms Iphigenie's earlier rescue by Diana from a piece of mythical baggage into an integral part of the play's structure, for it serves here as Iphigenie's guarantee of a more hopeful theology. Iphigenie alludes to her rescue at three key points as she struggles with the alternatives facing her. If she obeys Thoas and sacrifices the Greek prisoners, her family's bloody saga will continue into a new generation, but if she maintains her resistance, she will take on herself Diana's role of saviour and end the curse. The mythological stories thus determine the characters as the play shows them to us, and reflection on these stories takes on a motivating force in the chain of causes and effects.

But beyond this, the play suggests a continuity between the old stories and the new moral issue that Goethe introduces into his play. For Iphigenie is convinced that if she escapes by deceit she will lose the purity of hand and heart without which she cannot lift the family curse. The play thus fuses the blood-stained old myth with a modern moral consciousness. Even more remarkable is the closing theological modulation. When the meaning of the oracle is revealed, we feel that, in some sense, Iphigenie and her brother have actually become Diana and Apollo. Not only do the gods love mankind, human beings could themselves *be* gods if they could only show honesty and dignity in their behaviour towards each other (see Goethe's poem 'Das Göttliche' (Divinity), which was written at about the same time).

The plot of *Iphigenie auf Tauris* is thus neither a piece of classicistic pedantry nor a showcase for an admirable but static character. The events are real, and they hurl credible characters into crises which threaten their beliefs and their physical survival. Most daring, perhaps, is the transformation that Iphigenie undergoes in Act v. Her admission of the truth to Thoas has no primness about it. Rather, she first whips herself into an emotional frenzy, in which she expresses her anger towards Thoas but also her love and gratitude to him. After her behaviour in Act I, which had been chilly and reserved, this outburst comes as a remarkable reversal, but it is psychologically appropriate for it represents the character's breakthrough to a new self-understanding and a new moral commitment to others. The scene gives the play's conclusion an emotional complexity and truthfulness that make nonsense of most of the criticisms that have been levelled at it.

The resolution of the ethical and theological dilemma rests not only on Iphigenie's own decision but also on that of Thoas, who up to the end has the power to prevent the Greeks' departure. His surrender to Iphigenie's appeal has been declared by some critics to be implausible; one could equally well fault Shakespeare's *The Tempest* (another play dealing with a return from exile) by saying that ours is not a 'brave new world', and that Miranda will soon realize her mistake. Perhaps so, but the criticism is beside the point. Each play has the poetic power to make us believe, each time we see or read it, in its vision of hope, and that is surely enough. Similarly, the play has been criticized as evidence of Goethe's 'avoidance of tragedy'.[6] But this ignores its massive awareness of tragedy, for it admits the plausibility both of catastrophic events and of spiritual despair. It is precisely this awareness that makes the outcome of the drama so moving.

Like *Iphigenie*, *Torquato Tasso* was conceived for the amateur theatre group, but during Goethe's first decade in Weimar the work did not progress beyond a prose fragment (written in 1780). He resumed work on it in Italy, but it was only completed in summer 1789 after his return to Weimar. From its chronological position and subject matter – the misfortunes of a great Renaissance poet ending in estrangement from his courtly patrons – one might expect the play to be either a summation of Goethe's Italian experience or a reflection on his own experience at Weimar. But it contains little that we can connect to the preoccupations of Goethe's *Italian Journey*,[7] and Goethe's own situation in Weimar was quite different, for unlike Tasso he was entrusted by the Duke with extensive administrative responsibilities. The portrayal of Tasso's relationship with Princess Leonore von Este, on the other hand, probably has much to do with Goethe's relationship with Charlotte von Stein, which ended on his return from Italy.

Even more than *Götz* and *Egmont*, *Tasso* concerns the portrayal of a single character. When Tasso is not on the stage, the other characters talk about him. Thus the play has little that can be called action. Affairs of state, the normal sphere of action for noblemen like Alfons and Antonio, appear only at the margin. The sole practical issue at stake is whether Tasso should remain at Belriguardo, the Duke of Ferrara's country estate, or go elsewhere, and it is a surprisingly trivial issue for so lengthy a play, the solemn verse of which moreover creates the expectation of tragedy. (The use of tragic stichomythia for the dispute of the two Leonores in Act III over who should entertain Tasso is a blatant mismatch of content and form.) At the end, as the aristocrats depart leaving Tasso by himself, it is unclear whether the estrangement is to be temporary or permanent. Comparison to *Iphigenie* shows further that *Tasso* lacks a religious dimension, so that the poet's famous lines, 'Und wenn der Mensch in seiner Qual verstummt / Gab mir ein Gott zu sagen, wie ich leide' (And when the human being falls silent in his torment, a god has given me the power to say how I suffer; lines 3432–3) have no more than rhetorical force. It is not even possible to name any ethical issue that the work raises, for the theme of the incompatibility of poet and man of action, or the exchange between Tasso and the Princess over 'what is permitted' (lines 995–1048) are really no more than matters of social decorum.

Another consequence of the work's structure is that it appears to treat Tasso as the only problematic figure and to take the others for granted, as they themselves take for granted their own privileged existence. But the modern reader may well be reluctant to accept this perspective, not least when we consider what was happening in France as Goethe completed the work. What, we ask, is behind Antonio's unprovoked attacks on Tasso in the first two acts, and why is Antonio not called to account by the Duke? How benevolent a patron is this Duke? Does the Princess have Tasso's interests at heart? Is she exploiting him for some private emotional purpose, and why does she do nothing to help him in Act III? Is Antonio's offer of friendship in Act V sincere? In all these areas the play fails to deal satisfactorily with the issues that it raises. Particularly the later parts of the play seem to be written on the premise that courtly patronage offers Tasso the ideal conditions for his writing, and that the only source of disharmony is his own undisciplined and suspicious nature. And yet his two alleged outrages – drawing his sword on Antonio (Act II) and embracing the Princess (Act V) – can equally well be seen as responses to provocation, unwise perhaps but not incomprehensible. At the end we do not know what Goethe intends us to think, for he appears at once to be glorifying courtliness and also providing reasons for viewing it with suspicion.

The play has been defended both as a portrayal of an artist and as a portrayal of the conflict between artist and society. Neither interpretation is convincing, for Tasso is too specific an individual and his problems arise from too specific a constellation of circumstances for the significance of the action to be generalized in that way. The society of Belriguardo, moreover, is a very long way from being identical to society as such, and Tasso provokes the hostility of Antonio not because he is an artist but because he is a rival for female favour. The more recent interpretation that the play portrays the conflict between nature and culture is again unsatisfactory, as Tasso is not a very persuasive representative of nature. He has none of the qualities of Götz and Egmont, such as a love of physical exercise or of simple people. In fact, with his need for fine clothing and rich food, Tasso is no less dependent on courtly surroundings than his noble patrons, and thus it is hard to view him as a modern figure protesting against the restrictions imposed on him by a traditional society.

Despite all these difficulties, we should resist the temptation to belittle Tasso, for Goethe has created here a very particular mood of nervous strain in a small group of cultivated but overwrought individuals. On the one hand, the work harks back to the tradition of Renaissance pastoral, to which it contains several allusions. On the other hand, as a play of conversation rather than action, dealing with the rarefied conflicts within an isolated group, it anticipates the great modern playwrights, particularly Chekhov and Strindberg, whose works are full of broken characters like Tasso and who can create an emotional intensity out of all proportion to the external events that they show. Despite all reservations, therefore, Tasso still deserves to be called a great play, although one of a demanding and elusive kind, and its stature is revealed only if we avoid all attempts to reduce it to a formula.

Tasso is the last major work to be discussed here, for from here to the end of his life Goethe's chief energies as a dramatic writer were directed towards the completion of *Faust*. The remaining works can be divided into two categories, the plays dealing with the French Revolution and a group of allegorical texts. The most substantial play in the first group is *Die natürliche Tochter* (The Natural Daughter, 1803), but it was preceded by three quite interesting works. In *Der Groß-Cophta* (The Grand Kophta, 1791) Goethe returned to a plan of the previous decade to write a comic opera about the Necklace Affair, a scandal at the French court that had filled him with forebodings about the stability of the social order. The play follows the events of the scandal in a rather literal manner, but the comic mode prevails and the political questions that the play raises are quashed at the end by the arrest of the culprits.

Political discussion is similarly foreclosed in *Der Bürgergeneral* (The Citizen-General) and *Die Aufgeregten* (Agitation), both written in 1793, the second never completed. In both works, which are conceived as sequels to popular comedies by other authors, Goethe's strategy is to use characters already familiar to the audience to convey a message appropriate to the revolutionary situation. *Der Bürgergeneral* is rather feeble, and shows a ne'er-do-well called Schnaps who claims to be an emissary of the Jacobin party but who is really out to fill his belly at the peasants' expense. The plot of *Die Aufgeregten* is more wide-ranging, and it is one of the few works by Goethe in which we glimpse the reality of the German society of his time. The play shows how, in the revolutionary age, a typical dispute between gentry and peasants over feudal dues can become the spark for political violence. Emerging from these plays is a view that revolution is the outcome of foolishness in the lower class, self-importance in the middle class, and arrogance in the nobility. While conceding that the latter has often acted oppressively, Goethe still places his hopes in the existing order, which he believes could function well if each class observed its limits and performed its specific duties. Goethe's ideal (expounded much too didactically by the exemplary figures in these plays) is a society in which commoners do not need to involve themselves in public affairs since the latter are in the hands of enlightened nobles.

Though a completed five-act drama, *Die natürliche Tochter* (1803) is the only part of a planned trilogy to have been written and is not viable by itself. The plot is taken from a French memoir that appeared in 1798 and which Goethe read in the following year. The author was the illegitimate daughter of a nobleman, and her story concerns the family conflicts caused by her birth and her struggle (thwarted by the Revolution) to gain the social position due to her. Goethe intended to tell her story against the background of revolution, and to use the central character, whose name he ironically changed to Eugenie (well-born), to bring about a redemptive restoration of the social order at the end of the trilogy. The action of the completed part shows Eugenie's presentation to the King by her father the Duke, then her sudden abduction by hirelings of her half-brother. The third act consists largely of the Duke's lament over her falsely reported death. In the last two acts we see Eugenie escape banishment and likely death by agreeing to marry a provincial *Gerichtsrat* (legal counsellor) on the understanding that the marriage will remain unconsummated (for consummation would annul her claim to noble rank). The provisional quality of the conclusion is underlined by Eugenie's reference to her hope for a future 'resurrection'.

The completed trilogy could hardly have become a satisfactory treatment of the French Revolution, since political events are referred to solely from an aristocratic perspective. Nevertheless, *Die natürliche Tochter* is a work of considerable poetic power and looks back to *Iphigenie* in that it contains the motif of a woman's return from exile to heal the discords of her home. We can perhaps also hear an echo of Shakespeare's late romances *The Winter's Tale* and *Pericles*, in which female characters are falsely reported to be dead but return at the end to bring about a general renewal. Furthermore, Eugenie's breach of her father's pointless command not to open her cabinet of finery in Act II belongs more in a world of romance than in a tragic one. On the other hand, with its severe symbolic language and its abstract action (the country in which it takes place is never named), the play also looks forward to the Symbolist drama of a century later and to authors such as Maeterlinck and Hofmannsthal.

The remaining dramas of Goethe's middle and old age can be classified as allegorical works. They are of interest in part for the light they throw on *Faust II*, but also intrinsically, since they demonstrate the artistic path that Goethe took in the latter part of his life. As we have seen, he was already in 1775–86 required to plan courtly entertainments, a task that he sometimes accepted with ill grace. (Some texts from the masques of these years survive – see FA v, 435–57.) However, under the threefold impact of his experience in Italy, his observation of the political upheavals of his time and his scientific researches, the allegorical masque came to hold a prominent position in his later works. Allegorical pageantry, which underlies much of *Faust II*, was the artistic language that best expressed Goethe's convictions about the timeless and the transitory, about the unity of art and nature (see his sonnet 'Natur und Kunst' (Nature and Art)), about the fundamental law of polarity (*Polarität*) and intensification (*Steigerung*), and about the appropriateness of the traditional social order to the human condition. True, these works are a product of courtly culture as it had developed in Europe through the

Renaissance and the Baroque, and they might seem to represent both an aesthetic and a political dead end. Goethe's roots are in the past, and it was left to younger contemporaries such as Stendhal (b. 1783), Heine (b. 1797), and Balzac (b. 1799) to explore the new urban and bourgeois world that was taking shape. Moreover, the texts of the allegorical works are less self-sufficient than those of the earlier dramas, since costume, scenery, music and dance are all essential components of the festive event, and these are left to our imagination.

Such obstacles to appreciation notwithstanding, the allegorical works still represent the climax of a historical style. They may contain none of the human drama of *Egmont* or *Iphigenie*, but their artistry is still of a high order. We should note three completed works and one fragment. *Palaeophron und Neoterpe*, written for the birthday of the Dowager Duchess Anna Amalia in 1800, explores the relationship of permanence and change. *Was wir bringen* (What We Offer), which celebrates the opening of a new theatre in Lauchstädt in 1802, contains allegories of different dramatic genres, with the elevating function of art being symbolized by a magic carpet. *Des Epimenides Erwachen* (The Awakening of Epimenides) uses the myth of a Greek Rip van Winkle figure to celebrate the coming of peace in 1814. It contains 'daemons' of trickery and violence who represent the German experience under Napoleon's domination. The unfinished *Pandora* (1808), dealing once again with the return of a vanished female figure, is different from these in that it was not tailored to a specific occasion, so that, if completed, it could have stood on its own as a poetic drama. The poetry is notable for its use of a wide range of metres, and in its austere symbolic language the work looks forward to the world of the young Hofmannsthal. We can thus conclude this survey by noting that, although Goethe's development as a dramatist took him in the opposite direction from social realism, the victory of the latter has not been final. Though lacking the immediate appeal of his earlier dramas, and though rooted in a social reality that is now historic, Goethe's later works can thus still serve as a model for writers seeking an alternative dramatic and poetic language.

NOTES

1 Here as elsewhere I adopt Boyle's English version of the titles.
2 The young Goethe's frequent recourse to the dramatic mode of composition, though without any view to performance, is explained in Book 13 of *Dichtung und Wahrheit* in part as the author's habit of pursuing his private thoughts in dialogic form (HA IX, 576–7) and in part as a widespread tendency in the society in which he moved (HA IX, 594). Among further short dramatic texts of this period, which

cannot be discussed here, are *Hanswursts Hochzeit* (Hanswurst's Wedding), and the two 'artist dramas' *Des Künstlers Erdewallen* (The Artist's Earthly Pilgrimage) and *Des Künstlers Vergötterung* (The Artist's Deification).

3 Further texts in this genre are *Jery und Bätely* (1780, second version 1790), *Die Fischerin* (The Fisherwoman, 1782), *Scherz List und Rache* (Jest, Craft and Vengeance, 1784), *Die ungleichen Hausgenossen* (The Mismatched Household, 1786), and, from the next decade, Goethe's uncompleted continuation of Mozart's *Die Zauberflöte* (The Magic Flute, 1798).

4 Proserpina also appears as an episode in Goethe's comedy *Der Triumph der Empfindsamkeit* (The Triumph of Sensibility, 1777), an amusing skit on a contemporary fashion.

5 See Karl Maurer, *Goethe und die romanische Welt: Studien zur Goethezeit und ihrer europäischen Vorgeschichte* (Paderborn: Schöningh, 1997), pp. 25–32.

6 The phrase originates with Erich Heller's essay 'Goethe and the Avoidance of Tragedy', in his volume *The Disinherited Mind. Essays in Modern German Literature and Thought* (Cambridge: Bowes and Bowes, 1952), pp. 37–66.

7 The fragmentary *Nausikaa* (1787) was the only dramatic work to be conceived during Goethe's period in Italy.

5

JANE K. BROWN

Faust

Faust has been seen as the paradigmatic text of modernity almost since its conception. By 1836 Karl Gutzkow was claiming that Goethe was 'set by the gods as a boundary-stone to mark where the past ends and modernity begins',[1] while for Matthew Arnold he was the great manifestation of the modern spirit.[2] Innumerable critics have identified Goethe's most famous work as the beginning of this or that tradition. Whether or not one fully agrees with these characterizations, *Faust* is undeniably one of those rare works that capture some major turning point in our history. Composed over six decades, from 1773 to 1832, *Faust* comprehends far-reaching changes in philosophy, science, political and economic organization, industrialization and technology that might best be summarized as Europe's confrontation with the impact of secularization. Europe entered the eighteenth century with institutions and structures still defined in terms of a cosmos ordered by a divine principle; but increasingly the universe was felt to operate on its own and sometimes seemed entirely the product of natural processes. The resulting sense of crisis as the old institutions no longer corresponded to the naturalized world is reflected in political upheavals – the American and French Revolutions, the Napoleonic Wars, the Restoration and the July Revolution of 1830. In literature and the arts the upheaval is generally identified as Romanticism, in philosophy as the Kantian Revolution, in economics and technology as the Industrial Revolution. To understand *Faust* as modern one must thus read it against these various revolutions.

Goethe began *Faust* not in Germany, but in the Holy Roman Empire. By the time he finished it the Empire had been officially dissolved for twenty-five years and the German lands were well on the way to the consolidation that led to the modern nation-state of Germany in 1871. In the process Goethe, like all Europeans, had to reflect on the spectacular collapse of divine right monarchy in France and on the not always attractive birth pangs of democratic government. Goethe watched the French Revolution, career of Napoleon, and Restoration with profound ambivalence, and his concerns saturate *Faust*. There are passages of topical satire in scenes such as 'Walpurgis Night's Dream' and in the Emperor's restoration of his court after the dubious defeat of the alternative Emperor in Act IV of Part II. War lurks in the background throughout the play – in the soldiers and references to war in 'Before the City Gate', the military profession of Margarete's brother Valentin, military activity constantly alluded to in the first three acts of Part II, and explicit battle scenes in Act IV. More profound yet is the theme of revolutionary subversion implicit in the importance of Mephistopheles, the spirit who always denies and who always steals the show (HA III, line 1338).[3] Equally subversive is Faust's pact with the devil, which requires him to achieve salvation not by renouncing sin, but by pursuing it as far as possible. Faust and Mephistopheles are the successors to Milton's Adam and Satan, and Goethe was among the first to see Satan as a great revolutionary. Even where *Faust* operates with imagery of the older God-centred cosmos, its rhetoric betrays the presence of the new. The archangels in the 'Prologue in Heaven' celebrate the competing '*brother*-spheres' of the creation (244; my emphasis). The poet of the 'Prelude on the Stage' may hate the mobs to whom the director caters, but his poetry similarly speaks of the rights of humanity, conferred by Nature (136). By the end of Part II Faust himself has for all practical purposes replaced the Emperor as the ruler of active millions, and he was celebrated in this role by the Communist state in East Germany. Despite the fact that Goethe's own politics were often conservative, *Faust* embodies the revolutionary ethos of its time so profoundly that it has been seen as celebrating phases of that development that had not even been conceived at the time it was written.

Goethe represents various stages of the shift in economic power from landowning classes to bourgeoisie in the Industrial Revolution, which was just beginning in the early nineteenth century. Part I is set in the pre-industrial world of the German small town as it survived into the late eighteenth century. Act I of Part II offers a sophisticated analysis of the changing economics as a monetary system based on precious metal equivalence gives way to one based on signification and the authority of the nation-state. Act 4 sketches in passing life in the capital of a petty eighteenth-century German princedom, but then the newly restored Emperor grants Faust huge tracts of swamp which Faust drains and has settled, becoming himself the ruler of a productive people: power has passed to the rising technocratic class as the play recapitulates the economic evolution of its time. At the same time the last act contains prescient warnings of the dangers and potential inhumanity of the new regime. The modern nation-state that emerged on German soil from this process in 1871 was still officially an empire that accorded considerable respect to its old feudal class, but power actually resided in the hands of its industrialists. Small wonder that it adopted Goethe's *Faust* as its representative text.

German philosophy in Goethe's day was preoccupied with the gap between the subject, the self in its capacity as perceiver, and the object or non-self. Thus Faust appears repeatedly in the drama 'imprisoned' in small gothic chambers and literal prisons from which he longs to escape into nature, into the world, into a freedom to experience everything that can be known to the human spirit. German Romantics experimented with various models of mediation between subject and object, the most famous of which is Hegel's dialectic. Goethe completed *Faust I* at a time when he often discussed literature and philosophy with the active Romantic circle in Jena, which included, among others, Hegel (shortly before he wrote his *Phenomenology of Mind*). It is not surprising, therefore, to find innumerable contrasting principles at work in *Faust* that are brought into relationship with one another in various fashions, often dialectically.

In the generation before Goethe the sons of the rising middle class still normally studied theology at university, but the fashionable discipline for Goethe's generation was the more humanistic classical philology – a shift registered in *Faust* by the move from a traditional devil's-sabbath Walpurgis Night in Part I to a 'Classical Walpurgis Night' in Part II. Goethe's maturity saw the birth of new, even more human-focused disciplines such as linguistics, psychology and anthropology. At the same time history became a part of all disciplinary thinking in unprecedented fashion. No longer simply a repository of past information or a model to be emulated, history was now understood as an assemblage of cultures, each of which had its unique character and course of development. Classical antiquity, the ideal of European culture at least since the Renaissance, was now understood to have a history that could be studied, but never relived or recreated. The sixteenth-century setting so effortlessly created by Goethe in Part I becomes increasingly in Part II a gateway through which the play leads us ever further into a cultural past that is itself not static, but receding yet deeper from our view. From its evocation of wavering forms from the past in 'Dedication' (line 1), the play is preoccupied with memory and forgetting, with recovering the past to create a future, with making the fullest use of a present unfettered by the burden of memory. The essence of Faust's pact with Mephistopheles is to live each moment to its fullest and let it pass. Despite the framework of the 'Prologue in Heaven' the play has little concern with theology or with human life understood as occurring in a time that began with the Creation and will end with the Last Judgment. In *Faust* time is measured, as the hero himself recognizes at the beginning of Part II, by the throbbing pulse of human life (4679).

The making of *Faust*

The compilation of texts going back to early Christian times and now known as the 'Faust tradition' about the scholar who makes a pact with the devil was inspired by the stature of Goethe's text in the late nineteenth century. Most of its components – figures such as Simon Magus, Robert Diabolus, St. Cyprian, Theophilus and Cenodoxus – illuminate Goethe's *Faust* insofar as their stories entered into the legends that became attached to the name Faust, and primarily as indications of paths Goethe chose not to follow. The Faust legend in the narrower sense began in the later sixteenth century, when the scholar who makes a pact with the devil was connected to the historical figure Georg Faust (*c.* 1480–*c.* 1540), a notorious astrologer, alchemist, physician and magician who was expelled from various south German cities. In 1587 the *Historia von Dr. Johan Fausten*, the first of several chapbooks (collections of legends and anecdotes in the vernacular for a popular audience), appeared anonymously in Frankfurt, though it was evidently the work of a Protestant pastor; an expanded version of 1589 was reprinted 22 times by 1600. It was substantially revised in 1599, 1674 and again in 1725. This last was the basis for innumerable cheap pamphlet versions, in one of which Goethe probably first encountered his hero. The original chapbook appeared in English within two years of its first publication and was dramatized by Christopher Marlowe as *The Tragical History of Dr. Faustus*. Brought back to Germany by itinerant English players by 1608, the play was soon translated into German and became a standard among travelling troupes, and, in the eighteenth century, in ballet and puppet theatres – a form in which Goethe is also known to have encountered the material as a child.

The biographical backbone of the first Faust chapbook warns against the dangers of excessive knowledge, both scientific and historical, and thus expresses the ambivalence of the early modern age towards its expanding horizons. Faust's magic embodies the combination of knowledge, intuition and power that enthralled the Renaissance, when the lines between the occult sciences and other kinds of knowledge were still unclear. In the Middle Ages the church had demonized whatever aspects of antiquity it had not absorbed. The Renaissance successfully absorbed the classical material that came west after the fall of Byzantium in 1453, but still drew the line at magic as the work of the devil. Protestantism, with its increased emphasis on faith, only strengthened this tendency: knowledge led to pride and thus jeopardized the salvation of the soul through grace. The Faust myth as we know it seems to have been born from the conflict between the Renaissance thirst for knowledge of all kinds and the Reformation insistence on the purity of faith.

This conflict became the subject of high art when Gotthold Ephraim Lessing, leading critic and playwright of the German Enlightenment, proposed a Faust tragedy in 1759 as a possible German masterpiece. In order to encourage German dramatists to establish their independence from French and, to a lesser extent, English models in the theatre, Lessing suggested Faust in the seventeenth of his *Briefe die neueste Literatur betreffend* (Letters on Modern Literature) as a specifically German theme and published one scene of the play he had in mind. Goethe was not the only poet of his generation to follow Lessing's advice, for the older critic was widely admired, but his reputation as the greatest genius of the renascent German literature had been so firmly established by the success of *Die Leiden des jungen Werther* (The Sorrows of Young Werther) that *Faust* was recognized as Germany's new masterpiece as soon as word got out that Goethe was writing it.

Nevertheless, the Faust tradition constitutes but a fraction of Goethe's sources for *Faust*. From the first Goethe problematized the Faust material by explicit allusions to and parodies of other works. The affair between Faust and Margarete, the heart of Goethe's original conception, is stylized in terms of a seduction plot that was still recognizably English in Goethe's Germany, and even more in terms of the relation between Hamlet and Ophelia; the connection is marked by one of Ophelia's songs sung by Mephistopheles. The end of the 'Walpurgis Night' alludes repeatedly to *A Midsummer Night's Dream* and the masque in Act I of Part II draws in complicated ways on *The Tempest* – to mention only the most obvious of the Shakespeare allusions. At crucial moments, particularly in the pact scenes and at the beginning of Act IV, Milton's Satan stands behind Mephistopheles. Goethe similarly conducts a kind of interpretive conversation with Rousseau in the pact scene and in Faust's courtship conversation with Helen. At other times Goethe draws on the Spanish Golden Age dramatist Pedro Calderón de la Barca and on Dante. The play is saturated with biblical allusions, from the presence of the Book of Job in the 'Prologue in Heaven' to the last act of Part II. Biblical material appears so consistently and with such complex ironies that the drama constitutes an extended critique of the place of Christianity in European culture. Almost as pervasive are the allusions to classical antiquity, beginning with Virgil in the earliest stages of the play; in the later stages, particularly Part II, the canon expands to include Homer, Hesiod, Aeschylus, Sophocles, Euripides, Aristophanes, Herodotus, Apollonius of Rhodes, Lucan and Ovid. At times the allusions extend to opera, painting (primarily of the late sixteenth and seventeenth centuries) and sculpture from ancient Egypt to the seventeenth century. By anchoring his play so thoroughly in the European tradition, Goethe claims it for Germany, which had previously played but a marginal role in the classical revival in Europe, and simultaneously claims for Germany a place in that tradition. *Faust* is a comprehensive synthesis of European culture and as such is largely responsible for the widespread perception that Germany in the nineteenth and early twentieth centuries had reached the pinnacle of cultural development.[4]

Begun probably in 1773 and last corrected in 1832, *Faust* survives in four separate stages. The first, commonly known as the *Urfaust* (*Faust* in original form) and published only when a manuscript copy was discovered in 1887, probably represents the state of the manuscript when Goethe arrived in Weimar in 1775 and consists primarily of the tragedy of Margarete (or Gretchen). In Italy, more than a decade later, he revised most of this version into verse and added the scenes 'Forest and Cavern' and 'Witch's Kitchen'. He published most of it, but without the final scene, 'Dungeon', as *Faust. Ein Fragment* in 1790. In this form the play had a major impact on the German Romantics and also on Madame de Staël, who popularized this version in France and the English-speaking countries in *De l'Allemagne* (On Germany). Goethe returned to the play at Schiller's urging in 1797 and completed the remainder of Part I in 1806; it appeared in 1808. To this stage of the play belong the prologues, the second half of 'Night' with the Easter chorus, the pact scenes and the 'Walpurgis Night'. Although Goethe drafted parts of the Helen scenes and of the final scenes of Part II even before he finished Part I, he did not return in earnest to the manuscript until the mid-1820s; he published Act 3 (Helen) in 1827 and parts of Act 1 in 1828. In the summer of 1831 he sealed the completed manuscript of Part II for publication after his death, but made a few minor corrections the following January. It appeared in 1832 as the first of his posthumous works.

This long gestation has led many critics to assert that *Faust* cannot be understood as a unified work. The incompleteness of the *Urfaust* and *Fragment* has contributed to the sense of incoherence, although the unity of tone in the *Urfaust* has made it a favourite of critics since its recovery. Much work in the last generation has demonstrated the fundamental coherence of the text, but it is still helpful to understand the different stages of composition, for succeeding layers of the text elaborate and interpret their historical predecessors. The *Fragment* and even more so Part I transform the events of the *Urfaust* by recontextualizing them, so that a coherent document of the Storm and Stress movement becomes an equally coherent, if complex, document of the age of the French Revolution and German Idealism. Part II further elaborates, interprets and reinterprets the text of Part I from the point of view of the older and wiser survivor of the Napoleonic wars and their aftermath. Given the length of the play, some 12,000 lines, it is rarely performed complete. The habit, begun with the first performance in 1817, of extensive cutting has doubtless contributed to the perception that the play has no inherent structure. Given that *Faust* does not observe the traditional unities of action, time and place canonized by Aristotle, it is worth considering just what kind of tragedy it really is.

Its length and scope have prompted many readers to regard it as an epic rather than a drama. Three kinds of evidence support this thesis. First, Goethe never staged the play during his tenure as director of the Weimar theatre. Second, it describes all the stage action as it occurs, as if Goethe intended from the first to compensate for the likely absence of a visual realization. Third, the play constantly evokes milestones of European verse narrative. Allusions to the Bible, the *Aeneid* and Homer occur so frequently that many go unrecognized. The 'Prologue in Heaven' is explicitly modelled on the biblical Book of Job, the introduction of the Earth Spirit is equally clearly modelled on *Aeneid* III (192–9), and Faust's great monologue at the beginning of Part II in response to the rising sun evokes Dante in *terza rima*. The 'fortunate fall' in *Paradise Lost* stands behind the morally ambiguous pact in *Faust* and its Satan behind Mephistopheles, whose parody of the newly arrived devils in Hell (as in *Paradise Lost*, Book I) at the beginning of Act IV calls attention retrospectively to Milton's central presence even in the classical-romantic phantasmagoria of Act III: Faust's distribution of Greece to his Germanic followers echoes Milton's mapping of Christian devils onto their original pre-Christian locations (*Paradise Lost*, Book I, lines 376 ff.), and the identification of the narrative of the birth of Euphorion as a late imitation of the birth of Hermes repeats in reverse Milton's identification of Vulcan's fall as a late imitation of Satan's (I, 739 ff.). Milton evidently marks for Goethe the crucial dividing line between ancient and modern, and epic underpins the history of the European tradition even as Act III explicitly traces the history of tragedy.

Scholars who regard *Faust* in epic terms emphasize the generic uniqueness of the play, but it is wise to remember that Milton himself hesitated between writing *Paradise Lost* as classical epic or as baroque dramatic spectacular. The fact reminds us that dramas with *Faust*'s sweep 'from Heaven through the earth to Hell' (242) were still widely acknowledged and indeed performed in the seventeenth century, when court masque, municipally sponsored morality play, Jesuit school drama and opera dominated the European stage. Goethe was more aware than we are of the degree to which French neoclassical polemics had narrowed the options available to serious dramatists, and he himself still wrote numerous court masques and libretti. If *Faust* fails to observe the Aristotelian unities of time, place and even action, and ignores the simplest categories of causality, its tendency to represent the world in thematic, allegorical terms derives from the religious and court drama that was still vital everywhere in Europe in the seventeenth century and in remoter outposts of Germany into the late eighteenth. *Faust* is full of inset examples of these genres – the 'Walpurgis Night's Dream', the court masque and dumb show of Part II, Act I, the pastoral opera of Act III – and of allusions to practitioners of these forms, particularly to Calderón, the most formidable allegorical dramatist of both religious and secular stage in the seventeenth century. Such drama represents its figures and themes in recognizable relation to the cosmic context and so might best be thought of as 'world theatre'.

World theatre represents not what is real in the ordinary sense, but cosmic or eternal truths. Hence its audience judges the illusions on stage not for their reality, but as instruction about what is beyond human sight. It was the great achievement of Marlowe's *Dr. Faustus* to help shift English drama out of this allegorical mode into the form of drama more familiar to us, in which we focus on the psychology of the characters more than on their place in a larger context. Writing as he was in a world in which God had withdrawn from daily affairs, Goethe lacked the fundamental underpinnings for the genre. At the same time he had at his disposal all the techniques of the tragic tradition of the inner self Marlowe helped to establish. As a result, Goethe's world theatre looks quite different from that of his predecessors and must be regarded as a remarkable attempt to re-establish an outmoded genre on a new, post-Kantian basis in which cosmic allegory is replaced by symbolism of nature. For this reason the drama is often characterized as 'divine comedy' or 'mystery play'. Goethe subtitled it 'tragedy', but since world theatre must by definition affirm the cosmic order, tragedy in the normal sense of the term is impossible. It must be regarded here rather as a challenge to rethink our presuppositions about dramatic genre.

Issues in interpretation

In order to take account of both the inherent unity and the layered process of composition, it makes sense to approach each stage as a separate entity with its own agenda and thus treat *Faust* as four concentric texts, each of which encloses its predecessor in a web of elaboration and reinterpretation. Most scholarship has considered the stages as three distinct texts (with *Faust. Ein Fragment* taken as a slight variant of Part I), so that by reading the stages separately we shall be in one sense following a traditional model, yet diverging from it in seeing the stages, especially Part II, as elaborations of one another.

The *Urfaust*, composed between 1773 and 1775, is essentially a document of the Storm and Stress. As such, its central concerns are psychological. In the opening monologue, whose sources ultimately go back to Marlowe's *Dr. Faustus*, Faust rejects book learning in favour of magic. But the positive lights towards which he turns, first the moon shining outside his window, then the Macrocosm and Earth Spirit, evoke from him the language of eighteenth-century sensibility. Faust is interested primarily in his emotions, and his narrow gothic room, emblem of his dry intellectual world, offers no space for them to overflow. In this preoccupation with his feelings Faust resembles the hero of *Die Leiden des jungen Werther*, Goethe's novel of precisely the same years. Faust's extreme subjectivity explains why the love affair with Margarete, Goethe's original and most influential addition to the Faust legend, so quickly displaces the original plot. The scene between Mephistopheles and the student adumbrates the turn to love, and after a brief traditional episode from the Faust chapbook in 'Auerbach's Tavern' – into which Goethe inserts a few gratuitous love songs – the tumultuous love plot leaves ample scope for Faust's titanic feelings. Faust's speech welcoming the twilight in Gretchen's room in 'Evening' echoes both the rhyme sounds and motifs of his first emotional speech to the moon (2687–94).[5] Thus Gretchen, like Werther's Lotte, disappears as an individual in the plethora of emotions and ideals Faust projects onto her; her tragedy is that she does not really exist in the face of Faust's subjectivity.

The more obvious aspect of her tragedy is that she is seduced and abandoned by a lover above her in rank. Faust is another of the well-meaning but undependable heroes of the bourgeois tragedies popularized in Germany by Lessing (particularly *Emilia Galotti* of 1772), and indeed the Gretchen tragedy is the most compelling example of the genre in Germany. Goethe had Werther commit suicide with a copy of *Emilia Galotti* open on his desk, so it is hardly far-fetched to see Faust in the role of Lessing's indecisive prince, torn between his love for a pure woman and the evil advice of his scheming companion. Goethe translates this mode into the Shakespearean idiom popularized by his own *Götz von Berlichingen* (1773) with its often colloquial, abrupt language, occasional bawdiness, mixture of prose and verse, and use of crowd scenes. The intense subjectivity and rudimentary class consciousness of the *Urfaust* appealed especially to the vitalism of the late nineteenth century and contributed to its construct of 'the young Goethe'.

By the time Goethe returned to the manuscript he had become more critical of Werther's extreme subjectivity, as his revisions of the novel in the late 1780s reveal. *Faust* became more objective in a variety of ways. First, Goethe regularized the verse and versified some of the prose scenes, in particular 'Auerbach's Tavern'. It may not be obvious today that versification implies a reduction of subjectivity, but it clearly did for Goethe. The late 1780s is precisely the period in which he created his great blank-verse dramas of German classicism, and when he revised *Iphigenie auf Tauris* into verse he calmed, indeed repressed its more extreme emotions and even reduced the number of personal verb-subjects. Second, Goethe simply dropped the most pathetic scenes of the *Urfaust*: everything that came after 'Cathedral' – the scene with Valentin, the material that later became 'Gloomy Day. Field' and 'Night. Open Field', and 'Dungeon' – was laid aside. Third, he added two scenes composed in Italy, 'Forest and Cavern' and 'Witch's Kitchen'. Both change the course of the drama and also the meaning of much of the *Urfaust*.

'Forest and Cavern' introduces nature as the central theme and thereby redefines the significance of Faust's conjuring in 'Night'. In the *Fragment* the scene replaces the confrontation with Gretchen's brother Valentin as Faust's last appearance on stage and even incorporates Faust's speech from that scene beginning 'Was ist die Himmelsfreud in ihren Armen' (What use celestial joy in her arms, 3345–65). In the *Urfaust* the speech expresses Faust's remorse for Gretchen's seduction, but in 'Forest and Cavern' it is balanced by Faust's magnificent blank-verse prayer of thanks to the sublime spirit that gave him full access to nature. Now the speech expresses not Faust's remorse but a change of mood associated with Mephistopheles's arrival. The new scene marks a point of balance between two courses of action for Faust, indeed between two Fausts – the scholar and the seducer. Faust's description of nature is not simply the emotional overflowing typical of 'Night' but a reflection that connects passion and calm, perception and memory, in which the silver forms of the past (who exist independently of Faust) 'calm the severe pleasure' of his contemplation (3239). The tone contrasts dramatically with Faust's violent vision of Gretchen's destruction at his hands in the second (older) half of the scene. Since the spirit addressed seems to be the Earth Spirit that rejected him in 'Night', the speech retroactively gives the figures conjured earlier by Faust an objective existence they lacked in *Urfaust*, and a status independent of Mephistopheles. This is most obvious from the abrupt shift of mood that accompanies Mephisto's appearance at the end of the speech; but it is also evident from a changed stage-direction in 'Night' that Goethe has decoupled the magical evocation of the signs of nature from Faust's eventual partnership with the devil. In the *Urfaust* the Earth Spirit appears in a flame 'in appalling shape' (after line 481); in the *Fragment* the last phrase is omitted. As the spirit gains in dignity it is less an emanation of Faust's fevered sensibility and more the representation of a real nature with which Faust must come to terms.

'Witch's Kitchen' changes the conception of the play even more. Goethe placed it after 'Auerbach's Tavern', and at first glance it seems to continue

Mephistopheles's unsuccessful attempts to woo Faust with low pleasures on the way to the Gretchen tragedy: the 'pleasure' is Faust's rejuvenating draught or, as it is often understood, aphrodisiac. But something more important happens to Faust: while Mephisto and the apes perform an idiotic play about the world, Faust sees in a magic mirror a beautiful woman – a recumbent Renaissance Venus according to Goethe's own sketch of the scene. Faust reacts to it in the same language of transcendence and excessive emotion he uses with the magical signs and with Gretchen. Mirrors are common images of subjectivity; yet this magic mirror reflects not the self, but the vision projected by that self. Here is an explicit image of Faust projecting his vision of ideal beauty – or of the Ideal per se – onto something outside of himself; and the something onto which he projects it is a framed image. As Mephistopheles and the apes present a play within the play – a framed dramatic image – about nature, Faust creates his own image of the Ideal. Faust's subjectivity is contrasted with Mephisto's objectivity, but both find expression as aesthetic illusions. Because Faust is magically rejuvenated in this scene, in effect costumed for his encounter with Gretchen, all that follows, namely the Gretchen tragedy, is effectively transformed into a play within the play. Now the fact that Gretchen is the mirror onto which Faust continues to project his own vision reflects not only his subjectivity but also his creativity. In 'Night' Faust rejects the sign of the Macrocosm as 'play only' (454) and derides his scholarship as bombastic political tragedy (583); these references are easy to overlook, but once 'Witch's Kitchen' establishes aesthetic illusion as a vehicle for perception of the Ideal, they take on new significance, and it becomes necessary to read 'Night' differently, which, as we shall see, Goethe did in his revisions for Part I.

Because 'Witch's Kitchen' has so little mimetic significance it also makes the imagery of the play largely independent of the characters. The invocations of the Macrocosm and Earth Spirit both refer to drinking as a means of healing, achieving wholeness and unity with nature, and in 'Auerbach's Tavern' the spilt wine goes up in flame, the most powerful element of nature in *Faust*. But only in 'Witch's Kitchen' does Faust actually drink: the act both rejuvenates him and enables him to locate his ideal in any passing woman – 'With this drink in him, / He'll see a Helen in every woman', as Mephistopheles puts it (2603–4). Drinking is now an image of perception, and the terms in which the Ideal is to be perceived are explicitly classical. Here is the germ for Faust's preoccupation with Helen as the embodiment of classical antiquity in Part II. Furthermore, the appearance of this Venus/Helen figure in the mirror establishes the play's central image for the synthesis of real and ideal required for perception of the Ideal in the world: Faust gazes at the figure in the crystal mirror while Mephistopheles and the apes occupy themselves around the fire. In Part II the conception of Helen from the rape of Leda by the swan is figured three times as the lightning god Zeus (represented by Homunculus in the last scene of the 'Classical Walpurgis Night') coming to the woman in the water, which, in the first occurrence, is the 'fluid crystal of the wave' (6910) and in the second is a 'moist mirror' (7284). The marriage of fire and water that dominates most of Part II is thus first adumbrated in 'Witch's Kitchen'. Similarly, the mysterious and powerful old women who figure so importantly in the 'Walpurgis Night' and in Part II (the Mothers, Erichtho, Manto, the Phorkyads) are all prepared for by the witch of this scene, as are the low dark spaces of mysterious creation in Part II (the depths of the Mothers, Wagner's laboratory, the cave of the Phorkyads, the hut of Baucis and Philemon). Helen is first mentioned in the play at the end of 'Witch's Kitchen' and Faust is really set on his path to meet her through his rejuvenation there. The contrast between the scene's conceptual importance and its deliberate stylistic obscurity sets the agenda for Goethe's new conception of the play in the strongest possible terms: *Faust* now addresses the Romantics' epistemological dilemma that the Ideal can be perceived only in the chaos of Reality.

Faust I consists of the text of the *Fragment* with the restoration of 'Dungeon' (now revised into verse) plus additions that doubled the length of the text and made the 'tragedy of the scholar', as the first half of the drama is known, equal in impact to the tragedy of Margarete. The additions include the three prologues, the second half of 'Night', Faust's Easter walk, the pact scene and the 'Walpurgis Night'. Goethe wrote this material mostly in the late 1790s in a period when Jena, where he spent several months of each year, was the centre of German philosophy. It is thus natural that *Faust* in this form is the representative text of German Idealism. The three prologues frame the play to come in terms of the central epistemological issues of the period. 'Dedication' focuses on the poet's mediating role between present and past and thus introduces both the epistemological function of poetry and of memory, and also the worries about retaining access to the past brought on by the emergence of historicism in the later eighteenth century. The 'Prelude on the Stage' addresses similarly the mediating role of the dramatist between the poet's longings for eternal ideals and the director's insistence on fulfilling the demands of the day in the real world. The 'Prologue in Heaven', finally, with its ultimately unknowable God (so identified in the hymn of the archangels) represented by a stagy old man, questions the place of humanity in a universe in which God has been replaced by living nature. If the Lord of this prologue is certain that erring man can be saved so long as he strives, the devil is confident that he can win his bet: a universe in which the moral principle remains invisible behind the law of nature raises serious questions about the possibility of social justice. In this context Faust's seduction of Margarete becomes a more complicated moral problem.

In this 'tragedy of the scholar', Faust's course is no longer the outpouring of an increasingly isolated subjectivity but instead oscillates between imprisoning cells and open spaces to embody the idealist dichotomies of subject and object, of self and world, and of self and transcendental Other. The sequence of dichotomies culminates in Faust's recognition at the end of 'Before the City Gate' that he has two souls that pull him in opposite directions (1112); in answer to his prayer for a spirit to mediate between them the poodle that will become Mephistopheles appears. As a result the pact with Mephistopheles finally becomes necessary to Goethe's plot. Mephistopheles will now mediate, or eventually provide Faust with the wherewithal to mediate for himself, between his desire for knowledge of the unknowable Other (what the German idealists called the Absolute) and his desire for participation in the real world. Ultimately, the play shows us, the Other can be perceived only when embodied as nature or art. By placing all of the real world at Faust's disposal and often serving as a kind of stage manager, Mephistopheles reveals himself to be in this conception less a principle of evil than a principle of nature; he is, in fact, a nature spirit.

Under these circumstances the traditional pact with the devil is impossible, and Goethe substitutes instead a bet: Mephistopheles will serve Faust so long as Faust remains unsatisfied with anything the devil has to offer, that is, with anything the world alone has to offer. The traditional significance of the pact is subverted, since Faust must now embrace every temptation of the devil in order to be saved. More important is the specific formulation: 'Werd' ich zum Augenblicke sagen: / Verweile doch! du bist so schön!' (Should I ever say to the moment: / Tarry a while, thou art so fair!, 1699–1700). The word *Augenblick*, 'moment', contains in it the word for 'eye'. Such moments of temptation to make time stand still and lose the bet will be moments of vision, moments in which Faust somehow can 'see' the ineffable Absolute in the world. The bet articulates both the instability of any knowledge of the Other and also its dependence on an insight projected from within. Subjectivity is less a problem, as it was in the *Urfaust*, than a necessary component of knowledge. But the concept 'moment' is also important for itself. History is now temporality. As such it opens to the active mind an infinite realm of experience, but it also mandates impermanence in all things, including love. The shift from pact to bet thus advances the idealist critique of the possibilities and dangers of the now virtually complete secularization of European culture: the grounding of identity exclusively in the self on the one hand allows Faust the full development of his inherent capacities, but on the other hand leaves him to seek a basis for a knowledge of the non-self and for a morality grounded outside of the self. The dilemmas to which Rousseau and Kant had brought their century are here writ large.

Because, however, experience achieves its full significance for Goethe, as for Wordsworth, only in recollection, *Faust* transforms encounters with the world into 'staged' enactments of such experiences, so that the play becomes a series of plays-within-the-play, foremost among them the Gretchen tragedy. In the *Urfaust* the central axis was Faust–Margarete; now it is Faust–Mephistopheles, and we are offered less a depiction of typical modes of being than an allegorical analysis of specific themes and problems. In accordance with this shift, supernatural features take on greater prominence and become at the same time less shocking. It is in fact hard to imagine a less exciting scene than Goethe's 'Walpurgis Night': however much theatre directors have sought to make it otherwise, opera composers like Gounod and Berlioz recognized this truth and substituted ballets for it. Goethe's own poem, 'Die erste Walpurgisnacht' (The First Walpurgis Night), written shortly before the scene itself, treats the supernatural aspects of the celebration explicitly as a masquerade to hide the rites of druidical nature worship from superstitious Christians. If Mephistopheles is a nature spirit, his magic powers are really to keep the play moving efficiently, as when he explains that Faust could dig in a field for eighty years instead of drinking the witch's potion (2353–61). They also are a shorthand to express the basic relationships in the play: when Mephisto's wine turns to fire in 'Auerbach's Tavern' we recognize that wine is literally as well as figuratively 'fire-water' or 'spirits', and that everything in this play is to be understood allegorically. Even though God is ineffable, language and art in *Faust* carry meaning of the most important kind. Such certainty about the possibility of access to the order of the cosmos, however ineffable it may be, explains why Goethe can change the end of 'Dungeon'; instead of ending with Mephisto's condemnation of Gretchen, a voice from above declares her saved: in Part I *Faust* has become world theatre.

Faust II repeats structures and episodes from *Faust I*, but simultaneously broadens them as it unfolds their implications. The simplest way to recognize the analogies to Part I is to think of Part II as consisting of two parts: Acts I–III deal with Faust's recovery of Helen, his subsequent 'marriage' to her, and the birth and death of their son Euphorion; in Acts IV and V Faust returns to modern Germany and engages in the land reclamation schemes in which he completes his career. As Part I divides into the tragedy of the scholar (in which Faust renounces words for deeds) and the Gretchen tragedy, so Part II divides (symmetrically, we note) into the Helen tragedy and the tragedy of the man of deeds who finds his way back at the very end to the power of the master's word (11502, cf. 11423). The opening scene, 'Charming Landscape', like the prologues of Part I, introduces the general issues, which are still primarily epistemological and aesthetic. Act I repeats in the person of the Emperor the frustrations Faust experiences at the beginning of Part I in connecting his intense desires with a reality outside of himself. And as Faust's longings for knowledge turned into love for Margarete, the Emperor's longing for gold (and thus an orderly effective empire) mutates into a desire to see Helen, who then represents the Ideal also for Faust until Act IV. In a scene that reminds Faust explicitly of the witch's kitchen (6229) he descends to the Mothers to fetch her shade and sets the action of the next two acts in motion. Like Part I, Part II ends with salvation, this time Faust's; the return of Margarete to draw Faust ever onward in the wake of the Mater gloriosa at the end marks the parallel.

If the *Faust* of the 1790s focussed on the individual, Part II focuses on the social implications of idealism and historicism, and thus offers a sociological rather than anthropological perspective. Now Faust acts in the great world of the imperial court rather than in his narrow room or the imprisoning structures of the German petty bourgeoisie, and the drama offers various covert critiques of the state of European politics after the Restoration. This larger world appears in more particularized and varied detail, as one might expect in a drama whose central image for itself is the rainbow invoked at the end of 'Charming Landscape'. Faust is refracted and reflected in innumerable figures who engage in analogous quests – the Emperor, Homunculus who wants to become real, Euphorion who wants to climb and fly ever upward are obvious examples. Even Mephistopheles becomes a Faust analogue who quests for appropriate classical form in the classical Walpurgis Night and barely escapes being saved as he falls in love with the angels who rob him of Faust's soul at the end. Similarly the theme of striving, the essence of being human, is elaborated from seeking knowledge and comprehending the Other to seeking the well-springs of creative force within oneself. It also expands from the individual to the social dimension in the constant plays on the ambiguity of the German words *greifen/begreifen* ('grasp' in the sense of 'grab' and also of 'comprehend'). Part II is full of graspers: Faust causes an explosion by snatching at the shade of Helen in Act I; both Mephistopheles and Euphorion try to catch attractive young women; the courtiers try to grab the illusory trinkets of the Boy-Charioteer; griffins (German: 'Greif') talk about holding fast to gold; Faust's three mighty men cannot hold onto the gold they try to steal in Act IV; Helen's husband Menelaus is characterized as a pirate and the mighty men become pirates in Act V; Faust himself has his spoils of war displayed to please Helen; and the rape of Leda (mother of Helen) by the swan (Zeus) is described twice and finally re-enacted on stage as Homunculus breaks his vial at the feet of Galatea at the end of Act II in a splendid marriage of fire and water. And when Mephisto's narrative of the birth of Euphorion is identified by the chorus as a plagiarism of the Homeric hymn on the birth of Hermes, the entire allusive poetic method of *Faust* is identified as equivalent grasping. As a result, the already tangled moral questions associated with striving in Part I become infinitely more complicated.

Representation replaces perception as the central concern: it is imaged in the rainbow that can be comprehended but not literally grasped. The remainder of the Helen sequence explores in detail how such representations, which include money as well as art in all forms, can be produced and how they are to be understood. Taken literally they dissolve or become destructive by bursting into flame or exploding, as the shade of Helen does at the end of Act I. They are most effectively comprehended or grasped if one enters into the fiction, as Faust does when he dons medieval garb to meet Helen in Act III. In the last two acts the opportunities Faust generates for others to create their own world become the most concrete example of how human creative vision, which has replaced the visions of transcendent truth from Part I, can be realized in the world. Goethe confronts and complicates his own conviction of the autonomy of art with profound insights into the representational nature of all social existence: in *Faust II* all power, be it financial, military, political or technological, depends on the capacity to create illusions. History is no longer solely the real world in which the Ideal can be perceived in the Real, but, as a realm of successive illusions, is also the relentless destroyer of all human achievement. Nowhere is Goethe's critique of his own project more profound than in the play's encounter with classical antiquity. Because historicism had called into question the eternal classical ideal inherited by the eighteenth century, Goethe recreates his Helen by setting her into the context of the development of antiquity from ancient Egypt on, and by dismissing her to the underworld when she has served her purpose. She is both the great achievement of nineteenth-century philhellenism and a monument to its transience. Faust appears to lose his bet with Mephistopheles by savouring in anticipation the creative activity of his settlers, but ultimately he is saved to continue striving after death for an eternally receding ideal embodied in Margarete and labelled 'das Ewig-Weibliche' (the eternal feminine).

Part II differs from Part I in its more openly allegorical style and its indifference to the unity of action, tone or style. The tendency towards complicated allusions to other texts runs riot: Part II consists to a large extent of what might best be called 'friendly parodies', appropriations of texts and artifacts like sphinxes and griffins that span the history of European culture from Homer to Byron. So complex is the web of irony, parody and allusion in the final scenes that there is little agreement as to whether Faust's apotheosis is affirmative or nihilistic. The problem, of course, is the deliberate use of cosmic religious imagery, including paintings of the Assumption of the Virgin, to represent a world that is thoroughly secular, and in which the principles of physical and biological development have replaced the Christian God. In the spirit of human creativity celebrated in the play the older imagery takes on new meaning, and yet, as throughout *Faust*, the new necessarily and not always happily destroys the old. For as long as our culture continues to struggle between religious and scientific conceptions of its own existence *Faust* will continue to represent our own modernity.

NOTES

1 Karl Gutzkow, 'Über Goethe im Wendepunkte zweier Jahrhunderte', in *Ausgewählte Werke*, ed. Heinrich Hubert Houben (Leipzig: Max Hesse, n.d.), VII, p. 235. All translations are mine.
2 Matthew Arnold, 'Heinrich Heine', in *Essays in Criticism* (Boston: Ticknor and Fields, 1865), 157.
3 All further citations are by line number of this text.
4 The allusive aspects of *Faust* are analysed at length in my *Goethe's Faust: The German Tragedy* (Ithaca and London: Cornell University Press, 1986). For biblical allusions in *Faust* see Osman Durrani, *Faust and the Bible: A Study of Goethe's Use of Scriptural Allusions and Christian Religious Motifs in Faust I and II* (Berne: Lang, 1977).
5 For ease of reference for the reader working primarily with the final version of the play, all references to *Urfaust* and to *Faust. Ein Fragment* are to the lines' final position in *Faust I*.

6

T. J. REED

Weimar Classicism: Goethe's alliance with Schiller

Goethe's relationship with Schiller is a rare phenomenon in literature, an alliance of equals that stimulates the work of both but also transcends it in a common cause. The individualism inherent in creative writing is turned, in an extraordinary act of mutual tolerance, into understanding and cooperation. Each offers the other constructive criticism and practical example, they consult and collaborate. Their aim is not just to fulfil their own potential, but to establish new standards for German literary culture. Through theory and practice, and sometimes through satire and polemic, they create what came to be known as Weimar Classicism.

The contrast with earlier classicisms – this is the last one Europe would see – is striking. The French *grand siècle*, the Spanish *siglo de oro*, the Elizabethan and Augustan ages of English literature were all prolonged developments, rooted in a stable national society, concentrated in capitals and major cities, and in each case the work of several great names. The German version was created in just one decade within the borders of a small and insignificant duchy in a politically fragmented Germany that was not yet even a nation; and it was the doing of just two writers, whose contemporaries contributed little of significance or, often, actually opposed them. While it lasted, they were a powerful pairing, isolated but mutually sustaining: two was company.

Their friendship grew out of and in spite of a sense of acute difference, at first antagonism, on Schiller's side an actual love-hate which he compared to the feelings of Brutus for Caesar (to Körner, 2 February 1789). Goethe, ten years older and famous, had been the literary idol of Schiller's youth, but struck him on first acquaintance as egoistic and unapproachable. Schiller was also envious of the way Goethe's poetic career had been favoured by his easy personal and social circumstances, where he himself had risen from humble origins, been pressed by the Duke of Württemberg into an unwanted medical training, been forbidden after a first dramatic success – *Die Räuber* (The Robbers), 1781 – to write any more, and forced to flee his native duchy in the hope of living by his pen. That, in an age before copyright and systematic royalties, meant unremitting toil: hack-work, writing and editing journals and pot-boilers as a way to keep body and soul together, though it thereby kept the soul from writing what it really wanted to write. Schiller was proud of what he had achieved against these odds, and he was fiercely competitive; yet he also knew that Goethe's poetic genius was almost beyond competition. For his part, Goethe saw in Schiller, especially in that sensational first drama, a youthful wildness he himself had long outgrown and, equally unattractive, the disharmony with nature of an austerely analytical mind that had drunk too deep of Kantian abstraction. It seemed to Goethe they were absolute antipodes.

So the signs were not propitious. Yet by the start of the 1790s, Goethe badly needed an interlocutor, an equal – he can hardly have hoped for an ally. He had returned to Weimar in 1788 from two years in Italy with a renewed confidence in his grasp of realities and a new impetus to write. But he found his Weimar circle unsympathetic, even resentful of his long absence. He withdrew into himself, both intellectually and domestically: he had taken a resident mistress, Christiane Vulpius, which Weimar disapproved of. Schiller meantime was for him only a minor figure in the local background, someone whose historical writings had got him (with Goethe's support) a professorship at the local university of Jena. But then in 1794 Schiller absolutely needed Goethe. He was about to launch a new literary journal – *Die Horen* – in the hope of uniting all the best contemporary writers in one forum, a dream of cultural community dreamt in various forms by many eighteenth-century Germans as a substitute or even preparation for political unity. Eighteenth-century Germany had a mass of such journals, but Schiller meant his to subsume their readerships and ultimately to supplant them all as the focal point of literary culture. A formal invitation to Goethe to join this enterprise, followed by an opportune 'chance' encounter (Schiller may have engineered it) at a scientific society led to a first real meeting of minds. Conversation gravitated to Goethe's notion of the 'primal plant' (*Urpflanze*) which he insisted he could actually see in all individual plants and which Schiller insisted was a prior idea. This awkwardly confirmed their basic differences – Goethe's commitment to empirical realities as against Schiller's to mental structures – but they just managed to avoid dissension and glimpse common ground. Goethe's account of the meeting has attained mythic status, which is not to say that it lacks a core of truth.[1] A remarkable follow-up letter from Schiller of 23 August 1794, arriving nicely in time for Goethe's birthday on the 28th, showed how central the common ground was in cultural history and the psychology of literary creation. It re-read the two men's typological differences as complementarity and subtly suggested how much they had to offer each other.

Schiller's letter set the tone for all their later dealings. It was also the embryo from which in the following year he generated the most influential single critical essay in the language. *Über naive und sentimentalische Dichtung* (On Naïve and Reflective Poetry, 1795) presented in less than a hundred pages a theory of poetic types, a synoptic view of cultural change and its deepest causes from antiquity to modern times, and a new understanding from within of literary genres and forms. Goethe and he were the empirical material from which the psychological and historical theory was worked up, they were the contrasting halves of an ideal human and poetic wholeness. The conception shaped Goethe's self-understanding, as it has shaped the understanding of both poets ever since. Goethe was still speaking its language when, shattered by Schiller's premature death, he wrote: 'I am losing half of my existence' (to Zelter, 1 June 1805, HAB III, 7). They had not merely contributed each to a larger whole outside themselves; they had been engaged in a symbiosis that left the survivor feeling like a no longer viable organic remnant.

This, then, was immensely more than the mere dry working relationship to which critics have sometimes tried to reduce it. Various phases of German irrationalism and anti-intellectualism, from the Romantics onwards, have seen Schiller as unworthy of profound partnership with the intuitive, nature-blessed Goethe – a caricature of Schiller's own diagnosis of their typological difference. Nietzsche even objected to the linking of their two names with 'and' – see *Götzendämmerung* (Twilight of the Idols), §16. Post-1960s scepticism towards all canonical figures and phenomena was unable to swallow elevated claims of any kind. Yet a reading of the two men's correspondence shows how much more they were to each other than practical collaborators. It was a consciously embraced interdependence, an openness to stimulus by creative otherness, an acknowledgement and affirmation by each of what he himself was not, a commitment to 'mutual perfectibility' (Schiller to Goethe, 21 July 1797, MA VIII/1, 376[2]); and though they always retained the non-intimate form of address, 'Sie', it is impossible to miss the mutual cordiality that mingles with their responses to each other's work. Goethe speaks openly of his 'lively yearning to see and talk to [Schiller] again' (11 March 1795, 69), a week later is 'longing to see your latest work', and he signs off with 'farewell, and love me, it is not all on one side'. Schiller hails Goethe's domestic epic *Hermann und Dorothea* as a means whereby 'anyone who feels an affinity for you will have your existence, your individuality brought so close' and ends 'I embrace you with all my heart'(9 December 1796, 287). When they cannot meet, the exchange of letters is continual, it becomes a positive need, as witness Schiller's plaint: 'I have heard nothing from you for a long time, and have been long silent myself' (8 December 1795, 134). That sounds like a whole season of silence; in fact it is only ten days since both of them last wrote. The breaks in their correspondence when for a few days one is the other's guest in Weimar or in Jena are keenly anticipated and appreciatively remembered as intellectual feasts after which the 'spiritual nourishment' (Goethe, 12 May 1795, 75) is sorely missed.

It is hardly surprising that nobody else, even of those contemporaries who were sympathetic to their literary enterprise, could share this degree of closeness. Who could have matched them intellectually? Perhaps only Johann Gottfried Herder, a major cultural thinker and critic who had been the young Goethe's mentor and was now superintendent of the Weimar churches. But Herder already was and would increasingly become morose and grudging towards them and their undertakings; his 'pathological nature' meant he was 'lost to the good cause' (Schiller to Körner, 1 May 1797, NA XXIX, 70). Or perhaps Wilhelm von Humboldt, a man of outstanding intellect and range of learning, and a regular correspondent of them both? But Humboldt was ponderous and wooden in style, and ultimately not a creative mind (cf. Schiller to Körner, 6 August 1797, NA XXIX, 112), while his brother Alexander, the brilliant naturalist and explorer who might have been drawn in through him, and who even without that had a notable impact on Goethe the scientist, was constantly away working in the field. Christoph Martin Wieland was a writer from whom both Goethe and Schiller had earlier learned a good deal, and his elegance and wit were the nearest thing to European sophistication that eighteenth-century German writing could so far show. But he was now old and past his creative best, and in no mood to revolutionize the literary scene. None of those named, and nobody else at a further remove, had anything new and vigorous to offer, even if the central symbiosis of Goethe and Schiller had left room and need. At best they might be a supporting cast.

Symbiosis did not however mean the self-absorption of a two-man mutual admiration society. It had entirely practical outward effects. The alliance may have begun with theory, Schiller's typology of the 'intuitive' poet (Goethe) and the 'speculative' poet (himself), but the theory was itself a bait that lured Goethe into active creation and collaboration. He could hardly not endorse a theory that treated him so kindly, and hardly not work to confirm it further by joining Schiller in his literary campaign and by writing for his new journal. Equally, the typological theory had made Goethe curious to know more about Schiller's divergent character and poetic approach and ready to engage sympathetically with them. All this roused Goethe out of what might have turned into a lasting lethargy, for the lack of response from his Weimar circle after Italy had engendered a 'dark and hesitant mood' which he found difficult to get over (to Schiller, 27 August 1794, 17). Schiller provided him with the sounding board and support he had lacked, in ample measure and in various forms – lucidly stated general principles, perceptive comments on Goethe's work as it came from the pen, a sympathetic understanding and sometimes a vital clarification of major projects-in-progress such as *Wilhelm Meister* and *Faust*. Poetry came to life again in Goethe's own and his friend's practice. Halfway through the decade of their partnership Goethe could already draw the conclusion: 'You have given me a second youth and made me a poet again, which I had as good as ceased to be' (6 January 1798, 487).

Practical and stimulating in another way and on a larger scale was Schiller's activism, his drive to organize and proselytize and raise literary standards across Germany. But precisely the attempt to do this through the new journal emphasized their isolation. To begin with, the other contributors Schiller had signed up, a loose grouping of very uneven talents whom his publicity referred to hopefully as an 'estimable society', hardly came up to expectations in either quantity or quality. It was left to Goethe and Schiller themselves to write nearly half of the material published in the journal's first year (630 out of 1405 pages). On the other side, the public reception was negative – not altogether surprisingly, since the more vocal elements of 'the public' were those rival journals Schiller's conception aimed to make superfluous and the writers who had not been invited to join his 'estimable society'. Some of the criticisms from these sources were not without ground. Schiller had promised his journal would provide 'carefree entertainment', and break down the barrier between learned disquisitions and *belles lettres*; yet his own treatise *Über die ästhetische Erziehung des Menschen* (On the Aesthetic Education of Man, 1795) was a dense and demanding argument, with a strong flavour of Kantian and Fichtean thought and language. For elderly Enlightenment writers who had established a direct style as a medium for socially important debates ('popular philosophy'), this spelled obscurantism. Then, conventional morality declared itself shocked by the frank eroticism of Goethe's *Römische Elegien*, publishing which was one of Schiller's great coups in the journal's first year. Critics perpetrated the obvious pun that the journal's name *Die Horen*, which means 'The Graces', should read 'Die Huren', 'The Whores'. But even reasoned criticism struck Goethe and Schiller as unreasonable – as passé, benighted, short on principle, devoid of sophisticated insight. This concerted opposition began to demand a counter-stroke, and Goethe had the idea of writing a set of barbed epigrams in the manner of the Roman satirist Martial: unrhymed 'elegiac' couplets, hexameter plus pentameter. Schiller joined in with enthusiasm, and the planned hundred (Martial's *Xenia* had numbered 127) soon mushroomed to 750. The target had broadened too: beyond their immediate foes, Goethe and Schiller were now writing about virtually every cultural figure and phenomenon on the German scene, apportioning praise and blame (mainly blame) in the light of the criteria they were jointly evolving. For example, this riposte to Christian critics of Schiller's philosophical poem 'The Gods of Greece':

> Oh what a waste of the artist's splendid skill! If he'd only
> Carved his marble block into the shape of a Cross.
>
> (Xenion 279, 'Art's supreme purpose')

Or this, on the kind of play that first exploits immorality then moralizes:

> Dramatists are mine host, and the final act is the reck'ning:
> After vice has thrown up, virtue can sit down to feast.
>
> (Xenion 412, concluding the sequence 'Shakespeare's shade')

The *Horen* and *Xenien* episodes make clear how much Weimar Classicism was a process of struggle, how far it was from having a tranquil canonical status. Again unlike the classicisms of other literatures, it was never a stable and acknowledged literary mode, always an act of self-assertion, first against foot-dragging older contemporaries and later, hardly had Goethe and Schiller achieved widespread recognition, against subversion by a new generation, the young Romantics. (The classicisms of other literatures were separated from their Romanticisms by decades, if not centuries.) At this early stage in their rise, in the 1790s, Goethe and Schiller were still coming to terms with the nature of the German literary scene – discovering, indeed, that there was no one 'literary scene' in a country as fragmented culturally as it was politically. Hence the first line of Xenion 95, 'The German Empire': 'Germany? But where is it? The land just can't be located'. With no metropolis to concentrate literary activities and ambitions, every princely court, ducal residence or free city of the Holy Roman Empire had its own level (or lack) of cultural development, possibly had its own local writers, perhaps a theatre, a publisher, even a journal. Taking on an opposition that was so geographically scattered and whose backwardness was so internally diverse meant that Goethe and Schiller were waging war on several fronts at the same time. But the war did have a common target: they were waging it against 'Halbheit' in every department (Goethe, 21 November 1795, 126). That meant not just half-measures, doing things by halves, but work that allowed or emphasized only half the picture. The criticism is an exact reflection of their positive ambitions for their own work, since they had discovered they were themselves only partial poets and beings. But at least they were doing something about it, striving to complement each other, borrowing and balancing their divergent talents towards a potential ideal integration. In contrast, the writers scattered across Germany seemed to them to be stuck in the rut of partial abilities, partial commitments, partial visions of reality. It hardly mattered whether it was a cultivation of Christian spirituality at the expense of earthly experience (Friedrich von Stolberg), a dry rational-ism that neglected the emotions (Friedrich Nicolai), or smug moralizing that had no sense of ethical complexity. Moralizing, whether religious or secu-lar, turned writers into preachers. Sometimes morality was overspiced by a portrayal of the vices to be reformed (J. T. Hermes), sometimes evil and conflict collapsed into a sentimental resolution (August von Kotzebue, the most performed dramatist of the day). The seed of realism which the great pioneer Lessing had sown in his 'bourgeois tragedies', and which had borne lively fruit in the young Schiller's protest-play *Kabale und Liebe* (Intrigue and Love, 1784), had now degenerated into trivial imagings of everyday German life, works akin to twentieth-century soap-opera. All these in their different ways oversimplified the truth about humanity and, insofar as they were backed by dogma or convention or fashion, limited the freedom of art to treat life in its full complexity. It was both an illiberal and a superficial culture, lacking both of the two acceptable extremes, simplicity and sophis-tication. In Schiller's eyes, the public had 'no longer the unity of childhood taste and even less the unity of an achieved culture [*Bildung*]. It is midway between the two, and that is a marvellous time for bad writers, but all the worse for those who aren't simply out to make money' (15 May 1795, 77).

But it was not enough to satirize the mediocre work that was living off and confirming popular taste, or tastelessness. Two further things were nec-essary. The first was to show the foundation of principle on which the satire rested. For though a critical position was implicit in Goethe and Schiller's judgements, it needed to be spelled out if their polemic was not to seem merely gratuitous, ill-tempered, even envious of 'popular' writers. The sec-ond need was to show what they themselves could do by acting on their own principles. Without that follow-up, they were vulnerable to the charge of being unproductive know-alls.

Schiller took the lead in publicly formulating their position. His was the more analytical mind (that was central to his diagnosis of their difference) and he had engaged with critical problems almost since the start of his career, less from choice than through the tortuous development of his own writing. Critical reflection was a necessity, but not easy to live with; it was uncom-fortably double-edged, first disturbing his original creative drive, inhibiting it with self-observation and self-doubt, and then appearing as the only pos-sible – and laborious – means to restore it (to Körner, 25 May 1792). Schiller could not go back, only further on through the wood, which might get darker before it got lighter. He had also, under the influence of Kant's *Critique of Judgement* (1790), begun working on more fundamental aesthetic problems, a study that was intensified by a dual challenge: on the private level, to un-derstand and evaluate Goethe's work and creative character in relation to his own nature and difficulties, and on the public level to rethink how art might restore the wholeness and balance of human beings as potential citizens and thereby secure a future society against the violence and anarchy into which the French Revolution had descended. Schiller met the first challenge with *On Naïve and Reflective Poetry*, the second with the series of letters *On the Aesthetic Education of Man*.

Into the first essay's analysis of what shaped and differentiates ancient and modern writing, Schiller inserted a compact but comprehensive review of eighteenth-century literary culture, touching briefly but penetratingly on the serious German claimants to poetic standing and using the most prominent French and English writers of the century as reference points. He gleefully called this excursus 'Judgement Day' (to Goethe, 23 November 1795, NA XX, 130). Yet setting contemporary writers in this historical perspective meant showing that their failings were at least partly the necessary result of larger, suprapersonal causes. Post-Christian mankind had lost immediate contact with nature, was no longer unconsciously part of it as the ancients had been. That was writ plain across the face of all modern writing, dominated as it was by an awareness of loss and by a wistful or embittered aspiration to close the gap. The pervasive modern reflectiveness made this next to impossible: the harder you yearned, the deeper the problem became, there was no jumping over your own shadow back into innocence.

Schiller's essay had thus made a grand historico-cultural narrative out of the standard philosophical division between subject and object, perception and reality (and out of his own creative difficulties). It allowed, though, a direct application to practical criticism: how far and how well had a writer managed to earth thought and emotion in material substance, giving it a local habitation and a name and creating an illusion of tangible things and living people? Ultimately Schiller was posing the question of realism before the phenomenon or the term, in its modern sense, yet existed. But even as early as this, the relation to reality was a sound criterion for whether a writer had gone beyond conception to fulfilment and whether he had turned abstraction into poetry.

Schiller's finding was that contemporaries, Goethe excepted, mostly had not. He argues that the Swiss poet-scientist Albrecht von Haller 'is *teaching* rather than *portraying*' (NA XX, 454); in the nature poetry of Ewald von Kleist, 'reflection disturbs the intimate operations of feeling' (455); in Klopstock – still widely regarded as the leading poet of the day – there were 'no individuals, no living figures', his poetic impulse was 'too chaste, other-worldly, uncorporeal, sacred' (456–7). This criticism of the epic poem *Der Messias* (The Messiah), on which Klopstock's fame and authority rested, turns the *Xenien* rejection of Christian *content* into a matter of literary *form*.

'Chasteness', paradoxically, meant being unfaithful to the earthly element that was a necessary half of poetry. The phrase 'living figures' ('lebende Gestalten'), which has an obvious practical meaning in Schiller's criticism of Klopstock, also echoes the definition he gives of beauty as 'living form' ('lebende Gestalt') in the sixteenth of the letters *On the Aesthetic Education of Man* (NA xx, 355). He arrives at this deceptively simple formula by first analysing human beings down to their basic elements, the opposed impulses to form and to matter, which art can reconcile in free play. The integration of abstract and concrete, reflection and embodiment, which Schiller demands of art thus corresponds to the most fundamental human need and could restore lost psychic, social and ultimately even political balance.

That modern writers fell short of such integration was an inevitable consequence of their place in cultural history. Schiller's criticism thus tempers justice with mercy. He knows that the harmony which the 'naive' poets of antiquity could achieve before the Fall into Christian and post-Christian consciousness is no longer feasible for the 'reflective' poet, burdened as he is with the varied forms of reflection – religious, moral and epistemological – that make up modernity. Schiller gets concisely to their common root: 'We are never given the object, only what the poet's reflective understanding makes out of it' (NA xx, 452). But he sympathises with modern writers in their predicament; he is, after all, a modern himself. They have the harder, indeed infinite task of finding an adequate concrete form for limitless modern reflection. Schiller nevertheless insists relentlessly that they must strive to achieve that, taking as their example the perfection of ancient forms which were the closest to nature's perfection yet achieved by human art. These set an absolute standard, together with the works of the rare cultural throwbacks of modern times like Cervantes, Shakespeare, Molière – and now, on Schiller's own doorstep, Goethe. The great trio from the European canon he mentions by name; Goethe he celebrates unnamed in the ninth of the letters *On the Aesthetic Education of Man*, as a true follower of the Greek ideal, and unnamed again in the literary excursus of *On Naïve and Reflective Poetry*, but unmistakable because the titles of his works are given: *Werther, Tasso, Faust.* These are all, paradoxically, treatments of modern *sentimentalisch* (reflective) characters by a writer close to a recovered naivity, 'in whom nature operates more truly and purely than in any other, and who among modern poets perhaps stays closest to the sensuous truth of things' (NA xx, 459).

Which brings us back to the central matter of literature and the second thing that was necessary if the Weimar pair were to establish their position fully, namely the production of outstanding new works. For the *Xenien* affair was not an exercise of authority but only a claim to it, which so far was not publicly recognized but resisted. To many contemporaries the satire of the

Xenien seemed a violent overreaction, a misuse of both writers' talents, even an offence against the peaceful spirit of literature (which was greatly to overrate the peaceableness of literature, especially when innovators are set on making their mark). So the two partners now had to use those talents creatively.

Even without this strategic imperative, they were both at a point in their careers that demanded it. Goethe's productivity after he moved to Weimar in 1775 had flagged. In ten years, he produced nothing that could compare with his sensational youthful novel *Die Leiden des jungen Werther* (The Sorrows of Young Werther), his popular national drama *Götz von Berlichingen*, or his dynamic early poetry. The burden of his practical duties in the running of the duchy hampered all literary progress. He had important new conceptions – the dramas *Egmont*, *Iphigenie auf Tauris* and *Torquato Tasso*, the novel *Wilhelm Meister* – and he had brought with him from Frankfurt a far from finished *Faust*. But they were all as yet uncompleted. Goethe's early tendency to start writing on the spur of inspiration and then leave the project lying now had an administrative alibi. In his youth a household name, he was fading from public view, and he knew it. So in the months before leaving for Italy he planned a first collected edition. Revising and completing pieces for the eight volumes (published 1787–90) took much of his time and energy during his stay in the south, where he otherwise wrote only two poems, although he was also happy to remain silent, absorbing experience as a consciously long-term investment. But at least the completions he achieved over those two years already announced a more methodical writer than the genius who had dashed off *Götz* and *Werther* and the poems of his twenties. They showed a new orderliness, a concern for rounded form that was one precondition for classicism. Moreover the process of revising his earlier work aroused the creative appetite: 'I'm longing for our eight-volume edition to be complete so that I can move on to new works. You can imagine what a mass of material I've collected this year, more than I can ever hope to process' (to his publisher Göschen, 9 February 1788, WA IV, vol. VIII, 343). He also felt he had gained a new scientific, social and artistic purchase on the world. But what threads would lead through that 'mass of material' and help shape it? And where was the audience who would motivate and respond to the work that might result? Goethe's situation was part promise, part crisis.

So was Schiller's. It had taken him three years of struggle to complete his *Don Carlos* (1787) as the dramatic focus shifted from one character to another and his method painfully evolved from passionate identification with his figures and their ideals towards a more objective even-handedness. Since that traumatic experience, he had published no more plays or poetry, convinced that he first had to solve his problems at a theoretical level, and under pressure as always to turn out lesser things in order to survive. Some of this popular writing was at least on history, which secured him the Jena chair (thus bringing him into Goethe's orbit) and a more settled existence. Historical study also beneficially brought his imagination up against the hard world of *Realpolitik* that he would take on in the subjects of nearly all his later plays – Wallenstein, Mary Stuart, Joan of Arc, William Tell, the false pretender-tsar Dmitri. But at the end of the eighties, it was not clear when or whether he would rise clear of reflection and get back to poetic production. Like Goethe's, Schiller's career was on a knife edge between crisis and a fresh start.

Their partnership gave them renewed motivation and an audience that made up in quality of response what it lacked in quantity: each of them now had at least one responsive mind to write for. Then, they could be of direct help with each other's projects. Goethe had never yet worked at so inwardly intricate a structure as his novel *Wilhelm Meisters Lehrjahre* (Wilhelm Meister's Apprenticeship); Schiller had never taken on so large a mass of historical material as for his drama *Wallenstein*. Schiller put his critical acumen at Goethe's disposal and Goethe welcomed it, 'for though consciousness may not be capable of inventing, one needs consciousness all the more in long works' (25 November 1795, 131). And again: 'A hundred times, when talking to you about theory and practical examples, I had the situations in mind which I've now given you to read' – i.e. the manuscript of *Wilhelm Meister* –'and was tacitly thinking them through in line with the principles we have agreed' (7 July 1796, 20). It was not just a matter of the work's macrostructures; Schiller had a sharp eye for textual detail too. He commented on each new section of the novel in first draft, whereupon Goethe would 'alter and add' (to Schiller, 9 July 1796, 208).

It has sometimes been suggested that Schiller was positively intrusive and should not have burdened Goethe with his advice. Yet at a crucial late stage in the novel's genesis, Goethe begs him to 'read the manuscript first with friendly enjoyment, then with a critical eye and acquit me if you feel able. Many passages need fuller treatment, some demand it; for the demands this book is making on me are infinite and by the nature of things can't be fully satisfied, although it all has to be resolved somehow. My whole confidence rests on your demands and your absolution' – Schiller, then, functioned successively as a judge and a father confessor (25 June 1796, 181). Ten days later Goethe has had the requested help and is acting on it: 'Your objections have put me in a position to bring Book 8 [the last part of the novel] to completion' (5 July 1796, 199–200). And if further proof were needed of how highly he valued Schiller's input, there is the fact that Goethe asked for his advice yet again when he took out the old *Faust* materials that he had safely packed away in

1790 after publishing *Faust. Ein Fragment* in the Collected Writings: 'I'd be glad if you would have the kindness one sleepless night to turn over in your mind the demands that you would make of the whole work, lay them out before me, and thus as a true prophet narrate and interpret my own dreams to me' (22 June 1797, 359). Schiller has now become Joseph to Goethe's Pharaoh.

What Goethe gave Schiller in return was, by the nature of their typological difference, less clear-cut and explicit, less discursive, a specimen rather than a theory. As Schiller wrote in that crucial founding letter of August 1794, 'I was without the object for several speculative ideas, and you put me on the track of them' (13), that is, by what Goethe was and did, not by things he said. The creativity that Schiller could now watch in action from close by, the poetry he could admire all the more freely for having his own writing recognized, were, in the full sense of the word, object-lessons. He was avidly seeking models and materials for a more objective style. Where Goethe consciously needed consciousness, Schiller wanted to rid himself of an excess of it, so as to 'give only the object' (28 November 1796, 278) – something that, on his own showing, was strictly speaking possible only for a 'naive' poet. He looked for help to the Greeks, to Shakespeare, to the beneficially resistant mass of history, and now to Goethe as well: 'only the continual commerce with a nature so objectively the opposite of mine...could make it possible for me to go so far beyond my subjective limits' (5 January 1798, 486). All those influences went into the stylistic melting pot out of which, five hard years later in 1799, the *Wallenstein* trilogy emerged; but Goethe was the most immediate and the most intensely experienced of them.

Goethe also in the broadest sense gave support and understanding to this intensely active invalid (Schiller's health was broken before their partnership even began, and as an ex-doctor he had read the signs). There is a touch of tender concern in that request of Goethe's that Schiller should use a sleepless night to think through the *Faust* problem. Schiller's damaged constitution enforced a bizarre working routine that largely reversed night and day. One of his muses was Insomnia.

If the formula 'living form' in Schiller's account of beauty sums up the aesthetic ideal of the Goethe–Schiller collaboration, their attempt to integrate opposites, then the ethical core of their partnership is the idea of overcoming those 'subjective limits' and learning to live with difference. Living with difference does not mean wanting to iron it out. On one occasion when Goethe accepts a criticism of Schiller's, deprecates his own 'realistic tic' and urges his friend 'not to cease from the task of driving me beyond my own limits' (9 July 1796, 208), Schiller, so far from taking advantage of the concession so as to drive home his own critical point, almost takes back his objection for fear of undoing Goethe's 'poetic individuality'; for 'within its limits you must decidedly stay' (9 July 1796, 211). So there is a tension in Schiller between pursuing the ideal wholeness beyond all typological difference, and recognizing the distinctive individuality realized in Goethe's writing. Faced with the concrete instance, his instinct is to affirm it. Being in on the genesis of *Wilhelm Meister* gave Schiller a profound sense of the need to affirm: 'How vividly it has been brought home to me on this occasion that... when confronted with excellence there is no freedom but love' (2 July 1796, 187).[3]

This means that in practice the overarching ideal could only ever be approximated by the corpus of their joint and interdependent poetry. On that level, Goethe and Schiller certainly came closer to the ideal than any other two major poets. What other *pair* of great poets is there in literary history? For the English reader, Wordsworth and Coleridge spring to mind; but their partnership was only briefly harmonious, in the early phase that produced the *Lyrical Ballads*. Later, all was disharmony and bitterness. What made Goethe's friendship with Schiller so stable was, surely, that they had gone through a stage of mutual suspicion and hostility, had got it all out of their system and were clear about its deepest causes, before ever becoming partners. Their friendship was from the start a reconciliation.

It was tough as well as tender. It survived the potential frictions of an activity like organizing Weimar's theatre, a hotbed of intrigue and rivalry. Above all, in their poetic practice, they collaborated as closely as was compatible with remaining separate creators. Nobody knows for sure which of them wrote which of the *Xenien*. The ballad-writing of 1797 was a closely concerted exploration of the genre. The central works of the decade – *Wilhelm Meister*, *Faust*, *Wallenstein* – are all shaped and enriched by the respective non-author's input. In fact, so close did they come that, quite early in their collaboration, readers began to mistake the one's unsigned work for the other's. Goethe's comment states the possibilities and limits of their collaboration in a memorably cordial image:

> That people are now confusing our works I find very agreeable; it shows we are gradually sloughing off manner and making the transition to what is in a general sense good.[4] And then it's worth remembering that between us we can occupy a fine broad swathe if we hold on to each other with one hand and reach out with the other as far as nature has allowed us.
>
> (26 December 1795, 143)

This may not be the ultimate reconciliation of the naive and the reflective which the aesthetician Schiller dreamed of, but as a practical convergence it would do to be going on with.

Ten years later, Goethe used much the same image to mourn his dead friend. His plaintive question, 'Who will reach out his hand to me as I sink in the real?' ('Schemata zu Schillers Totenfeier', MA vi/2, 567) shows how much and in what way he missed Schiller. It could of course be argued that this itself, like so many of Goethe's interpretations of himself and the classical phase, bears Schiller's imprint. That is not to say it is wrong. What came to dominate, however, in the literature of the succeeding decades was not at all the unmitigatedly 'real', but rather the fantastic, in the thinking and writing of the Romantics. Some of Goethe's own later work bears the same mark (he even found himself developing an interest in the Christian Middle Ages the Romantics so enthused over). But periodically he set his face publicly against Romantic trends, especially in the memoirs of his *Italienische Reise* (Italian Journey, 1817/29) where he documents the Italian foundations of his classicism. And in his later years he drew ever more on his memories of Schiller and their partnership for support. Schiller's letters especially were 'an unending treasure . . . and, just as they helped us to progress, one must read them again so as to be kept from backsliding' (to Wilhelm von Humboldt, 22 June 1823; HAB iv, 68). Publishing these exchanges would, he says, 'make fully visible and comprehensible our joint and inseparable activity, and show that neither of us can be understood without the other' (to Sulpiz Boisserée, 29 September 1826; HAB iv, 204). It was admittedly 'amusing to see' how, immediately after the 'grand fanfare of the *Horen* . . . there was an embarrassing shortage of copy. And yet, if it hadn't been for the drive and thrust of that time . . . German literature would now look completely different.' As for his own self, 'I really don't know what would have become of me without Schiller's stimulus' (to Schultz, 10 January 1829, HAB iv 312). That leaves little room to doubt how much the shaping of this phase, both personal and historic, was Schiller's work.

NOTES

This essay restates the argument, though with much altered detail, of my chapter 'Schiller und die Weimarer Klassik' in *Schiller-Handbuch*, ed. Helmut Koopmann (Stuttgart: Kröner Verlag, 1998).

1 See 'Glückliches Ereignis', HA x, 538–42.
2 Further references to the Goethe–Schiller correspondence will be to this volume by page number only.
3 Cf. the comment of the French philosopher Alain on the nature of their friendship as revealed in the letters: 'Each gives the other the only help which one nature can give to another, which is to confirm it and ask it to remain itself. It is not much to accept beings as they are, and we always have to come to that; but wanting them as they are, that is true love.' 'Poètes', in *Propos*, Paris: Gallimard, 1958, pp. 523–4.

4 At the back of Goethe's mind here, no doubt, is the hierarchy sketched in his brief essay of 1789 about the development of artists, 'Einfache Nachahmung der Natur, Manier, Stil' (Simple Imitation of Nature, Manner, Style). The last stage, he there says, rests 'on the deepest foundations of knowledge, on the essence of things as far as it is given to us to know it in visible and graspable shapes' (HA XII, 32). He may well have thought that Schiller's philosophical and his own scientific knowledge separately and jointly met that condition.

7

LESLEY SHARPE

Goethe and the Weimar theatre

Goethe was Director of the Weimar Court Theatre from 1791 to 1817 and steered it from comparative insignificance to national importance, as a theatre where a repertoire of literary merit was combined with a style of playing predicated on a classical aesthetic. This style, in its decisive departure from the realistic tendencies of the contemporary German stage, aroused controversy and dissent, both in Goethe's day and after. Whether a rare flowering or a theatrical dead end, the Weimar theatre under Goethe, particularly during the years of collaboration with Schiller (1798–1805), was at the very least a highly significant experiment that raised the national level of debate about theatrical performance. Goethe's major plays were not, on the whole, written with the stage in mind, nor did he take on the directorship of the theatre in order to put them on the stage, for they formed only a tiny part of the repertoire. His concern was, within the constraints imposed by the means at his disposal, to bring to audiences the great plays of world literature in a vivid yet elevated style and thus take German theatre out of its provinciality.

German theatrical life underwent huge changes in the course of the eighteenth century. For the first half the commercial theatre with dedicated buildings hardly existed. Theatrical life was divided between the courts and the non-aristocratic sector. The former was served largely by French theatre companies and Italian opera companies, and there was only limited access for members of the bourgeoisie. The latter was served by the *Wanderbühne* (travelling companies), which had no permanent home and had to move regularly from place to place. Though their status improved in the course of the century, actors were excluded from the stratified hierarchy of respectable occupations and led a precarious existence. The courts were eager for theatre and opera but as they favoured French drama and Italian opera, French being the language habitually spoken at many German courts, there was consequently little interest in encouraging German literary products. The *Wanderbühne* had a broad international repertoire drawn from many sources. Though the use of fixed texts grew in prevalence in the course of the century, there was still a strong tradition of extemporization on the basis of a scenario. Moves were made in the middle of the century to improve the standard of acting. The famous actor Konrad Ekhof, for example, founded an acting academy in 1753 linked to Ackermann's renowned troupe in Hamburg. By the later decades of the century the feeling was widespread among the educated bourgeoisie that the way to improvement lay in the notion of a 'national theatre', an institution or group of institutions that would help raise public taste by putting on mainly German plays of literary merit to a high professional standard. A repertoire should be developed that reflected German contemporary attitudes and self-perception. The most famous, though short-lived, national theatre experiment was that conducted in Hamburg. It was a project sponsored not by a court but by a group of citizens and thus in theory had the freedom to develop a repertoire in tune with bourgeois taste. The critic and playwright Gotthold Ephraim Lessing was resident critic at the Hamburg National Theatre and his *Hamburgische Dramaturgie* (1768–9), which includes his devastating assault on the French classical tradition, arose from this short-lived venture.

The 'national theatre' concept was one of the most potent cultural ideas of the second half of the century. It sprang not only from the desire to raise the nation's cultural prestige after many decades of French hegemony, but also from a belief in the theatre's potential as a vehicle of enlightenment. All through the eighteenth century apologists for the theatre had stressed its usefulness as a school for morals, as a source of wisdom about life and human nature, even (though this was more controversial) as a necessary mirror to hold up to tyrants. The national theatre movement gained a further political dimension by becoming the focus for hopes of greater cultural cohesion in the German states: as Friedrich Schiller put it in his speech of 1784, 'Was kann eine gute stehende Schaubühne eigentlich wirken?' (What can a good standing theatre actually achieve?): 'If we had a national theatre, we would become a nation'(NA xx, 99). Yet there was always a significant gap between the vision and tastes of the pioneers of theatre and theatre criticism and those potential audiences. Goethe's careful attempts at reform of the repertoire in Weimar mirrored those of reformers before him and encountered the same problems of audience resistance. Goethe and Schiller, it must be stressed, held a much more complex view of the nature of aesthetic education than that often put forward by those who claimed a direct moral influence for the theatre. They firmly rejected the idea that the stage should preach to the audience. For them art itself was ennobling and capable of refining those receptive to it. It should not, they believed, be subordinated to didactic ends.

The Hamburg National Theatre experiment proved that subsidy was necessary, and that an alliance of court and commercial patronage might give a national theatre a chance of success. There were enlightened courts willing to support the idea of such a theatre with a German repertoire. For one thing, the cost involved in paying for French and Italian companies made a home-grown substitute attractive. Such a compromise had been tried out with some success in Weimar before Goethe's arrival, when the Dowager Duchess Anna Amalia invited the renowned Seyler-Ekhof troupe after the collapse of the Hamburg venture to come to Weimar in 1771. They stayed until fire destroyed the royal palace, including the theatre, in 1774. From Weimar the troupe was able to move to Gotha and work under similar conditions. It was on this basis of patronage and support for a non-courtly repertoire that further national theatre experiments, for example in Vienna and Mannheim, were established. These experiments set the precedents for Duke Carl August's founding of a court theatre under Goethe's direction in 1791.

Amateur theatre

When Goethe arrived in Weimar there were two amateur groups who helped, at least provisionally, to fill the gap left by the palace fire and resulting departure of the Seyler-Ekhof company. A court group, which performed mainly French plays in French, was led by Count Putbus, and a commoner group by Friedrich Bertuch, a leading figure in Weimar's commercial life. After Putbus's death in September 1776 the court group came to an end, and in October 1776 Carl August asked Goethe to take over direction of the amateur productions. Within a short time he had drawn the court and commoner groups together in joint ventures. A small budget was granted to the project. The repertoire was mixed and international: Voltaire, Destouches, Goldoni, Aristophanes, along with German authors such as Lessing, J. J. Engel, Bode, Einsiedel and Seckendorff (the last three being Weimar writers and translators). Goethe himself was much performed: *Erwin und Elmire* (with music by Anna Amalia), *Die Geschwister* (Brother and Sister), *Die Mitschuldigen* (Partners in Guilt), *Lila*, *Der Triumph der Empfindsamkeit* (The Triumph of Sensibility), *Das Jahrmarktsfest zu Plundersweilern* (The Fair at Plundersweilern), *Die Laune des Verliebten* (The Lover's Spleen), *Jery und Bätely*, *Die Fischerin* (The Fisherwoman). Until 1780 performances were held in an adapted ballroom, and thereafter the newly constructed playhouse was used. They were also put on at the country palaces of Ettersburg and Tiefurt and in the Wittumspalais. Performances were rehearsed with care and much effort was put into the creation of special effects, whose success was often due to Johann Martin Mieding, court cabinet maker, whose sudden death in 1782 is commemorated in Goethe's poem 'Auf Miedings Tod' (On Mieding's Death).

The only professional performer in the amateur theatre was the singer and actress Corona Schröter. In 1776 she accepted the invitation to come to Weimar as court singer to Anna Amalia. Her most famous performance, and Goethe's, was in the original prose version of his *Iphigenie auf Tauris* (1779), in which she played the title role and Goethe played Orest. From the point of view of later developments in the theatre in Weimar this was the most significant production of the amateur theatre years and points forward to aspects of Goethe's approach as director of the court theatre. Apart from the fact that the play itself is an adaptation of a classical model, costumes and set were designed with an eye to a unified style and to the harmony of the visual effect.

The court theatre

By 1782 Goethe's administrative commitments in Weimar were such that there was no time for amateur dramatics and productions ceased. From 1784 onwards opera and drama were provided by the company of Joseph Bellomo, which had requested permission to play in Weimar. He gave three performances a week, a mixture of opera, *Singspiele* (an earlier form of operetta), chivalric dramas and plays set in a contemporary non-aristocratic milieu, of which some were comedies, some serious plays. In exchange for these commitments he had use of the theatre and of the court musicians. The court and musicians' families were granted free admission, though this financial loss was offset by the provision of a subsidy by the royal family. Court dissatisfaction grew over the years at the indifferent quality of the productions and when Bellomo announced in 1791 that he was moving on, Carl August, no doubt inspired in part by the example of nearby Gotha, as well as by the creation of 'national theatres' in Vienna and Berlin, decided to create his own court theatre.

Goethe was not enthusiastic about assuming the directorship of the theatre and regarded it as an interim solution. It was not easy, however, to attract a director of calibre away from more prestigious and secure theatres to the little provincial town of Weimar, and in the event he remained in the post until 1817. From his deputy Kirms he had careful financial advice and control. Johann Friedrich Kranz was appointed musical director and an actor, Franz Joseph Fischer, was engaged as director of rehearsals. Later this task fell to one of three actors in turn on a weekly basis and later still to one of the established actors, Anton Genast, whose recollections, recorded by his son Eduard, provide many insights into the productions. Carl August respected the fact that Goethe wished after his Italian sojourn to remain free of the administrative burdens that had oppressed him in the early 1780s. Though he brought natural gifts, an interest in acting, and some experience to the task, the theatre, being a transitory art form, was at odds with his commitment to scientific work, while the frequent feuds among the actors caused distracting disputes. He attempted, nevertheless, to sound hopeful about raising the standard of performances, particularly with regard to a clear and precise speaking of lines without incongruous dialect features or extemporization (see his letter to Reichardt, 30 May 1791; HAB II, 137). The actors were engaged on one-year contracts, and for the remainder of the season from May 1791 Goethe took over much of Bellomo's repertoire. After the first year, however, he dispensed with the services of most of the company, retaining only a few and engaging a number of new actors. Even so, the funds available for the theatre were not such as to allow him to engage outstanding actors and he relied on bright newcomers and experienced but lesser talents to carry the repertoire. The Weimar emphasis on ensemble playing can be seen as a response to limited funds and talent as well as an attempt to achieve a unified aesthetic effect.

Goethe's first years as director show a cautious and pragmatic approach to the repertoire, deriving in part from a lack of suitable plays and from the recognition that Weimar had only a small base of potential theatre-goers. The town itself had approximately 6,500 inhabitants in 1790. Though loud and unruly inside and outside the theatre, the students of Jena, the university town about twelve miles from Weimar, were an important element of the potential audience. Goethe's long-term aim was to recreate an international repertoire, for one of the effects of the 'national theatre' movement with its encouragement of indigenous playwrights, and the introduction of dramas with bourgeois settings, was a loss in the range of the repertoire in the latter decades of the eighteenth century. The Duke provided a subsidy that covered about one third of the theatre's costs. Admission was no longer free to members of the court and Goethe attempted to extend and retain the loyalty of potential audiences by introducing the season ticket. There were usually three performances a week, on Tuesdays, Thursdays and Saturdays, with lighter fare often provided at the weekend in order to boost audiences. The summer seasons, particularly at Bad Lauchstädt, a spa some thirty miles from Weimar, were an important source of additional income. One way of winning audiences was by ensuring the flow of performances of operas and *Singspiele*. There was no separate opera company, however, and singers and actors had to double up. Another way was by making use of the abundant supply of plays by August Wilhelm Iffland and August Kotzebue, who specialized in comedies and dramas (as opposed to tragedies, which were hardly played at all). Many of their plays were the equivalent of the *drame* advocated in France by Diderot, that is the play with a contemporary setting and non-aristocratic characters that had elements of realism and the sentimental and avoided a tragic outcome. The general popularity and ready availability of such plays for performance resulted in the dominance of an acting style on the German stage that was in direct opposition to the stylized kind of performance required by the classical revivals and verse dramas of the later Weimar repertoire. When Goethe took over as director of the theatre this realistic acting style was all many of the actors, particularly the younger ones, knew.

By the mid-1790s Goethe's commitment to the theatre was flagging and he cast around for someone to replace him. One possibility was Iffland, an actor as well as a playwright and for many years already a leading light at the Mannheim National Theatre. Though Iffland's plays were not what Goethe admired artistically, his ability as an actor was outstanding. He was invited to make a series of guest appearances in Weimar in 1796 (he guested again in 1798, 1810 and 1812), one of his roles being Egmont in Goethe's drama, which Schiller adapted at Goethe's request. Iffland was indeed poised for a new venture, but it was Berlin, not Weimar that drew him away from Mannheim. Nevertheless, his guest appearances at the Weimar theatre were regarded as extremely important by Goethe, for his skill and professionalism both boosted Goethe's enthusiasm for the theatre and gave the actors some much-needed experience of acting of a higher standard. The visit also inaugurated the theatre partnership of Goethe and Schiller through the *Egmont* adaptation. Schiller had written no plays since completing his *Don Carlos* in 1787, devoting himself instead to historiography, aesthetics and philosophy. The request to adapt *Egmont* helped to bring him back to the theatre at a time when he was turning his thoughts to his *Wallenstein* project. Goethe bore Schiller's ruthless changes to his original with stoicism, though his play is considerably altered in character as a result.

The fact that in Schiller he had an ally in his aesthetic outlook, whose gift was to write plays that required the kind of stylized and less naturalistic acting Goethe strove for, opened up for Goethe the possibilities of the theatre. In the period from 1798 to Schiller's death in 1805 the two men worked together to realize their vision of a nobler kind of theatre, one that through artistic merit, not through didacticism, would elevate the audience and actors. In 1799 Schiller moved from Jena to Weimar expressly to be closer to the theatre. He translated and rehearsed, as well as providing a play of his own each year up to his death. In this shared mission there were three key and interlinked factors: repertoire, actors and audience. The staging of the three parts of *Wallenstein* in December 1798 and January and April 1799 initiated attempts at this more idealized performance, which culminated in Schiller's experiment in reviving the chorus in his *Braut von Messina* (Bride of Messina). Gradually the repertoire grew more ambitious and varied. Of course Iffland and Kotzebue continued to be important components, but by the early 1800s their works were leavened not only by Schiller's plays and by a number of Goethe's but also by several international additions, including Terence's *The Brothers* (in Einsiedel's version), Shakespeare's *Macbeth* (in Schiller's verse translation) and *Julius Caesar* (in A.W. Schlegel's verse translation), Gozzi's *Turandot* and Racine's *Mithridate* (in Bode's version). As far as opera was concerned, Mozart was a particular favourite of Goethe and the proportion of opera performances devoted to him increased over the years. Other much-performed opera and *Singspiel* composers were Cimarosa, Paisiello and Dittersdorf.

The presence of French classical drama in the repertoire began with Goethe's translation at Duke Carl August's request of Voltaire's enlightenment drama *Mahomet*, which the duke had seen in Paris in 1775. Carl August's request to see it on the Weimar stage embarrassed Goethe, who felt little affinity with French classical works, but he complied with a blank-verse translation or adaptation. The performances in 1800 were not a great success and indeed aroused some hostility in the non-aristocratic members of the audience, as French classical drama was associated with the French cultural hegemony the Germans felt they had successfully thrown off and more recently with the French *ancien régime* and its tyranny.[1] Yet Goethe followed *Mahomet* with *Tancrède*, which was felt to be more suitable to adaptation, and Schiller, who had been particularly sceptical about the *Mahomet* project,[2] went on to translate Racine's *Phèdre*, which thereafter enjoyed a long life in the Weimar repertoire.

An important impetus to help him overcome his uncertainty about how to approach the *Mahomet* translation and about what such a project might bring for the Weimar theatre was provided by the letters written from Paris by Wilhelm von Humboldt on the contemporary French stage. Goethe was so struck by Humboldt's comments that he published them as an essay entitled 'Ueber die gegenwärtige französische tragische Bühne' (On the contemporary French tragic stage) in his art history journal, *Die Propyläen* (The Propylaea). Humboldt readily admits that French classical theatre seems unnatural to German audiences. To the French spectator, nature is defined by order, control and propriety. Humboldt takes an anthropological approach to the perception of drama in the two cultures. Whereas the French, he argues, are trained and accustomed to respond to a work of dramatic art in the round, to the visual and aural qualities and not just to plot and character, German audiences lack this response to the sensuous. Thus French dramatic performance achieves a much higher degree of artistic roundedness and completeness. Humboldt bases much of his comment on the acting of the renowned François-Joseph Talma. Talma's great gift is to combine the three vital aspects of classical drama: the visually interesting in posture, expression of feeling, and solemnity. Talma departs when he feels it necessary from what Humboldt sees as the very formal and conventional style of French drama that leads to the presentation of emotions but not of individual characters. So while Humboldt does not in any way revert to advocacy of the French classical tradition, he does suggest how such drama in performance can achieve something of the fusion of real and ideal, nature and art, that Goethe was hoping to achieve on the Weimar stage.

The repertoire was one vital factor in the strategy of the theatre, but two others were also vital: the audiences and the actors. At the beginning of his period as director, Goethe remained pragmatic about the mix of offerings at the theatre. As more demanding experiments crept into the repertoire, other more popular pieces were still given ample space and were by no means replaced by the 'new' repertoire. Rather, playwrights such as Iffland and Kotzebue made the experiments possible by shoring up the income of the theatre to the point where there was a little leeway for something less immediately appealing to the generality of theatre-goers. A desire to educate the audience's taste was always balanced with pragmatism, but the desire was there and it led to a certain ambivalence in Goethe's attitude towards the audience, an ambivalence shared by Schiller. Their artistic aims demanded that they invest confidence in the audience, and yet experience told them both that audiences, particularly in a provincial town with restricted experience of professional theatre, were often not receptive. Goethe pursued a rhetoric in his writings on the theatre in which the audience is held in high regard, as in his piece 'Weimarisches Hoftheater' (Weimar Court Theatre), written before the première of Schiller's translation of Gozzi's *Turandot*: 'One can show the audience no greater respect than by not treating them as rabble' (MA VI/2, 696–7). Whereas, as he goes on to say, an ill-educated public wants immediate thrills and gratification, an educated public is prepared to bring higher expectations to the play. The performance is a collaboration between actors and audience: 'If versatility is desirable in the actors, it is equally so in the audience' (700). This can be seen as part of a process of making the audience feel it should want better. Schiller enters into this rhetoric too, for example in his preface to *Die Braut von Messina*, where he explains the use of the chorus in modern tragedy: 'The usual assertion that the public drags art down is untrue; the artist drags down the public, and whenever art has declined, it has declined as a result of artists. The public requires nothing other than receptivity, which it indeed possesses...and when it has begun to content itself with what is bad it will be bound to stop demanding the excellent, even if it has been given it' (NA X, 7). Schiller's words sound like an indictment of Kotzebue and his audiences. Yet while Goethe knew how to be flexible in order to sustain audience support, he could be determined when he believed the experiment was an important step in broadening audience receptivity and the actors' capabilities. The staging of two plays by the Schlegel brothers, A.W. Schlegel's version of *Ion* and Friedrich Schlegel's *Alarcos*, serves as a case in point. It was at a performance of *Alarcos* that Goethe famously ordered the audience not to laugh ('Man lache nicht'). His prestige and standing with the court meant that he could treat audiences with an imperiousness that cast doubt on the viability of the theatre under anyone's direction but his.

The third factor was the actors. Most actors of the time were trained or gained their experience in playing repertoires mainly composed of plays with a contemporary bourgeois setting. One of the particular challenges of the Weimar repertoire was the speaking of verse, whereas most actors were used only to prose and still frequently relied on extemporizing if their memories failed them. The naturalistic style that predominated in the theatre at the time had encouraged the actors in a sloppiness of pronunciation and memorizing that in Goethe's view had to be overcome. Even when, as in the case of *Mahomet* or the Schlegels' dramas, he doubted the appeal of the play itself, he believed the practice of speaking verse was vital to the actors, just as hearing it was vital to the audience.

The promotion of verse as a medium for drama was not simply a means of bringing German drama up to the status of classical, Shakespearian or French classical drama. Nor was it simply a slavish adherence to convention. Rather it was an important element in the anti-naturalistic tendency of the Weimar style and the Weimar theory of art. In his prologue to *Wallenstein*, spoken before the première of the first part of the play, *Wallensteins Lager* (Wallenstein's Camp), Schiller playfully asks the audience to indulge his use of rhyming verse (he used the form of doggerel known as *Knittelvers*), saying it is a way of ensuring the integrity of the dramatic illusion (lines 129–38). The play creates an illusion but breaks it by its own manifest quality as a work of art. This awareness of art as art is vital to aesthetic appreciation and to any aspiration to higher artistic effect. This same point is argued in Goethe's dialogue 'Über Wahrheit und Wahrscheinlichkeit der Kunstwerke' (On Truth and Verisimilitude in Works of Art), published in the *Propyläen*.

A principle of the Weimar theatre from its inception was that of ensemble playing. The German theatre had long been dominated by the virtuoso actor, while the general standard of acting otherwise often left much to be desired. Actors, moreover, were quite restricted in the range of roles they were prepared to take on. The assignment of roles, indeed the writing of popular plays, was dominated by the *Rollenfach* – the group of related stock roles that an actor could be called on to perform. The principle of ensemble playing was announced on the new theatre's first evening in the prologue preceding the performance of Iffland's *Die Jäger* (The Huntsmen):

> Denn hier gilt nicht, daß einer atemlos
> Dem andern hastig vorzueilen strebt,
> Um einen Kranz für sich hinwegzuhaschen
> (MA IV/I, 192)

For here it is not a case of one breathlessly trying to overtake the other in order to snatch at a wreath for himself.

This principle was, of course, easier to apply in a situation where there were no outstanding actors, but even those who were most prominent in the company had to show flexibility, as Anton Genast recalls: 'Under Goethe's direction the actors were not allowed to lay claim to certain types of role, and even the leading actors could not refuse to accept the role of messenger if it was to the benefit of the whole. He demanded that everyone should put art above his precious ego.'[3] He also recalls that, by the time of Schiller's involvement, Goethe was much more frequently to be seen at rehearsals. He directed the older actors with some consideration, in order not to offend them, saying, "'That's not bad at all, though I had imagined the moment more like this; we'll think about it until the next rehearsal and then perhaps our views will coincide." Young actors he spoke to more directly, saying, "Do it like *this* and then you will achieve the right effect." '[4]

Concern about the standard of acting led Goethe to set up classes for young actors. In this way he was able to bring on talented newcomers and create the possibility of longer rehearsal times. His *Regeln für Schauspieler* (Rules for Actors), dating from 1803, arose from his own notes and from those taken by two new actors, Karl Franz Grüner and Pius Alexander Wolff. Some twenty years later his companion and helper Johann Peter Eckermann arranged the notes and published them, a process that naturally gave them a certain air of inflexibility. What the *Regeln für Schauspieler* show, amongst other things, is his concern for harmony of style, and to achieve it he had to exercise a degree of control over productions that was unusual in his day. He states clearly one principle of the theatre: 'Stage and auditorium, actors and audience together make up a whole.' The actors were to remember that their playing should not imitate the real but express the ideal and that nothing ugly or unseemly should take place out of a mistaken sense of realism. They should even bear themselves in everyday life in such a way as to express this grace and dignity, so that on stage it should appear natural, as an extension of their normal bearing. Much attention is given to the speaking of verse, which should be deliberate and clear, and enhance the meaning of the speeches. The actors must never speak to each other in such a way as to give the impression they have forgotten the audience is there. They must never speak to the back of the stage. With such rulings Goethe decisively goes against the realistic trend established by Diderot for the mixed genre of the *drame*. The actors' posture should always be erect, the upper arm close to the body, the chest held out. Such directives remind one of antique statuary as interpreted by Winckelmann, and of neoclassical painting. After the usual reading rehearsals of new plays great care was taken with the position of the ensemble on stage and with graceful and harmonious groupings and movement.

The death of Schiller in 1805 marked the end of an era in the Weimar theatre. Goethe continued to aim for the same kind of aesthetic effects, though in 1806 the theatre was threatened with closure when the French occupied Weimar after the Battle of Jena. Fortunately, the frugality of Kirms provided enough in reserve for its continuation. In 1807 the company gave a series of guest performances in Leipzig that was generally well received and confirmed Goethe's achievement with the company, though complaints about the stiffness of the performances were also heard. In 1807 he also began a singing school for the training of opera singers. Notable successes in the repertoire of these later years were the plays of Calderón, in particular *Life is a Dream* and *The Constant Prince*. A famous failure was Kleist's comedy *Der zerbrochne Krug* (The Broken Jug), premièred at the theatre in 1808. The playwright was so outraged that he considered challenging Goethe to a duel. The precise extent of and reasons for this failure are not clear, contemporary reports giving conflicting impressions, some not unfavourable to the play. Certainly Goethe's decision to chop the one-act play into three sections and precede the whole with an opera must have damaged the momentum of the play, in which a village magistrate is finally revealed as the guilty party in the trial conducted on stage.

Goethe's interest and involvement in the theatre waxed and waned in the last decade of his directorship. As with every acting company there were feuds and rivalries, and though he tried to maintain civil relations Goethe had periodic difficulties with Caroline Jagemann, the leading actress and the duke's mistress, who behaved as though her theatrical obligations were a matter of her own whim. In 1808 there was a crisis over Paer's opera *Sargino* when Jagemann went over Goethe's head and appealed to Carl August against the dropping of the opera, in which she was one of the two leads. When Carl August rejected Goethe's compromise, he asked to be relieved of the directorship. Things were patched up with a new arrangement that assured him of his jurisdiction over theatre matters, subject to regular consultation with the duke. In 1817 Goethe submitted another request to be relieved of his duties, the consequence of controversies over the choice of a Kotzebue play for the duchess's birthday celebrations. The duke again refused, reorganizing the administration of the theatre, separating the opera from the drama and giving Goethe overall responsibility for the latter.

The final straw for Goethe came soon after in March and April 1817, when the duke, again at the instigation of Caroline Jagemann, gave permission to a performer from Vienna named Karsten to present a French melodrama entitled *Aubri de Mont-Didier's Dog or The Forest near Bondy*, which featured a poodle in a leading role. Goethe's unhappiness at the pressure put on him to accept this performance caused him to withdraw to Jena, where he frequently went in order to work in peace. While he was there the performance went ahead and Carl August anticipated his resignation with a letter relieving him of his duties in the theatre. Whether or not Goethe wanted the duke to anticipate his wishes in this way is a moot point, for in the preceding months he had put renewed effort into the theatre. The fact that he had not in fact requested to be relieved of the directorship suggests that Caroline Jagemann finally got her way and prompted the duke to step in while the situation was still unclear. The actual theatre building was later destroyed by fire in 1825.

Any attempt to appraise the impact of Goethe's theatrical experiment on the development of German theatre is hampered by his stature and reputation, which allowed him to push through certain productions that would never have come off elsewhere. Along with Wolfgang Heribert von Dalberg, director of the Mannheim National Theatre, he was one of the first nonacting superintendents, who stood outside the productions and imposed on them an artistic vision. Something of the problems faced by such a director, who had to reconcile the playwright's talents with the need to entertain, must find ironical expression in the 'Prelude on the Stage', one of the framing scenes to *Faust* and written in the later 1790s. It was to be expected that dissenting voices would be raised, given that the theatre struck out in a direction opposed to that of the majority of theatres of the time. One of the most influential critical reviews was entitled *Saat von Göthe gesäet dem Tage der Garben zu reifen* (Goethe's seed, sown to ripen for harvest day) and appeared anonymously in 1808 as a comment on the guest performances in Leipzig of 1807. It was in fact written by a certain Carl Reinhold, himself a former actor with the Weimar company:

> The players are under no circumstances allowed the slightest movement that might betray an individual characteristic or a marked passion; they are not supposed to act at all but rather to speak, and they are regarded as having reached their true goal and perfection if they should succeed in turning every performance into a reading rehearsal in full costume.[5]

Yet the practice of verse-speaking and the consequent dignity acquired by the performance were possibly the theatre's most lasting legacy, without which the verse drama of nineteenth-century playwrights such as Grillparzer and Hebbel could hardly have been created. The Weimar ideal of a theatre that combined high aesthetic standards with an international repertoire was perpetuated through three men in particular, Pius Alexander Wolff, Karl Grüner and Joseph Schreyvogel. Wolff, one of the two actors for whom Goethe had made the notes that form the basis for the *Regeln für Schauspieler*, was acknowledged by Goethe himself to be his most faithful disciple in artistic matters. It was a blow for Goethe and the Weimar theatre when he and his wife left in 1816 for the Königliche Schauspielhaus in Berlin, but he took the Weimar style with him. The other young actor who received the *Regeln für Schauspieler*, Karl Grüner, absorbed the principles of ensemble playing and of concern for harmonious visual effects, particularly in the staging of crowd scenes, and applied them during his period in Vienna at the Theater an der Wien and at the Burgtheater. He and Joseph Schreyvogel, who was dramaturge at the Burgtheater from 1814 to 1832 and had met Goethe and Schiller during a two-year stay in Jena in the 1790s, shared Goethe's vision of an international repertoire. Grüner also introduced two particularly successful and long-lived productions to the Vienna theatre world, his stagings of *Götz von Berlichingen* and Schiller's *Wilhelm Tell*. Thus the Weimar theatre came to influence the leading theatrical centre of the German-speaking world in the nineteenth century. The Weimar experiment could not claim to have grown out of or produced a true fusion of literary excellence and theatrical creativity. Yet its contribution to a more aesthetically ambitious and professionally exacting theatre tradition was, given the restricted means and limited talents, remarkable.

NOTES

I am grateful to the British Academy for awarding me a grant under their Small Grants in the Humanities scheme and thus enabling me to carry out the research for this chapter.

1 For reception see MA VI/2, 922–3.
2 See his letters to Goethe of 15 October 1799 and 8 January 1800, NA XXX, 106 and 136.
3 Eduard Genast, *Aus dem Tagebuch eines alten Schauspielers*, 2nd edn, vol. I (Leipzig: Günther, 1862), p. 100.
4 Ibid., p. 86.
5 *Saat von Göthe gesäet dem Tage der Garben zu reifen. Ein Handbuch für Aesthetiker und junge Schauspieler* (Weimar and Leipzig: n.pub., 1808), p. 27.

8

Goethe's prose fiction

In many ways Goethe does not strike one as a born storyteller. There is little in his prose fiction of that teeming materiality we have come to expect from the great European novelists of the eighteenth and nineteenth centuries. Yet the narrative mode evidently meant a great deal to him because he wrote prose fiction throughout his long creative life. And he was a remarkably sophisticated witness to the emergence of the various forms of modern narrativity, particularly the novel.

Admittedly the tradition of German novel writing of the late eighteenth and nineteenth centuries which he helps to inaugurate does not figure in the pantheon of established European 'classics'. Within the broad compass of narrative realism, with its wholehearted acknowledgement of the omnipresence of social life, German fiction tends to figure as at best a marginal presence. But all the same it has valuable insights to offer; most particularly, German writing of this period sustains and is sustained by an urgent dimension of reflectivity, one which invests the narrative process with an unmistakable intensity of theoretical self-commentary. Three of Goethe's theoretical comments on fiction can serve to focus the particular contribution he makes to this tradition. In one of his maxims and reflections he observes: 'Der Roman ist eine subjektive Epopöe, in welcher der Verfasser sich die Erlaubnis ausbittet, die Welt nach seiner Weise zu behandeln. Es fragt sich also nur, ob er eine Weise habe; das andere wird sich schon finden' (The novel is a subjective epic, in which the writer asks for permission to treat the world in his own particular way. The only question is whether he has a particular way [Weise]; everything else will take care of itself; HA XII, 498). This is a very casual and relaxed statement about a very casual and relaxed literary genre. The double meaning of the word 'Weise' – 'way' and 'melody' – suggests that the universe of modern novel-writing is in Goethe's eyes democratic and multivocal – lyrical and prosaic, profound and banal. Yet he does not content himself with simply upholding a narrative ethos of genial pluralism. In a letter of 27 September 1827, in which he is ruminating on the kind of statement the novel can make, he observes:

> Da sich gar manches unserer Erfahrungen nicht rund aussprechen und direkt mitteilen läßt, so habe ich seit langem das Mittel gewählt, durch einander gegenübergestellte und sich gleichsam ineinander abspiegelnde Gebilde den geheimen Sinn dem Aufmerkenden zu offenbaren. (HAB IV, 250)

> As a very great deal of our experiences cannot be straightforwardly said or directly conveyed I have for a long time now chosen the technique of revealing to the attentive reader the secret meaning by virtue of structures which are linked to, and as it were look at and mirror, one another.

This is an intriguing remark, for it suggests that beneath the surface casualness of the novel there is a complex subtext; the realistic foreground, we might say, is accompanied by a metaphorically sustained metatext.

All of this may sound somewhat forbidding – poles apart from the wealth of socio-psychological particularities that fill the pages of Dickens or Balzac. Yet perhaps it is not quite as bloodless as it sounds. In respect of *Die Wahlverwandtschaften* (The Elective Affinities) – but I think we can take the remark to be general in its application – Goethe speaks of his aim as being 'sociale Verhältnisse und die Konflikte derselben symbolisch gefaßt darzustellen' (to portray social circumstances and the conflicts between them through symbolic comprehension, HA VI, 638). What the remark implies is that Goethe as narrator does have a lively sense of society, but society defined not as materiality, not as streets, houses, furnishings; rather, as mental furniture, as the signs and tokens at work in the socialized psyche of men and women. And thereby Goethe helps to inaugurate a potent tradition of novel-writing, one which can serve to differentiate our sense of how literary realism, with its concern to express the social definition of human experiences, can function.

'Novelle' and Novellen

Goethe's *Novelle* (1828) is, in some ways, a strangely stilted story, stilted both in its events and in its characters. The setting is contemporary with the time of writing – the early nineteenth century – and we find ourselves in a small German principality. The recently married prince leaves with his courtiers on a long-awaited hunt. His young wife is left behind, attended by an uncle and Honorio, a young equerry. There is a discussion of plans to restore an old castle, making it a site safe for recreational purposes. The three figures ride towards the castle, crossing the marketplace of the town where wild animals are on display in cages. They rest above the old castle, only then to find their peace violently disturbed. A puff of smoke appears in the marketplace, and the Princess recalls a previous, terrifying fire of which she has heard frequent accounts from the uncle. In the confusion two of the wild animals have escaped; the tiger appears and runs in panic up the hillside. Honorio shoots the tiger. The lion takes refuge in the old castle. But violence is not necessary. The young boy, part of the family in charge of the wild animals, calms the frightened animal by playing his flute and singing. On this image of order restored the story closes.

Most readers have felt that *Novelle* works with a movement from order into violence and back into order. The exposition stresses the harmony of the social world, and we end with a vision of harmony that embraces the animal world, the social world and (in the song of the boy) the divine world. Moreover, as various hints indicate, Honorio is in love with the Princess, and in the course of the tale he learns to overcome what could be a socially and psychologically disastrous infatuation. Yet the thematic cluster concerning Honorio's passion is very understated; this is because Goethe's tale is a masterpiece of subtextual statement. Constantly, in a profusion of subtle links, parallels and echoes, the text sketches in its true theme: the dark side of the socialized, that is repressed, imagination of civilized men and women. Time and time again the fantasy images have to do with violence, sadism, blood-letting. The hunt is occasioned neither by concerns of security nor by the need for food, but simply by the desire for sport. This recreation is, then, an act of war, a 'Kriegszug' (HA VI, 492) against the peaceful animals of the forests. The wild animals displayed in the cages are not wild; long captivity has made them docile. But, as the uncle points out, the people who go to the side-shows want to see not what is before them but what is depicted in the posters advertising the attractions – one of which shows a tiger about to maul a black man. Yet even the uncle is not proof against the disturbing phenomenon which he so acutely diagnoses, because one of his favourite anecdotes is of the earlier fire on the marketplace. The result is that, when a second fire breaks out, the Princess can see only terrifying images – both of the fire and of the wild animals. The tiger that runs towards her is frightened, not vicious; but in her mind's eye she registers the violent image from the poster. By giving chase, Honorio angers the animal. He kills it and offers the Princess the hide in an archetypal gesture of male prowess. And the Princess recalls his skill in cavalry sports and displays; he is particularly adept at impaling the mock-up head of a black man as he gallops past. The reference to the black man recalls the poster of the tiger. The story is remarkable for the density of its subtextual statement; and in the process it interrogates the mentality of socialized men and women.

In my view, *Novelle* is a masterpiece. It also has a certain exemplary force by virtue of its title. Initially Goethe planned to call the story 'Die Jagd' (The Hunt). But finally he decided on the simple generic designation – *Novelle*. In a famous remark to Eckermann of 29 January 1827 he sketches in the implications – 'denn was ist eine Novelle anders als eine sich ereignete unerhörte Begebenheit?' (for what else is a Novelle but an unheard-of event that has occurred?). The observation has all the hallmarks of a casual comment. That sketch of a definition draws marvellously economic attention to a particularly suggestive constellation: the story combines the intimation of the exceptional (wild animals on the loose in early nineteenth-century Germany) with an assertion of plausibility ('eine sich ereignete Begebenheit'), by which one could understand that the laws of familiar material and social causality are respected. The exceptional moment crystallizes the mentality of everyday living and experiencing.

If we look at the earlier work entitled *Unterhaltungen deutscher Ausgewanderten* (Conversations of German Emigrants, 1795) we can see Goethe exploring the possibilities of the 'Novelle' form. He takes the governing structural model, a frame narration housing a series of tales, from Boccaccio's *Decameron*. Goethe transposes this generic constellation to the modern world. The threat to order and civil society (in Boccaccio, the plague in Florence) is now the French Revolution. Once again the telling of tales is seen to have an educative force. And the stories told, which thematize the interplay of order and chaos, include simple ghost stories, moral tales which explore the capacity for self-control vested in mature men and women, and an extended fairy tale. None of these works is, in my view, in the same league artistically as *Novelle*. But they show Goethe experimenting with the possibilities of the short prose form. And they show him constantly interrogating and thematizing modes and forms of narration.

Die Leiden des jungen Werther

Die Leiden des jungen Werther (The Sorrows of Young Werther, 1774, second edition 1787) is a novel in letter form. It was an extraordinary bestseller – the first to issue from Germany. Its success was due to the fact that it was utterly attuned to the contemporary discourse of *Empfindsamkeit* (sentimentalism). The name Werther itself is unusual; all the other principal characters are given Christian names – Lotte, Albert. But Werther has simply his surname; and it implies some kind of value (*Wert*). Precisely what this value might be is something that will haunt us throughout the novel.

At the beginning Werther is alone; but far from being oppressed by the lack of human society, he rejoices in his rapturous connectedness to the natural world around him. The letter of 10 May begins: 'Eine wunderbare Heiterkeit hat meine ganze Seele eingenommen, gleich den süßen Frühlingsmorgen, die ich mit ganzem Herzen genieße' (A wonderful serenity has taken possession of my entire soul like the sweet spring mornings which I enjoy with all my heart, HA VI, 9). We note the constantly asserted reciprocity between Werther and nature, the expressions of likeness, kinship, and of wholeness (*gleich* and *ganz* are key words). Yet inseparable from this splendour is an intimation of danger, of an experiential energy so great that it threatens to overwhelm the expressive capacity and coherence of the self. Werther finds it difficult to draw; he is aware of being engulfed by a force that he cannot contain. The great sentence that dominates the second half of the May 10 letter, which passionately instances examples of natural beauty as emblematic of religious exaltation, is wonderfully expressive. Borrowing from particular forms of contemporary rhetoric (and specifically from the homiletic or sermonizing tradition), Werther's outpouring rises magnificently to the challenge of finding words for the tumult within him. However, as we follow the sequence of the letters, we witness a pattern of degeneration and decline. The letters, initially at any rate, are addressed to a friend; but increasingly we lose any sense of interpersonal communication. The traffic flows all one way, and the result is desperate claustrophobia. We could trace a number of themes throughout the novel – Werther and nature, Werther and love, Werther and religion, Werther and art. Common to all four strands is a process of ever greater disintegration as Werther slides into a paranoid condition. His inability to make compromises, to find some kind of sustaining balance between self and world means that increasingly he tries to make the world in his own image – or to discount it entirely. Ominously, in the letter of 24 July in Book I he writes: 'alles schwimmt und schwankt so vor meiner Seele, daß ich keinen Umriß packen kann' (everything swims and floats before my soul – so much so that I cannot get hold of any outlines, 41). The dreadful solipsism of the Werther mentality blights his relationship to everything outside himself, whereby only those experiences are admissible that corroborate the self. His understanding of religion becomes a near-blasphemous identification of himself with Christ. Something similar holds true of his relationship to Lotte. Clearly she is profoundly drawn to him; but one particular remark, to the effect that it is only because he cannot possess her that he is so obsessed with her, is particularly telling (103–4). Perhaps, then, Werther is in love with love rather than being in love with another person who is genuinely perceived as other. All of which makes Werther into one of the most intense psychological novels ever written. It culminates, with unforgettable cruelty, in a botched suicide. Werther in his last days spends more and more time envisaging and creating the scenario for a noble, decorous, beautiful death. But the reality is anything but that; it is foul.

Werther's name, as we have noted, implies value. The title of the novel, which refers to poor Werther, implies compassion. What are we to make of him? At one level, our answer will no doubt be framed in psychological terms. We register both the intensity and the monstrosity of the uncompromising self. Yet we can also hear the character of the protagonist as one that expresses a profound philosophical dilemma: that of the acutely self-aware, self-reflective spirit who is in quest of simple, integral, unifying experience. When, for example, Werther writes in the letter of 16 June of the sheer beauty of Lotte dancing, he expresses a vision of a body and a consciousness in perfect union. As many commentators have registered, the image of the dancer at one with the dance constantly recurs in nineteenth-century European literature as the palpable physical expression of a desperately longed-for ontological wholeness. Precisely that glimpse of wholeness contrasts brutally with Werther's sense of having to live in fragmented and fragmenting self-awareness, of being a mere spectator at a puppet theatre: 'Ich spiele mit, vielmehr, ich werde gespielt wie eine Marionette und fasse manchmal meinen Nachbar an der hölzernen Hand und schaudere zurück' (I play along, or rather, I am played with like a marionette and sometimes I grasp my neighbour by his wooden hand and recoil in horror, 65). At such moments one hears the central issue of this remarkable novel as one that has very little to do with erotic entanglement – and a great deal to do with the displacing force of human self-consciousness.

Part of our uncertainty as to how we are to evaluate Werther derives from the formal organization of the novel text. The bulk of the novel consists of Werther's letters; and they constitute not a dialogue but a monologue (this, precisely, is the formal correlative of his psychological sickness). But as Werther's mood darkens there is, as a simple matter of plausibility, the need for an editor figure to step in to order Werther's often incoherent and undated final jottings. At one level, then, the 'Herausgeber' is a dispassionate onlooker, someone who, for example, gives an account of Werther's suicide, who reports events as facts occurring in a world of outward cause and effect. When the novel shifts us from Werther's letters to the narrative of the editor, the effect is both shocking and liberating. At this level of structural statement, then, our text passes judgement on Werther as we move from inwardness to outwardness. Yet it is important to stress that the editor is anything but a strident or censorious judge; rather, he is deeply sympathetic to Werther. He introduces himself as the assiduous compiler of Werther's letters, thereby legitimating both himself as documentary agent and the authenticity of the text that follows (that is to say: the fiction is that these are genuinely the letters that Werther wrote). But the documentary mode gives way to a more assertive, buttonholing one: we are told that we will be grateful to have this record of Werther's temperament because we will not be able to deny him our tears and admiration. The plural mode of address – *ihr* – then contracts to singular – *du* – as the individual reader is urged to make this little book his or her friend, although a note of warning is sounded about allowing the book to replace all other human contact. The 'little book' is, as it were, pressed into our hands, but it comes with a health warning. We are urged both to identify with Werther and to keep him at arm's length.

Precisely this disquieting ambivalence is at the very heart of Goethe's great novel. It is worth noting that Werther remained an uncomfortable text for Goethe throughout his life. He never read from it in public; his own responses to the Werther figure range from the censorious to the justificatory. Moreover, the events in the novel were – and were known to be – scandalously close to real-life events (involving Goethe himself and a young woman by the name of Lotte Buff who was engaged to a man called Kestner). At one level Goethe was, of course, fully justified in resenting prurient questions as to 'where he got his novel from'. At another level, he knew that the suggestion of indiscretion was part of the book's power. (It does, after all, depend centrally on the fiction of personal, private letters being made public. Moreover, for the details of Werther's catastrophic end Goethe drew on a much talked-about suicide of the time; he even went so far as to request an account of that suicide from none other than Kestner himself.) Goethe's own relationship to Werther was, then, nothing if not ambiguous; and some of that ambiguity is transferred to us, the readers.

It is also noteworthy that he wrote two versions of the novel. The first, of 1774, is the more passionate and immediate; the second, of 1787, is more withdrawn in tone, and is more sympathetic to the Albert figure. Yet, in my view, Goethe's attempt to redress the balance of sympathies makes matters more, rather than less, complex. The second version, for example, introduces the 'Bauerbursch' figure, the young farmhand who loves his mistress, a widow, and believes himself to be encouraged by her. When he discovers he has a rival, he kills him. That Werther identifies with the young man and even seeks to support him before the judicial authorities is a measure of his sickness. At the same time the little social cameo suggests that the issue of passion denied an outlet has broader socio-cultural implications than simply one young man's emotional inadequacy. Similarly, although he is a solipsistic figure, Werther's life and death are not bereft of a social dimension.

He is an intelligent, gifted, lively young man of bourgeois upbringing – and he is unable to find any social activity worthy of his talents. In part because he cannot express himself through social interaction he tries to write a self into being through his letters – just as he tries to write a loving self into being to make up for the lack of an actual relationship. Above all else – and here we reach the last strand of statement in this extraordinarily sophisticated novel – he is an intensely literary person and persona. When he and Lotte first become acquainted, they share the experience of the thunderstorm by invoking the name of the major contemporary poet, Klopstock, whose famous poem 'Die Frühlingsfeyer' (Spring Celebration) contained a much-admired evocation of a thunderstorm. At the end of his life, Werther, in his stage-managed suicide, leaves Lessing's play *Emilia Galotti* open on his desk. His literary predilections move in the course of the novel from Homer to Ossian. In other words, Werther is a novel about a culture in which secular literature acquires cult status; and it is therefore deeply appropriate that it, too, became a cult book. In a quite uncanny way Werther, as text, thematizes and prefigures its own success. And that dimension of self-consciousness compounds our sense of the text's destabilizing energy. To this day, Werther has lost none of its power to engage and unsettle its readers.

Die Wahlverwandtschaften

Albeit in very different ways, *Die Wahlverwandtschaften* (The Elective Affinities, 1809) is also a text that can play havoc with its readers. The events all take place on the estate of Eduard, a minor aristocrat, and his wife Charlotte. They invite two friends to join them – the Hauptmann (captain) and Ottilie. Each partner in the marriage becomes increasingly attracted to one of the newcomers, and the passions unleashed take a terrible toll, for the novel ends with the death of both Eduard and Ottilie. At one level the novel is about passion and nothing else; it is a love tragedy in which, to an extent that the characters themselves only dimly apprehend, subterranean currents of emotion and desire carry all before them. At another level, it is a forbiddingly and ferociously cerebral novel. The result is utterly paradoxical: an abstract novel about visceral experience.

Perhaps one should begin by spelling out the levels of statement at which the events unfold before us. At one level, we seem to be concerned with matters that are at the very least mysterious, if not magical. We are confronted by a superabundance of unexplicated patterning. Eduard and Ottilie have complementary migraine headaches, their handwriting is uncannily similar. Ottilie can intuitively accompany Eduard's utterly erratic flute-playing.

There is the goblet with the entwined initials E and O, the fact that Eduard planted the plane trees on the day of Ottilie's birth, and Ottilie's seemingly miracle-working powers after her death. Yet parallel to these weighty intimations of the mysterious we have a whole strand to the novel that conveys the existence of – and validates – the human capacity for self-control, for moral choice, for (to put it at its most modest level) common sense. Much of the implication of destiny and fate is associated with the love of Eduard and Ottilie; whereas Charlotte and the Hauptmann, although they too are overtaken by feelings that they can neither understand nor control, live and oblige themselves to live in a world of explicit moral choices. Once we heed this cognitive dimension, we find ourselves both aware of and, perhaps, offended by Eduard's headlong propensity to make every incident, scene, object, utterance symbolic of his ineluctable destiny to love Ottilie. And finally, there is a level of thematic statement which has to do with nature, nature both within and outside the human sphere.

All these three levels of thematic statement – the supernatural, the moral, and the natural – partake of and derive from sustained patternings within the statement of the novel text. By any standards, *Die Wahlverwandtschaften* is overdetermined as a narrative. The cluster of names itself speaks volumes: the women characters are called Charlotte and Ottilie; and the Hauptmann's name is Otto, Eduard's name as a child. Small wonder that the child is called Otto. The name itself is a palindrome, and, like all patterns in the novel, demands to be read both forwards and backwards. Added to which, the initials of the four main characters (as they are usually named in the novel, and in the order of their appearance in the narrative) spell E-C-H-O. At times one begins to wonder if one is not, in fact, reading a conundrum, an experiment, rather than a novel. But, infuriatingly, the text outflanks us here and suggests precisely this possibility. In a remarkable opening gesture – 'Eduard, so nennen wir einen reichen Baron...' (Eduard, so we are going to call a rich baron..., HA VI, 242) – we sense that we may be in the realm of conjecture and contingency. Moreover, the title of the novel is echoed, mirrored, discussed and thematized in the text. There is cerebration at every turn but it does not seem to clarify or explain, still less control, events. There is only a hall of mirrors before us and – in so far as we are prepared to enter the text – all around us.

How do we find our point of entry into the text? There are a few pages of exposition before the E-C-H-O constellation comes into being. Once we have negotiated that conjectural, opening sentence, we seem to be on relatively safe ground. We might even be in the world of a Jane Austen novel as husband and wife move around their property. Discussion initially centres on the estate, but then turns to the possibility of inviting the Hauptmann to join them. Charlotte is unwilling to change the balance of their lives. But Eduard presses the case, arguing that both of them are mature, self-aware people, and that, by that token, they are equal to handling the changes in emotional temperature and chemistry that might ensue. But his wife responds: 'Das Bewußtsein, mein Liebster, ist keine hinlängliche Waffe, ja manchmal eine gefährliche für den, der sie führt' (Consciousness, my dear, is not an adequate weapon – sometimes it can even be dangerous for those who wield it, 248). This is one of those moments where, by implication, the theme and manner of the novel interlock. As events will show, self-consciousness is no defence against emotional turmoil. Moreover, we the readers will find that we are reading a highly self-conscious novel and that we are frequently aware of our own role as interpreters. But we too find it difficult to achieve clarity and stability of understanding. In a sense, we might say that *Die Wahlverwandtschaften* means too much for its own – and for our – good.

The Hauptmann is invited to join Eduard and Ottilie; and it is the resulting threesome that one evening discusses the notion of elective affinities, processes of bonding and re-bonding in chemistry. Above all, what is at issue is the possibility that a particular compound can be fractured by the appearance of a third substance which then bonds with one of the previously conjoined substances – almost as though some kind of choice were being exercised. At one level, the discussion amongst the three friends genuinely does concern recently discovered chemical processes. At another level, the characters ceaselessly make metaphorical links between the behaviour of chemical substances on the one hand and the chemistry of human attraction on the other. And, as soon as one formulates the matter in this way – in terms of 'human chemistry' – one finds oneself asking whether that, too, is a literal or metaphorical statement. Are men and women subject to the laws of material reality in the same way, and to the same extent, that the chemical substances are? If so, what is the force of 'Sitten und Gesetze' (customs and laws, 272) in the human sphere? Are they merely more complex forms of material processes, or do they truly bespeak a dimension of experience in which men and women have at least a measure of cognitive and ethical autonomy? Charlotte at one point likens the chemical substances not just to blood relatives, 'Blutsverwandte', but to spiritually kindred entities, 'Geistes-und Seelenverwandte' (273) – but then herself insists on the all-important differences between a chemical experiment on the one hand and the complex choices of human behaviour on the other:

Diese Gleichnisreden sind artig und unterhaltend...Aber...wenn [der Mensch] hier mit den schönen Worten Wahl und Wahlverwandtschaft etwas freigiebig gewesen, so tut er wohl, wieder in sich selbst zurückzukehren und den Wert solcher Ausdrücke bei diesem Anlaß recht zu bedenken.   (275)

These metaphorical terms are appealing and entertaining... But... if [we] have just been fairly generous in our use of the lovely terms choice and elective affinities, we would do well to look into our hearts and at this juncture seriously think through the value of such expressions.

Here we touch the central issue. Charlotte warns against thoughtlessly playing with analogies; crucially, human beings are creatures who discriminate, who reflect ('bedenken'), who make and act upon distinctions. Yet she herself has warned against placing great trust in the human capacity for reflectivity and self-consciousness. Perhaps thinking merely compounds the complexity? The rest of the novel sustains a dialectically open debate about cognitive autonomy in human affairs.

As soon as Ottilie enters the novel, the seemingly ineluctable agency of human attraction takes hold – and it works not just through material agencies but also through mental processes. In the extraordinary scene of spiritual adultery, where husband and wife, Eduard and Charlotte, have intercourse but are spiritually unfaithful to each other, Goethe explores the complex role of mental processes, of images and fantasies in human eroticism. Consciousness, then, would seem to make possible not only human choice but also human craving and fantasizing. Late in the novel, after the death of the child, Ottilie decides to go no further in the relationship with Eduard. When she decides to assert herself, she repeats the phrase 'Ich bin aus meiner Bahn geschritten' (I have strayed from my path, 462, 476). It is her one great moment of reflectivity and self-analysis in the novel; it is also a supreme moment of moral choice. Yet it is also accompanied by the relentless process of starving herself to death. We find ourselves caught between two understandings of her behaviour at this juncture. On the one hand, we have the clear sense that human self-consciousness enables the workings of free will and moral choice; and on the other, that human self-consciousness can be largely, if not entirely, controlled by compulsive behaviour, by self-loathing and, in this particular case, anorexia.

Thus far I have been highlighting the philosophical implications of *Die Wahlverwandtschaften*, treating the text as some kind of experimental model of the philosophical workings of human desire. But the characters involved in this experiment cannot, in the last analysis, abstract themselves – or be abstracted by us as readers – from the particular historical and social context of their lives. And, viewed under this aspect, the experiment emerges as the expression of lives that are curiously aimless, bereft of any truly engaging social activity. As members of the minor aristocracy, Edward and Charlotte aspire to be architects of the world around them, but their attempts at finding renewal in their listless domain are doomed; and the doom extends even to the figures who come from a different (bourgeois) social world and are in quest of a fuller life – the Hauptmann, and, most particularly, Ottilie. Death lurks everywhere. The significations of both the religious and the aristocratic universe atrophy at every turn; nature at times assumes a vengeful aspect; and the energy driving the plot forward seems to be some kind of malignant fatality that carries everything and everybody with it. The philosophical profundity of the novel interlocks with its sombre social diagnosis: those who experiment with life rather than living it may uncover all manner of mysteries in the domain of human cognition; but those mysteries, once given full sway, can take a terrible toll.

The 'Wilhelm Meister' novels

That conjoining of philosophical and historical issues is also characteristic of the great narrative project which occupied Goethe throughout his life – the sequence of novels centred on the figure of Wilhelm Meister. *Wilhelm Meisters Theatralische Sendung* (Wilhelm Meister's Theatrical Mission, written between 1777 and 1785) is, in my view, the most engaging. It is a splendid novel of adolescence and concerns a young man who seeks fame and fortune in the theatre. There is much social and psychological realism in the ironic narrative mode which acknowledges both the idealism and the immaturity of the eager young man, both the excitement and the tawdriness of the theatre. Goethe never published the novel. Rather, he left it as a fragment and then returned to it, deriving from it the first five books of *Wilhelm Meisters Lehrjahre* (Wilhelm Meister's Apprenticeship, 1796).

The novel opens with a cameo portrait of the frustrations and tensions within the bourgeois family:

> Es war einige Tage vor dem Christabend 174– als Benedikt Meister Bürger und Handelsmann zu M–, einer mittleren Reichsstadt, aus seinem gewöhnlichen Kränzgen Abends gegen acht nach Hause ging. Es hatte sich wider die Gewohnheit die Tarock Partie früher geendigt, und es war ihm nicht ganz gelegen, daß er so zeitlich in seine vier Wände zurückkehren sollte, die ihm seine Frau eben nicht zum Paradies machte. Es war noch Zeit bis zum Nachtessen, und so einen Zwischenraum pflegte sie ihm nicht mit Annehmlichkeiten auszufüllen, deswegen er lieber nicht ehe zu Tische kam als wenn die Suppe schon etwas überkocht hatte.   (MA, II/2, 9, and HA VIII, 487)

> It was a few days before Christmas Eve 174– when Benedikt Meister, citizen and businessman of M., a medium-sized free city, left his convivial circle at

around eight o'clock and went home. His game of taroc had finished earlier than usual, and it did not really suit him to return so early to his four walls which his wife did not exactly make into a paradise. There was still time before supper, and she tended not to fill such an interval with pleasantness, for which reason he preferred only to get home when the soup had already boiled over.

It is a splendid opening – vivid and immediate. From all this one senses keenly how and why Wilhelm, as a young person starved of affection and good humour at home, will set his heart on a career in the theatre. In the *Lehrjahre* this opening phase of socio-psychological portrayal is cut altogether, and the novel is thereby robbed of a particular dimension of social specificity.

The novel of Wilhelm's theatrical aspirations dominates the first five books of the *Lehrjahre*. What then follows is the interpolated manuscript, the 'Bekenntnisse einer schönen Seele' (Confessions of a Beautiful Soul), in which a woman gives her account of how she came to find fulfilment in a religious calling. In the final two books of the novel Wilhelm becomes more and more associated with the so-called 'Turmgesellschaft' (Society of the Tower), a progressive secret society made up of both aristocratic and bourgeois members who seek to further a variety of social projects. Moreover, the ethos of the Society seeks to acknowledge both the virtues of the aristocratic appreciation of style and aesthetic semblance and the bourgeois belief in hard work and practical achievement. The sequence of events which, it has to be admitted, is not the most arresting aspect of the novel, is a strange mixture of the episodic and the providential. Natalie, to whom Wilhelm becomes betrothed at the end of the novel, is a shadowy figure. She is associated with images that mean a great deal to him – with his grandfather's art collection, with a compassionate figure who is represented in the picture of the ailing son of the king, and with the so-called 'beautiful Amazon' who helps Wilhelm and the theatrical troupe after they have been attacked by robbers in Book IV. This benign agency seems to be watching over Wilhelm. But the benignity also has its ruthless side. Wilhelm becomes deeply attached to two figures: Mignon the waif, and the Harper (as it turns out, the Harper is her father – but the union from which Mignon comes is incestuous). They are touching, forlorn creatures; the words they speak and the songs they sing all express homelessness and longing. They embody the possibility that pathology and disarray can have an immense poetic appeal – but both figures are written out of the novel at the end. The poetry of their being is inseparable from their doomed condition. And the whole thrust of the plot, while in its episodic profusion it does not allow Wilhelm himself to have much sense of being master of his own destiny, yet conspires to protect and fulfil him, to fit him for life. His apprenticeship years may feel eventful; but in the last analysis they are sheltered, and Mignon and the Harper have to be dismissed from his experiential world.

The first five books, comprising the so-called 'Theaterroman', show Wilhelm extending his personality in a great number of ways. He leads a bohemian life and comes into contact with many people whom polite society tends to shun. (This is particularly true of his sexual experience; it is noteworthy how often he encounters androgynous figures.) He also extends himself imaginatively by playing out various roles. The theatre obliges Wilhelm to ponder the relationship between idea and reality, between reflecting and doing. At the end of the 'Theaterroman' Wilhelm is enriched and more mature than he was. And yet he drifts away from the theatre; there is no spectacular repudiation. It is simply that he has outgrown a necessary but circumscribed phase of his life.

The 'Bekenntnisse einer schönen Seele' that follow introduce Wilhelm to a life of concentrated inwardness. Not that this is asserted as an unequivocal value; but it propels Wilhelm towards that greater concern for ideas and ideals that will characterize his dealings with the Society of the Tower. Yet curiously, even in that final phase of the novel, Wilhelm's development is tentative rather than forthright. He is admitted to membership of the Society, he is allowed to browse in the archive in which the various stories of the development and growth processes of individual members of the Society are stored. Yet he feels none the wiser. At times he can even be irritated by the Society's fondness for maxims and pithy sayings. A mere three pages from the end of the novel he laments his lack of any sense of clarity and wisdom. That everything culminates in a happy ending has more to do with good fortune than with any sureness of understanding on Wilhelm's part.

Given that our hero has no little difficulty in making sense of his own experiences, it is perhaps understandable if we the readers are also left a shade perplexed. But at least certain aspects of cultural and philosophical context can give us a measure of interpretative orientation. In discussion with his bourgeois friend Werner, Wilhelm explains some of the socio-psychological parameters of his experience, and in the process he makes an all-important distinction between the *Bürger* and the *Edelmann*. The nobleman expresses everything through the representation of his own person, whereas the bourgeois expresses nothing and is not meant to express anything through his personality. The former may and should engage in semblance; but the latter should only be – any semblance on his part is ludicrous or tasteless. The former should be active and cause things to happen; the latter should achieve and produce. And the common assumption is that there neither is nor should be any harmony in his being because he has to be useful in only one particular way (HA VII, 291). Wilhelm is, as it were, in quest of a bourgeois role for himself, but does not quite know where to find it. Precisely because of his uncertainty his life expresses many forms of bourgeois culture – and they are centrally part of the historicity of the *Lehrjahre*. The second half of the eighteenth century in Germany was an age that was passionately concerned with the need to found a national theatre; and the discovery of Shakespeare was a powerful force in the energizing of cultural debate at the time. Moreover, Pietism in particular provided a discourse of intense inwardness – both religious and psychological. This element of personal self-scrutiny and self-expression contributed to a culture in which diaries, letters, memoirs were particularly in favour. Finally, the last two books of the *Lehrjahre* embody the whole theme of the secret society. This was an institution that was germane to both social and cultural life. One thinks, for example, of the various subgroupings within late eighteenth-century society – the Freemasons, the Illuminati, the various orders and brotherhoods, both progressive and sinister. (One needs only to contrast Mozart's *The Magic Flute* with the novels of the Marquis de Sade to sense the full spectrum of the issues involved: secrecy could be the emblem of humane initiatives but also of exultant perversity.) *Wilhelm Meisters Lehrjahre* embodies and takes issue with late eighteenth-century social and cultural life in ways and to an extent that are not self-evident to its readers nowadays.

Finally, *Wilhelm Meisters Lehrjahre* is a central text in the evolution of the modern German novel, not least because for many practitioners and commentators it acquired the status of a canonical *Bildungsroman*. This genre has often been claimed to be the chief German contribution to the European novel. At one level it is a type of narrative close to the concerns of European realism, addressing as it does the psychological and social rites of passage of an adolescent as he (and most usually it is a 'he') makes his way through the adult social world, seeking to find a place for himself. What, however, is particular about the German *Bildungsroman* is that the issues are framed less in terms of practicality (of which the realist novel speaks) than with a view to a philosophically differentiated definition and exploration of the interplay of self and world. The *Bildungsroman* protagonist does not have to worry where the next meal is coming from; his counterpart in realist fiction does. In the *Lehrjahre*, Wilhelm speaks of wanting to develop the self that he has and is: 'mich selbst, ganz wie ich da bin, auszubilden, das war dunkel von Jugend auf mein Wunsch und meine Absicht' (HA VII, 290). Within this self-definition, Goethe's novel is remarkable in its scrupulous understanding of the complex and largely diffuse processes of individual development and growth. What Wilhelm himself does not understand is comprehended by the novel itself: namely that he takes on a certain more-than-individual, and by that token exemplary, stature. And it is Wilhelm's ordinariness that makes him – and the novel in which he figures – deeply representative of late eighteenth-century bourgeois culture in Germany. The tentativeness is part of the novel's truth. The project of human perfectibility is, admittedly, in evidence; but it depends for its realization above all else on good fortune rather than rational, goal-directed thinking.

The notion of journeying is omnipresent in *Wilhelm Meisters Wanderjahre* (Wilhelm Meister's Journeymanship, 1821 and 1829).(The governing metaphor is, of course, that of the guild structure of professional training which decreed the sequence of apprentice, journeyman, and master.) Wilhelm, now married to Natalie, is instructed by the Society of the Tower to stay no more than three days under one roof. Hence, the whole ethos of the novel is not one of possession, stability and certainty – but rather of movement, change, pluralism. And the novel sustains this ethos not only thematically but also formally by moving back and forth between various discursive and narrative worlds. We have short tales or 'Novellen', we have letters, papers of various kinds, maxims. And there is no clear principle of superordination or subordination. There are three story lines that tend to reappear in the novel and are, by that token, more constitutive of the total narrative work than are the self-contained tales. We have the evolving relationship between Wilhelm and his son Felix, a relationship that culminates in a scene where Wilhelm, having learnt the skills of a 'Wundarzt' (surgeon), is able to save his son from the consequences of an accident; we have the unfolding love between Felix and Hersilie; and there is another love story involving Leonardo and Nachodine. But, apart from occasional moments, none of this is handled with any particular urgency or intensity. Indeed, in one sense *Wilhelm Meisters Wanderjahre* is largely uninterested in storytelling as an absorbing process of sustained chronological and psychological import. Characters come into and go out of focus for no particular reason. Sometimes they are key agents in a story, sometimes they are peripheral figures in somebody else's story, sometimes they are narrators. There is a profusion of narrative processes in evidence, but not much storytelling that generates substantial characters or events. For this reason the exceptions to the rule are particularly noteworthy. The tale 'Der Mann von fünfzig Jahren' (The Man of Fifty) has powerful moments of experiential authority – particularly when the theme of ageing, and the attempt to hide ageing by the use of make-up, are being explored. But such moments are rare and merely remind us of a traditional narrative universe that we seem to have left far behind us. For the most part, the *Wanderjahre* is sustained by narrative garrulousness, by a climate of ongoing narrativity with little or no human interest being generated along the way. We seem to be, in many ways, close to Flaubert's notion of the 'livre sur rien'.

There is an editor figure, yet his function is not (as in, say, *Werther*) to authenticate the text we are reading. Rather, he confirms the fundamentally textual nature of the universe in which we find ourselves. In consequence, we are asked not to surrender to the mimetic power of fictions, but to read and re-read as active participants, as co-makers of the archive which we have entered. In a sense the *Wanderjahre* believes in the human community as an aggregation of stories, of attempts to convert experience into discursivity of various kinds. And the novel ends: 'Ist fortzusetzen' (To be continued, MA XVII, 714), thereby implying that narrativity, discursivity is a ceaseless process, one sustained without any conclusion in prospect.

There is no master narrative in the *Wanderjahre* to which all the component parts are subservient. Even those which look conceptually authoritative – such as, for example, the maxims – merely thematize the question whether, in a universe of texts, there can be any privileged, metatextual realm. All of this brings the *Wanderjahre* close to a postmodern universe of pantextuality. Yet there are tendencies in the novel which resolutely pull in the opposite direction. There is, for example, a socio-economic theme, a consistent discussion of the position of handicrafts – spinning and weaving – that are threatened by the inroads of new technology. Moreover, we note the persistent educative theme of the 'pädagogische Provinz'. And behind the half-heartedly told stories a didactic thrust can be heard which condemns passion as an aberration. In consequence, the *Wanderjahre* exhibits a strange combination of postmodern irony with a kind of hectoring pedagogy in the service of self-discipline and renunciation. The upshot, in my experience as reader, is of having to deal with a highly sophisticated exercise in narrative sclerosis.

All of which may seem a harsh judgement. And I want, in conclusion, to differentiate that harshness by suggesting that, if we take the *Wanderjahre* not so much as a novel text in its own right but as part of the larger *Wilhelm Meister* project, then it acquires both cogency and interest. In the *Meister* novels Goethe has, in exemplary form, produced a summary of the possible modes of the modern novel – from the socio-psychological realism of the *Theatralische Sendung* on the one hand to the self-reflective ironies of the *Wanderjahre* on the other. In their enormously influential theories of the novel both the philosopher Hegel and the aesthetic theoretician Friedrich Schlegel sensed the extent to which Goethe was able in his fiction to acknowledge both the materiality and the mentality of the modern world; the novelist was, as it were, both storyteller and philosopher. Similar claims have been advanced for Goethe's narrative achievement by such key twentieth-century theoreticians of the modern novel as Bakhtin and Lukács. Perhaps this fact can help us to gauge the scale of Goethe's achievement as a writer of prose fiction. In the constant reworking process of the *Meister* project he found generic expression for the various forms of modern narrative subjectivity. The rewriting process itself, the sense of a shifting dynamic of signification was utterly central to his diagnosis of the modern. Goethe's *Meister* project is a key witness to the rise of the modern novel – not least because it has its own novel theory built into it, thanks to its consistently self-thematizing narrative mode. Moreover, as I have sought to suggest, Goethe produced three undoubted masterpieces – *Werther*, *Die Wahlverwandtschaften*, and *Novelle* – masterpieces that are not simply erratic individual achievements but also have a certain generic force. The confluence in Goethe's creativity of a life-long interest in narrativity on the one hand with a readiness to experiment with the emergent generic possibilities of modern prose fiction on the other is a signal achievement. Goethe is not widely acknowledged as one of the canonical – that is, indispensable – makers of modern fiction. It is time he was. Because, like so few other great writers, his narrative practice also is his narrative theory.

9

DENNIS F. MAHONEY

Autobiographical writings

When Goethe first drew up a schematic diagram for his planned autobiography in October 1809, he had just completed work on his novel *Die Wahlverwandtschaften* (Elective Affinities), whose formal elegance contrasts all the more glaringly with the moral and societal crisis depicted therein. In the years since the death of Schiller in 1805, Goethe had witnessed the dissolution of the Holy Roman Empire, the defeat of Prussia, and the reorganization of the political map of Europe by Napoleon. His mother had died in 1808, removing yet another link to his childhood and youth. Under these conditions he undertook the re-examination of his life and career as a writer from the vantage point of a sixty-year-old interested in imbuing individual stages of his life with historical significance.

It is in this context that the title *Aus meinem Leben: Dichtung und Wahrheit* (From my Life: Poetry and Truth, 1811–33) assumes its meaning: while not neglecting factual information (*Wahrheit*), Goethe is above all concerned with the refashioning and interpretation of his recollections (*Dichtung*). In the process, the specific events and individuals depicted in Goethe's autobiographical writings become paradigmatic not only of important stages in the individual development of the poet, but also of significant moments in the social, cultural, religious and literary life of German-speaking Europe. Although writing at a time when European Romanticism, in the wake of Jean-Jacques Rousseau's *Confessions* (1766–70), was celebrating individualism, particularly as mirrored in poetic genius, for much of *Dichtung und Wahrheit* Goethe chooses instead to focus on the events and persons that helped shape his inchoate youthful self. In those autobiographical works dealing with his life after 1775, Goethe becomes even more guarded about revealing personal details. In the *Italienische Reise* (Italian Journey, 1816–29), for example, one looks in vain for information on the biographical basis for his erotic *Römische Elegien* (Roman Elegies, 1795), although Goethe simultaneously encourages and frustrates such expectations with interspersed accounts of his (chaste) encounters with an unnamed Milanese maiden. But while present-day readers are likely to be disappointed by Goethe's reticence about his private life, they are amply repaid by the vignettes of life in Frankfurt; these provide a far greater sense of the particulars of eighteenth-century life than do Goethe's novels, including *Wilhelm Meisters theatralische Sendung* (Wilhelm Meister's Theatrical Mission, 1777–85), and rank among the supreme accomplishments of German prose writing.

Organized in four parts of five books each, *Dichtung und Wahrheit* treats Goethe's childhood and youth in Frankfurt (published in October 1811); studies in Leipzig and Strasbourg (November 1812); encounters with the Storm and Stress generation and his own ensuing literary productions (May 1814); and the decision to travel to Weimar breaking off his engagement with Lili Schönemann (published posthumously in 1833). The astrological motifs incorporated in Goethe's account of his birth at the stroke of noon on 28 August 1749 imply an individual in harmony with the cosmos. Not to be forgotten, of course, is that Goethe also notes that he came into the world taken for dead, through the incompetence of the attending midwife, and that only through repeated efforts did he glimpse the light of day. This near-fatal mishap, however, causes his grandfather to promote better training for midwives, and so young Wolfgang's birth already proves a boon to his surroundings (HA IX, 10). A further example of this linkage of public and private life occurs in the discussion of the disquieting effects of the Lisbon Earthquake of November 1755 upon the optimistic world view not only of the adults around him, but also of the six-year-old Goethe himself (HA IX, 30–1). Goethe had received through Bettina Brentano his mother's recollections of young Wolfgang's reaction to this natural catastrophe, which depicted him as being quickly able to come to terms with it, on the grounds that God knew that immortal souls could not be damaged by an evil earthly fate. In *Dichtung und Wahrheit*, however, Goethe stresses the young boy's doubt in God as loving father, thereby indicating his distress at the destruction of public order that Europe was experiencing in the aftermath of the French Revolution, and laying the groundwork for his treatment of that amoral world force he calls the Daemonic in Part IV of his autobiography (HA X, 175–7).

Significant not only for Part I of *Dichtung und Wahrheit* is its motto from the Greek playwright Menander that the person who does not get thrashed does not get educated; throughout the autobiography of his youthful development Goethe takes care to point out moments of desolation and despair as well as accomplishments. The pomp and circumstance of the coronation of the young Emperor Joseph II – the last such imperial coronation to take place in Frankfurt – contrasts, for example, with Goethe's physical and emotional collapse when Gretchen, his first young love, is apprehended, charged as an accessory to criminal fraud, and expelled from Frankfurt at the end of Book 5. The selection of this name, of course, also awakens associations with the unfortunate heroine of the first part of Goethe's *Faust* (1808). At other times in the narrative, the reader's attention is directed explicitly to Goethe's transformation of disappointments and personal failings in life and love, such as with Friederike Brion in Sesenheim, into literary portrayals of betrayed lovers and faithless suitors in dramas such as *Götz von Berlichingen* (1773) and *Clavigo* (1774): 'Ich setzte die hergebrachte poetische Beichte wieder fort, um durch diese selbstquälerische Büßung einer innern Absolution würdig zu werden' (I continued the customary poetical confession, in order to be worthy of an inner absolution by means of this self-tormenting penance; HA IX, 521–2). The language of confession links Goethe's autobiography with the tradition established by St Augustine and emulated by the Pietist autobiographies of the seventeenth and eighteenth centuries; but Goethe's 'fragments of a great confession' (HA IX, 283) depict the development of an approach to life and literature that is cognizant of traditional ecclesiastical authority but also freed from its constraints.

The writing and publication of *Werther* (1774), as treated in Part III of *Dichtung und Wahrheit*, serve as milestones in the development of a new aesthetic, but they also document the point where the young Goethe fully becomes aware of the gulf separating him from the bulk of his readers and critics. Many want to know only the 'real' details behind the story; others rush to extremes and either imitate Werther even to the point of copying his suicide or else condemn both the immorality of his actions and the laxness of his creator in not presenting a more explicit moral message (HA IX, 588–94). In writing this section of *Dichtung und Wahrheit* nearly forty years after the initial publication of *Werther*, however, Goethe went beyond a mere lament on the gulf between reader and author. With the help of narrative techniques developed by him and other authors of the Classic-Romantic generation, he could employ *Dichtung und Wahrheit* as a school for further developing the type of active and well-disposed reader whom the narrator imagines as his ideal audience in the preface to this work (HA IX, 8). In telling the tale of his own education as a reader Goethe has built into the narrative a morphology of growth that runs parallel to the development of German literature throughout the course of the eighteenth century, making *Dichtung und Wahrheit* into 'der Entwicklungsroman des Lesers' (the novel of development of the reader).[1]

If the first three instalments of *Dichtung und Wahrheit* correspond both in content and form to patterns in *Wilhelm Meisters Lehrjahre* (Wilhelm Meister's Apprenticeship, 1795–6), even more daring experiments in the blending of autobiographical narrative with novelistic techniques are yet to come. By Part IV of *Dichtung und Wahrheit*, the narrator has become more like the 'editor' of the 1829 version of *Wilhelm Meisters Wanderjahre* (Wilhelm Meister's Journeymanship), in that he provides literary and non-literary documents within the text with a multiplicity of perspectives and allows the reader the task of drawing conclusions from them. Previous generations of scholars have understood such a practice – which is true in even more extreme form for *Zweiter römischer Aufenthalt* (Second Stay in Rome, 1829), the third and final part to *Italienische Reise* – as indicative of a loss of interest or ability on Goethe's part as he strove to bring these autobiographical writings to their conclusion. Robert Gould offers a different perspective: 'It means that the autobiography is openly presented as anything but a complete and factual account of the past. Rather, it is meant to be seen as a literary artifact dependent on choices made by the narrator.' Such an understanding of 'autobiography as text and manipulation of text'[2] is underscored by Goethe's ending *Dichtung und Wahrheit* with a quotation from his own drama *Egmont*, as his youthful self makes the decision to travel to Weimar rather than to proceed on the journey to Italy his father had urged upon him. In his commentary on this image of the charioteer attempting to guide the 'Sonnenpferde der Zeit' (the sun-horses of time; HA x, 187), Erich Trunz points out that Goethe begins and ends *Dichtung und Wahrheit* with an image of the sun, and the same observation is made by Benedikt Jeßing. But whereas for Trunz the emphasis is on the difference between one's fate at birth and the mature individual's response to the world (HA[4] x, 652–3), Jeßing stresses the radical uncertainty of the meaning of life as the concluding message of Goethe's work.[3] By ending the autobiography of his youth with a highly theatrical, but also multivalent piece of 'Dichtung', Goethe thus leaves it to his readers to compose their own interpretation of the significance of his life's trajectory.

Such readers, of course, have the benefit of knowing that Goethe's journey to Italy did take place, albeit only after more than a decade of work as a court official in Weimar; that Goethe's autobiographical writings avoid the depiction of these years reveals not just the reticence of the privy councillor, but also the extent to which Goethe's stylization of his life affected his choice and treatment of subject matter. In 1816, 1817 and 1829, Goethe instead published three further instalments to his autobiographical project, which since 1829 bear the collective title *Italienische Reise*. Beginning with the first volume, which deals with the unannounced journey from Carlsbad into Italy during September and October of 1786 and then the four months of his initial stay in Rome, Goethe edited his original travel journal, as sent to Charlotte von Stein, and also letters from Italy to friends and associates in Weimar such as Duke Carl August, the Herders, and Charlotte von Stein herself. Such sources were ideal for conveying a sense of immediacy and authenticity, as Goethe well knew from his *Werther*, whose revised version he had finished in the summer of 1786. A careful comparison of the autobiographical sources with the finished product, though, makes evident how Goethe refashioned them in order to advance a message of the restoration of his spiritual wellbeing through life in Italy and contact with Greek, Roman, and Renaissance art – and not simply through freedom from his official duties and accumulated personal frustrations in Weimar. Given that in the years after 1814 Goethe was at odds with Carl August's attempts at liberalization in the Grand Duchy of Saxe-Weimar, and given the Duke's intrusions upon Goethe's direction of the Weimar theatre, the time may well have been ripe for such an autobiographical return journey to Italy.

The focus on classical and Renaissance art has its own significance, however. Whereas Goethe's positive mention of his youthful enthusiasm for Gothic architecture in Book 9 of *Dichtung und Wahrheit* was meant to provide encouragement for Sulpiz Boisserée's attempts to complete the Cologne Cathedral (HA IX, 382–8), he wrote *Italienische Reise* as a secular rejoinder to the sectarian 'Nazarene' school of art championed by many German Romantics in the decade after 1810. The year 1816 saw the publication not only of the first volume of *Italienische Reise*, but also of the polemical essay *Neudeutsche religiös-patriotische Kunst* (New-German religious-patriotic art), co-authored with Johann Heinrich Meyer, whom Goethe first met in Rome in November 1786. It does Goethe's autobiographical works a disservice to regard them as objective statements about literary and art history, let alone as unembellished accounts of his life and travels. On the contrary: once one recognizes the programmatic intent behind his artistic credo, one can delight in his deliberate impudence in relating, in his entry for 25 December 1786, that he has recently procured the plaster cast of a colossal bust of Jupiter before which he now can pay his 'Morgenandacht' (morning devotion, HA XI, 151)!

One serious drawback to Goethe's depiction of his artistic conversion in Italy, however, is that great stretches of it lack the sense of productive tension between himself and his surroundings that characterizes *Dichtung und Wahrheit*. Nicholas Boyle points out an apparent exception to this pattern in Part II of the *Italienische Reise* that nonetheless quickly conforms with the general rule. In the entry for 23 March 1787 Goethe describes his initial astonishment and discomfort upon viewing the three Greek temples in Paestum, some fifty miles south of Naples: 'Ich befand mich in einer völlig fremden Welt' (I found myself in a completely foreign world, HA XI, 219); within the space of an hour, however, Goethe 'succeeds in getting on to a friendly footing with inhabitants of a strange world, separated from his own by over two thousand years of history'.[4] Within the structure of the *Italienische Reise*, this (purportedly) first encounter with classical Greek architecture serves as a prelude to further revelations in art, literature, geology and botany during his stay in Sicily, which then becomes the 'key' (HA XI, 252) to Goethe's Italian experiences. For the Sicilian and Neapolitan segments of the *Italienische Reise* he destroyed the bulk of the original documents upon the completion of his narration, making it more difficult for critics to distinguish between 'Dichtung' and 'Wahrheit'; nonetheless, Boyle succeeds in proving that Goethe did not visit Paestum in March of 1787, but rather only after his return from Sicily in mid-May of that year. Why this change in dating? 'Goethe wanted to conceal that even after spending six weeks in Sicily he could still find pure doric architecture completely strange.'[5] If one looks closely enough, there are other indications that Goethe's self-constructed myth of untroubled happiness in Italy is just that – a myth. Numerous episodes in the Sicilian portion of the *Italienische Reise*, such as Goethe's visit to the bizarre art collection of the Prince of Pallagonia in Palermo, hint at a deep-seated ambivalence and uneasiness about his experiences on the island.[6] Such imperfectly concealed contrasts between the master plan of narrative and the discordant details, which testify to the effort Goethe invested in the construction of his imaginary Italy, are perhaps of greater interest to today's readers than the finished myth itself.

'Auch ich in Arkadien!' (I, too, in Arcadia, HA XI, 7), the motto to the first two volumes of *Italienische Reise*, originally had been an emblematic inscription in seventeenth-century painting that referred to death's presence even in the idyllic pastoral landscape of Arcadia; only in the course of the eighteenth century did the speaker of 'Et in Arcadia ego' come to be understood as that person, living or dead, who had experienced earthly bliss (cf. HA[4] XI, 575–7). In the final scene in *Italienische Reise*, however, a sense of the transience of beauty and happiness re-enters Goethe's landscape, and with powerful results. As early as 31 August 1817 he had written of his pain on departing from Rome (HA[4] XI, 677–8). Not until 1829, however, did he bring *Zweiter römischer Aufenthalt* to a conclusion with a revised version of his farewell to Rome that ends, rather than beginning, with a quote from Ovid's *Tristia* in which the Roman poet recalls his final night in Rome (HA XI, 556). As Horst Rüdiger observes, this quote implies that, for Goethe, a return to Weimar is akin to exile at the edge of Roman civilization; Rüdiger also points out, though, that in his revision of the original draft Goethe eliminates the specific comparison between himself and the poets Ovid and Tasso, the latter being the subject of the unfinished drama Goethe was bringing back from Rome in April of 1788.[7] As Duke Carl August had died in June 1828, several months after Goethe's resumption of work on *Zweiter römischer Aufenthalt*, it would have been impolitic to the point of impiety to indicate too directly that the Duke, in calling him back to Weimar, was exercising sovereign power over his court poet.

Earlier that decade, Goethe had already skirted the boundaries of what for him was politically permissible. In his *Campagne in Frankreich 1792 / Belagerung von Mainz* (Campaign in France 1792 / Siege of Mainz, 1820–2) – whose grimly ironic opening motto is 'Auch ich in der Champagne!' (I, too, in Champagne, HA x, 188) – death has a more than metaphorical presence, as Goethe witnesses the misery and destruction unleashed by the wars of the French Revolution. Encouraged by the French émigré nobility to expect an easy march to Paris and rescue of the imprisoned King Louis XVI, the Prussian army is checked by the cannonade at Valmy, decimated by dysentery, and forced to retreat in October of 1792 through the rainy countryside it has just ravaged. By the end of October French armies advance as far as the Rhine and occupy the city of Mainz, in which German adherents of the French Revolution proclaim a republic. Although Mainz is retaken by the Prussians and Austrians the following summer, the departing French revolutionary leaders warn that they will be back (HA x, 387); indeed, the concluding sentence of *Belagerung von Mainz* alludes to the catastrophic defeat of the Prussian army at the Battle of Jena in 1806 (HA x, 400), which was commanded by the same general, the Duke of Brunswick, who had been in charge in 1792–3.

Goethe had accompanied these earlier expeditions at the behest of Duke Carl August, who had responded to Goethe's radical reduction of the duchy's armed forces during his tenure as Minister of War by becoming commander of a Prussian cavalry regiment in 1787. In the postscript to a letter from Verdun and Luxembourg in mid-October of 1792 to his fellow minister Christian Gottlob Voigt, Goethe reacted to the report that the Privy Council had declared the conflict to be an imperial war by remarking: 'Wir werden also mit der Herde ins Verderben rennen – Europa braucht einen 30jährigen Krieg um einzusehen was 1792 vernünftig gewesen wäre' (So we will rush into destruction with the rest of the herd – Europe needs a Thirty Years War in order to recognize what would have been sensible in 1792, HAB II, 159).

Such explicitness is not a part of Goethe's method in *Campagne in Frankreich*. Thomas P. Saine, in particular, has pointed out the euphemisms, vagueness and indirection of the narrative, where Goethe often says one thing and leaves it to 'the initiated reader' to come to the opposite conclusion, as when he has the Duke of Brunswick express the hope that Goethe will make it clear that his forces have been defeated by the weather, not by the foe (HA x, 264).[8] A principal motif of *Campagne in Frankreich*, however, is the inability of both the émigrés and the leaders of the German expeditionary force to grasp the gravity of the revolutionary threat. In a famous passage from Johann Peter Eckermann's *Gespräche mit Goethe in den letzten Jahren seines Lebens* (Conversations with Goethe in the final years of his life) Goethe expounds the view that a great revolution is never the fault of the people, but rather of the rulers, who have the obligation to be perpetually just and perpetually alert (Eckermann III, 4 January 1824). In portraying both the French princes and the Prussian high command as inattentive military leaders, therefore, Goethe in effect blames them for the ensuing chaos unleashed upon Europe.

By way of implicit contrast, Goethe's optical studies, which he continues even while observing the effects of 'cannon fever' (HA x, 233–4) upon his own person at Valmy, coincide with his goal of seeing clearly in political, personal and literary matters. It is this facility which enables the narrator, when asked, to provide the oft-quoted evaluation of the significance of the military standoff at Valmy: 'Von hier und heute geht eine neue Epoche der Weltgeschichte aus, und ihr könnt sagen, ihr seid dabei gewesen' (From here and today begins a new epoch of world history, and you can say that you witnessed it, HA x, 235). In the *Belagerung von Mainz*, Goethe has his military comrades recall and repeat these words (HA x, 365), so as to underscore their significance. While Saine is correct in casting doubt on the biographical accuracy of such prescience,[9] within a work that is literary as well as autobiographical ('Dichtung' as well as 'Wahrheit') Goethe can place Valmy at the beginning of 'a chronic cycle of revolution and counter-revolution, violence and counter-violence' against which he is to set his own individual efforts as poet and scientist.[10] For this reason, Goethe closes *Campagne in Frankreich* with a discussion of literary works like *Der Groß-Cophta* (The Grand Kophta, 1791) and *Hermann und Dorothea* (1797) that attempt to depict objectively both the moral bankruptcy of the French aristocracy and the anarchy unleashed by the revolutionary wars (HA x, 356–61).

Such 'retrospective vision'[11] in *Campagne in Frankreich* also characterizes the depiction of Goethe's visits to friends such as Friedrich Jacobi who have not seen him since his return from Italy; they are disappointed when the Goethe they meet does not correspond to their old image of him and show little or no interest in his latest scientific and literary works: 'Man kann sich keinen isoliertern Menschen denken, als ich damals war und lange Zeit blieb' (One cannot imagine a more isolated person than I was then and remained for a long time, HA x, 313). This impression is reinforced at the conclusion of *Belagerung von Mainz* when Schlosser, his brother-in-law and friend of his youth, breaks out in derisive laughter at the mention of an essay on the theory of colours that Goethe had composed during the siege and that calls for a society to investigate the phenomenon from a variety of perspectives:

how naive to imagine that in Germany any type of common effort could take place! (HA x, 399).

This gloomy conclusion to *Belagerung von Mainz*, however, is implicitly preparing for a treatment of Goethe's friendship and literary partnership with Schiller. In 1817 Goethe had already published 'Glückliches Ereignis' (Fortunate Event), an account of the July 1794 conversation with Schiller on the metamorphosis of plants that signalled not only the disparity in their approach to nature, but also the fruitfulness of the resulting intellectual exchange: 'und so besiegelten wir, durch den größten, vielleicht nie ganz zu schlichtenden Wettkampf zwischen Objekt und Subjekt, einen Bund, der ununterbrochen gedauert, und für uns und andere manches Gute gewirkt hat' (And so through the greatest, perhaps never completely resolvable conflict between subject and object we sealed an alliance that continued unbroken and that brought much good for ourselves and others, HA x, 541). In 1828 and 1829, Goethe provided a record of these benefits by publishing their correspondence. The circumstances of its publication, to be sure, also supply an insight into Goethe's capacity as hard-nosed businessman. In a letter of 11 June 1823 to his publisher Cotta, Goethe mentions that in recent weeks he has gathered together Schiller's letters to him from 1794 to 1805, which he regards as 'den größten Schatz, den ich vielleicht besitze' (perhaps the greatest treasure I possess, HAB iv, 66). By this point Goethe had offered Charlotte Schiller a small sum for the acquisition of his letters to her late husband, which she rejected on the grounds that this would have denied the Schiller children proper recompense from their publication. After long and at times fractious negotiations involving Cotta, Goethe and the Schiller family, with Wilhelm von Humboldt serving as mediator, an agreement was reached in March 1824 that named Goethe as editor of the correspondence, with all royalties to be divided equally between him and Schiller's heirs. By August 1826, Goethe reported to Cotta that the manuscript was ready for publication, but further wrangling over royalties delayed the final signing of the contract until March 1828.

There is no doubt that Goethe invested a good deal of time and labour in the preparation of these letters for publication. In contrast to his editorial shiftings and shapings for the *Italienische Reise*, however, here there was no need for extensive revisions, because both partners had already written their letters with the consciousness that they were likely to be published some day. Although these letters are much more than autobiographical documents, their studied concentration on aesthetic issues contrasts markedly with the more intimate and wide-ranging correspondence that Schiller enjoyed with Körner and Goethe with friends such as Knebel and Zelter. Within the *Tag- und Jahreshefte* (Annals, 1830), Goethe's account of his activities between

1749 and 1822, this partnership with Schiller serves as a sign of the transition in German culture from the 'aristocratic anarchy' (HA x, 443) of disparate sub-groups to the coordinated efforts in the arts and sciences taking place in Weimar and Jena alike. While entries for the period between 1795 and 1805 record in summary form the accomplishments of these years, Goethe refrains from any extensive discussion of them, referring instead to the recently published correspondence with Schiller (HA x, 444) – yet another indication that he regarded these letters as an integral part of his autobiographical project.

The Goethe–Schiller correspondence has enjoyed deserved acclaim ever since its publication; Schiller's profound analysis of *Wilhelm Meisters Lehrjahre* in his letters from early July 1796, and Goethe's letter of 8 December 1798 on the poetic significance of astrology for the *Wallenstein* trilogy, to mention just two examples, demonstrate vividly how these two great writers benefited each other. The *Tag- und Jahreshefte*, by contrast, are yet another work from Goethe's later years that has traditionally been regarded as an artless compilation of disparate materials, drawn in this case from Goethe's extensive diaries and correspondence and edited with the help of Friedrich Wilhelm Riemer, Goethe's long-standing associate in philological matters, and Eckermann, whose services Goethe had already engaged upon his arrival in Weimar in June 1823. Georg Wackerl, however, points out a salient feature of the *Tag- und Jahreshefte*, which begin not with the birth of the poet, as does *Dichtung und Wahrheit*, but rather with the mention of 'zeitig erwachendem Talent' (timely awakening of talent; HA x, 429) and cover in one paragraph the years 1749 through 1764, which required five books in *Dichtung und Wahrheit*.[12] Goethe is able to pass with relative speed through these years because in this autobiographical project he is concerned not with the development of his talents, as treated in *Dichtung und Wahrheit*, but rather with their employment, as he remarked to Eckermann in their conversation of 27 January 1824. And while specific literary works are mentioned both before and after the watershed year of 1789, at which point the annalistic organization of material begins, much more attention is given to Goethe's participation in the intellectual life of Jena and theatrical productions in Weimar.

Personal feelings are not entirely absent from this 'life as work' approach to autobiography, but once again indirection is the preferred method. In the account of his reaction to Schiller's demise, Goethe tells of his attempt to defy death by completing Schiller's unfinished drama *Demetrius*; only after his poetic imagination fails him does true desolation set in: 'Meine Tagebücher melden nichts von jener Zeit; die weißen Blätter deuten auf den hohlen Zustand' (My diaries report nothing from that time; the white pages indicate the empty condition; HA x, 472). Another blank spot occurs at the close of the annals for the year 1806; Goethe mentions the foreboding and even despair in the air as Prussian military leaders convene in Jena for the upcoming battle against the Napoleonic army, but refrains from an account of the battle and its aftermath (including, of course, Goethe's marriage with Christiane Vulpius, whose life and death receive no mention anywhere in the *Tag- und Jahreshefte*). Characteristically enough, the entry for 1807 – and with it volume II of the annals – begins with the notice that the theatre had reopened late the previous year, as a sign that life was returning to the town and duchy of Weimar (HA x, 496). Activity, in this case artistic activity, is depicted as the exemplary response to life's travails; a production in 1807 of *Torquato Tasso*, undertaken only half-willingly by Goethe at the urging of his theatre company, proves to be 'eine freundliche, den innigsten Frieden herstellende Kunsterscheinung' (a friendly phenomenon of art, producing the innermost peace; HA x, 497). One is reminded here of the Viennese determination to rebuild the State Opera House before all else in the aftermath of World War II, but also of Tasso's words at the conclusion of Goethe's drama: 'Und wenn der Mensch in seiner Qual verstummt, / Gab mir ein Gott zu sagen, wie ich leide' (And when the man becomes mute in his torment / A god gave me to say how I suffer, HA v, 166). Even more than was the case in *Dichtung und Wahrheit*, the 'man' Goethe in his later years preferred either to keep his feelings to himself, mask them in poetry, or allow others, such as Eckermann, to record them for him.

Goethe's characterization of the *Tag- und Jahreshefte* as *Ergänzung meiner sonstigen Bekenntnisse* (Supplement to my other Confessions) could also be applied to Eckermann's *Gespräche mit Goethe*. Not only do these conversations coincide with the years left untreated in the *Tag- und Jahreshefte*, but they also provide the type of detailed information on Goethe's life and opinions that Eckermann had wished for the latter work and that Goethe largely refrained from providing.[13] In the aforementioned conversation of 27 January 1824, for example, Goethe expatiates on why he has become so taciturn in describing his later years: where is the audience to whom he would feel inclined to speak comfortably and at length? It is precisely this function that Eckermann exercises ever since describing his first visit to Goethe on 10 June 1823 as the fulfilment of his dearest hopes and dreams. In the ensuing days and years, he composes the image of Goethe as the vigorous, benevolent Sage of Weimar that was to counteract the then-current views of him as unapproachable Olympian or servant of princes and contribute to the establishment of the Goethe cult of the later nineteenth and twentieth centuries.

In his letter to Eckermann of 12 October 1830, Goethe indicated that he wished no speedy publication of these conversations, but would be willing to go through and edit them so as to increase their value – a clever way of ensuring that this work would not appear until after his death, when it could serve as a kind of capstone for his autobiographical edifice. Following Goethe's severe illness in late November 1830 and ensuing resolve to complete the remaining parts of *Faust* and *Dichtung und Wahrheit*, Eckermann notes in his final entry for 1830 that he has abandoned plans to edit these conversations with Goethe's help – which appears symptomatic of Eckermann's seemingly self-abandoning service to Goethe. But by including his exchange of letters with Goethe in the *Gespräche*, Eckermann shows his own slyness, as this serves as a signal that he is a sufficiently important individual for Goethe to enter into a correspondence with him. And by recording discussions with Goethe on *Faust*, Part IV of *Dichtung und Wahrheit*, and *Wilhelm Meisters Wanderjahre*, Eckermann puts himself in a role analogous to Schiller in the latter's promotion of Goethe's literary production.[14]

Indeed, there is a collective character to much of Goethe's autobiographical oeuvre. For the early stages of *Dichtung und Wahrheit*, Bettina Brentano served as a conduit for his mother's recollections of her young son. In composing *Campagne in Frankreich*, Goethe made use of the memoirs of others in recalling a time whose details he had banished from his own memory. In the autobiographical work from the final years of his life, Goethe relied increasingly on editorial assistance in the compilation of material, and even on the inclusion of pieces by other people in the text proper, such as segments from Karl Philipp Moritz's essay 'Über die bildende Nachahmung des Schönen' (On the creative imitation of the beautiful, 1788) as an example of the conversations on art and aesthetics that took place during his second sojourn in Rome (HA XI, 534–41). One could, of course, be cynical and speak of the phantasm of 'Goethe' as a composite image. I prefer, however, to shift the focus and end this essay with Goethe's reflection in Book 9 of *Dichtung und Wahrheit* when he observed that Sulpiz Boisserée and others were taking up interests that he had not pursued since his youth: 'dann tritt das schöne Gefühl ein, daß die Menschheit zusammen erst der wahre Mensch ist, und daß der Einzelne nur froh und glücklich sein kann, wenn er den Mut hat, sich im Ganzen zu fühlen' (then there occurs the beautiful feeling that only humanity together is the true human being, and that the individual can be cheerful and happy only if he has the courage to feel himself in the Whole; HA IX, 387).

NOTES

1 See Gisela Brude-Firnau, '*Aus meinem Leben: Dichtung und Wahrheit*', in Paul Michael Lützeler and James E. McLeod (eds.), *Goethes Erzählwerk: Interpretationen* (Stuttgart: Reclam, 1985), pp. 319–43, p. 331.

2 Robert Gould, 'The Functions of the Non-Literary Quotations in Part 4 of *Dichtung und Wahrheit*', *German Life and Letters* 44 (1991), 291–305, pp. 301, 303.
3 'Dichtung und Wahrheit', in *Handbuch* III, 315.
4 Nicholas Boyle (with additional material by John Kington), 'Goethe in Paestum: a Higher-Critical Look at the *Italienische Reise*', *Oxford German Studies* 20/21 (1991–2), 18–31, p. 19.
5 Ibid., p. 30.
6 Peter Boerner, '*Italienische Reise*', in Paul Michael Lützeler and James E. McLeod (eds.), *Goethes Erzählwerk: Interpretationen* (Stuttgart: Reclam, 1985), pp. 344–62, pp. 355–9.
7 Horst Rüdiger, 'Zur Komposition von Goethes *Zweitem römischen Aufenthalt*: Das melodramatische Finale und die Novelle von der "schönen Mailänderin"', in Stanley A. Corngold et al. (eds.), *Aspekte der Goethezeit* (Göttingen: Vandenhoeck & Ruprecht, 1977), pp. 97–114, pp. 100–2.
8 Thomas P. Saine, 'Goethe's Novel: *Campagne in Frankreich*', in William J. Lillyman (ed.), *Goethe's Narrative Fiction: The Irvine Goethe Symposium* (Berlin: de Gruyter, 1983), pp. 193–223, p. 212.
9 Ibid., pp. 200–2.
10 Richard Fisher, '"Dichter" and "Geschichte": Goethe's *Campagne in Frankreich*', *Goethe Yearbook* 4 (1988), 235–74, p. 239.
11 Ibid.
12 Georg Wackerl, *Goethes 'Tag- und Jahreshefte'* (Berlin: de Gruyter, 1970), pp. 88–9.
13 Ibid., pp. 32–8.
14 For a stimulating discussion of the psychodynamics of Eckermann's relationship with Goethe see Avital Ronell, *Dictations: On Haunted Writing* (Bloomington, IN: Indiana University Press, 1986), pp. 63–191.

10

DANIEL STEUER

In defence of experience: Goethe's natural investigations and scientific culture

Goethe's views on the systematic investigation of nature were informed by his belief that science once developed out of poetry, and that one day these two human faculties might well meet again to their mutual advantage (cf. HA XIII, 107). Against the background of this belief, his own contributions to the study of organic form and transformation (morphology), to optics and the science of colour, to geology and mineralogy, and to meteorology must be seen as an attempt to maintain the unity of human knowledge and experience, and the unity of humankind and nature. He differed from the more speculative of the Romantics through his insistence on empirical evidence and demonstration, and from the positivist tendency of the emerging natural sciences through a highly developed consciousness of theoretical issues. This chapter portrays the specific nature of Goethe's natural investigations, concentrating on morphology and the theory of colour as the most important areas of his activities. It will argue that, ultimately, the relevance to us of Goethe's scientific activities lies in methodological issues rather than individual results. His balancing of analytical and synthetic procedure makes it possible to extract elements from the totality of nature without losing sight of its unity. Goethe insists on a continuous dialogue between experience and theoretical abstraction, and on the phenomena themselves providing the true teachings of nature. This is a necessary corrective to the idea that scientific theories are the expression of something more fundamental than the phenomena themselves. The indivisible association of knowledge and respect for the object of knowledge is at the heart of Goethe's approach.

The habit of a lifetime

Goethe never saw himself as first and foremost a poet, with only a secondary interest in nature: this public perception, he said when reflecting on the history of his botanical studies in 1817, ignored the fact that he 'diligently cared, with great attention, for nature in all its physical and organic manifestations, and pursued his serious reflections continuously and with passion' (HA XIII, 167). Before his arrival in Weimar, his contributions to Lavater's *Physiognomik* around 1775 may be seen as the prelude to his systematic osteological, anatomical and morphological studies, pursued with Justus Christian Loder in Jena from 1780 onwards. By then a cabinet minister, his responsibilities included the mining affairs of the duchy, and put him in touch with geologists, notably Johann Karl Wilhelm Voigt and Friedrich Wilhelm Heinrich von Trebra. In 1784 two important essays resulted from these interests, one on the intermaxillary bone in humans, the other on granite ('Über Granit'), while his Italian journey led to the publication of three further pieces between 1788 and 1790, 'Einfache Nachahmung der Natur, Manier, Stil' (Simple Imitation of Nature, Manner, Style), *Das römische Karneval* (Roman Carnival), and *Versuch die Metamorphose der Pflanzen zu erklären* (Essay Explaining the Metamorphosis of Plants), which, according to Goethe, show his inner development at the time and the attitude he took towards nature, society and art (HA XIII, 102–3). Taken together, these three essays show that Goethe saw the emergence of true artistic style, of human customs and of natural form as governed by analogous principles. In all three cases polarities are mediated in a process of repetition with variation, leading to an intensification and, as the developmental end-point, a form which rests in itself. However, while art and society are thus half nature, half culture, natural form (and formation) provides the unifying frame.

His return from Italy was followed by a long period of sustained investigations ending with the publication of *Die Wahlverwandtschaften* (Elective Affinities) in 1809 and *Zur Farbenlehre* (Theory of Colour) in 1810 (though the central ideas were established by 1801). After that, though Goethe never stops observing, collecting, and following developments in the sciences, there is a shift in emphasis towards self-reflective analysis of his path in science and a renewed interest in the poetic foundations of human thought. Both the *Naturwissenschaftliche Hefte* (Scientific Notebooks) and *Zur Morphologie* (On Morphology), published between 1817 and 1824, combine the presentation of his research during the previous thirty years with aphorisms, poems and autobiographical sketches, thus attempting to make disciplinary boundaries permeable, just as the *Noten und Abhandlungen zum besseren Verständnis des West-östlichen Divan* (Notes and Essays on the *West-Eastern Divan*) let poems and poetics permeate each other. The theory of language behind the latter locates the foundations of meaning in primordial tropes which hardly deserve the name because of their intense amalgamation with specific forms of life; they are constitutive of a culture, and not accidental to it. These remarks on language and on translation can be seen as a seal to Goethe's ironic and poetic epistemology (cf. HA II, 179–80, 186, 255–9).

Goethe's last major piece of writing on science, *Principes de philosophie zoologique* (HA XIII, 219–50), takes the debate between Geoffrey St. Hilaire and Georges Cuvier as an opportunity once again to present his ideas on the two principal approaches in science – the analytic, moving from individual empirical data to the whole, and the synthetic, working from a totality (which is not given to the senses) towards individual cases – , to recapitulate the history of comparative morphology, and to warn against misleading metaphors employed in the debate, such as *unité du plan, embranchement* and *matériaux*, which suggest that organisms are constructed in an additive way.

The passionate subject and its objects

Goethe was a passionate scientist, and his conviction that scientific activity is intrinsically related to self-delusion did not diminish this passion. Rather, he takes account of this fact by never losing sight of the moment at which experience – whether simple observation or technically aided experiment – is turned into theory: it is here, at the turning point from experience to judgement, that all man's inner enemies lie in ambush – imagination, impatience, jumping to conclusions, complacency, inflexibility, prejudice, laziness, carelessness, fickleness – ready at any time to lead astray both the man of action and the seemingly dispassionate observer (see 'Der Versuch als Vermittler von Objekt und Subjekt' (The Experiment as Mediator Between Object and Subject; HA XIII, 15)). Accordingly, for Goethe psychology, epistemology and experimental practice must be seen in context. This is exemplified by the structure of *Zur Farbenlehre*, the first, didactic part of which presents Goethe's own findings and methodological reflections. The second part is a critical analysis of Newton's *Opticks* as an example of a lack of theoretical awareness and the rhetorical use of scientific language and experiments. And the third part gives a historical account of ideas and theories of colour and light, thus relating the first two parts. Human knowledge appears as a result of the mediation between the individual's direct experience of nature, and the tradition from which the researcher comes. Goethe's epistemology is a form of perspectivism, but one contained within the limits of sensual experience. He talks of nature without being a naive realist, and he stresses the influence of the individual's mode of apprehension (*Vorstellungsart*) without falling into radical subjectivism:

> [Man] may elevate his mode of apprehension as high above the common one as he wishes, he may purify it as much as he likes, still, as a rule, it remains nothing but a mode of apprehension; that is: an attempt to comprehend several

objects in terms of some intelligible relation, which, strictly speaking, they do not possess. Hence our inclination towards hypotheses, theories, terminologies and systems, all of which we cannot disapprove of because they are necessary products of the way our own nature is organized. (HA XIII, 15–16)

Mediation between subject and object remains the starting-point, the end-point and – most importantly – the task. As we shall see, Goethe's idea of research as a process of ongoing mediation amounts to an ironically modified version of Kantian transcendental philosophy, a version in which the stable categories and modes of apprehension are resolved into a dialogue between *a priori* reasoning and experience. This makes discussion of his work difficult, but also attractive and still relevant to our own age.

Science between 1780 and 1850: formalization and temporalization

Goethe's research falls into the period 1780–1850, sometimes referred to as the Second Scientific Revolution. The first saw the rise of empirical investigations together with the application of mathematical models, culminating in Newton's *Philosophiae Naturalis Principia Mathematica* (1687). All through the eighteenth century, these activities were still summed up as Natural Philosophy and Natural History, and only during the so-called second revolution did the term 'science' crystallize. This period was characterized by two tendencies: formalization and temporalization.

The overall result of formalization was the levelling out of qualitative differences within natural phenomena in favour of ever more abstract (formal) entities. The attitude of the Baconian sciences, beginning with experience and working on the basis of *a posteriori* reasoning, was replaced by that of the classical *a priori* sciences, such as rational mechanics, geometry and astronomy. This reversal becomes strikingly apparent when comparing the Aristotelian concept of motion with Newton's. Whereas Aristotle held that a body moves as long as a force acts upon it to overcome any resistance to that movement (and empirically resistance is always present), Newton began from the ideal and hypothetical case of a body in frictionless movement, and postulates that it continues with uniform velocity in the same direction unless a force acts upon it. The aim is no longer to describe existing entities but measurable effects, and theoretical models are only auxiliary tools to construct a mathematical system to describe these effects. In consequence, the meaning even of fundamental terms is identified with a measurable quantity (metrification); the experiment is taken not as a demonstration of a natural phenomenon, but as a way of confirming the quantitative mathematical model; and finally, knowledge, as an *adequatio rei et intellectus*, a correspondence between subject and object, is replaced by successful prediction and control.[1]

In this context, the programmatic paper by the physicist and physiologist Hermann Helmholtz, *On the Conservation of Force* (1847), is an interesting case. It had developed from an attempt to find a common basis for animal heat and physical heat, and ended by identifying all natural phenomena as manifestations of one underlying force assumed to be located in point-like atoms. Johann Poggendorff, publisher of the *Annalen der Physik und Chemie*, at first rejected it as 'pure philosophy', which shows that the oppositional lines did not run only between a qualitative and a quantitative approach. Poggendorff was not at all against the use of mathematics, but he opposed 'the practice of most mathematical physicists of assuming without empirical evidence the existence of hypothetical entities and then making them the foundations of physics'. This was also Goethe's criticism. However, Poggendorff's idea of physics was to locate natural laws 'as revealed by instruments in experimental researches, focused on number and measure'.[2] And this is the strict opposite of Goethe's conviction that the human body is the most precise physical instrument (HA XII, 458).

Parallel to the formalization of natural investigations, the spatial arrangement and interpretation of phenomena as practised earlier in natural history was re-interpreted into temporal sequences, but, in the case of biology, without a change in the logic of the descriptions and classifications, which were still based on similarity. Neither Darwin nor other evolutionary biologists added theories of transformational principles based on biological organization, rather than the ultimately statistical argument of natural selection, to this re-interpretation of the diversity of 'form' into a temporal sequence. Thus phylogenetic trees, allegedly presenting the evolutionary relationship of organisms, grew in abundance without any criteria being given to explain how, for example, animals consisting of many similar segments (such as earthworms) led, by way of reduction, to animals with only few or no distinct body segments, or vice versa. Once again, Goethe, often referred to as one of the founding fathers of comparative morphology, was, as we shall see, more cautious than his followers in the conclusions he drew from his morphological studies.

Goethe, then, was sceptical of formalization in so far as he distrusted *a priori* speculation and abstraction, and critical of temporalization in so far as he distrusted historical hypotheses. And he criticized the replacement of the human body as the touchstone for knowledge by apparatuses. The motivation behind all three points of criticism is the insistence on the logical priority of human experience over whatever intellectual system or practice is built upon it. His attitude arose from a spirit of discrimination and from an entirely 'this-worldly' epistemology: before retreating into metaphysical abstractions, see how far you can get with your senses and a conscious use of language. Truth, for Goethe, was a pluralist concept, but in each of its forms dependent on language (and, hence, tradition), on sense experience, and on an individual's critical mind to bring the two together.

Morphology as a universal approach

Morphology and metamorphosis for Goethe were both objects of investigation and the medium of reflection because the same principles that govern the change of form in nature also apply to intellectual transformations in the history of knowledge. Remembering in 1817 his attempts at surveying the versatility of plants using Linné's nomenclature, he asks the reader to imagine him, as a born poet (to him not a contradiction to being a born scientist) who strives to mould his expressions as closely as possible to the object in mind (HA XIII, 160), being asked to use a prefabricated terminology, a kind of semantic type-case from which to construct the forms (*Gestalten*) in question. Here, as elsewhere, Goethe remains aware of the empirical residue which results from the incongruity of a clearly defined conceptual language (with stable categories) on the one hand, and the dynamic and mobile phenomena of living nature on the other, without, however, denying the need for it, or, in this case, the merit of Linné. But just as nature is versatile and in a constant process of becoming, so the language of the investigator must be flexible and open to variation and change. In his 'Schlussbetrachtungen über Sprache und Terminologie' (Final Reflections on Language and Terminology), concluding the first part of the *Farbenlehre*, Goethe reminds the reader that all language is essentially symbolic and uses tropes, especially in the context of things which should be called 'activities' rather than 'objects' (as is clearly the case with, for example, colours and morphogenesis, i.e. the development of form). He suggests a conscious and pluralist use of metaphysical, mathematical, mechanical (including the related corpuscular) and moral modes of expression, and he warns against a substitution of signs for the phenomena themselves. A physicist should carefully avoid turning empirical intuition (*Anschauung*) into concepts and concepts into words, and then treating these words as if they were objects (HA XIII, 482; §716) – a process which exemplifies the greatest danger to all inquiry into physics, namely to take what is derivative as primitive and thereby to confuse the abstract result of enquiry with fundamental phenomena (HA XIII, 482; §718).

According to Goethe's own method, investigations should begin by observing the phenomena as they appear in everyday life. The next step should be to bring them under general empirical categories, and these, in turn, under scientific categories. At each step – and this is crucial – the laws and rules implied in these categories reveal themselves not through words and hypotheses to the understanding, but through the phenomena to the senses ('dem Anschauen'; cf. HA XIII, 367–8; §175). This distinguishes a process of abstraction which remains anchored in reality from one in which words take the place of phenomena. The *Urphänomen* (primordial phenomenon) of a particular set of natural phenomena, the end-result of Goethe's method, provides the anchor insofar as (a) it can be experienced (it is real), (b) it contains the conditions necessary for the appearance of this class of phenomena (it is identical with them, and can therefore symbolically stand for them), and finally (c) it is an ultimate point of knowledge (and therefore ideal, but in an entirely this-worldly sense). The simple signs of a scientific language should designate such a primordial phenomenon, such as, for example, the '+' and '−' of the magnet. *Urphänomene* thus indicate the observable limits of human insight into nature, and they are situated at the ever controversial border between science on the one hand, and philosophy and religion on the other. The concept of the *Urphänomen* therefore sums up Goethe's methodological position vis-à-vis science.

Goethe rejects the idea of any precision – linguistic, mathematical or otherwise – which would be alien to the real object, and as reality itself is poetic, so it is poetic language that is needed to express the subtler aspects of it. Only a language formed, informed and transformed by experience can do justice to it, just as only a mind formed, informed and transformed by the objects of this world can hope to speak such a language. We know ourselves only in so far as we know the world. We perceive the world only within ourselves, and ourselves only within the world. 'Every new object, well perceived, discloses a new organ within us' (HA XIII, 38). Living knowledge is the result of this reciprocal formation.

Morphology of organic beings

Goethe's interest in morphology was ultimately directed at the transformational principles governing the universal metamorphosis taking place in nature. It is ironic, therefore, to see in his comparative work on animals a strong fixation on those structures which allow only limited or no further modification of form: bones. Both the 'discovery' of the intermaxillary bone in humans and the vertebrae theory of the skull concern the skeleton. In the *Tag- und Jahreshefte* (Annals), Goethe dates his renewed interest in anatomy to an *aperçu* in 1790: walking on the Lido in Venice, Götze, his servant, shows him a sheep's skull which has burst in such a way as to remind Goethe of his old conviction that the bones of the skull are metamorphosed vertebrae, and which also demonstrates how amorphous organic masses become more and more organized through their opening towards the outside and transformation into organs of sense (HA X, 435–6). The existence of the intermaxillary bone in humans, on the other hand, had been a matter of ongoing dispute, in which, ultimately, the unity of nature and the question whether humankind stands out from the rest of creation had been the issue. The Frenchman Felix Vicq d'Azyr rediscovered the bone in 1780, and subsequently published on it in 1784. Goethe reached his conclusion around the same time, in 1783/4. Priority, however, is not of the essence here. Goethe evokes the concept of the 'Great Chain of Being' when writing about the large gap between the bones in turtles and elephants: yet 'a sequence of forms can be placed between them which links them' (HA XIII, 195). And the same holds true for the walrus and humans. The controversial nature of the bone's presence in the latter is due to its close condensation with neighbouring bones, making the seams hard to find. On the one hand, Goethe (and this is the most interesting passage of his text) attributes this to the teething process and the resulting need for the implicated bones to direct their growth toward each other and thus to form tight bonds (HA XIII, 194–5). On the other hand, he defines the bone by its relation to the incisors (and vice versa), thereby foreshadowing the quasi-geometric and architectonic *Bauplan* approach of later morphology, which views and describes organisms as collections of individual and separate traits, and which, as we have seen, he criticised explicitly in his discussion of the academy debate.

This contradiction can be pushed further. After his Lido *aperçu*, Goethe aimed to set up an osteological type which was meant to serve at least two purposes: first, to allow a systematic comparison between descriptions made by different anatomists in different places and at different times without the risk of confusion between individual parts, and second, to represent a common type, symbolic of organismic principles and running through all organic beings. (In fact, Goethe concentrated largely on mammals.) The first of these aims is more or less uncontroversial; comparative anatomy needed a '*tertium comparationis*' (LA I, vol. IX, 141), a canonical model, serving as a prototype against which to compare individual species (cf. LA I, vol. IX, 172, 181). Goethe stresses that this model can never be a single species, as the individual can never represent the whole. It must be an idea, but an idea derived from experience, and representing those parts which are common to all animals. In so far as each new empirical finding changes the picture slightly, this amounts to a permanent movement between the rational and the empirical.

The second aim, however, is more complex; it assumes that the skeleton lays the foundations for all higher organic *Gestalt* (HA XIII, 210; *Gestalt* is the fixed form of an organism at a particular stage as opposed to the living developing form), that through the skeleton the definite character of every *Gestalt* is eternally preserved for us (HA XIII, 62–3), and that the construction of bones is the clearly visible scaffolding of all *Gestalten*, which, if correctly perceived, makes it easier to recognize all other parts (HA XIII, 180). If Goethe mocked the Newtonians for their *idée fixe* that refrangibility is responsible for all optical and chromatic phenomena, then this sequence of statements, running from 1795 through to 1824, should demonstrate that he never abandoned his own assumption of the primary significance of the skeleton. This, and not his method, kept him from formulating any transformational principles which would be more satisfactory than, for example, the idea of a 'budget' (HA XIII, 244), whereby nature cannot add to one part of an organism without taking away from another.

Despite this limitation, Goethe claims to have tried 'a description of individual bones, but in their constructive, integrative context', because 'naked numbers and measurements dissolve all form' (HA XIII, 210). The self-referentiality of the organism means that none of its parts is 'mechanically added or provoked from the outside', notwithstanding the reciprocal influence between organism and environment (cf. his second attempt at a metamorphosis of plants, LA I, vol. X, 66). From the start, Goethe was aware of the inherent conflict within the emerging life sciences, which depended on dissection in order to learn about the parts yet thereby destroyed the very phenomenon of organic composition. The skeleton cannot be looked at in isolation, and the fluid, soft and hardened elements of an organic body 'must be looked upon as one', as a unity (LA I, vol. IX, 135–6).[3] Only 'by virtue of this concept' can we hope to fill the gaps of physiological knowledge (195).

Goethe's morphology rejects teleology. For Goethe the proper question to ask was not for what purpose a particular part of an organic being exists, but how that part develops within the totality of the organism. 'Every creature is its own reason to be. All its parts have a direct effect on one another, a relationship to one another, thereby constantly renewing the circle of life; thus we are justified in considering every animal physiologically perfect... We will not claim that a bull has been given horns so that he can butt; instead, we will try to discover how he might have developed horns he uses for butting' (HA XIII, 177; trans. Douglas Miller).[4] Goethe remains within the conceptual framework of Kant's *Critique of Judgement*, which juxtaposed the discursive nature of our understanding (forcing us to conceive of an organismic totality as the result of the competing forces acting within it) with a non-discursive, intuitive and god-like understanding which could draw a conclusion from the concept of a whole to the necessary relation of its parts (§77). However, Kant speculates, there may be a kind of intellectual intuition which would unite teleology (*nexus finalis*) and mechanical explanation (*nexus effectivus*), and Goethe appropriates the idea of such archetypal intuition for his own enterprise, not without stressing Kant's assessment of it as a rather risky venture for human understanding (cf. HA XIII, 30–1; and *Critique of Judgement*, §80).

This risky task, for Goethe, is the task of morphology: to derive, by application of the concept of 'physiological perfection', from the perception of a whole (an organism) the necessary relation of its parts. A purely mechanical mode of explanation may be appropriate in the case of, for example, a clockwork, where the movements of individual parts cause and explain those of other individual parts (though this does not explain why the parts have been arranged in a particular way). But when applied to organic beings the mechanical explanation ignores the necessary interrelation of all parts with all other parts which constitutes the identity of the organism. While for Schelling and other natural philosophers this identity was grounded in an idea, for Goethe it was given in experience. Thus, in his morphological work he tried to disprove Kant's pessimistic view that it is categorically impossible to find, in nature, explanatory principles (*Erklärungsgründe*) for organic forms (*Zweckverbindungen*; cf. *Critique of Judgement*, §77); it would be irrational ('schlechterdings ungereimt'), Kant had said, to assume that some day a Newton of the organic realm would stand up and explain the existence of even a single blade of grass without recourse to teleological principles (§75). Kant's evaluation is correct as long as Newtonian physics and natural laws are taken to be identical: biological form indeed asks for a different mode of explanation. What is at stake here is a conceptual difference, not an empirical one. Biology and evolutionary theory have subsequently ignored this difference, which cannot simply be overcome by the statistical argument of long time-spans of random mutations.

The history of morphology in the nineteenth and twentieth centuries bears this out.[5] The change introduced by the reductionist programme of the 'physicalist physiologists' (Du Bois-Reymond, Brücke, Ludwig, Helmholtz), effectively brought about a science of physiology, independent of biology, and, through an institutional separation, resolved the problem of anatomy, morphology and physiology all working within one discipline: 'Organic physics was to be [the physicalist physiologist's] lever in redefining the discipline of physiology in such a manner as to exclude...*Bauplan* practitioners of the morphological approach'.[6] But it also separated form and function, and obliterated the phenomenon of organismic self-referentiality, whereas previously morphology had been 'essential to physiology because organisation was one of life's defining characteristics'.[7] Physicalist physiologists either subsumed earlier morphology under their paradigm, or, like

Du Bois-Reymond, disparaged it through ridicule. Much nineteenth-century reference to Goethe as an intuitive anticipator of later scientific insights there-fore ignores the methodological abyss between him and nineteenth-century science, which had in the meantime converted the phenomena of form and organization into geometry and physics.

The counterfactual *Urphänomen*

Goethe's *Urpflanze*, the *Urphänomen* of plant organization, rests on the idea of the 'leaf' as the basic organ whose modifications lead to the various parts of one plant as well as to the different plants. As in the case of the animal kingdom, the idea of metamorphosis is thus developed in two dimensions: within the individual organic being, and across organic beings. When Goethe expounded his theory to Schiller, Schiller reacted by saying it was an idea, not an experience. And Goethe replied that in that case he should be glad to have ideas without knowing it, and even to be able to see them with his own eyes. That, according to Goethe, was precisely the point which, at that moment, separated them (cf. Goethe's famous account of the conversation, HA x, 540–1). But the opposition between them was not a real one. What Goethe had in mind was not a single plant corresponding to the *Urphänomen*, and hence an empirical representation of a Platonic idea. Rather, he believed that if one looks at individual plants as differing manifestations of a construc-tional and developmental principle, a model encapsulating this principle (and thereby all possible transformations of the leaf) would appear to the inner eye, not through arbitrary intuition but as a consequence of systematic em-pirical observations. The following lines from the poem 'Die Metamorphose der Pflanzen' (Metamorphosis of Plants) illustrate this:

> Alle Gestalten sind ähnlich, und keine gleichet der andern;
> Und so deutet das Chor auf ein geheimes Gesetz,
> Auf ein heiliges Rätsel. Oh könnt' ich dir, liebliche Freundin,
> Überliefern sogleich glücklich das lösende Wort!
>
> (HA xiii, 107)

All forms are alike but not identical, and thus they point to a secret law, a sacred mystery. If only I could pass on to you, sweet friend, the crucial word that solves it.

Goethe would like to give the solution explicitly, in one word, but he cannot. He knows that he does not possess the principle of biological organization, but he also knows that it must exist.

The irony in his recollections proves his awareness of this conflict. In the *Italian Journey*, he tells a story of modern man. Setting off to the public gardens of Palermo to pursue his 'poetic dreams', he is captivated by a 'spectre' of a quite different kind, his pet idea, his 'Grille', of the *Urpflanze*. Maybe he can find it here? For it must exist! Without such a common pattern, how could he recognize something as a plant? Goethe here enters into a Socratic dialogue with himself. But his self-mocking tone shows that he knows that the question is wrongly put. Spectre (*Gespenst*) is a term used by Newton, and adopted by Goethe in the service of his polemic against him; here, Goethe uses it against himself, and concludes with a sigh of resignation: 'Why is modern man so lacking in concentration, why so tempted to tasks he can neither rise to nor fulfil?' (HA XI, 375). And immediately afterwards, with gentle self-irony, he presents his optimistic letter to Herder, written from Naples in 1787. Nature herself shall envy him for his *Urpflanze*, with this model it will be possible to invent plants which are not just flights of fancy but possess inner truth and necessity: 'The same law will be applicable to all other forms of life' (HA XI, 375). Alas, the mature Goethe knew that this law cannot be explicitly given, it can be demonstrated only by pointing to individual forms. The final conclusion is left to the observer.

Form, for Goethe, was a transcendental category. His appropriation of Kant – contemporaries called it 'a strange analogy of the Kantian mode of thought' (HA XIII, 28) – includes the transcendental argument. Goethe, however, turns it against itself: by what process of abstraction is Kant able to formulate his argument? Answer: by abstracting from some of the qualities, such as form or colour, that are as essential to the human senses as are space and time, and by placing the faculty of human insight (*das Subjective Erkenntnisvermögen*) in the position of a detached object (cf. WA II, vol. XI, 376). Goethe replaces the resulting fixed division between subject and object with a dynamic model of experience. Through this move experience is allowed to correct the immutable categories of philosophy, and the result is an ironic transcendental philosophy which is aware of the constitutive function of modes of apprehension and of conceptual *a prioris*, without looking at them as unshakable foundations once and forever given.[8] The gap between idea and experience is acknowledged by Goethe; yet the idea exists only in so far as it communicates with experience. In this play of reciprocal influence, the individual retains the right to face nature independently of preconceived ideas. In a letter to Schiller (10 February 1798, HAB II, 329), Goethe points out the analogies between scientific and theoretical behaviour on the one hand, and practical behaviour in everyday life on the other. In both cases, man is forced to be selective, he must be concerned, not with what is, but with what should be: 'Now the latter is always an idea, and he is concrete in a concrete situation; and so he continues, in never-ending self-deception, in order to give to what is concrete the honour of an idea.' From here, Goethe's criticism of Newton becomes almost self-explanatory.

Goethe's *Farbenlehre* and Newtonian optics: the spectrum as spectre

Newtonian optics, for Goethe, was the paradigm case of a dogmatic and ossified theory. Newton's intention had been to connect and subordinate the study of light to that of mechanics; his *aperçu* had been the proportions of the elongated spectrum produced by a beam of sunlight when viewed through a prism, as this contradicted the established laws of reflection and refraction.

Newton's procedure in his *Opticks* (1704) is to set up a number of definitions and axioms, and then to present experiments which are interpreted on the basis of this *a priori* framework. He assumed that colour is an accidental property of 'rays', associated with their 'refrangibility', and the arrangement of experiments around his *experimentum crucis* (a single decisive experiment that settles the truth or falsehood of a hypothesis or theory) was meant to prove this. However, the only way to identify 'rays' is their colour. In a colourless spectrum no parts could be singled out, hence no conclusions could be drawn with regard to the projection of the original image after refraction. Such conclusions are possible only if there is an image, and Goethe is therefore right to point out that Newton, slipping in and out of empirical and theoretical statements, turns the relation between evidence and conclusion upside down through the way he constructs the relation between hypothetical 'rays' and observable light and colours. Goethe does not criticize the fact that Newton starts from theoretical premises, but that he moves neither from principles to experience, nor from experience to principles, using instead a 'mixed style of delivery', by assuming as known what would need first to be introduced, derived, explained and demonstrated, and then mentioning only those phenomena which seem to suit his theory (LA I, vol. v, 2; §6).[9]

What, then, are the hallmarks of Goethe's investigations as opposed to Newton's? Most importantly, his point of departure is visible nature. From his observation of coloured shadows in 1777 (HA XIII, 348; §75) to the final, yet still provisional, *Entwurf einer Farbenlehre* (Sketch of a Theory of Colour), as he titled the didactic part, Goethe remains firmly within the realm of experience, making repeated attempts to persuade his readers through the inclusion of black-and-white and coloured charts to see with their own eyes, and repeat the experiments themselves (HA XIII, 321). Goethe's arguments rest on the entire sequence of phenomena thus presented. He neither accepts the idea of an *experimentum crucis*, nor does he begin with conceptual definitions of light and colour. In his preface, he declares that we try in vain to express the essence of an object. What is given are effects, in other words phenomena, and just as we fail if we try to describe someone's character in direct terms, instead of portraying his deeds and actions, we must present a synopsis of colour phenomena if we wish to understand their essence: 'Colours are the deeds of light, deeds and sufferings' (HA XIII, 315). And when Goethe later in the introduction rhetorically asks himself for a definition of colour, he again evades an answer, saying he can only repeat that colour is law-like nature with respect to the sense of the eye (HA XIII, 324).

Thus, the appearance of colour is a procedural phenomenon, depending on light and the eye alike. With respect to the conditions under which colours appear, Goethe's theory is contained in the *Urphänomen* of atmospheric colours (see below), whereas his *Farbenkreis*, the circle of colours consisting of two triangles – green, purple and orange, and yellow, blue and red (or crimson) – gives a synopsis of the lawful relationships and the harmonies between the different colours. These apply to all three classes of colour phenomena which his mature theory distinguishes – physiological, physical and chemical colours:

> We first looked at colors insofar as they are a property of the eye, dependent on effect and counter-effect in the eye. We then turned our attention to colors as observed within colorless media. Lastly, we took note of colors which were undeniably a property of external objects. We called the first type of colors physiological; the second, physical; and the third, chemical. The first are entirely ephemeral, the second are transient but always linger for a time, and the third may be held constant over long periods.
>
> (HA XIII, 325; trans. Douglas Miller)[10]

Physiological colours belong in some cases (for example after-images) entirely, in others (for example colour contrast, coloured shadows) partly to the eye (cf. HA XIII, 329; §1). After looking at a dark cross, the eye will produce the after-image of a white cross (darkness and light); after looking at a blue cross, it will produce an orange one because complementary colours (those opposite each other in the colour circle like green and red, yellow and purple) harmonically call for each other, invoking the totality of the colour circle. Combinations of colours with a common neighbour, for example yellow and red, Goethe calls characteristic harmonies, and they can be seen as representing individuality within the totality. 'Negative harmonies' are produced by neighbouring colours. A special status is given to the combination of yellow and blue which Goethe calls 'common harmony', though according to his own definition it qualifies as a characteristic combination. But yellow and blue are ingredients of the *Urphänomen* of all colour phenomena.

This *Urphänomen* of the colour of the earth's atmosphere already belongs to the first class of physical colours, those which need some colourless material basis in order to appear but which are not permanent (as is the case with chemical colours). This first class of physical colours, in turn, are the dioptric colours, which result from refraction and are associated with a turbid medium. With relative light (the sun) on one side, and relative darkness on the other, we then see blue appear next to the darkness, and yellow next to the light, owing to the mediation of the turbid medium. The blue sky thus becomes the symbolic representation for the minimal conditions necessary for colour to appear. And red (or crimson) is the climax of the mediation between blue and yellow (the basic polarity), a process Goethe called intensification (*Steigerung*), a term developed from a suggestion made by Schiller in 1798 that the development from blue to blue-red, and yellow to yellow-red is an *Intension*.

Goethe presents the chromatic *Urphänomen*, together with a general explanation of the notion, immediately before discussing prismatic phenomena. For if the turbid medium becomes more or less transparent, we arrive at the second class of dioptric colours where that phenomenon is of paramount importance which goes 'under the artificial name of refraction' (HA XIII, 369; §179). Goethe stresses that refraction is not in all instances accompanied by coloured phenomena. Only if an image is shifted will colours appear. In the simple case of a white patch on a dark ground viewed through a prism, the white (main image) will be shifted (as a *Nebenbild* or secondary image) across the dark, resulting in blue, and the dark on the other side will be shifted across the white, resulting in yellow. This is in line with his *Urphänomen*, and all other, more complicated, phenomena (including Newton's experiments) are explained on this basis.

Following his *aperçu* when looking through a prism in 1790, the criticism of Newton and the importance of physiological colours – those belonging to the eye itself – rise in importance; in fact, Goethe's emphasis on the human eye and vision, and his rejection of Newton's *experimentum crucis* follow from each other. Newton's prismatic experiments dealt exclusively with physical colours, and his conclusion is, even though he expresses it cautiously under the heading of a query, that '[n]othing more is requisite for producing all the variety of Colours, and degrees of Refrangibility, than that the Rays of Light be Bodies of different sizes.'[11] In other words, within this corpuscular theory (which considers light to consist of discrete particles), colour is the epiphenomenal sensuous effect of a quantitative cause and thus radically subjective. In opposition to this, Goethe's expectation of a white wall coloured when seen through the prism, not only led him to his *aperçu* that a boundary is necessary in order to produce colours (where boundary means a circumscribed area, or *Bild*), he was also inclined to look for universal principles, of the subjective as well as objective world, governing the interaction of these images in the production of colour. After all, though man is 'the most important earthly object' (HA XIII, 369; §181), he is still part of this ensemble of objects – this 'farbigen Abglanz' (coloured reflection, *Faust II*, line 4727) in which all life presents itself to us, in short: nature.

Neither modern colour science nor philosophy offers a clear decision in favour of Goethe's or Newton's theory of light and colour, as the need to include the eye, the observer and various environmental factors, as well as physical properties of light below the perceptional level, is by now generally asssumed. And Goethe's theory as such is no more coherent than Newton's. If Newton dogmatically postulates 'rays', without justifying the materiality of light, Goethe dogmatically postulates secondary images whose materiality lets them act as a turbid medium. And occasionally, though maybe less often than Newton, he omits a thought or observation which would produce difficulties for his theory, for example the question of why the secondary image is shifted sometimes more, sometimes less, depending on its colour. This is at least evidence that the phenomena of refraction and of colour are not as independent of each other as Goethe wanted them to be.

However, as far as awareness of methodological issues is concerned, Goethe wins hands down. He at least provides a framework within which colour is not an occult appendix to the material world, but an integral part of it, and in which perceiver and perceived inhabit the same space. Every intentional look one takes at the world is already imbued with theory, he states in his preface. But one should theorize consciously, with 'self-awareness, with freedom, and – to use a daring expression – with irony' in order to avoid the 'kind of abstraction of which we are afraid', and to achieve a useful, lively empirical result (HA XIII, 317). We can take from this passage two subtle points. One is Goethe's admission that his own theory is just that, a theory with its characteristic blind spots, and that its results should therefore be looked upon with the same ironic distance that all individual modes of apprehension deserve. The other is that Goethe was not critical of abstraction as such, but only of a particular type of abstraction, that which does not lead back into practical life.[12]

Goethe within the history of science

There seems to be a growing consensus amongst historians of science that the division between empirical science, based on experience and experiments, and speculative Romantic *Naturphilosophie*, based on ideas, is an invention of the later nineteenth century, and the image of a misguided quasi-science which turned into real science is increasingly replaced with a much more flexible image of complex paradigm shifts.[13] From this perspective Goethe's natural investigations are simply part of the history of natural investigations.

With respect to an explanatory morphology and to a theory of the organism, Goethe's work is still relevant, precisely because the phenomena in question do not yield to a purely instrumental approach. And his *Farbenlehre* will remain significant as a monument of resistance to the absurdities of a reductionist philosophy of nature which explains phenomena by denying them independent existence and a logic of their own. His other, extremely varied writings, though often corrected in the past in their empirical detail, bear witness to a project of science and an epistemology which take nature as a hypothetical unity, including the investigator and observer. The dialectic between object and subject that follows from this acknowledges the anthropomorphic character of knowledge, and it therefore insists on continuous reflection and revision of theoretical premises.

Modern science is early on characterized by a dichotomy. On the one side, there is Goethe's understanding of Baconian science as grounded in experience as the touchstone for knowledge, on the other there is the Baconian project of domination over nature as the ultimate goal. The latter, according to Gernot Böhme, is nearing its end. It is simply no longer possible to believe, as C. P. Snow did when talking about the two cultures (that of the scientist and that of the man of letters), that a proper understanding and implementation of science and technology by non-scientific intellectuals and decision-makers will automatically lead to human and social progress. The changes in the history and philosophy of science since Snow's famous lecture in 1959 confirm this. The criticism of a historiography based on the idea that the internal cognitive development of science guarantees rationality and progress, beginning with the work of Hanson and followed by Kuhn and Feyerabend, has led to a constructivist view of science. Science is no longer seen to approximate a true representation of nature, but to construct its own objects through its conceptual and technological procedures. Competing theories are seen to be evaluated for their fit not with nature but with theoretical fashions and the policies of funding bodies. The anthropology of knowledge which has thus emerged, and which very much resembles Goethe's contextualization of scientific activity, does not amount to a complete relativism. But the empirical content of scientific knowledge is perceived to be highly mediated through the institutional practices of the state, the university and, not least, the economy, and scientists are seen as investing their work with personal, professional and traditional predilections. This development includes the role of the experiment and the laboratory in general.[14] As a result, science will be judged more and more in terms of the way it affects our being – body and mind. The kind of abstraction Goethe feared and that flourished after his death relied on a climate in which science and knowledge were in no need of justification beyond their technical applicability. In so far as today's problems are seen as inherent to the application of technology and rationalist philosophies and not just as side-effects of their misuse, there is now a need for further justification.

NOTES

1 See Michael Heidelberger, 'Wandlungstypen in den Baconischen Wissenschaften im Deutschland des frühen 19. Jahrhunderts', *Philosophia Naturalis* 20. 1 (1983), 112–26.

2 Timothy Lenoir, 'Laboratories, Medicine and Public Life in Germany 1830–1849. Ideological Roots of the Institutional Revolution', in Andrew Cunningham and Perry Williams (eds.), *The Laboratory Revolution in Medicine* (Cambridge: Cambridge University Press, 1992), pp. 14–71, p. 60.

3 For a recent attempt to revise morphology and evolutionary theory on the basis of the hydraulic nature of organisms see W. F. Gutmann, 'Constructional Principles and the Quasi-Experimental Approach to Organisms', in N. Schmidt-Kittler and K. Vogel (eds.), *Constructional Morphology and Evolution* (Berlin and Heidelberg: Springer Verlag, 1991), pp. 91–112. For a criticism of morphology under the Darwinian paradigm from a structuralist perspective, which assumes that 'pre-Darwinian morphologists [sought] a system of transformations, and ... that such a system is potentially intelligible in terms of the "laws" or "rules" responsible for its generation', see G. Webster and B. C. Goodwin, 'The origin of species: a structuralist approach', *Journal of Social and Biological Structures* 5 (1982), 15–47, p. 17.

4 *Goethe's Collected Works*, vol. XII: *Scientific Studies*, ed. and trans. Douglas Miller (Princeton University Press, 1995), p. 121.

5 See E. S. Russell, *Form and Function. A Contribution to the History of Animal Morphology* (London: John Murray, 1916) and Peter J. Bowler, *The Non-Darwinian Revolution* (Baltimore and London: Johns Hopkins University Press, 1988) for an overview and discussion of the development of morphology. For an illustration of how nineteenth-century *Bauplan* logic is now transposed onto molecular structures see Peter W. H. Holland, 'The Future of Evolutionary Developmental Biology', *Nature* 402 (Supplement), 2 Dec. 1999, 41–4. For a critical discussion of the role and the explanatory limits of geneticism see Evelyn Fox-Keller, *Refiguring Life. Metaphors of 20th Century Biology* (New York: Columbia University Press, 1995), and Richard Lewontin, *The Doctrine of DNA. Biology as Ideology* (Harmondsworth: Penguin, 1993).

6 Lenoir, 'Laboratories, Medicine and Public Life', p. 56.

7 Lynn K. Nyhart, *Biology Takes Form. Animal Morphology and the German Universities, 1800–1900* (Chicago and London: University of Chicago Press, 1995), p. 45.

8 For more detail see my 'Morphologie und Moderne: Goethes ironische Erkenntnistheorie und die Frage nach dem Organismus', in Heike Bartel and Brian

Keith-Smith (eds.), *Nachdenklicher Leichtsinn. Essays on Goethe and Goethe Reception* (New York and Lewiston: Mellen, 2000), pp. 39–55.

9 See D. L. Sepper, *Goethe contra Newton. Polemics and the Project for a New Science of Colour* (Cambridge: Cambridge University Press, 1988), pp. 129–30.

10 Goethe, *Scientific Studies*, ed. and trans. Douglas Miller, p. 165.

11 Isaac Newton, *Opticks or A Treatise of the Reflections, Refractions, Inflections & Colours of Light* (New York: Dover Publications, 1952), p. 372.

12 See D. Steuer, *Die stillen Grenzen der Theorie. Übergänge zwischen Sprache und Erfahrung bei Goethe und Wittgenstein* (Cologne, Weimar and Vienna: Böhlau, 1999).

13 See, for example, Andrew Cunningham and Nicholas Jardine (eds.), *Romanticism and the Sciences* (Cambridge: Cambridge University Press, 1990), and Stefano Poggi and Maurizio Bossi (eds.), *Romanticism in Science. Science in Europe, 1790–1840* (Dordrecht, Boston and London: Kluwer, 1994).

14 See Bruno Latour and S. Woolgar, *Laboratory Life: The Construction of Scientific Facts* (New Jersey: Princeton University Press, 1986), and Karin Knorr-Cetina, *The Manufacture of Knowledge. An Essay on the Constructivist and Contextual Nature of Science* (Oxford: Pergamon Press, 1981). Also David Gooding, Trevor Pinch and Simon Shaffer (eds.), *The Uses of Experiment. Studies in the Natural Sciences* (Cambridge: Cambridge University Press, 1989).

11

BARBARA BECKER-CANTARINO

Goethe and gender

Goethe created poetic and complex female and male characters in his key works. But because he viewed his works as 'fragments of a great confession' (HA IX, 283), biographical accounts of Goethe's relationship with women coloured the readings of his works for almost two centuries; moreover, they were often marked by a condescending attitude towards the women in Goethe's life, an exclusive focus on and a naive adoration of the poet as a great man. Goethe's Faust and his concept of the 'Eternal Feminine' were seen as the loftiest ideal of modern German man, and the poet's biography was constructed along a string of ever-fascinating sexual experiences with women. In recent decades, such hagiography has given way to spirited studies of Goethe's relationship to women, who are seen as personalities in their own right with contributions to literary culture. Feminist and gender studies have produced new readings of his female (and male) characters in their gender roles and relationships. They have started a lively debate about Goethe's representations of gender dichotomy, his sophisticated gender discourse, his negotiations of femininity, masculinity, androgyny, homoeroticism and male bonding in the patriarchal setting of his age.

Mistresses, muses and literary women

Goethe's famous love poem 'Willkommen und Abschied' (Welcome and Farewell), written during his courtship of Friederike Brion in 1770/1, is paradigmatic for Goethe's many intense relationships with women. The many short attachments were emotionally and erotically charged encounters with the other, inspiring him to poetic creation as an immediate expression of experience (*Erlebnislyrik*). There would then follow a sad farewell and lasting separation. From his mother, Frau Aja, a great storyteller in her letters, he would inherit 'die Frohnatur und Lust zu fabulieren' (her cheerful spirit and joy in story-telling, HA I, 320), but after he had left Frankfurt for Weimar in 1775 he would very rarely see her again before her lonely death in 1808. His symbiotic bond to his sister Cornelia, born only fourteen months after Johann Wolfgang, was severed when Cornelia was married in 1773 and died of depression in 1777. In his friend's fiancée, Charlotte Buff, whom Goethe met while attending the Imperial Court at Wetzlar in 1772, he encountered the sensitive, motherly woman he would immortalize in the figure of Lotte in *Die Leiden des jungen Werther* (The Sorrows of Young Werther, 1774). But unlike Werther, Goethe would go on to new adventures. His engagement to the Frankfurt patrician Lili Schönemann ended when he accepted Duke Carl August's invitation to Weimar in 1775, where soon his most famous relationship began, the platonic affair with Charlotte von Stein. The break with Frau von Stein, who inspired Goethe to great poetry and whom he immortalized in the figure of Iphigenie, came in 1788 when he returned from his Italian journey and began his liaison with Christiane Vulpius. And there were many more relationships of 'welcome and farewell' with mostly young and sexually attractive women. Most were well educated and talented, and Charlotte von Stein or Marianne von Willemer were poets in their own right even though their works were totally overshadowed if not absorbed by Goethe.

Goethe's affair with Christiane Vulpius, a lower middle-class woman whom he took into his house when she bore his (only surviving) son in 1789, became the talk of Weimar society, as did his publication of the *Römische Elegien* (Roman Elegies), in which he freely incorporated his erotic adventures in Italy. Christiane Vulpius was never accepted in court circles, nor did she take part in Goethe's social life and literary activities, but always lived in the back part of the house, the servants' quarters. Goethe came to rely on Christiane's companionship and married her in 1806 while Napoleonic troops occupied Weimar. She had efficiently organized his household affairs and supervised his large, hospitable *Haus am Frauenplan*; the marriage guaranteed ownership and legitimized his son. Christiane then fulfilled until her lonely death in 1816[1] the essential functions of the housewife and mother, important for Goethe's daily and family life, a fact he gratefully acknowledged. In 1813, on the 25th anniversary of their first meeting, Goethe dedicated the popular poem 'Gefunden' (Found) to Christiane. The folksong-like poem tells the story of finding a beautiful little flower in the shadow of the forest; when the 'Blümchen' softly protests at being broken off, the 'I' of the poem digs it up and transplants it into his garden where it continues to prosper and multiply.

In his autobiographical accounts Goethe was himself the focal point at all times in his relationships with women. But he felt less comfortable with independent, literary or artistic women, because he thought in terms of conventional gender roles of separate spheres for men and women, as Schiller had described them in his poem 'Das Lied von der Glocke' (The Song of the Bell, 1799): the man goes out into the hostile world of work, the chaste wife serves quietly within the house. Such notions of gender roles served above all as a line of demarcation for Goethe's own identity as a male; his sense of masculinity was ever-present in his poetic work. They are also reflected in contemporary natural law philosophy. In his *Grundlage des Naturrechts nach Prinzipien der Wissenschaftslehre* (1796; trans. as *The Science of Rights*), Fichte deduced the 'natural' role of the female thus: 'Woman, in making herself the means to satisfy man, gives up her personality . . . Her own dignity requires that she should give herself up entirely as she is, and live to her choice and should utterly lose herself in him.'[2] Biological sex was the scientific premise for gender difference, the division of mankind into male and female; the 'natural' state of the adult female was marriage and she was then deduced to be exclusively the male's property. The female has ceased to lead the life of an individual by becoming a part of his life; man, according to Fichte, finds the 'whole fullness of humanity' in himself, while woman can never achieve such an overview. When she is married, 'the state abandons all claim to consider the woman as a legal person . . . the husband becomes her legal guardian'.[3] In philosophical and legal terms, Fichte has reduced woman to man's property, he has taken away autonomy (as an individual and as a political person) from her, subsuming her existence under that of the male.

With the concept of the 'naturally' dependent female under male tutelage, there was no place for independent literary women in the aesthetics of German classicism, and their writings were considered dilettantish. In Goethe's and Schiller's thinking during the 1790s, dilettantism was a key concept, being an imperfect form of art that approximated but did not achieve the essence of art. The two men planned to collaborate on an essay 'On Dilettantism' which was to appear in their journal *Propyläen*, but it remained a fragmentary sketch. In the detailed outline the dilettante was defined as one who confused art with its content, was innocent and clung to the subjective. Dilettantism, they believed, was a pervasive phenomenon, and the amateurish producers of much pseudo-art were everywhere; they were mere superficial and mechanical imitators of the real art on which they fed. In this scheme of Goethe's and Schiller's, women's writing figured as a prominent example of pseudo-art, though it was in the good company of Klopstock, of Wieland's lasciviousness and Bürger's 'Geleier' (din). Most non-classical art seemed to fall under the verdict of 'dilettantism', but only in the case of women's writing was sex being used as a grouping and distinguishing characteristic. This critical standpoint devalued women's poetic production as lacking in aesthetic quality, a value judgement that influenced later literary historians as long as gender difference was perceived as it was in the age of Goethe.

In 1806 Goethe reviewed three novels by women authors for the prominent literary journal *Jenaische Allgemeine Literaturzeitung*, among them the anonymous *Bekenntnisse einer schönen Seele, von ihr selbst erzählt* (Confessions of a Beautiful Soul as Told by Herself, 1806).[4] The title alludes to Goethe's 'Beautiful Soul' whose confessions are in Book 6 of *Wilhelm Meisters Lehrjahre* (Wilhelm Meister's Apprenticeship, 1795–6). Goethe acknowledged the novel's sensibility and pleasantly entertaining character, placing it in the sphere of trivial literature. Probably assuming the author to be a man, as did many contemporaries, he wrote: 'We certainly would have preferred to title this work "Confessions of an Amazon"... For here we see a mannish woman [*Männin*]... a strict, though not unpleasant person, a virgin, a virago in the best sense whom we esteem and honour without being actually attracted by her' (WA, I, vol. XL, 375–6). Besides clearly drawing a line between this novel and his own writings, he criticized especially the heroine's independent lifestyle and her companionship with several women, which he viewed as subordination to other women (a jab at possible lesbianism). He also criticized the novel's low aesthetic quality ('nicht ganz ästhetisch', 375), and he was particularly upset about its moral implications ('sittliche Wirkung'). Thus he sternly admonished the female readers: 'She [the heroine] is neither a daughter, nor a sister, nor a beloved, nor a wife, nor a mother, and thus one cannot anticipate in her the housewife, nor the mother-in-law, nor the grandmother. Since she cannot be all by herself, has to associate with somebody and has to govern and to serve at the same time, as is woman's nature, her existence has to be that of a governess and a lady companion, not a very desirable position for a woman' (376). Goethe then recommended this book for female readers as a contrasting picture to their own lives by which they could examine their own aspirations, and he predicted that these readers would 'mostly disagree with the amazon' (377). He could perceive and, at the same time, wanted to reinforce only the dominant female role model of the beloved, wife and mother: woman as defined by her utility to the male (as beloved and wife) and to society as a whole through her biological function (as mother). This fixed role concept prevented him from even attempting to understand the novel's different value system and aesthetics. His inflexible notions about gender roles and gender differences coloured his perception of literary women and their work. Goethe criticized another of the three novelists, Caroline Paulus, whose pen name was Eleutherie Holberg, for allowing her heroine to philosophize, and worse, for finding arguments against natural law philosophy which propagated the separate spheres for male and female as 'natural' gender roles. Goethe then proceeded to set down rules for what was appropriate for the 'female pen' and strongly suggested supervision by male writers (383–4).

Goethe excluded women from an active role in aesthetic production: the female author could not be a creative genius. For Goethe, genius presupposed an autonomous subject and woman could not be such an autonomous subject because she lacked the anthropological prerequisites. She herself was beauty, served as matter and material for beauty, while the genius was merely symbolically present in the work of art as a union of reason and feeling. A genius could create, he could prescribe for nature the rules which, by way of reason, were inherent in him: the male was the creator of art, the female was his muse, his inspiration.

Goethe's sense of masculinity and his role as a male was an integral part of his aesthetics. The 'other' (the female) was of little interest to him unless she could be absorbed into his own work and be subsumed under his masculine creativity. Thus in the *West-östliche Divan* the poet Hatem sings of his beloved Suleika's poetic talents:

> Von den Dichterinnen allen
> Ist ihr eben keine gleich:
> Denn sie singt mir zu gefallen,
> Und ihr singt und liebt nur euch.
> (HA II, 74)

> Songstresses all, whoe'er ye be,
> None equals her who soars above.
> For she does sing to pleasure me,
> You but yourselves can sing and love.

Ironically, Marianne von Willemer's fine poems were submerged into Goethe's *Divan* collection. For Goethe and his age, literary women were to serve as muses, not to write as independently creative individuals. If they were to write, they had better stay within the confines of the 'female pen', which nineteenth-century critics would segregate into 'women's literature'.

Gender politics and male bonding: from *Götz* to *Hermann und Dorothea*

The Western literary tradition knew two basic, diametrically opposed female character types: Eve, the vehicle of misogyny, and the idolized Mary figure. Imbued with the moral and religious values of the Jewish-Christian tradition, women were either evil, witch-like, destructive creatures or pious, loveable heroines. While bourgeois drama and Lessing provided models for 'mixed', psychologically more realistic characters, Goethe in his first drama

Götz von Berlichingen (1771) juxtaposed the ambitious social climber Adelheid, whom he paired with the fickle weakling Weislingen, to the pure, loving Elisabeth, Götz's loyal wife and mother of his son. Yet the drama's action centres on a large, male cast and a male desire to bond with other men. The women are ornamental, empathetic creatures who uphold the moral standards and intuitively sense oncoming disaster without being able to avert it. Fighting for justice and the world of politics are clearly the men's domain, and evil, ambitious Adelheid dares to dabble in it, her political intrigue bringing about her own and others' destruction.

Goethe experimented with the sentimental young woman as a lovable and loving heroine closely attached to and supportive of a man: examples are Klärchen in *Egmont* (1787), Lotte in *Werther*, Marie in *Clavigo* (1774), or Stella and Cäcilie in *Stella* (1775). Goethe's sentimental heroine, whose literary models were figures such as Richardson's Clarissa, Rousseau's Héloise, and Sophie La Roche's Sophie Sternheim, was steeped in love and erotic entanglement with the opposite (never her own) sex, while social circumstances – class difference, a betrothal, a fickle lover – complicated the plot and led to the demise of the heroine (*Clavigo, Stella*). While Goethe's figures stayed within the traditional gender roles and relationships, which greatly narrowed women's actions, they played out a gentle, sentimental 'battle of the sexes', a drama of power, loyalty, betrayal, deceit, erotic attraction, genuine feelings, love, sacrifice and selflessness. In his early works, Goethe shifted the comedy of manners into a comedy of gender, an exploratory play with gender relations expressed as sentiments, love and sexuality.

In *Iphigenie auf Tauris* Goethe moved away from such playfulness to philosophical concepts. Iphigenie – the lonely woman in the play – is no longer sexually engaged with men but in Goethe's rewriting of the myth reconciles the warring males. Abducted to the desolate island of Tauris by the goddess Diana when her father was to sacrifice her for victory in the Trojan War, Iphigenie has served as priestess and persuaded King Thoas to abolish blood sacrifice. When Thoas wants to renew the ancient custom and orders the sacrifice of two strangers, Iphigenie refuses and tells the truth: the strangers are her own brother Orest and his companion. Thoas grudgingly lets them go. Trusting in humanity, Iphigenie can break the spell of warfare among nations and generations. It is also a story of ending bloody gender battles (mother Klytemnaestra had taken a lover in her husband's absence and had slain the latter upon his return; son Orest had avenged his father by killing his mother, then was pursued by the Furies in revenge for his matricide). Iphigenie's sisterly, feminized act of trust, truth and courage ends the inherited gender wars, but at a price: as Iphigenie refuses to marry Thoas, she refuses the bond to the other sex (and with it family, and children). Iphigenie stands apart from the sphere of male action; as a priestess she leads a pure life in a religious realm. Goethe later called his Iphigenie 'verteufelt human' (devilishly human),[5] recognizing the pitfalls of idealization: Iphigenie is the virgin priestess who appears superhuman, more an allegory of humanity than a woman of flesh and blood. She preserves her purity throughout the play, refusing the older, fatherly Thoas's marriage proposal as well as the plea of Pylades, her brother's friend, for help in escaping Thoas. As if to avoid incestuous relationships, she suppresses her own desires in order as it were to purify Orest, Thoas and herself. Gender has been purged of sexual desire, power struggle and violence; the monstrous genealogy of her forefathers has been expunged. At what price? Desire, love, sexuality, procreation have given way to an almost autonomous woman, a sister, a sterile priestess.

A few years later in his seminal novel *Wilhelm Meisters Lehrjahre*, Goethe created a large number of female figures, all of whom owe their significance in the novel to their relationship with Wilhelm and his world. The novel thrives on an intricately designed gender system, first the less stringent gender order of the actors' world, then the order of separate spheres in the bourgeois society dominated by the secret Society of the Tower. This all-male Society gradually surfaces as the propelling social order through which Goethe gives patriarchy a voice in this fictional world.

A highpoint is the ceremonial episode in which Wilhelm is finally initiated into the Society. Here he meets his father's spirit and is authenticated in his paternity. Wilhelm wanders between and comes to fill both roles, father and son: this ceremonial scene, reminiscent of a Masonic initiation rite, plays out the ritual of patriarchy. The scene begins with former strangers (now turned friendly companions) revealing their identity as members of the Society, and explaining their guiding role in Wilhelm's life. Then the old King of Denmark – we are immediately reminded of Wilhelm's earlier performance of Hamlet and his fateful encounter with the king's ghost who had proclaimed himself to be his father's – appears before Wilhelm: ' "I am your father's ghost", said the figure in the frame, "and I depart in peace, for all I wished for you has been fulfilled more than I myself could imagine . . . Farewell, and remember me when you partake of what I have prepared for you"'(HA VII, 495). This meeting of son and father, a first climax in this ritualistic scene, signals a fruitful relationship, a sort of blessing from the father, a passing on of the father's heritage to the son. Now the Abbé, Wilhelm's guiding, helpful mentor and a father surrogate, hands him his 'Certificate of Apprenticeship', a collection of allegorical, moralistic aphorisms to guide Wilhelm, the 'true student' of art and life, in his advancement to the stage of 'Meister' (master). Master and father (with their respective corollaries of student and son) are key concepts of patriarchy, embodying power as well as the promise of (individual) achievement, of continuity of the bloodline and (material, artistic, intellectual) inheritance. Male bonding and male desire, which overcome generational conflicts, rivalries and competitive confrontations, are celebrated in this Goethean vision of Wilhelm's rite of passage into manhood, into the all-male Society of the Tower.

There is another important aspect to this rite of passage into patriarchy: Wilhelm's coming into fatherhood. In a matter 'that is close to [Wilhelm's] heart and should be so' – the heart being a reference to the emotional, personal, essentialist aspect of the hero's being – Wilhelm asks the right question: ' "Very well, then! You strange wise men, whose sight can pierce so many mysteries, tell me if you will: is Felix really my son?" "Praise be to you for asking that question!" exclaimed the Abbé, clapping his hands with joy. "Felix is your son! I swear it by all our most sacred mysteries. Felix is your son, and in spirit his deceased mother was not unworthy of you. Take unto yourself this lovely child from our hands, turn around and dare to be happy" '(HA VII, 497).

Thus Wilhelm receives his son from the hands of the patriarchal order and he explicitly acknowledges this confirmation of his paternity. For when Felix appears this very moment on the scene, 'his father rushed towards him, folded him in his arms and pressed him to his heart. "Yes, oh yes," said Wilhelm, "you are indeed mine! What a gift this is from Heaven that I have to thank my friends for. Where have you come from at this moment, my child?" "Don't ask," said the Abbé. "Hail to you young man. Your apprenticeship is completed, Nature has given you your freedom" ' (HA VII, 407). Nature has legitimized Wilhelm, the male order has confirmed his (biological) paternity.

This is, indeed, a curious appropriation of procreative labour by the patriarchal Society of the Tower, for in the politics of reproduction the natural mother has conveniently been obliterated. We recall that Felix was the illegitimate child of the actress Mariane, Wilhelm's first great love, whom he had deserted before she bore 'his' son, believing her to be unfaithful and promiscuous. Mariane, the mother, fades from the narrative and eventually dies. But 'fate' would have it that Wilhelm meets the orphan Felix and befriends him like a father. Yet Wilhelm cannot quite bring himself to believe the old servant woman's story assuring him of his paternity – women's, especially old women's stories are unreliable, appear mysterious and untrustworthy to the male hero. Only his male mentors of the Society can speak the truth.

In the initiation ritual of the Society of the Tower, history is made symbolic, for rituals are not merely empty or hollow but inscribe and bestow meaning. As a living symbol of patriarchy, the Society reconfirms Wilhelm's paternity and thus authorizes his masculinity. This rite of passage signifies both a climactic fulfilment (being assured of biological progeny) and a mission for his future (raising his son). Wilhelm has become a worthy link in the eternal chain of patriarchy. The mother's procreative role is taken over by the patriarchal order and bestowed upon Wilhelm. Mothers (notably Wilhelm's own) are absent from this ritual, as women are excluded from the Society. Women as autonomous subjects (human subjects in the way male individuals are conceived) are written out of this order, assigned a subordinate role in the novel's text. For women are domesticated into useful, cooperative females subordinate to the needs of males.

The women in *Wilhelm Meister* totally lack the men's inner connection, bonding and organized society. They are a colourful array of socially and individually differing women, and represent aspects of what was considered traditional femininity in the eighteenth century such as love, fertility and sexuality (the actress Mariane bears Wilhelm's child, but in an affair out of wedlock); love, sentimentality, and artistic dilettantism (the actress Aurelie dies of a broken heart and of confusing subjectivity with art); love, pleasure, and sensuality (Philine freely acts out her sexual desires); and love, creativity and poetry (Mignon). Mignon is of unstable gender, a boyish young girl, at first abused by her adopted father, then sexually attracted and slavishly attached to Wilhelm, who rescued her by buying her. 'Mignon' was also the French word for the favourite boy among aristocrats of the Rococo era, and Goethe thinly disguised other sexual constellations, including child abuse and pederasty, in this figure, who upsets the otherwise neatly separated spheres of male and female. Mignon aspires to maleness and to an incestuous symbiosis with her father-substitute Wilhelm, but (in the realistic part of the novel) refuses to accept her biological change into a woman and dies. The mysterious Mignon also embodies aspects of poetic creativity and genius, here closely linked to a homoerotic desire, which, however, fades away and dies in the sexually sober and normative second part and is replaced by Wilhelm's marriage.

The 'Confessions of a Beautiful Soul' serve as a transition to a somewhat changed, more orderly gender system firmly under patriarchal control in part two of the novel. The Beautiful Soul's life-story consoles dying Aurelie and prepares Wilhelm for introduction into life in bourgeois society (or more accurately, the gentry), after he has left the theatre, the world of art and illusion. In the manuscript the 'Beautiful Soul' tells of her turn to God, leaving profane love behind, and of intentionally remaining unmarried and cultivating her pious soul; but in the end she is not allowed to become the guardian of her orphaned nephew and niece (who later turn out to be Lothario and Natalie). The 'Beautiful Soul' is dead, her lesson is one of spiritual guidance and quietude, but her life is not a role model for the novel's women. Rather, she represents a sterile woman who has refused to assume her female role as beloved and mother subjected to the father/husband. The novel's surface narrative integrates her in her religious devotion only as beautiful imago, that is to say as a dead saint – Wilhelm sees her picture in Natalie's house and recognizes her – while the deep structure of the continuing narrative eliminates her as a female role model, casting her as a barren, undomesticated and potentially castrating female.

For all the women characters in the second half of *Wilhelm Meister* appear to have been domesticated: Therese is dedicated to educating children, Natalie becomes Wilhelm's wife, and even coquettish Philine arrives on the scene married and pregnant. Subverting this pattern, Mignon's mysterious story is finally unravelled and she must die. With all the irony in the narrative style, there is a noticeable shift towards the orderly gender division in bourgeois society (though the story is set mostly on country estates).

During the decade following the French Revolution, Goethe joined the chorus of conservatives who wanted to save the country from the revolutionary upheavals by strengthening the family unit and asserting their maleness as head of the household. His epic *Hermann und Dorothea* (1797) likewise propounded a patriarchal family idyll. Well-to-do Hermann takes a poor refugee girl into his house after a short encounter with her homeless companions, who are fleeing the horrors of the French Revolution. She believes herself to have been hired as a maid, but the captivated Hermann elevates her against his father's objections to be his bride, as he can point to her virtues and capacity for work in the household. Dorothea is the model mother/housewife who fits the proverbial line: 'Dienen lerne beizeiten das Weib, nach seiner Bestimmung' (Women should learn in their youth that fate has designed them for service, HA II, 494). She joyfully accepts her role as maid/housewife/beloved, just as Hermann rejoices in his newfound ownership of his bride: 'Du bist mein: nun ist das Meine meiner als jemals' (You are mine: now that which is mine is mine more than ever, HA II, 516). With this nationalistic epic – the name Hermann harks back to Germany's founding hero, the Teutonic Hermann – Goethe celebrated gender roles: Dorothea – 'god's gift' expelled from revolutionary France – becomes the model, modest mother/housewife, property of Hermann and contributor to his wealth, business and ownership. Meanwhile, Hermann explicitly rejects a 'modern', educated woman who can play the piano, knows how to dance, and has literary interests. Goethe's message was in consonance with what other poets of the 1790s such as Schiller, Herder, or Johann Heinrich Voß were preaching. The success of *Hermann und Dorothea* on publication surpassed even that of *Werther*, and it remained the most widely read work among the German bourgeoisie in the nineteenth century.

Gretchen between witch and infanticide: the patriarchal Faustian world and the 'eternal feminine'

Generations of readers and critics of *Faust I* (1808) have seen in Gretchen a sign of selfless, idealized femininity, who can ultimately redeem Faust. But when we look at the drama's gender system, Gretchen's story appears to be cast as one of seductive and (self-)destructive female sexuality, anchored in the symbolic witch-scenes and the sexual revelry of the Walpurgis Night. It is also a story of infanticide (excluded from the representational level), and of confinement in the patriarchal 'Faustian world'. Gretchen's supposedly 'female' voice is, indeed, quite different from Faust's eloquent self-presentation in soliloquies and dialogue; but it is a voice shaped and controlled by Goethe according to late eighteenth-century notions of gender. Goethe imagined a celebration of patriarchy in an atavistic interpretation of woman's sexuality and body, while concurrently scripting a seemingly progressive, universal significance for his Faustian man and world.

The 'Witch's Kitchen' is intimately linked to notions of gender. The witch's brew, which instantly rejuvenates Faust to make him both appealing to and desirous of woman, causes him to confuse carnal desire and enjoyment (the realm of the body) with love and sublime beauty (the realm of the mind). The beautiful, nude female image in the witch's magic mirror suggests woman's connection to the realm of the witch, the link being her body, the site of her sexual power, ostensibly a locus for male confusion and disempowerment. The illusion both stimulates and (much later) elevates Faust. It is this dualistic, powerful image of the female – a refraction of the Eve/Mary dichotomy – which the magic mirror presents and which the 'Witch's Kitchen' (Goethe's addition to the Faust legend, as is the Gretchen story) inscribes into Faust's soul or universe. With this image before him, Faust immediately afterwards encounters and courts Gretchen.

As the seduced innocent, Gretchen serves as a representation of male power and prerogatives over the female body, as a sign of *his* redemption. As a child-murderess she becomes a prisoner of her procreative role. Thus she is doomed in every aspect of her own possible being: as a woman, lover and mother. Her infanticide surfaces only covertly in two symbolic visions in the 'Dungeon' scene, when she is imprisoned awaiting public execution. Gretchen is no longer able to distinguish between her fantasies and reality, between past, present and future; she appears helpless and insane in terms of the realistic world, yet for Faust, Gretchen now represents a possible lethal threat, a past he desires to forget in order to proceed with his exploration of life and self. In the opening of Part II, Faust will reappear, purged and refreshed by a long sleep, and will continue his symbolic journey. Not so Gretchen. In killing her own child, she has forfeited her right to live in this world; as infanticide she is punished by society in kind for her crime. Her death, demanded within Faust's patriarchal world, is an act of ultimate self-destruction, of killing her child and giving herself up as a sacrifice for her lover, who can thereby go free and, more important, continue experiencing life. Thus Gretchen's active role in this Faustian world is to destroy herself and her child, where ironically childbearing is the 'natural' *raison d'être* of woman. Gretchen then atones for this crime and self-annihilation as a woman by accepting society's punishment: death by execution, which, in the religious connotations of the drama (introduced by the Lord's appearance in 'Prologue in Heaven') signifies deliverance to the Father. Her death sentence and her final willing acceptance of her fate clear the way for Faust to continue his creative experimentation with life without being burdened by Gretchen's 'small world'. Faust has, as it were, incorporated woman's story into his own.

Gretchen's destruction (that of mother and child) merely prompts a change in the medium of the drama; the realistic setting and the philosophical, magical and theological discourse that informs much of *Faust I* give way to a vast symbolic and poetic panorama in Part II. Here woman is transformed into an aesthetic and mythic mode, culminating in the abstraction of the 'Eternal Feminine'. Like the Mothers, the guardians of life albeit living in the underworld, and Helen of Troy, everlasting art and beauty,[6] the 'Eternal Feminine' is a construct, a male fantasy of man's own creativity. In the much-quoted final lines of *Faust II*, 'Das Ewig-Weibliche / Zieht uns hinan' (the Eternal Feminine leads us on), a feminine maternal principle[7] – whatever that might be – has become an aesthetic or religious *medium* for Faust's transcendence into a higher world, just as Gretchen in Part I was a 'helpmate' for man's redemption.

When critics claim general truthfulness to life for the *Weltanschauung* in the *Faust* drama, this claim of universality needs to be qualified: it is an androcentric, patriarchal view of an equally patriarchal text with a well-defined gender dichotomy. Not only does the text centre on Faust's views, aspirations, progress and growth, it also employs the female as subservient, instrumental and secondary, as conceived for male interests. Such an appropriation signifies an assertion of male power: woman's creative potential, childbirth, has been taken away and transposed onto a seemingly voluntary self-sacrifice of the female for the male, for *his* redemption. In the reduction of woman to those elements which remain subservient to and controllable by male interests lies the ultimate conquest, destruction and exclusion of her procreative, life-giving function. 'Power', Foucault remarks with reference to the sovereign's patriarchal power, 'was essentially a right of seizure; of things, of bodies, and ultimately life itself; it culminated in the privilege to seize hold of life in order to suppress it'.[8] Such a patriarchal power moulds Faust's encounter with Gretchen and is inscribed into the imaging of the female in *Faust*. Gretchen's story is complex and in its patriarchal version depressingly perceptive of what Goethe scholars have aptly called the deepest drives of western civilization.

Only fairly recently in the history of two hundred years of Goethe scholarship has feminist criticism opened up the way to read patriarchy in Goethe and the culture and literature of his age. The *Faust* drama can be regarded as Goethe's most sophisticated and final word on the subject of patriarchy. It is a concept which figures as an unconscious as well as at times explicit idea in his writings. The dimension of gender looms large in the age of Goethe. His poetic imagination of male–female relations, male and female characters, and masculinity and femininity are shaped by his notions of patriarchy, gender roles and hierarchy. Feminist theory and gender studies have enabled us to view Goethe and his writings with new eyes and to discover layers of meaning obscured by hagiographic interpretations. Only a great artist like Goethe can stand the test of changing readers' interests and critical attitudes and only great works yield new levels of meaning and pleasure for the reader and critic.

NOTES

1 After many travels and absences during the last decade of her life, Goethe never visited his wife during her severe illness, did not take his leave of her and did not attend her funeral. See Sigrid Damm's meticulously researched bestseller *Christiane und Goethe. Eine Recherche* (Frankfurt am Main: Insel Verlag, 1998).

2 *The Science of Rights*, translated by A. E. Kroeger (New York: Harper and Row, 1989), p. 401.

3 Ibid., p. 418.

4 The novel had appeared anonymously at Friedrich Unger's in Berlin; the author was in fact the publisher's first wife Friederike Helene (1754–1813), a well-known novelist and translator.

5 In a letter to Schiller of 19 January 1802, HA VIII, 405. The meaning of 'verteufelt human' has been debated: contemporaries took it to mean 'exceedingly human' and gave Iphigenie model status; it could be a negation of the possibility of any humane action; and it could be taken literally as referring to the play's non-Christian setting and mentality.

6 Wilhelm Emrich, *Die Symbolik von Faust II. Sinn und Vorformen* (Bonn: Athenäum, 1957), 2nd edn, p. 325.

7 Such terminology can unfortunately still be found in the commentary of the Frank-furter Ausgabe (FA I, vol. VII/2, 816–17). See also the subjective and uncritical reading in Erich Neumann, *Das Ewig-Weibliche in Goethes Faust* (Heidelberg: Winter, 1985), p. 306.

8 Michel Foucault, *The History of Sexuality*, trans. Robert Hurley (New York: Random House, 1980), vol. I: *An Introduction*, p. 104.

12

BEATE ALLERT

Goethe and the visual arts

The visual arts were for Goethe a subject of intense interest and concern. His work on them is not restricted to the writings on art and art theory collected in the five relevant volumes of the Frankfurt edition (FA I, vols. XVIII–XXII); it also includes drawings, sketches, colour plates, copper engravings, illustrations to his theatre productions, portraits and scientific illustrations. Over his lifetime he produced an enormous body of texts on visual art, architecture, sculpture and painting. He knew personally many of the most talented artists of his time and had an intimate knowledge of much western and later also oriental art history. As a result of his travels in Italy and throughout Europe, he became acquainted with numerous prominent art experts, and through his initiatives as publisher, art critic and administrator he tried to promote certain artistic ideals and to influence the content and spectrum of ongoing artistic endeavours. He recommended travel to Greece, to the ruins of Paestum in Italy, and across Sicily in order that people might participate in his insights into the aesthetics of classicism, yet he also drew attention to the importance of local history as documented in both high art and popular culture, and his own literary work liberally mixes colourful scenes from the carnival and the marketplace, local history and everyday life.

Better known himself as an art collector and an art critic than as an artist, Goethe experimented with new approaches to visual art and created a new awareness of the importance of motion and colour in the various processes of seeing. In his optical studies he explored new methods of visualization and used these insights in his art criticism and stage directing. He thought of images as living organisms and of art history as an incomplete process that requires the active participation of the viewers and readers. He made a conscious effort to break down the binaries of artist and art critic, production and reception of a work of art, and thus is a pioneer in questioning certain culturally ingrained theoretical assumptions about such divisions and about the aesthetic process, which in his view must be understood in interactive and subject-related rather than in any fixed terms. No description, he argued, could ever do justice to experiencing an artwork. He worked with engraving, etching, watercolours, pencil, ink and oil, and carefully studied numerous techniques and artistic media. In order to gain a deeper understanding of the artists' subject matter, he often turned to the natural sciences. For him nature and art history existed in a complementary or dialogic relationship. He linked seeing with other sense perceptions such as the tactile, thereby questioning the splitting of senses he perceived in the dominant discourse on seeing in his own time and culture, the Cartesian scopic regime and Newtonian science. Though sceptical of theory, he could not avoid theorizing, and his discourse on visuality and multi-sensory perception provides insights that are still important for contemporary theoretical debates on the visual.

Goethe's approach to the visual arts was shaped by many influences, including his father's art collection and his various instructors. From 1758 to 1761 he had engraving lessons from Johann Michael Eben, in 1765 painting instruction from Friedrich Oeser, teacher of the great art historian Johann Joachim Winckelmann, at the Academy in Pleißenburg; in 1768 he learned etching techniques from Johann Michael Stock in Leipzig, the year of his first visit to the Johanneum in Dresden where he became keenly aware of Dutch art. The following year he went to the 'Mannheimer Antikensaal' where he first saw a copy of the Laocoon group, a sculpture of a father and his sons being attacked by monstrous snakes. In May 1770 he attended an exhibition of Gobelin tapestries based on the patterns by Raphael. Continuing his legal studies the same year in Strasbourg, he documented in 'Von deutscher Baukunst' (On German Architecture) the lasting impression made by the city's Minster. He also met Johann Gottfried Herder at this time. The idea of art as an expansion of one's own sense perceptions became formative to his critical approach. In 1774 he met Johann Caspar Lavater who involved him in the study of portraits, though Lavater avoided the intricate related questions concerning the problematic relations between inner and outer features of a character, the construction of social norms, and cultural diversity. From the beginning the complexity of Goethe's discourse on the visual makes any narrative about it fragile and framed in ways that may not do justice to his dynamic contributions on verbal–visual relations.

Goethe's work on the visual is conventionally divided into four distinct periods. The first, 1749–86, covers his early years, the important breakthrough to the Storm and Stress movement, and his first decade in Weimar. The second period, 1786–98, involves his travels to Italy and the works associated with the move from Storm and Stress towards the formation of 'Weimar Classicism' ('Weimarer Klassik'). The third period, 1798–1805, is considered the peak of Goethe's classical production. It is associated also with the failed *Propyläen* (Propylaea) venture, which was a collaborative effort – involving Goethe, Johann Heinrich Meyer, Wilhelm von Humboldt, Karoline von Humboldt and Schiller – to establish a journal and cultural centre to enhance productivity among visual artists. The fourth period, 1805–32, covers the time from Schiller's death. Goethe's work on the visual finds expression in *Über Kunst und Altertum* (On Art and Antiquity), a journal that consists of a very large body of texts by Goethe, Meyer, Humboldt and others. There are art-historical essays, notes, drafts, letters, poems and sketches. There are also documents concerning art collections, for example a collection of precious gems by the Dutch philosopher and art critic Franz Hemsterhuis, and transactions related to it. There is an elaborate and at the time surprising commentary on Johann Heinrich Wilhelm Tischbein's cycle of idylls, a collection of forty-five pictures by the painter, whom Goethe had met many years earlier in Italy. In order to do justice to the question of the development of Goethe's thinking on art, one must also consider all the late works, including *Die Wahlverwandtschaften* (Elective Affinities), *Faust II*, and especially his *Farbenlehre* (Theory of Colour) with its shift from optics to chromatics.

This periodization is not without its difficulties. There are debates on whether Goethe's Italian and post-Italian classicism differed from eighteenth-century neoclassicism, or represented a distinct position of 'Deutsche Klassik', whether the material in the *Italienische Reise* written after 1805 reflects only some modifications to Goethe's classical approach to art, or if this work documents actual counter-classical tendencies. Goethe's writings after Schiller's death or beginning with *West-östlicher Divan* and his intensified interest in early German painting after 1814 also indicate a move away from classical ideals. That year he first became familiar with the collection of medieval and Dutch art assembled by the brothers Boisserée in Heidelberg and after a second visit in 1816, he reported enthusiastically on the collection in *Über Kunst und Altertum* (FA I, vol. xx, 70–98).

The so-called 'Helen act' in *Faust II* also plays a key role in this debate on counter-classical tendencies. During his 'high classical' period around 1800 Goethe was doubtful how his vision of Helen as the noblest embodiment of beauty could be realized in the context of the Faust drama, but after 1810 he saw the Middle Ages in a new light and had a more differentiated understanding of antiquity, so that, in contrast to his earlier version, he later emphasized the distant otherness in the Greek archaic image and in the language of the Helen figure.[1] According to Richard Alewyn it is a 'pathos of distance' that characterizes the conception of the revised version of 1826/7,[2] to which Goethe first gave the title 'Helena, klassisch-romantische Phantasmagorie', perhaps indicating a reconciliation between ancient and modern and even a mediation between Weimar Classicism and Romanticism.

While numerous scholars have emphasized the various distinctions outlined above and discussed the changing movements that Goethe initiated
and established, others have challenged chronological linearity as the exclusive or even a relevant structuring device. They address instead the multiple
voices coexisting in Goethe's work, including his paintings, and consider
the tensions in his dynamic oeuvre as analogous to those present in a living
organism or artistic performance. Numerous critics have recently drawn attention to Goethe's strategies of evasion. There are elements that do not
fit any monocausal or centripetal pattern of imagination and argumenta-
tion in his work. Scholars inspired by his *Farbenlehre* (Arthur Zajonk and
others) favour an approach according to which opposites should no longer be
viewed as mutually exclusive but rather as complementary. Goethe's concept
of after-images (which explores what one sees with the eyes closed and how
these images result from the colours previously seen) implies that colours
interact dynamically in the various processes of visual perception and that
modes of perception in general are inseparable from what is actually seen, a
process which was important to Nietzsche's interactive concept of truth and
which still engages critics interested in Gestalt psychology, phenomenology
and cognition. Goethe's work from this perspective is one of simultaneously
coexisting diverse levels of discourse and his encounter with the visual poses
challenging methodological and theoretical questions that go far beyond the
immediate concerns of Goethe reception.

Goethe's productions as a visual artist have recently attracted new attention and become easily accessible in print.[3] These works used to be neglected
in Goethe scholarship, although Goethe worked very hard to become not
only a poet but also a painter and in doing so to challenge the traditional
hierarchy among the verbal and the visual. He based his aesthetic writings
on a heightened awareness of sense perceptions and a new approach to visuality. His contributions as practitioner of the visual arts range from simple
pencil sketches to coloured etchings which he extravagantly mounted in gold
frames, from casual notebook drawings to stylized products of self-conscious
art; they include many portraits, landscape paintings, and illustrations to scientific studies. Adaptations of his theory of metamorphosis and its influence
on visual art of the nineteenth and twentieth centuries have recently been examined by Christa Lichtenstern, who has linked his work with such artists
as Paul Klee, Willi Baumeister, Henry Moore, Salvador Dali, and André
Masson.[4] Despite his extensive travels, Goethe did not personally know
some of the painters and individual works that are perhaps considered the
most important today.[5] He lived in Rome for months but never met Canova.
And because he never went to Paris, when discussing works of art based there
he had to rely on reproductions and the judgement of others. He never saw

any of Jacques-Louis David's works in the original although he may have had the opportunity to do so, and he may not have had first-hand knowledge of the output of Goya and Turner.[6] When he first visited the Johanneum in Dresden in 1768, he almost overlooked the Italian masters and ignored the precious collection from antiquity. Furthermore, Goethe was disappointed with his own achievements as an aspiring painter. Though he found painting often much more compelling and personally necessary than writing, he always kept a critical distance from his somewhat sobering achievements in the visual arts. But this makes his contributions as a painter and art critic no less important or interesting, and perhaps even more likeable, particularly if we look at some of his writings that can be interpreted beyond the level of the author's explicit intentions.

Architecture, sculpture, painting, style

Goethe's work on architecture is best illustrated with reference to his essay 'Von deutscher Baukunst' (1772). It has been considered the manifesto of the Storm and Stress movement, advocating freedom of art over restrictive rules, the artist as genius, and the artwork as a live organism, always in process. Goethe tried to visualize the building he saw, the Strasbourg Minster, from its inception by the first architect who began building it through all the periods of restoration and reconstruction. He compared this formative process of reconstruction in the realm of culture with growth in nature, and made the study of history and science integral to his art-theoretical pursuits. He established an 'aesthetics of genius' (*Genieästhetik*) that no longer adhered to the normative poetics of the time but offered a new sense of freedom to the artist who creates his own world. In contrast to the contemporary Rococo with its emphasis on an aesthetics of ornament, he rejected redundant 'Schnörkel- und Muschelwesen' (curlicues and shell-like ornamentations) and favoured more basic and dynamic lines. At the same time, he invented an 'aesthetics of production' (*Produktionsästhetik*) that gave the viewer or recipient of an artwork an active role in the construction of its meaning. Also, he promoted art history against its own traditional methodology: instead of analyzing a work of art to the point of fragmentation, Goethe proposed the reconstruction of the work in the direction of what he called a living 'whole'. He developed a model of reading a building, or an approach to seeing artworks and images, which is not assertoric, and which is neither intrusive nor controlling. He thus anticipates an aletheic approach to seeing, that is, one that does not isolate what is seen from its context and cannot be conceptualized in terms of subject/object binaries. Goethe can be linked with Merleau-Ponty and phenomenology in his critique of what is considered the tyranny of a dominant controlling gaze and in emphasizing the importance of the viewer's own positioning in relation to what is seen.[7]

Experiencing the Strasbourg Minster became formative to Goethe's approach not only to visual art but to all poetic writing. He thought of its columns as majestic trees (FA I, vol. XVIII, 113), thus suggesting art as a second nature in an ongoing process of construction and reconstruction. By this he meant not a mimetic reproduction of what already exists in nature, but the creation of something artistic yet in tune with nature's perfect sensibility and capacity for change. His essay is on one level a hymn to Erwin von Steinbach (d. 1318), principal architect of the Minster, yet on another level it is devoted to all talented architects, inventors and creators. In order to draw attention to the dynamics mediated, the life itself, he suggested a type of language similar to Gothic architecture, a term that gained new meaning in Goethe's context. Before Goethe, the word 'Gothisch' was used in a pejorative way and had negative connotations in German art history. Goethe argued that the term had made him expect something completely different from what he actually experienced when he saw the Minster, namely a 'deformed, ungroomed monster' (FA I, vol. XVIII, 114), yet what he saw was the completely harmonious sum of a thousand details that together formed a 'Gestalt', a body of art with its own integral characteristic features, its own life. He suggested on the basis of his own experience that the term 'Gothic' should now be associated with 'German architecture', a notion that became the source of much critical debate before it was eventually rejected. But it explains why 'Von deutscher Baukunst' is variously translated into English as 'On German Architecture' or 'On Gothic Architecture'.

The essay, whose genesis was long and complicated, was first published anonymously in November 1772 in Frankfurt, then the following year under the title 'Von deutscher Baukunst. D.M. Ervini a Steinbach'. In the same year Herder published it along with his own critical comments in his collection *Von Deutscher Art und Kunst: Einige fliegende Blätter* (Of the German Way and Art: Some Flyers). Many years later, in *Über Kunst und Altertum*, Goethe returned to the topic, first with the 1817 essay, 'Alt-Deutsche Baukunst' (Old-German Architecture) and later in 1823 with a second 'Von deutscher Baukunst'. This complicated publication history of interrelated material is exemplary in revealing multiple layers of intertextuality. Today even the 1773 essay is no longer interpreted just as a manifesto of the Storm and Stress movement but also as a document that reflects features of Weimar Classicism, for example in the definite traces of Winckelmann's dictum of 'edle Einfalt' (noble simplicity) and 'stille Größe' (silent greatness).

Other essays, such as 'Von Arabesken' (On Arabesques) and 'Baukunst' (Architecture), reflect Goethe's approach to architecture not only in terms of ocularcentrism, as something that should look good, but also with respect to other sense perceptions. In the 1795 'Baukunst' he emphasized that architecture is not primarily for the eyes but for all senses involved in body motions, comparing the pleasant sensation one may have dancing to a rhythm with the feeling one should experience when entering a well-built house, even with one's eyes closed (FA I, vol. XVIII, 368). His attempts to de-prioritize seeing in favour of multi-sensorial perception imply important aspects of cultural criticism that have only recently begun to emerge in Goethe scholarship.

Goethe's work on sculpture was similarly pathbreaking in terms of visual theory. He considered the human body as the most desirable object/subject of art and dissolved the object/subject binary, especially in his 1798 essay 'Über Laokoon' (On Laocoon). Experts of Goethe's time debated the literary traditions of the myth behind the famous sculpture. That was not of much interest to Goethe, who believed that everything an artwork meant was actually presented within it. He was aware of the contemporary debate over whether Laocoon was screaming or not. In 1755 Winckelmann had given the classicist's answer in arguing for silence through application of his 'noble simplicity' and 'silent greatness'. Goethe followed Winckelmann's idealistic account, but added a new awareness of visual effects such as light, dawn, distance, motion, and opening and closing of the eyes when seeing the sculpture.

Goethe's commentary on Laocoon begins with the statement that a real artwork – like a work of nature – remains beyond the grasp of reason, though it can be seen or felt and has a definite effect on the senses. Nor can its essence be expressed in words. Goethe explains that he does not want to write about the sculpture as if the verbal could reproduce the visual; his commentary should be understood in addition to the sculpture and not as a replacement for it. He also argues that if one wants to speak about one excellent piece of art, one must speak about art in general, for each artwork contains all of art. And all 'high' works of art represent human nature. Goethe avoids notions of the divine and of evil and anything not 'present' in the actual artwork. He is not interested in the literary sources, comments and legends surrounding the Laocoon sculpture and he argues that it represents nothing but a father with his two sons in danger of being killed. He notices that the three figures express various degrees of fear and suffering and that together they represent a 'tragic idyll' (FA I, vol. XVIII, 493), well-balanced and harmonious. As many of his interpretations of visual art suggest, he seems to have a tendency to avoid the topic of death, and Goethe often called images harmonious which for many other observers were not.

What makes Goethe's approach even more interesting is that he also proposes a choreography of seeing. He suggests that one should stand at a distance from the Laocoon group and close, open, and then close one's eyes again. This procedure will have the effect of bringing the statue to life, as if the motion that was frozen in the moment of the sculpture could visually continue without interruption. As if he is contributing to his studies of after-images, which play an important role in his *Farbenlehre* (where he elaborates on what is seen with the eyes closed in relation to the colours seen just before closing them), he offers an approach to reading the Laocoon sculpture in terms of motion and experimentation, an approach characterized by dynamic relations between subject and object, to the extent of dissolving these binaries by an open-ended process of seeing and by involving the viewer actively in the construction of meaning. Goethe also points out that there is a combination of action and passion, of conflicting emotions, in the Laocoon statue, which creates a vivid expression, though one that would be hard to find in any real-life situation. Long before Jean Baudrillard and others he thus suggested a model of art as simulation where things are experienced as 'real' but do not represent anything mimetic or given outside of the specific media.

Goethe's approach to painting is best exemplified in the essay 'Einfache Nachahmung der Natur, Manier, Stil' (Simple Imitation of Nature, Manner, Style), considered a central text of Weimar Classicism. It is among the first results of Goethe's Italian journey and reflects his discussions with the writer Karl Philipp Moritz. It addresses Goethe's approach to the imitation of the beautiful and different stages in the evolution of art and aesthetics in terms of various subject–object relations between artist and nature. It exemplifies Goethe's approach to the problem of mimesis. The essay begins with the remark that the 'simple imitation' of nature is a suitable approach to painting, especially to the production of still lives and landscapes. Even a painter of limited talent could achieve 'pleasant results' this way. Artists who wish to paint landscapes must therefore learn how to observe carefully, to study nature, and to engage in copying nature as closely as possible, and this should be carried out only by those of a calm and stable temperament. Such activity could then lead to 'satisfactory results', even if such an approach to painting may appear pedantic or inappropriate to more talented artists. More talented artists, Goethe goes on, do not need to adhere this closely to the imitation of nature. They can follow the spirit rather than the letter of mimetic principles and find a language for themselves that has its own integrative effects. Free to invent their own manner of expression, they paint what is in their soul when they see nature; they can thereby give the surrounding objects a distinctive form, and their pictures offer a sense of autonomy. Their artistic 'language' is called 'manner'.

It is only when the imitation of nature is accomplished and the effort to find a comprehensive and characteristic language about it is successful that art can then achieve, according to Goethe, the highest form: 'style'. His devotion to the paintings by Jacob Philipp Hackert and his interest in Salomon Gessner and Georg Forster are intimately connected with their shared search for style and an approach to visual art that would go beyond traditional mimesis and mannerism. Art at its most cultivated stage requires careful in-depth studies of the objects of nature and their evolution in history, together with a so-called 'free' subject or creator, and it can then achieve a synthesis between imitation and manner in style. These are according to Goethe the stages in the evolution of art and culture. Knowledge of nature is important in this regard because even in Goethe's terms art cannot rely solely on immediate sense perceptions. The sciences, therefore, inform artistic production and are integral constituents in the development of advanced art. They provide a better understanding of growth, evolution and transformational processes in nature. For this reason, according to Goethe, the advancement of the sciences is indispensable for the advancement and cultivation of art. He demanded that the natural sciences and artistic production correlate and he was innovative in his own time in his attempts to initiate interdisciplinary border crossings.[8]

Goethe as art critic

What clearly marks a distinction between the critical discourse on Goethe's writings in general ('the verbal') and that on his contributions on the visual in particular, is that scholarship on the verbal tends to portray Goethe more often as an initiator of movements and as a source of completely new ideas, whereas the discourse on the visual discusses him as someone responding to visual art and the artists he came into contact with, thereby emphasizing his reflective role as a mediator and critic. But as we have seen above, it is Goethe's discourse on the visual that actually challenges these distinct categories since he empowers the recipients to participate in the construction of an artwork's meaning. It has also been debated whether Goethe actually had any immediate influence on the visual artists of his time and how influential, if at all, one should consider his own paintings.

It is questionable to what degree Goethe's achievements as a painter were really taken seriously by any contemporary artist and the term 'dilettantism' has often been used of his efforts as a visual artist. There is no doubt, on the other hand, that the *Propyläen* had an influence on art education and art politics. The journal has been considered a failure as it existed only from 1798 until 1800, yet the entire venture had wide-ranging effects on the production and distribution of art. While it was intended as a way of facilitating communication among artists and critics throughout the German-speaking regions at a time of political fragmentation, it initially limited such intellectual exchange by imposing a firm value system drawn from Greek antiquity on contemporary art. It seems contradictory that Goethe actively contributed to such a regulating procedure after having challenged conventional rules earlier in the context of the Storm and Stress movement, when he was a spokesperson for the free artist and the liberated individual. The *Propyläen* venture included public competitions among visual artists for prizes awarded by a jury consisting of Goethe and his friends. It served as an incentive and filter to celebrate the so-called 'best' artists, but also as a defence mechanism in the fight against the rise of Romanticism.

Goethe's anti-Romanticism seems to be the programmatic undercurrent for much of his art criticism and visual theory up to his very last works and has served as a simplistic matrix in much scholarship on his relations to visual art. We know that Philipp Otto Runge, who had sent one of his works to the *Propyläen* competition, was so insulted by Goethe's critical response that he rejected classicism as a whole. Goethe also tried to influence Caspar David Friedrich against what he perceived in his work as the influence of Romanticism with its extreme 'Eigensinn' or subjectivity (see his 1816 essay 'Ruysdael als Dichter' (Ruisdael the Poet)). Goethe interpreted Ruisdael's paintings in terms of an 'art of expression' (*Ausdruckskunst*), in contrast to Friedrich's 'art of imagination', and argued, for example, that Ruisdael's famous painting 'The Jewish Graveyard' reflected a continuity from the fragmentary to the living – thus ignoring death and everything problematic in this painting for the sake of an imposed harmony. Friedrich was not in any case to be changed by Goethe. One notes, however, that he actually won one of the last competitions of the *Propyläen* and that Goethe simply had to acknowledge his outstanding talent.

There is agreement that Goethe did have an influence on art criticism and art history, if not on the artists themselves, because his criteria became normative for the influential art historian Heinrich Wölfflin and others in preserving classical ideals and promoting the paradigm of a forced separation between art theory and art history. Art was conceived of as 'autonomous' and as timeless. Despite the attempts by others to incorporate historical and cultural concerns, the Winckelmann–Goethe–Wölfflin paradigm became dominant and dangerous in art history. The negative influence of art politics in these terms can be illustrated by the fact that Runge and Friedrich were almost forgotten until the influential 'Ausstellung Deutscher Kunst aus der Zeit von 1775–1875' (Exhibition of German Art from the Period 1775–1875) in the Berlin Nationalgalerie in 1906. It has been argued, however, that Goethe actually entered into dialogue with the theorists of Romanticism and that the critical reception of Romantic art in the German-speaking world may not have resulted from the prejudices of Goethe and his followers alone but also from other factors in the process by which art history was constructed.

Goethe acknowledged a gap between the visual and the verbal and questioned facile equations and simplistic analogies between them. He particularly challenged the notion of translatability among the senses. He believed in a mutual illumination of sense perceptions and disciplines, insisting on the importance of the actual experience of seeing art when writing about it and basing his art-theoretical considerations on what he thought of as concrete experiences. He attempted to bridge the gap between the specific and the whole, between the concrete experiences of the senses and more abstract thoughts, via so-called 'symbols' (FA I, vol. XIII, 207). He proposed that it was possible carefully to approximate meanings via these 'symbols' that should at the same time, however, leave the inexplicable open without naming and thus destroying it. Unlike allegories, which draw analogies between remote things that are then ideally connected by an act of imagination, Goethe asserted that symbols expressed something real but momentary in the flux of time. While these symbols have attracted some interest in the context of semiotics they have ceased to be considered the guarantors of the eternal or the stabilizers of apparently timeless ideals.[9] They are features of an ongoing search for truth, such as in *Faust II*, or elements in a process that reflects the open-endedness of language and can well be associated with what Charles Sanders Peirce, Umberto Eco and others have called 'unlimited semiosis'.

In his introduction to the *Propyläen* Goethe wrote: 'Nature is separated from art by an enormous gulf which even the genius cannot overcome without other resources. Everything we perceive around us is only raw matter' (FA I, vol. XVIII, 461). In the moment an artist works on an object in nature, this object no longer belongs to nature: it is created entirely fresh and belongs to the realm of art. The visible cannot be reduced to a perceptible thing. This is one aspect – as Gilles Deleuze has pointed out – that Foucault treasured in Goethe's approach to art.[10] Many contemporary critics are still engaged in attempting to decipher how these worlds of the natural and the artistic connect and differ for Goethe. It has been argued that Goethe made visual art and literature belong to quite different spheres and that whereas the visual arts represent perfection in a way that is no longer to be traced today via any acceptable premises, literature for Goethe has always had to do with the contradictions of life and has been the medium of the indeterminable. While the visual and the verbal differ, I do not believe that Goethe's approach to the visual is any less complicated than his approach to the verbal, for his discourse on the visual demonstrates similar tensions and contradictions. While he insisted that art should be a 'second nature', or a creative effort that counters the ongoing loss of nature in the process of history, even for him it operates on more than one level, being itself not free from the flux of time and also always dependent upon its recipients to bring it to life.

Goethe considered both the production and reception of an artwork as activities that counter death and are vital in every culture. During his middle period of classicism, he argued that each artwork represents something 'whole' – nature in its process of growth and evolution (on this also see the essay 'On Arabesques') – yet he noticed in his later work, especially *Faust II*, that such completeness is only an ideal that can never be fully attained. But even then and in his *Über Kunst und Altertum* he maintained a distance from the Romantic movement as he saw it by insisting that it is not only imagination but concrete sense experiences that are needed in understanding visual art. Meaning to him must be based on an artwork's immanent vernaculars. In particular, Goethe criticized the Romantics' approach to religious art and argued that pictures mean only and precisely what is represented regardless of any external parameters, legends or imaginary links to something beyond what is actually shown in the image. His 1817 observations on Leonardo da Vinci's celebrated picture 'The Last Supper', 'Abendmahl von Leonard da Vinci zu Mayland', focuses on the specific moment which is, according to Goethe, presented in the picture regardless of its written underpinnings. His description claims to avoid abstraction but is nevertheless an interpretation of signs that at least in Goethe's time seemed to have culturally stable designated meanings. Today we can no longer rely on any such stable signifiers such as he set out to find in the folds of the apostles' garments, their facial expressions, or their gestures in the picture. Even in the context of well-established Goethe scholarship, which itself appears at times as a coded network, we do well to raise questions that link his work productively with our own senses.

Goethe was not only an advocate for seeing and for the eyes, he placed ocularity in the much broader context of multi-sensory cognition within which the tactile gains new importance in the discourse on the senses. His approach to visual art is characterized by the importance of three-dimensional haptic or tactile qualities, a discovery of light and shadows interacting with other features of a painting, and new attention to motion and processes of viewing. Architecture and sculpture served for Goethe as models for all artworks, yet his approach cannot be characterized primarily with respect to structural features. His most innovative contribution to art and aesthetics consists perhaps of his awareness of seeing in motion, visuality as integral to multiple sense perceptions, and his interest in colour, 'coloured shadows' ('farbige Schatten') and 'after-images'. His *Farbenlehre*, as has often been argued, may have resulted from his misunderstanding of Newtonian optics, yet recent scholarship suggests that Goethe may not have been wrong to estimate it as his most daring and advanced achievement. His colour plates and experimental illustrations deserve as much attention as his landscape drawings, portraits, and images commenting on history, mythology and drama.

This alternative approach to the visual can be traced in Goethe's poetry, where he found a poetic solution to the notion of living images. The process of an image that turns from being an object of observation to an empowered subject in its own right is presented, for example, in Goethe's poem 'Amor als Landschaftsmaler' (Amor as Landscape Painter, first published in 1788). Theodore Ziolkowski has argued that this poem was influenced by Claude Lorrain's painting 'The Mill' (1646), yet it is a perfect example of Goethe's own aesthetics of production in which the artist, observer and reader successfully participate in a creative act.[11] The poetic 'I' is staring into a fog as if it was a grey canvas, and is perhaps about to paint something when a boy joins him and in fact shows the expected master, who then turns into an observer, how to paint. Soon there are flowers close to a river, blue mountains, and many beautiful colours. When the boy adds a beautiful girl to his painting, the observer makes enthusiastic comments admiring the skills of the young creative artist, the boy. While he is speaking, there is motion in the image, wind in the trees, waves on the water, and suddenly the picture comes alive: the girl slowly begins to move and steps out of the frame. The poem ends with an open-ended question to us, the readers: 'Glaubt ihr wohl, ich sei auf meinem Felsen / Wie ein Felsen, still und fest geblieben?' (Do you believe I remained on my rock, like a rock, still and fixed? FA I, vol. I, 353). Goethe dissolves the expected hierarchies between master and student and challenges the notions of a controlling subject and passive, mute object together with their usual gender implications; he brings motion into the culturally imposed parameters set around the process of seeing and changes it into something open-ended. The boy is the master, not the old self, and the girl steps out of the frame, no longer objectified by any gaze but completely alive and moving on her own.

The complexity of Goethe's thinking on visual art and its development are not matters therefore that can be answered exclusively either on the basis of Goethe's art production and art criticism, or in the context of his specific contributions on architecture, sculpture and painting. Not only do they involve the much broader contexts of his fiction, drama and poetry, but they are also intimately connected with his botanical studies; his observations on geology and stone formations; his interest in the shapes and colours of clouds; and his important *Farbenlehre*, with its long-ignored ramifications and theoretical implications even for postmodern visual theory, semiotics and film. Despite all the attention that has been paid to the subject, the complexity of Goethe's discourse on the visual and its significance for contemporary debates continue to surprise and challenge us.

NOTES

1 Ingrid Strohschneider-Kohrs, 'Bilder und Gegenbilder der Antike-Rezeption', in *Poesie und Reflexion: Aufsätze zur Literatur* (Tübingen: Niemeyer, 1999), pp. 249–76, p. 260.
2 Richard Alewyn, 'Goethe und die Antike', in *Probleme und Gestalten. Essays* (Frankfurt am Main: Suhrkamp, 1982), pp. 255–70, p. 270.
3 See Günther Bergmann, *Goethe – Der Zeichner und Maler. Ein Porträt* (Munich: Callwey, 1999); Petra Maisak, *Johann Wolfgang Goethe – Zeichnungen* (Stuttgart: Reclam, 1996); and Sabine Schulze (ed.), Goethe und die Kunst (Stuttgart: Hatje, 1994).
4 Christa Lichtenstern, *Die Wirkungsgeschichte der Metamorphosenlehre Goethes. Von Philipp Otto Runge bis Joseph Beuys* (Weinheim: VCH, Acta Humaniora, 1990).
5 See Sabine Schulze's introductory chapter to *Goethe und die Kunst.*
6 Ibid., p. 10.
7 See my 'Hidden Aspects of Goethe's Writings on Color, Seeing, and Motion and their Significance for a Feminist Visual Theory', in Laura Doyle (ed.), *Bodies of Resistance: New Phenomenologies of Politics, Agency, and Culture* (Evanston: Northwestern University Press, 2001), pp. 144–91.
8 See Ernst Osterkamp, *Im Buchstabenbilde: Studien zum Verfahren Goethescher Bildbeschreibungen* (Stuttgart: Metzler, 1991); Uwe Pörksen, *Raumzeit: Goethes Zeitbegriff, abgelesen an seinen sprachlichen und zeichnerischen Naturstudien* (Mainz: Akademie der Wissenschaften und der Literatur / Stuttgart: Steiner, 1999); and also the contribution by Kremer in *Handbuch* III, pp. 564–70.
9 See Clark Muenzer, '"Ihr ältesten, würdigsten Denkmäler der Zeit." Goethe's "Über den Granit" and his Aesthetics of Monuments', in Richard Fisher (ed.), *Ethik und Ästhetik: Werke und Werte in der Literatur vom 18. bis zum 20. Jahrhundert. Festschrift für Wolfgang Wittkowski zum 70. Geburtstag* (Frankfurt am Main: Lang, 1995), pp. 181–98.
10 Gilles Deleuze, *Foucault*, trans. and ed. by Seán Hand (London: Athlone, 1988), pp. 58–9.
11 'Die Natur als Nachahmung der Kunst bei Goethe', in *Wissen aus Erfahrung. Werkbegriff und Interpretation heute. Festschrift für Herman Meyer*, ed. by Alexander von Bormann (Tübingen: Niemeyer, 1976), pp. 242–55.

13

W. DANIEL WILSON

Goethe and the political world

By the time of Goethe's death in 1832, many of the characteristics of the modern age were evident: revolution, parliamentary democracy, political parties and human rights. However, the political world in which Goethe grew up and matured was essentially premodern; the eighteenth century saw only the first stirrings of the modern national state and its political institutions. The Treaty of Westphalia (1648) had cemented the status quo, in which hundreds of sovereign states sought increasing autonomy under the loose umbrella of the Holy Roman Empire – which, as the joke went, was neither holy nor Roman nor an empire, but rather a weak federation, approximately coextensive with German-speaking territories. Because the Empire was an impediment of sorts to the rise of the national state, it was seen as a political dinosaur by Prussophile nationalist historians in the nineteenth and twentieth centuries, and indeed by many thinkers in the eighteenth. However, more recent historians, critical of this nationalist heritage, have begun to valorize the Empire as the protector of rights, diversity and regionalism, as opposed to the faceless centralism and bureaucratization that characterized larger national states like France. There is certainly some truth to this view, which sees the Empire as a sort of model for European union today. At least in theory, any municipality could, for example, plead its case before an Imperial court in Vienna or Wetzlar if it felt that its absolutist ruler was infringing established rights – only one more reason that historians increasingly shy away from the term 'absolutist', with its suggestion of unimpeded princely power. But these legal avenues were not as accessible as such historians suggest. In practice, the Imperial courts often sided with the princes, and the courts' notorious costs and delays of decades – Goethe himself experienced them as an intern in Wetzlar – discouraged such legal actions. Nevertheless, this weak counterbalance to princely authority led even many contemporaries to speak boldly of German 'freedom', by which they meant not the new liberal concept of individual rights and popular sovereignty, but the system of checks on autocratic power in the institutions of the Empire. In retrospect, it seems clear that 'freedom' had become a political alibi for intellectuals who were powerless to effect fundamental change.

Goethe had even more reason than most Germans of his day to favour the status quo. He grew up not under princely authority, but in an 'imperial free city', Frankfurt on the Main. However, the absence of a prince, court or powerful nobility should not lead us to associate such cities with democratic or even proto-democratic states. They were controlled by another kind of elite, prominent burghers from a few long-established families – and Goethe's was one such family in Frankfurt. It is characteristic of Goethe's sense of privilege that when he received his patent of nobility in Weimar, after having left his home town, he had the sense that he was only being recognized for a status that he had always possessed: 'We Frankfurt patricians had always considered ourselves equal to the nobility' (Eckermann III, 26 September 1827). Goethe's identification with the ruling elite remained with him for the rest of his life. To be sure, he later was beholden to a princely government and a court that were alien to his roots and of which his father utterly disapproved. But distrust of the lower classes, whether of the rebels of the Frankfurt Fettmilch uprising before Goethe's birth, the uppity peasants of Saxe-Weimar, or the Jacobins of revolutionary France, remained a constant of Goethe's political outlook, both before and after his removal to Weimar. It was thus not a huge break with his past when he allied himself inextricably with the interests of Duke Carl August of Saxe-Weimar-Eisenach.

The myth prevails, however, that when Goethe left his non-monarchist home town in 1775, at the age of twenty-six, he switched allegiances from a sort of youthful revolutionary élan to deference to princely authority. In truth, the pre-Weimar Goethe had merely toyed with social or political dissidence. He was no more revolutionary than his first novel's hero Werther, who seems to reject the boundaries between classes – or, more accurately, between estates – only to say in the next breath that he realizes they are necessary, and expresses frustration merely because they stand in the way of his very individualistic striving for self-realization; the context, after all, is that Werther wants to enjoy the company of a noblewoman (MA 1/2, 250). The entire movement of young upstarts that figures in literary history as 'Storm and Stress' was a literary revolt, not a political one. They criticized certain social ills in feudal society and the absolutist state, but without the vaguest programme for eliminating them – their stillborn political critique paled in comparison with the bold affronts of an Enlightenment writer such as Lessing. Symptomatic of the ambivalence that Goethe felt towards the power structures of his day is the transformation of his manuscript *Gottfried von Berlichingen* into the published play *Götz von Berlichingen* (1773), the work that made him famous and the version that is still usually read today. In the unpublished *Gottfried*, Goethe portrayed the cause of the rebellious sixteenth-century peasants with marked empathy, but within a year and a half he had transformed the relevant scenes so thoroughly that in the published version the peasants seem like bloodthirsty monsters without the slightest hint of a lofty struggle against feudal abuses.[1] This pattern is repeated in other works: whenever the pre-Weimar Goethe shoots off barbs at (usually unidentified) princes, it is in passages that remain in his drawer. Though he gained a reputation as a firebrand, it was based mainly on the diffuse rebelliousness that permeated works of the Storm and Stress writers, and on the (mis)conception that he had advocated suicide or had challenged rationalist social and ethical norms in *Die Leiden des jungen Werther* (The Sorrows of Young Werther, 1774). Any sense that the young Goethe challenged the feudal and absolutist order was misplaced.

To be sure, much of Goethe's textual politics is decidedly non-absolutist, even if not anti-absolutist. It is no accident that the heroes of both *Götz* and especially *Egmont* – a tragedy that bridges his early life stages, begun before his move to Weimar and finished only in Italy in 1787 – are noblemen. Goethe conceived the counterweight to absolutist authority not in the lower classes or even his own middle class, but in the aristocracy. This was an older model, shared even by Lessing, that invested hope in a revival of the nobles, who still had the residual power, in their estates (*Landstände*), to authorize taxation. Thus, many thinkers of the day advocated not overthrowing the monarchist order, but slowing the accretion of power by the absolutist state by strengthening the only existing institution that had the potential to exert its influence. The telos of history casts this hope as a regressive, conservative one, since the future seems to have rested with the middle class, democracy and revolution. But to many thinkers in the eighteenth century whose dramatic heroes are always nobles, the only realistic hope for an 'opposition' to abuses of monarchist power rested in the ancient prerogatives of the relatively independent landed nobility, particularly if they avoided the temptation to accept courtly sinecures. Goethe's valorization of this model extended even to the period of the French Revolution; in his anti-revolutionary plays *Die Aufgeregten* (Agitation, written 1792 or 1793) and *Der Bürgergeneral* (The Citizen-General, 1793), the positive foil to revolutionary nonsense are the landed nobles, who act like enlightened and benevolent fathers towards their peasants. In these plays the prince remains invisible, decidedly ignored in the search for a stable antidote to revolutionary violence. At this point, Goethe seems to have given up hope for meaningful change through the system of so-called 'enlightened absolutism', and sought instead the impetus for reform from what could be called 'enlightened feudalism', on a local level and out of reach of the baleful influence of the court.

Goethe's own political activities, however, clash glaringly with his literary turn away from princes. He remained steadfastly loyal to the principle of monarchist authority from his arrival in Weimar in 1775 to his death, even when his duke found himself in conflict with the local nobility. Goethe arrived in Saxe-Weimar as a favourite of the new, eighteen-year-old duke, Carl August (1757–1828), but within a few months found himself appointed Legation Councillor with a seat in the four-member Privy Council, the highest governing organ in the duchy. The duke's appointment of Goethe was controversial not only because the infamous writer seemed to seduce the immature duke into a few months of wild escapades, victimizing the duchy's citizens, but also because Goethe was seriously underqualified for the highest position in the state, which was usually filled by experienced administrators. The senior Privy Councillor, Jacob Friedrich von Fritsch, even threatened to resign and was persuaded to stay on only after intensive cajoling by the ducal family.

Within a short time, Goethe's detractors had to admit their mistake. He threw himself into his new responsibility with vigour and determination. The next nine years – until his virtual withdrawal from the daily work of the Council in the spring of 1785 – found Goethe so immersed in the minutiae of absolutist government that he published very little literature and was written off by the world of letters as a complete loss. In meetings two or three times a week, Goethe took part in at least 11,000 different cases decided by the Council, many of which involved extensive study of documents, writing of protocols, memoranda, essays, and often occasioned fact-finding journeys to the far reaches of the duchy or diplomatic trips abroad. A small double principality with a population of about 100,000, Saxe-Weimar-Eisenach had no differentiated ministries; the Councillors had to decide on all sorts of issues, from the design of new uniforms for the military and a decision on a new well for Weimar to the momentous questions of foreign affairs in a state that was dangerously subject to the whims of larger powers such as Prussia and Saxony. As if that were not enough, Goethe found himself appointed head of the Mining Commission (1777), the Roads and War Commissions (both 1779) and the Ilmenau Tax Commission (1784), and beginning in 1782 he was the de facto director of the financial authority (the *Kammer*).

Our knowledge of Goethe's work in the commissions is hampered by the loss of most of the relevant files during the Second World War, but his more important work, in the Privy Council, is relatively well documented. The files do not always give an adequate picture of the real events and decision-making processes, since oral deliberations were seldom protocolled. Furthermore, most remain unpublished. The projected edition of Goethe's official writings (*Amtliche Schriften*) has not been completed (in particular, the commentary to the documents from the first decade in Weimar has never been published), and in any case, the overwhelming majority (perhaps 95 per cent) of the decisions in which Goethe participated are not documented in his own writings, but merely by his initialled assent on manuscript drafts of edicts and the like. The serious researcher of the political Goethe must therefore work in the State Archives in Weimar, and most of this work has yet to be done. Nevertheless, clear patterns, especially as they are flanked by evidence from Goethe's letters, diaries and recorded conversations, have emerged from scholarship to date.

The first concerns the area of 'reform'. The foremost scholar of the duchy policy in the agrarian realm – the battleground of attempts to effect change within the feudal system – suggests that this term ought not even to be used for agrarian policy in Saxe-Weimar, since the government had no underlying conception of fundamental change.[2] In other areas, too – legal structures, economic policy, taxation – the trend seems to have been towards modest improvements born from a spirit of rational analysis and – sometimes – Enlightenment thought. However, the image of a 'social reformer' Goethe that one finds in some modern scholarship is overblown.[3] None of these measures threatened the feudal or absolutist status quo, and most of them did not even aim to alter it much. They represent a sort of patchwork response to crises. They stem from the notion that the monarch is a sort of paternalist *Landesvater* responsible for the wellbeing of his subjects, who remain political children, unable to represent their interests in institutional ways.

This view of Weimar's subjects as passive children did not take account of the determined protest and unrest staged by some of the duchy's subjects, who were anything but docile and satisfied with this paternalist regime or the feudal system. To be sure, the only subjects who were organized well enough to represent their interests effectively were students who were banded together in quasi-Masonic secret societies, and peasants organized in their villages, whose rights and responsibilities vis-à-vis their feudal lords were guaranteed by ancient compacts. Throughout most of the four decades in which Goethe was a member of the Privy Council (1776–85 and, less intensively and regularly, 1786–1816), both of these groups provided a constant source of headaches for the government.[4] The peasants, in particular, had firm legal grounds for their claims, and in the background lurked the threat of a lawsuit against the government before an Imperial court. Despite this threat, the Weimar government – like those in comparable German territories – pursued a consistent policy of undermining and curtailing the peasants' rights wherever possible. The area in which this struggle was most heated was feudal duties, especially the unpaid labour that the peasants owed their lords (*Frondienste*). Since the feudal lord was very often the duke himself, and the state's finances rested on the backs of the peasants, the government was constantly confronted with strikes and even violent protest against its encroachments on the villagers' rights. We are unaware of Goethe's oral arguments in such cases. But his political responsibility is clear: newly examined documents show that, along with the duke and the other councillors, he ordained punishment of protesting peasants, even when the government's own judicial authority pointed out the illegality of restrictions on the peasants' 'rights' and 'freedoms'.[5] The notion of human rights, as it was widely debated in Germany until the French Revolution introduced a new concept, was focussed precisely in this area of peasant struggles against infringements on their privileges. A heterodox writer such as Gottfried August Bürger attacked such abuses energetically, but Goethe's alliance with his duke prevented him from even considering writing such critical texts.

Another recently discovered area of his official activities where Goethe found himself in direct contradiction to the discourse of his contemporaries concerned the war in America. In his play *Kabale und Liebe* (Intrigue and Love, 1784), Friedrich Schiller bitterly criticized the sale of peasants to the British for use against the American rebels, a practice carried out in half a dozen German states. Weimar did not participate in the large-scale commerce in entire regiments – it hardly had enough peasants even to consider this path – but it did sell individual prison inmates as soldiers to the British.[6] We have evidence that only a few of these inmates agreed to the transaction; the others – as well as homeless 'vagabonds' – were sold without their consent. Saxe-Weimar prided itself on adherence to the rule of law, but in this case, clearly defined punishments were arbitrarily transformed into a potential death sentence. Goethe's involvement in these transactions was greater than that of the other Councillors, since he was also head of the War Commission and made promises to the 'recruiters'. His involvement contradicts the impression he later gave in his autobiography, that he had supported the American War of Independence (MA XVI, 750).

The deepest contradictions, however, are between Goethe's professions of a humane ideal (*Humanität*) and these official activities. In the earliest version of his grand play *Faust*, for example, Goethe had portrayed the piteous fate of an unmarried woman who killed her newborn child from fear of disgrace – infanticide was one of the central obsessions of the Storm and Stress, a paradigm of individual self-realization in conflict with encrusted and inhumane social norms. However, when the duke asked his Privy Council to consider eliminating the death penalty for infanticide, all of them, including Goethe, voted to keep it.[7] This decision sealed the fate of a woman who had been waiting for execution; the Council apparently feared civil unrest at the execution, for it ordered extraordinary security measures. A local intellectual called the execution, in November 1783, a 'state murder'.[8]

We should hardly be surprised at such contradictions, if that is indeed what they are. The Privy Councillor Goethe obeyed different dictates from those of the young writer Goethe. And yet in all of these instances, the politician found himself in opposition not only to modern hindsight judgements, but also to central discourses of his own day, even in his own government. He clearly was not in the vanguard or even the mainstream of political thought in the eighteenth century.

The same is true of his attitude towards the French Revolution, which was easily the most important political event in his life. For at least a decade after 1789, he hardly wrote a work on which the Revolution did not leave its mark, and the literary project of 'high classicism', the pact between Goethe and Schiller between 1794 and 1805, had a clear antirevolutionary impetus. Here, too, Goethe found himself in disagreement with most of his intellectual contemporaries. Though they generally viewed a revolution as unnecessary in their land of 'enlightened' princes, most German thinkers enthusiastically welcomed the upheaval in France as the dawn of a new age, a cataclysm that would supposedly convince unenlightened German princes to change their ways and urge enlightened ones to move towards even more fundamental reforms. Goethe portrays this initial high-minded – and, in his view, naive – idealism at the beginning of Canto Six of his counter-revolutionary verse epic *Hermann und Dorothea* (1797), but he himself never shared this enthusiasm of his contemporaries. Though he saw clearly that the French monarchy and aristocracy had brought about its own demise, he repeatedly claimed that the 'apostles of freedom' were wolves in sheep's clothing who merely wanted to gain power for themselves. Of course, the revolutionary terror – even though it was triggered mainly by the interventionist wars of the monarchist states – seemed to confirm Goethe's interpretation, and by this time most of the Revolution's German adherents had long since changed their minds. Goethe never ceased to express his sentiment that the Revolution crushed the natural order of things and had nothing to offer in its place but chaos and brutality. The bewildering events in France cemented his conviction that the common people could never rule themselves, that under the surface lurked violence and greed that only firm and assured autocracy could keep under control.

In Saxe-Weimar, the effects of the Revolution were deep and wide.[9] By 1792–3, when the French revolutionary troops drove the German coalition armies out of France and threatened even to take Eisenach, which was on Weimar territory, the Revolution was greeted with considerable enthusiasm by individuals in all strata of Weimar society: peasants, burghers, nobility, students and professors in Jena, and intellectuals such as Johann Gottfried Herder. For a few weeks in the fall of 1792, the populace of Eisenach saw the expected French invaders as liberators, not as the enemy. Such enthusiasts almost uniformly did not want to see their duke and the established order overthrown. Rather, they hoped that the French would force Carl August to introduce reforms they had demanded for decades. The Revolution did not convert these Germans to its ideology, but rather lent them the courage to voice more brazenly their old complaints against isolated aspects of the feudal order. Their issues were not revolutionary, but were the same as in prerevolutionary times; they were merely voiced with more energy and less fear than before. Similarly, the students in Jena were infected with revolutionary fervour, but for them the goal was merely the autonomy of their secret societies, which they saw as an issue of 'academic freedom'. The government responded by branding such protesters – and in particular textile workers in Apolda, who rose up against oppressive conditions in 1793 – as 'sans-culottes'. This distortion gave the government licence to take extraordinary measures to suppress potential dissent and opposition. The government used spies, sent troops to Apolda, and inhibited the free expression of ideas. These measures were hardly draconian, and reflect similar strategies in other territories – except that in the criminalization of student secret societies Saxe-Weimar took the lead, with Goethe in the vanguard. Furthermore, these security measures were present in various forms long before the French Revolution. This pattern belies the persistent myth – propagated by the Weimar government – of a basically contented populace that was stirred up by 'alien' ideas from France and even by mysterious French 'emissaries'. In fact, dissidents during the period of the French Revolution targeted the same abuses as before 1789. The unrest emerged from home-grown Weimar protests that were merely given new energy by the revolutionary events and the approach of French troops.

Goethe accompanied Duke Carl August, general of a Prussian regiment, on the ill-fated Austro-Prussian campaign against the new French republic in the autumn of 1792. He saw first-hand the ignominious defeat of the disciplined but mercenary troops of the monarchist order at the hands of the first modern army fired by zeal for the cause of the masses. From this point on, Goethe almost always saw the Revolution through the lens of war. And even if his security mentality and his identification with the feudal and absolutist order provide little with which moderns can sympathize, Goethe was far-sighted in his categorical rejection of war. Even when it was designed to restore the monarchical order in France, Goethe abhorred war as a policy tool. When the Privy Council voted – in his absence – for Saxe-Weimar to join in declaring that the war against France was an Imperial war requiring the participation of all territories in the Empire, Goethe expressed his open dismay: 'So we will run headlong into our ruin with the rest of the herd', he wrote in 1792, 'Europe needs another Thirty Years War to understand what would have been prudent in 1792'.[10] His words stand as an ominous prophecy of the decades of war unleashed by the First Coalition War in that year. And Goethe never changed his opinion that war was far worse than the alternatives.

Paradoxically, Goethe remained to the end an admirer of one of the most prominent contemporary warmongers, Napoleon Bonaparte – despite the French emperor's dismantling of the Empire and the old regime in Germany, to which Goethe was so attached. This adulation, which has embarrassed German nationalists ever since, should probably be seen as part of Goethe's fascination with the strong personality of genius, but also as a function of his admiration for an unabashed representative of autocratic power at a time when the authority of monarchs was becoming unhinged. Even with the growing cogency of liberal thought in the second half of his long life, Goethe never abandoned the view that rulers should not allow their subjects to meddle in affairs of state, since government was a matter of authority, represented by the aura of the prince. His subjects, by contrast, were not schooled in the intricacies of government and were driven by base passions; they were easily duped by demagogues and thus an incalculable political danger. Their dabbling in politics was mere intrusion, in Goethe's eyes. He was consequently a lifelong opponent of freedom of the press, even when it was introduced in the new Weimar constitution of 1816 – and needless to say, he opposed the introduction of the constitution itself and treated the new parliament with open contempt. Weimar's freedom of the press did not, admittedly, go very far; those intellectuals who took it seriously soon found their journals prohibited and were in some cases themselves punished.

In other areas, too, Goethe had no patience with the new trend to recognize human rights. Though his attitude towards Jews was ambivalent – it has been interpreted variously as indifferent or anti-Semitic – he clearly opposed Weimar's introduction of new rights for them in 1823. He condemned a new law allowing intermarriage of Christians and Jews as 'absurd' and 'grotesque'. Already in 1808 he had refused to intervene in the heated debate in his hometown, Frankfurt, over limited new rights for Jews; one of the proponents of such rights earned from Goethe the epithet 'Humanitätssalbader', a sort of humanitarian driveller (to Bettine Brentano, 20 April 1808, WA IV, vol. xx, 50).[11] This term speaks volumes for the contradiction between Goethe's lofty ideal of *Humanität* and his illiberal political precepts.

Given his rejection of any participation in government by free citizens in the public sphere, Goethe's only real alternative to tyranny was the principle of 'enlightened absolutism' (or, as it is sometimes known in the English-speaking world, 'enlightened despotism'). It was the responsibility of enlightened advisers to inculcate wise principles of government in the monarch, who was enjoined to develop a strong sense of his weighty duty to keep the common weal in mind and to resist the temptation to exploit and abuse his power for his own personal pleasure. Goethe's poem on the occasion of the duke's twenty-sixth birthday in 1783, 'Ilmenau', is the paradigmatic expression of these beliefs. He admonishes the duke to lead the people with a strong hand towards their own happiness. Of course, Goethe recognized that not all princes lived up to this ideal, and in particular, a good prince might be succeeded by a benighted one (as was soon to happen after the death of Frederick the Great in 1786 and the ascension of Frederick William II to the Prussian throne). The resulting pessimism regarding the vagaries of royal succession found expression in some of his works – with a remarkable gendered twist. In *Die Aufgeregten* the enlightened countess is the daughter of an evil count and the mother of a boy who seems to be developing the same way as his grandfather. Margarete of Parma, the regent of the Netherlands in *Egmont*, is more humane than her king, Phillip II of Spain. In both cases, the women are not true rulers, but merely stand in for the men in an interregnum, even though the women would obviously be better suited to the task. In other works, too, Goethe never seems to have been quite able to portray an ideal reigning prince. In this sense we find a familiar pattern, in which Goethe worked out his doubts and ambiguous attitudes in the subtle logic of literature, even when he felt inhibited from expressing those doubts in non-literary texts.

Even his relationship with Carl August was fraught with crises. Goethe found himself repeatedly compelled to admonish the duke to rule and behave more responsibly, often in tones rather less rarefied than those of 'Ilmenau'. The duke's passion for hunting, in particular, often drove Goethe to distraction. Finally, on 26 December 1784, he relayed the frustration of the peasants in the area of the Ettersberg, where the duke's wild boar roamed freely, destroying crops, protected from any intervention by the peasants. The other major passion of the duke was his military, and here Goethe managed one of the few true reforms of his political career, halving the size of the already minuscule Weimar 'army' – but only against the will of Carl August. And Goethe participated only grudgingly in Carl August's diplomatic forays on behalf of a *Fürstenbund*, a league of central German princes that would provide a counterweight to the two 'superpowers', Prussia and Austria. Goethe saw the folly of such efforts, and believed that the duke should concentrate his energies in the domestic sphere rather than constantly travelling around in pursuit of the glory of diplomatic success.

The related rise of German nationalism was another trend for which Goethe had no taste. The uprising against Napoleon in 1813 left him cold, and even after the French emperor's defeat in 1815 he proudly wore the medal that Napoleon had bestowed upon him. It is not difficult to see where Goethe's opposition to nationalism was rooted. At this early stage, German nationalism was allied with liberal efforts to gain constitutional rights (it was also allied with some Romantics, which may be a secondary reason for Goethe's distaste for it). Since Goethe saw in this twin movement of nationalism and liberalism a threat to absolutist order, he rejected it. Another reason for his attitude was his genuine conviction that large states were anathema to the development of rich culture and paternalist politics; the most obvious contemporary example was Prussia, whose mechanical militarism and bureaucratization Goethe condemned when he visited Berlin and Potsdam on a diplomatic mission in 1778. Goethe remained loyal to the house of Saxe-Weimar to the end. He had been schooled in the thought of Justus Möser, the Osnabrück functionary who sang the praises of the diversity and relative freedom of the German small states within the Holy Roman Empire. It was a book of Justus Möser that lay on the table at the first meeting of Goethe and Carl August in 1775, and a conversation about it ensued, leading to the duke's invitation for Goethe to visit Weimar. Despite the rise of nationalism, parliamentary democracy and revolution, Goethe never betrayed the principles of Möser.

The contemporaries of the older Goethe were not kind to his political reputation. Only three years after his death, Ludwig Börne coined the famous term 'Fürstenknecht' for him – lackey of princes. It is easy to counter all political critique of Goethe with the argument that his views were those of his environment, but Wolfgang Rothe has cogently argued against this: 'The banal excuse, that he was only a child of his times and cannot be measured with today's yardstick, is historically inaccurate: Goethe was not representative of his time, but rather a nonconformist. He did not conform to the liberal and constitutional tendencies of the early nineteenth century, and he alienated himself from the intellectuals of Germany and in the end found himself completely isolated.'[12] And, it should be added, he was in a minority position among intellectuals already in the first years of his service to the duke, when the call for human rights (variously understood) and reforms became increasingly vociferous. Rothe rightly counters the trend to instrumentalize Goethe politically in practically every age and ideology. Goethe was a declared foe of ideologies, which has not kept even democrats from claiming him as their own – Thomas Mann was only the most famous example, in the founding year of the two German states and Goethe year 1949, but even on the occasion of Goethe's 250th birthday in 1999, Katharina Mommsen declared Goethe the spiritus rector of the constitution of the Federal Republic of Germany.[13] The political scientist Ekkehart Krippendorff is perhaps more justified in stressing the value of Goethe's opposition to war and nationalism,[14] but his valorization of the supposedly humane values of Weimar absolutism as a model for today has drawn equally justified criticism;[15] it is a view that could be voiced only by ignoring the details of Goethe's activities as Privy Councillor. Goethe's greatness lies not in his political values, but in his poetic achievement.

NOTES

1 See W. Daniel Wilson, 'Hunger/Artist: Goethe's Revolutionary Agitators in *Götz*, *Satyros, Egmont*, and *Der Bürgergeneral*', *Monatshefte* 86 (1994), 80–94.
2 Rosalinde Gothe, 'Goethe, Carl August und Merck: Zur Frage der Reformansätze im Agrarbereich', *Goethe-Jahrbuch* 100 (1983), 203–18, p. 215.
3 The most influential – but by no means the only – example of this trend is Dieter Borchmeyer's handbook *Weimarer Klassik: Portrait einer Epoche* (Weinheim: Beltz Athenäum, 1994; 1st edn 1980).
4 See my *Das Goethe-Tabu: Protest und Menschenrechte im klassischen Weimar* (Munich: Deutscher Taschenbuch Verlag, 1999), chapters 2 and 3 (peasants) and chapter 4 (students).
5 Ibid., pp. 88–9.
6 Ibid., chapter 1.
7 *Goethes amtliche Schriften: Veröffentlichung des Staatsarchivs Weimar*, 4 vols., ed. Willy Flach and (vols. 2–4) Helma Dahl (Weimar: Böhlau, 1950–87), vol. 1, pp. 245–51.
8 *Das Goethe-Tabu*, pp. 7–8.
9 Ibid., chapters 2–5.
10 Letter to Voigt, Luxemburg, 15 Oct. 1792, *Amtliche Schriften* 2/1, p. 301.
11 On the context, see W. Daniel Wilson, ' "Humanitätssalbader": Goethe's Distaste for Jewish Emancipation, and Jewish Responses', *Goethe and German-Jewish Culture*, ed. by Klaus Berghahn (forthcoming).
12 Wolfgang Rothe, *Der politische Goethe: Dichter und Staatsdiener im deutschen Spätabsolutismus* (Göttingen: Vandenhoeck & Ruprecht, 1998), p. 132 (my translation).
13 Katharina Mommsen, *Goethe und unsere Zeit: Festrede im Goethejahr 1999 zur Eröffnung der Hauptversammlung der Goethe-Gesellschaft im Nationaltheater zu Weimar am 27. Mai 1999* (Frankfurt am Main: Suhrkamp, 1999).
14 Ekkehart Krippendorff, *'Wie die Großen mit den Menschen spielen': Versuch über Goethes Politik* (Frankfurt am Main: Suhrkamp, 1988).
15 See the critique of Krippendorff by Rothe, *Der politische Goethe*, pp. 26, 102, 231ff., and the exchange between Krippendorff and Wilson in *Frankfurter Rundschau*, Aug. 14, 1999 (special issue on the 250th anniversary of Goethe's birth), p. 22.

14

H. B. NISBET

Religion and philosophy

Throughout Goethe's childhood and adolescence – as he tells us in his autobiography *Dichtung und Wahrheit* (Poetry and Truth) – the main focus of his religious awareness was the Bible, which he learned to read not only in Luther's translation but also in its original languages (HA IX, 124–8). He derived early poetic inspiration from it (HA IX, 140–3) and later described it as the main source of his moral education (HA IX, 274). His father's copy of the Vulgate stood on his desk throughout his later years (HA[12] IX, 731). Although he therefore had little sympathy with those who, like Voltaire, ridiculed the Bible as a tissue of absurdity and superstition (HA IX, 274–5 and 510), his own reading of it was by no means uncritical. After his encounter with Herder in 1770, he came to regard the Old Testament not only as a rich repository of ancient poetry – both he and Herder produced their own translations of the Song of Songs – but also as a historical and anthropological document affording valuable insights into primitive oriental society (HA IX, 129–35 and 511). It followed from this that the Old Testament and its doctrines were of limited relevance to other ages and cultures, including that of modern Europe: their religious significance remained primarily local and Judaic.[1]

Goethe's relationship with the New Testament and Christianity is altogether more complex, given that Christianity was still a powerful force in European culture. He took his last recorded communion at the age of twenty-one, and later described himself as 'not anti-Christian or un-Christian, but decidedly non-Christian'.[2] But as this formulation suggests, he still found something to respect in Christianity. After early dissatisfaction with the routinized observances of orthodox Lutheranism, he was drawn for a time into Pietist circles, whose emotional style of worship seemed to him closer to the spirit of early Christianity (cf. HA[12] XII, 694); he even underwent something akin to a conversion experience.[3] This involvement with Pietism reached its climax during his convalescence from serious illness in 1768–70, under the guidance of Susanna von Klettenberg, an older friend of the family who later became his model for the pious lady whose confessions occupy Book 6 of *Wilhelm Meisters Lehrjahre* (Wilhelm Meister's Apprenticeship). His Pietistic phase soon passed, but he continued to value the ethical content of Christianity as a religion of love and mutual forbearance: he had this in mind when, a few days before his death, he told Eckermann: 'However much . . . the human spirit may enlarge its bounds, it will never surpass the sublimity and ethical culture of Christianity as it shines and sparkles in the gospels.'[4] From around 1770 onwards, however, Goethe became increasingly aware that he could not accept many of the central tenets of Christianity. With his basically optimistic view of human nature, he rejected the dogmas of original sin (HA x, 44) and eternal punishment (HA xii, 229–30). He also disliked the Christian preoccupation with death, countering the time-honoured dictum *memento mori* with the rival injunction 'Gedenke zu leben' ('Remember to live'; HA vii, 540). His main objections, however, concern the divinity and atonement of Christ, to which he at times takes outspoken exception.[5] Like the hero of *Die Leiden des jungen Werther* (The Sorrows of Young Werther) he feels no need for a mediator, wishing instead to know God directly (HA vi, 85–6); he also finds the image of the crucified Christ aesthetically and morally repugnant, pillorying it in the *Venezianische Epigramme* (Venetian Epigrams) of 1790 (nos. 7 and 21, HA i, 176 and 179). The sharpness of his attacks on Christian supernaturalism from the 1770s to the early years of the following century was, however, largely a response to the persistent proselytizing of his pious friends Johann Caspar Lavater and Friedrich Heinrich Jacobi. Typical in this respect is his letter of 9 August 1782 to Lavater, to whom he declares:

> *You* consider the gospel as it stands to be the most divine truth. But an audible voice from the heavens would not convince *me* that water burns and fire extinguishes, that a woman can bear a child without a man, or that someone can rise from the dead; on the contrary, I regard these as blasphemies against the great God and his revelation in nature.[6]

It is plain from this and other similar utterances that Goethe was not an atheist – although he occasionally liked to style himself as such in order to shock the curious or those who tried to convert him.[7] He simply refused to recognize any of the Christian churches, or indeed the Bible itself, as the ultimate authority in religious matters, and when he read Gottfried Arnold's *Kirchen- und Ketzergeschichte* (History of Churches and Heretics, 1699–1700) during his Pietist phase in Frankfurt, he found himself in sympathy with numerous heretics (HA ix, 350). During his Storm and Stress period, this interest led to a series of plans for dramas and other literary works on such figures as Mohammed, Prometheus, Ahasverus – and, of course, Faust (cf. HA x, 45–8). The archetype of most of these figures was the fallen angel Lucifer, around whose rebellion against God the young Goethe constructed a speculative cosmogony (HA IX, 351–3), influenced by various hermetic and alchemical works, such as Welling's *Opus mago-cabbalisticum* (1735), which he read during his convalescence (HA IX, 341–2). Apart from Faust, the most representative literary embodiment of this spirit of religious defiance is Prometheus, as depicted in Goethe's poetic monologue of that title (HA I, 44–6). Prometheus expresses the divine creative power inherent in human beings; this glorification of self-assertive subjectivity – the poem ends significantly with the word 'ich' – is also, of course, part of the Storm and Stress cult of the creative genius. The defiance of Prometheus points forward to that paganism which Goethe liked to flaunt during and immediately after his journey to Italy, telling Fritz Stolberg, for example, that 'I personally hold more or less to the doctrine of Lucretius and confine my pretensions to the sphere of [this] life' (2 February 1789, HAB II, 109). In keeping with the sexual liberation he experienced in Italy and during his subsequent liaison with Christiane Vulpius, this paganism has strong erotic overtones, most memorably present in the *Römische Elegien* (Roman Elegies) and *Venezianische Epigramme*; the defiance of conventional morality implicit in these works is again in large part a reaction to Christian disapproval (cf. Jacobi's comments in *Gespräche* II, 21). Goethe's belief that divine powers are inherent in human nature finds less combative expression in that doctrine of *Humanität* which he developed in conjunction with Herder during the 1780s, and which is already foreshadowed in the first version of *Iphigenie* (1779). This doctrine is the central theme of his unfinished religious epic *Die Geheimnisse* (The Mysteries, 1784–5), in which a secret quasi-monastic order, epitomized by its leader Humanus, embodies the finest ethical aspirations of mankind as recognized by different religious cultures. The supernatural claims of the various religions are, however, conspicuously absent. Even Goethe's belief in personal immortality, which gained in strength in his later years, is based on secular rather than religious premises: he derives it rather from the Leibnizian concept of the indestructible monad or the Aristotelian entelechy than from Christian revelation.[8] The primary model for Goethe's classical humanism remains, however, the ancient Greeks, who endeavoured, as he puts it, 'to deify man rather than to humanize the deity' (HA XII, 136; cf. HA XII, 103).

In this glorification of the best qualities in human nature – Iphigenie's ethical nobility is a good example – Goethe's debt to the Enlightenment is obvious. Nevertheless, this represents only one side of his mature religiosity, which is focussed not only on the subjective aspects of human nature but also on the objective realm of nature as a whole. He found intellectual support for his own religion of nature, the elements of which are present in his literary works from the early 1770s onwards (see, for example, Werther's letter of 10 May, HA VI, 9), in the pantheism of Spinoza, whose *Ethics* (1677) he first studied in 1774. He was attracted to Spinoza for various reasons – not least because Spinoza had long been stigmatized as a heretic or even an atheist; but as Goethe later admitted, the attraction was essentially an attraction of opposites (HA X, 35). He certainly shared, in very general terms, Spinoza's belief in the oneness of everything, in an immanent god, and in the central role of love;[9] but he also found Spinoza's serene detachment and universal determinism an anchor and refuge in the turbulent years of his own early manhood. And although he told Jacobi that the one book which corresponded most closely to his own view of nature was Spinoza's *Ethics* (21 October 1785, HAB I, 488–9) his own pantheism was a far cry from the latter's abstract rationalism, for it had a strong intuitive and emotional basis in his experience of visible nature. He confessed in 1785 that he had never read Spinoza's writings consequentially ('in einer Folge') or attained an overall view of his system, preferring instead to seek the divine 'in individual things' and 'in plants and stones' (to Jacobi, 9 June 1785, HAB I, 476). In so far as Goethe's pantheism does have a philosophical foundation, it is far closer to Herder's dialogues *Gott* (God) of 1787, in which Spinoza's universe is energized by Leibnizian dynamism, than to the *Ethics* of Spinoza himself.

It is above all in his scientific works, the first of which were composed in the course of discussions with Herder on Spinoza and the natural world in the mid-1780s, and in his late philosophical poetry that Goethe's nature pantheism is most fully expressed. Nature is not the work of a transcendental god: it has its own creative principle within itself, whose laws and regularities are the object of scientific enquiry (cf. HA XIII, 31–2). Spirit and matter, thought and extension, are equally divine and equally necessary (letter to Knebel, 8 April 1812, HAB III, 180); and far from concealing God, as Jacobi believed, the natural universe reveals him (to Boisserée, 2 March 1828, HAB IV, 271) – not, however, in that teleological evidence for design to which rational theologians had been fond of appealing, but in archetypal forms which it is the business of the scientist to identify and describe in their endless metamorphoses. In his later years, Goethe resorts increasingly to the medium of poetry – even within his scientific writings (cf. HA XIII, 32 and 34–5) – to express these views, which at times approach a kind of nature mysticism. This philosophico-religious wisdom is seen to its best advantage in the collection of poems he published in 1827 under the title 'Gott und Welt', including poems such as 'Prooemion', 'Parabase', 'Dauer im Wechsel' and 'Eins und Alles'. His preference for poetic expression, as distinct from discursive prose, is an essential feature of his late religiosity, and it derives in part from a conviction – perhaps reinforced by Kant's doctrine that our knowledge of the natural world is confined to phenomena, whereas the thing-in-itself is unknowable – that there is an ultimately unfathomable quality about existence, including the natural world, which sets a limit to our enquiries (HA XIII, 34). We must indeed pursue the latter as far as they will go, but the limit is reached when we encounter those archetypal phenomena (*Urphänomene*), such as magnetism or the production of colour from light and darkness, which cannot be further reduced (cf. maxims 19 and 20 in HA XII, 367). At this point, we must simply accept and venerate them (cf. maxim 718 in HA XII, 467). The older Goethe regards this attitude of veneration or reverence (*Ehrfurcht*) as existentially valuable, whether it is directed – as the educators of the 'Pedagogic Province' in *Wilhelm Meisters Wanderjahre* (Wilhelm Meister's Journeymanship, 1829) inform us (HA VIII, 154–8) – at what is above us, what is beneath us, or what is on the same level as ourselves. These three kinds of reverence, we are told, are to be found in varying degrees in different religions, but Goethe adds to them a fourth kind in which all the others are said to be implicit, namely reverence for ourselves – not as individuals, in a spirit of self-satisfaction, but for the divine principle within us as human beings. The precise significance of this doctrine need not concern us here, but in the context of Goethe's religious thought, two things stand out: firstly, the reverential attitude itself is more important than its object, which in this case appears to include all of creation; and secondly, its trinitarian expression marks this doctrine out as yet another of Goethe's religious models constructed in conscious divergence from equivalent models in Christian theology, such as St Augustine's *ordo caritatis* (see editor's commentary in HA¹² VIII, 615). Once again, the object of attention is immanent rather than transcendental: the religion of the Pedagogic Province is in fact a later version of the religion of humanity described in the fragment *Die Geheimnisse* (see above, p. 221).

The older Goethe's stress on the religious attitude as distinct from any definable object of worship is in keeping with a distrust of theology, and indeed of theory and abstraction in general, which characterizes his thought from an early stage. It is evident in his essay 'Zwo wichtige bisher unerörterte biblische Fragen' (Two Important but Hitherto Unanswered Biblical Questions) of 1773, in which he interprets the Pentecostal gift of tongues not as a miraculous multilingual facility but as an inarticulate language of personal religious feeling (WA I, vol. XXXVII, 186–90); and more famously, it informs Faust's reply to Gretchen's question whether he believes in God: 'Ich habe keinen Namen / Dafür! Gefühl ist alles; / Name ist Schall und Rauch, / Umnebelnd Himmelsglut' (I have no name for it! / Feeling is all; / Name is sound and smoke, / Obscuring heaven's glow'; HA III, 110). His distrust of religious dogma is compounded by his belief that no doctrine can retain its original form for long: all verbally transmitted material is subject to constant modification by changing circumstances, so that interpreters of the Bible, for instance, can rarely agree on the significance of anything they interpret (HA IX, 509; cf. HA X, 40). For the same reason, he views all Christian churches with distrust, describing their history as 'a product of error and violence' (*Gespräche* III/1, 603).

In his attitude to confessional differences, Goethe is again in tune with the Enlightenment. He remains a lifelong advocate of tolerance, and rebuffs the intolerance of Lavater with the words 'in our father's pharmacy there are many prescriptions'.[10] His Lutheran upbringing taught him to be critical of the Catholic Church, but his criticisms are tempered by recognition of the socially constructive function of popular Catholic festivals (HA X, 423–8 and XI, 484–5 and 515), and in later years by a recognition that the numerous sacraments of the Church of Rome may offer a greater enrichment of life than the austere Protestant liturgy (HA 9, 289–93). Admittedly, he had only contempt for those German Romantic poets who converted to Catholicism (cf. *Gespräche* II, 301–2) and for the neo-Catholic medievalism of the Romantic movement in general;[11] but this reaction has less to do with religious prejudice than with what he saw as a confusion of aesthetic and religious values in Romantic art, and with his own preference for classical art. His religious tolerance should not, however, be confused with indifferentism. He found much to admire in all the major religions, including Islam and Hinduism, and used their iconography and discourse, detached from specific dogmatic ends, as a rich source of poetic symbolism and allusion: *Faust* and the *West-östliche Divan* are only two of the most familiar examples.

No coherent religious system can be extracted from Goethe's writings and sayings. He remained open to the most diverse religious currents, drawing upon them in different ways as his own preoccupations and poetic productions required. In his famous statement that he was a pantheist in science, a polytheist in poetry and a monotheist in ethics,[12] he was not defining precise ideological differences – on another occasion, he in fact described himself as an atheist in science and philosophy, a pagan in art, and a Christian by emotional inclination (*Gespräche* III/1, 36–7). He was simply pointing out that no one set of doctrines can do full justice to the complexity of the universe and of human existence, although all of them have their distinct value if they are approached in a sympathetic and non-dogmatic spirit.

In a brief account of his philosophical development, Goethe declared that he had no aptitude ('kein Organ') for philosophy as such (HA XIII, 25). As already noted, he was never at ease in the realm of abstractions, whether in theology, art, science or philosophy. In his opinion, truth is apprehended for the most part directly, by means of observation and intuition (*Anschauung*).

In distancing himself from formal philosophy, he often describes his own 'innate methodology' (HA x, 520) in these terms, also declaring that philosophy is of value to him only in so far as it confirms conclusions he has already reached in his own intuitive manner.[13] His *Maximen und Reflexionen* are full of remarks of this kind, and of warnings against the use of theories divorced from experience, such as the following: 'Theories are usually the over-hasty conclusions of an impatient understanding which is anxious to get rid of the phenomena and replace them with images, concepts, and often indeed only with words' (maxim 548 in HA xii, 440). The fundamental concept in his philosophical thought – as in his religious thought – is accordingly nature, both as the object of our experience and as the ground and substance of our own being. Nature, which Goethe often describes as a mother, consequently includes mind as well as matter, and any disparagement of 'mere' nature by Kantian idealists such as Schiller was guaranteed to offend him (cf. HA xiii, 29).

Nevertheless, his dismissive remarks on formal philosophy should not be taken too literally. They may be due in part to his early encounters with the philosophical orthodoxy of the German universities in the mid-eighteenth century, namely the systematic rationalism of Christian Wolff, which he later described as 'alien, unpalatable, and ultimately superfluous' (HA ix, 273). This aversion may also help to explain why he took to reading hermetic and cabbalistic works by Paracelsus and others during his convalescence in 1768–70 (HA ix, 341–2); and while the main impact of this reading was on *Faust*, on which he began work soon afterwards, it must also have enlarged his knowledge of philosophy, especially of the neo-Platonic tradition to which most of these works belong. This in turn prepared the way for his reception of Leibniz and Spinoza, both of whom owe much to that same tradition.

At any rate, Goethe gradually acquired an extensive knowledge of philosophy, and during the middle decades of his life he devoted considerable time to philosophical studies, especially of Kant and German Idealism. Fichte, for example, commented after meeting him in 1794 that, in conversation, Goethe had given as clear and concise an outline of his (Fichte's) system as Fichte himself could have done (Grumach iv, 88). We have already seen how, in 1774 and again in 1784–5, he looked to Spinoza for philosophical support for his basic convictions concerning God and nature. But Spinoza's metaphysical principles were too general to provide a philosophical framework for the detailed studies of comparative anatomy, botany, and other aspects of natural history to which he devoted much of his energy during the 1780s. Here, the metaphysics of Leibniz, with its doctrine that all natural forms are links in a continuous chain of being, stretching upwards from the simplest elements of matter through all living forms to the human species, and perhaps on to the denizens of higher worlds, was much more useful. In the first place, it could easily be reconciled with Spinoza's monism, for there is no abrupt transition between matter and mind in Leibniz's cosmic hierarchy. Furthermore, Leibniz's monadology – which played no part in the more mechanical system of his disciple Wolff – provided a universal dynamic principle which accorded well with the vitalism of late eighteenth-century biology. And thirdly, Leibniz's gradual series of related forms, each differing only slightly from its predecessor, provided a ready-made basis for that 'natural system' of plant and animal classification which Goethe, along with other post-Linnaean taxonomists, hoped to establish.

Exactly when and how he first encountered Leibniz's thought is impossible to establish. But Leibniz's popular works, especially his *Théodicée* and *Monadologie*, were so widely known throughout the eighteenth century that Goethe cannot have failed to encounter them by the 1770s at the latest, and their substance became a permanent part of his world view. (For example, Leibniz's monadology and theodicy underpin the ostensibly religious framework of *Faust*.) Leibniz's principles provided the foundation for the work of eighteenth-century naturalists such as Charles Bonnet, and for the comprehensive account of the natural world in Herder's *Ideen zur Philosophie der Geschichte* (Ideas on the Philosophy of History), with both of which Goethe was demonstrably familiar by the mid-1780s. His own theories of comparative anatomy and botany, and of the gradual metamorphoses of basic forms, are undoubtedly informed by Leibniz's vision of nature.

Goethe's attachment to observation and experience, to what a friendly critic once described as his 'gegenständliches Denken' ('objective thinking'; HA XIII, 39), gives his thought a pronounced empirical basis which is lacking in all of the philosophers so far mentioned. He was himself aware of this fact, and in the course of his empirical work on colour in the 1790s he looked for philosophical support to the father of British empiricism, Francis Bacon, whose thought, along with that of Spinoza, Schiller and Kant, he once described as a decisive influence on his own philosophical development (*Gespräche* II, 1105–6). In his essay 'Der Versuch als Vermittler von Objekt und Subjekt' (The Experiment as Mediator between Object and Subject; the title was supplied by later editors), he recommends what is essentially Bacon's method of induction, whereby observations based on experiment are arranged in cognate series until the essential quality common to them all can be identified (HA XIII, 19–20). During the first decade of the following century, however, his work on chromatics led him to qualify his admiration for Bacon considerably. For firstly, he realized that the product of Baconian induction is an abstract concept (such as Bacon's definition of heat as motion), whereas Goethe, with his habitual distrust of abstractions, had now come to believe that inductive generalization should itself culminate in a concrete observation in the shape of a single archetypal phenomenon (or *Urphänomen*), such as the production of colour at the intersection of light and dark images, which incorporates the essential qualities of all the other phenomena in the same field of enquiry (HA XIII, 367–8; cf. HA XIII, 25). And secondly, his historical studies of the Royal Society convinced him that Baconian inductionism had encouraged an indiscriminate approach to observation, purportedly seeking to avoid prior assumptions but in fact opening the door to premature theories such as Newton's theory of refraction, of whose falsity Goethe was now convinced (HA XIV, 90, 136–53, and 155).

For all its apparent concreteness, the *Urphänomen* also has an ideal quality about it. As an archetypal form or regularity inherent in natural phenomena, it is, as it were, an idea of nature itself, and Goethe explicitly says on various occasions that nature 'operates according to ideas' (LA I, vol. X, p. 277; cf. *Gespräche* II, 705). His position here is akin to that of Plato, in that he derives all phenomena from an archetypal idea or form; but he is even closer to Plotinus and neo-Platonism, for unlike Plato's Ideas, Goethe's ideas of nature are not transcendental entities, but immanent principles active within the natural world. At the same time, however, the *Urphänomen*, as an ultimate generalization and universal principle by which all particular observations can be guided, is akin to Kant's 'regulative ideas', an affinity which Goethe himself appears to have noticed (HA XIII, 30–1).

Goethe's relationship to Kant's philosophy is complex and unconventional. On the one hand, he was in no doubt that Kant was the greatest philosopher of the age, whose influence on German culture was incalculable (conversation with Eckermann, 11 April 1827). On the other hand, he was never entirely at ease with the abstraction and technicality of Kant's system, and had much greater difficulty reconciling it with his own blend of intuitive empiricism and neo-Platonic metaphysics than he had with the thought of Spinoza, Leibniz or Bacon. But Kant was too important to ignore, and soon after his return from Italy in 1788 Goethe began to inform himself about his philosophy with the help of the philosopher Karl Leonhard Reinhold and others; he also read the *Critique of Pure Reason* for himself. In his scientific practice, he could readily concur with Kant's doctrine that our knowledge of the natural world is confined to phenomena – although, as we have already seen, he still felt free to indulge at times in that very kind of speculation on monads, entelechies and other metaphysical entities which Kant had attempted to outlaw. His study of Kant also made him more conscious than before of the distinction between subjectivity and objectivity, and of the constitutive role of the subject in all cognition (HA XIII, 26–7; cf. letter to Schultz, 18 September 1831, HAB IV, 450). The part of Kant's system which he had least use for was his moral philosophy, with its rigorous dualism of moral freedom and natural determinism, and one of his recurrent criticisms of Schiller is that the latter often placed excessive emphasis on this opposition (cf. conversations with Eckermann, 14 November 1823 and 18 January 1827). The work of Kant which he found most congenial was the *Critique of Judgement*. It appealed to him not only because it confirmed his long-held antipathy, already nurtured by Spinoza and Bacon, towards teleological explanations of natural phenomena; it also seemed to endorse the opinion he had formed in Italy that art and nature are parallel realms, and that the successful work of art, like the natural organism, is an end in itself, not the instrument of any external purpose.[14] Characteristically, it is this third and last of the *Critiques*, in which Kant attempts to draw together and reconcile those realms of nature and freedom which he had so rigorously separated in the first and second, that appeals most to Goethe's sense of the harmony and oneness of the universe.

Goethe was personally acquainted with all the leading post-Kantian German Idealists – with Fichte, Schelling and Hegel during their periods in Jena, and with Schopenhauer through his mother Johanna, who was a prominent member of Weimar society from 1806 onwards. In his official responsibility for the administration of the university, Goethe acquainted himself with the writings of Fichte's Jena period (1794–9), but found he had little common ground with Fichte's radical subjectivism. After Fichte's abrasive behaviour led to his dismissal from the university, Goethe ceased to have regular contact with him – although there are possible allusions to some of his ideas in *Faust* (cf. Boyle II, 763 and 767).

Schelling, on the other hand, had much in common with Goethe. The philosophy of nature was of central importance in his system, and he treated the development of nature and its processes as parallel to that of mind or spirit: the mind simultaneously acquires knowledge of itself as it acquires knowledge of nature. Schelling also acknowledged his debts to Spinoza and Leibniz – the former in his philosophy of nature, the latter in his philosophy of mind and consciousness (cf. Boyle II, 665–7). All of these attitudes were congenial to Goethe, who frequently sought Schelling's company during the latter's time in Jena (1798–1803) and discussed his own scientific work with him at length; Schelling's concept of polarity as a productive principle throughout nature also encouraged Goethe to formalize his own equivalent doctrine (cf. HA XIII, 48). But Schelling's attitude was too dogmatic for Goethe's liking, and his *Naturphilosophie* contained too much abstraction and speculation; nor could Goethe endorse Schelling's typically Romantic privileging of art and aesthetic experience as the culmination of his *System des transzendentalen Idealismus* (1800). The qualified admiration for Schelling which he retained for the rest of his life was due primarily to the central importance of nature in the latter's philosophy (cf. letter to Boisserée, 2 March 1828, HAB IV, 271).

Goethe's relationship with Hegel and Schopenhauer, on the other hand, was more distant. He respected them both, not least because both defended his anti-Newtonian theory of colour at a time when it was almost universally condemned by the scientific establishment.[15] But Goethe could never be happy with Hegel's systematic doctrine that the content of all areas of experience, including art and religion, can be fully articulated in rational discourse; and although he reacted positively when Hegel expounded some of his ideas to him in conversation, he found Hegel's published work abstruse and uncongenial (to Knebel, 14 November 1827, HAB IV, 260) and eventually ceased to take any interest in it (*Gespräche* III/2, 158). In the course of his contacts with Schopenhauer, he read several of the latter's works, including *Die Welt als Wille und Vorstellung* (The World as Will and Representation, 1819). Not surprisingly, Schopenhauer's nihilism and pessimism left no discernible mark on Goethe's thinking.

So much for Goethe's attitude towards earlier and contemporary philosophers. His own views on metaphysics, epistemology and scientific method have already been discussed in connection with his response to Spinoza, Leibniz, Bacon and Kant. It now remains to look in conclusion at his position with regard to other areas of philosophy.

On ethics, we have seen that this was the one part of Kant's system with which Goethe could not come to terms, and that he had similar difficulty with Schiller's moral philosophy in so far as it reflected Kant's ethical dualism. Goethe's own moral philosophy is not systematic. As already noted, he comments positively on Christian morality and on Spinoza's doctrine of universal love; but the affective ethics of sensibility is also a powerful influence. It is significant in this connection that the morally exemplary characters in his literary works, from Iphigenie and the pious lady in Book 6 of *Wilhelm Meisters Lehrjahre* to Ottilie in *Die Wahlverwandtschaften* (The Elective Affinities) and the transfigured Gretchen at the end of *Faust*, are all female: their ethics are ethics of the heart rather than of the head. As in the literature of sensibility, the moral values in question are also closer to the middle-class conception of virtue than to the courtly ethos of honour and reputation: the heroines of *Hermann und Dorothea* and *Die natürliche Tochter* (The Natural Daughter) are in this respect typical. Goethe's personal reflections on ethical matters are predominantly practical and specific to particular situations: his *Maximen und Reflexionen* contain hundreds of observations of this kind, the accumulated wisdom of common sense and long experience, for which he finds the apophthegm or aphorism a more appropriate vehicle than the ethical treatise.

His political principles – for one can scarcely speak of his political philosophy, since his works contain nothing resembling a comprehensive theory of politics – are similar in this regard. He shows great respect for custom and tradition (*Götz von Berlichingen* and *Egmont* are obvious examples), but he also inherits the *Aufklärung* belief in moderate reform, initiated by an enlightened government from above rather than in response to popular pressure from below; and he has only distrust for political theory as soon as it is divorced from practice. The political theorist to whom his own moderate conservatism most closely approximates is Justus Möser, whose role in the administration of the Bishopric of Osnabrück was not unlike Goethe's role in Weimar; the appreciative comments in Goethe's autobiography on Möser's writings underline his sympathy with the latter's political thinking (HA IX, 596–8 and especially X, 52–3). As in political matters, Goethe's distrust of abstract theory is apparent in his attitude towards history: for although he lived in the golden age of philosophies of history – from Montesquieu, Rousseau and Condorcet to Herder, Kant and Hegel – he regarded all such schemes with scepticism, discerning no rational plan or progress in history, but for the most part disorder and contingency.

Although Goethe reflected profoundly on art in general and on the poetic and visual arts in particular, he again has no systematic theory of art and aesthetics. His philosophical reflections on art date largely from the years after his return from Italy, where he had engaged in long discussions on art and beauty with Karl Philipp Moritz, in the course of which, as he later acknowledged (letter to Riemer, 19 August 1829, HAB IV, 339–40), he laid the foundations of his own classical aesthetics. Like Moritz, Goethe came at this time to regard 'art' – over and above its embodiment in each of the individual arts – as a creative activity in its own right, and with a profound cultural significance (see Boyle I, 498–500 and 553–4). The kind of art they had in mind – like Winckelmann before them – was classical art, the art of ancient Greece and its neoclassical derivatives. True art is analogous to nature – not nature in the raw as in naturalism, but an ideal, normative nature whose highest expression is beauty, described by Moritz as 'das In-sich-selbst-Vollendete' ('that which is perfect in itself'); or as Goethe later put it, classical beauty is the aesthetic equivalent of the *Urphänomen* in nature (conversation with Eckermann, 18 April 1827). Moritz published his conclusions in the treatise 'Über die bildende Nachahmung des Schönen' (On the Creative Imitation of the Beautiful, 1788), an extract from which Goethe included in his *Italienische Reise* (HA XI, 534–41). Goethe wrote no aesthetic treatise of his own, although he did outline his classical programme for poetry and the visual arts in various shorter essays on specific topics, of which 'Einfache Nachahmung der Natur, Manier, Stil' (Simple Imitation of Nature, Manner, Style, 1788) and *Winckelmann* (1805) are among the most important. But unlike Moritz – and, for that matter, Schiller – he continued to believe that beauty can never be defined conceptually, but only felt or created (cf. conversation with Eckermann, 18 April 1827). He was accordingly perfectly happy to be classified in Schiller's *Über naive und sentimentalische Dichtung* (On Naive and Reflective Poetry, 1795–6) as the 'naive' type of artistic genius who creates for the most part spontaneously and without reflection, unlike Schiller himself, for whom rational reflection was an essential part both of the creative process and of aesthetic theorizing.

To conclude: Goethe was neither a philosopher nor a theologian, but few poets of any age or culture can rival him in the breadth of his knowledge of philosophy and religion. This knowledge was not merely an adjunct to his poetic, scientific, autobiographical and other works. It fructified and enriched almost everything he wrote.

NOTES

1 HA IX, 135–6; cf. WA I, 37, pp. 181–6.
2 See his letters to Susanna von Klettenberg, 26 August 1770, HAB I, 115, and to Lavater, 29 July 1782, HAB I, 402.
3 Letter to Langer, 17 January 1769, HAB I, 84; cf. HA IX, 334–5.
4 See his conversation of 11 March 1832; cf. letter to Zelter, 7 November 1816, in HAB III, 376; also HA XII, 229 and 239.
5 Cf. his letter to Herder, *c.* 12 May 1775, in HAB I, 182–3.
6 HAB, I, 403; cf. letters to Jacobi, 21 October 1785 and 10 May 1812, HAB I, 489 and III, 191.
7 Cf. *Gespräche* III/1, 36–7; also letter to Jacobi, 5 May 1786, HAB I, 508.
8 Cf. *Gespräche* II, 700–77 and conversation with Eckermann, 1 September 1829.
9 Cf. *Ethics* Part V, Prop. XXXVI and Corollary.
10 Letter to Lavater, 4 October 1782, HAB I, 408; cf. HA XII, 228–39.
11 WA I, vol. XLVIII, p. 122; cf. *Gespräche* II, 406–7 and 409.
12 HA XII, 372; also letter to Jacobi, 6 January 1813, HAB III, 220.
13 Cf. letter to Jacobi, 23 November 1801, HAB II, 423.
14 HA X, 286–7; also letter to Zelter, 29 January 1830, HAB IV, 370.
15 On Hegel, see *Tag- und Jahreshefte*, 1817, in HA X, 520; on Schopenhauer, see Goethe to Schopenhauer, 23 October 1815, HAB III, 328–9.

15

GERHART HOFFMEISTER

Reception in Germany and abroad

For much of his adult life, Goethe had a dominant position in the Republic of Letters in Germany as well as abroad. No one who amounted to anything, whether it was Kleist or Heine, Scott or Byron, Musset or Saint-Beuve, Mazzini or Pushkin, could possibly bypass him and his work. Admirers and opponents alike would agree on one point: 'He disposes of the poetic world, like a conqueror of the real earth.'[1] Confronted with his monumental stature and output, they took a position either in favour of Goethe or against him, sometimes even switching sides in the course of their careers. As a result, Goethe became a controversial figure both for poets and critics, for Germans as well as for Europeans. But what has been his enduring impact?

By the end of his life, Goethe felt less accepted by German than by European contemporaries, who between 1827 and 1831 not only sent him birthday gifts (medallions and books) from Paris, Moscow, and Scotland (Carlyle in 1831), but also published three reviews of his 'Helena' tragedy (*Faust II*, Act III) in the same year (*The Foreign Review*, Edinburgh; *Le Globe*, Paris; *The Moscow Messenger*, 1828). Goethe was delighted, since this lively response seemed to confirm his venture to promote *Weltliteratur* (world literature) as a network of communication among intellectuals and peoples across national frontiers. For him *Weltliteratur* was neither the sum of all national literatures nor the ever increasing canon of world masterpieces, rather he conceived of it as a dynamic process of rapprochement among European nations – above all Britain, France and Germany – with the goal of breaking down the walls of national prejudices that hampered peaceful coexistence in the wake of the Napoleonic Wars. To realize this social function of literature, Goethe called upon contemporary authors to serve – along with himself – as mediators and facilitators across the frontiers in periodicals, translations and memoirs. He hoped this common market of ideas would eventually manifest itself in a greater sense of understanding and tolerance, first among the intellectuals and thereafter also among the peoples. By favouring foreign authors such as Lord Byron and Manzoni at the expense of German Romantics, however, Goethe heightened the controversy that surrounded his reputation, for as a young man his outlook on life and literary practice (see his Storm and Stress works of the 1770s) had not been so far removed from that of the Romantics, whom he now viewed with deep concern from the vantage point of an Olympian patriarch in Weimar. Goethe had not only become an ambivalent figure in the eyes of others, but he had himself matured and had developed negative views about Romantic poetry, although in fact his poetic output shows a surprising affinity to Romanticism.

These controversies surrounding Goethe's reputation are exacerbated by the fact that German literary critics have seen Goethe's literary situation vis-à-vis Romanticism in a different light from foreign scholars. For German literary historians Goethe went through three major stages, from the Storm and Stress via Weimar Classicism to his later style. In Germany Goethe is associated most closely with 'Klassik' (classicism), which he understood as a bastion of high moral and aesthetic standards modelled on the ancients and upheld in the face of the corroding trends of Romanticism. But viewed from outside Germany, the 'Age of Goethe' is seen as part of the 'Age of European Romanticism'. Accordingly, to foreign critics Goethe appeared to be the key figure in the struggle to build a cultural identity for Germany, and an outstanding representative of the new 'Romantic Movement' that swept across Europe from the 1770s onwards, breaking down the poetic conventions of classicism. Whether Goethe himself and German literary historians agreed with this assessment or not, Goethe as scientist, artist, and author of *Die Leiden des jungen Werther, Götz von Berlichingen, Faust,* and *Wilhelm Meister* came to be regarded as central to the creation of Romantic ideas and innovative literary practices. As early as 1904, the literary historian George Saintsbury in his *History of Criticism and Literary Taste in Europe (1900–1904)* considered Weimar Classicism and Jena Romanticism from Klopstock to Heine as integral parts of European Romanticism, but it took an additional seventy-six years for German critics to revise their traditional insistence on the antagonism between Weimar and Jena in favour of a single interdependent period of Classicism-Romanticism.[2] Even the notion of a cultural lag between a dominant German and a receiving Romance literature can, according to Virgil Nemoianu's masterly work, be laid to rest; in *The Taming of Romanticism* (1984) he demonstrates the synchronism of the Romantic movement in Europe from its dawn in the 1760s and 1770s (Wood, Young, Rousseau, Goethe) to High Romanticism around 1800.[3] Goethe played a pivotal role in this process, because, by breaking down classicist conventions in his early masterpieces (*Götz von Berlichingen,* 1773; *Die Leiden des jungen Werther,* 1774), he undermined the supremacy of French culture in Germany, replacing it with a new priority: the discovery of 'inward forms', native traditions, and 'the reproduction of the world around him through the world within'. For this reason he appeared to many as a Romantic and Weimar as the seat of German Romanticism.[4]

Goethe's position in 'Romantic' Germany

Goethe's position in German cultural development from the Storm and Stress onwards rapidly took on ironic dimensions. Had he not been the young rebel who had recreated the myth of total self-emancipation from all possible constraints in the glorious role-poem 'Prometheus' (1774)? Had he not rejected the imitation of foreign styles in favour of 'Gothic' art in 'Von deutscher Baukunst' (On German Architecture, 1772)? Yet during his last thirty years the mature author intentionally and programmatically turned against Romanticism in all its excesses.

The more influential the Schlegel brothers became with their message of 'the arbitrary rule of the poet' (*Athenäum* no. 116), the more inroads Wackenroder's and Tieck's *Herzensergießungen eines kunstliebenden Kloster-bruders* (Outpourings of an Art-Loving Friar, 1797) made, the more polemical grew Goethe's broadsides against the mysticism of the Romantics, against their chaotic, if not downright grotesque forms, and their absurd content: 'Ancient works are like sculptures, true and real; Romantic art is deceptive as the images of a magic lantern ... Thoroughly ordinary subject matter receives a wondrous appearance through Romantic treatment, its "coating" constituting everything, its foundation nothing' (*Gespräche* II, 329). For him, art was to be created by analogy with nature and inspired by the ancients. If this precept were not strictly observed, art could easily become the product of a severe fever, as was apparently the case with Wackenroder and his overly pious followers, blasted in the Weimar manifesto *Neu-deutsche religiös-patriotische Kunst* (New-German Religious-Patriotic Art, 1817). In *Die romantische Schule* (The Romantic School, 1836) Heinrich Heine, from his anticlerical standpoint, interpreted this essay as a revolution in German letters that established Goethe as a canonical figure, victor over all Romantics who harked back to medieval Christianity. On this latter score Heine was mistaken; Goethe, unsuccessful in his attempt to redirect his contemporaries' poetic energies away from a dangerous fusion of religion and nationalism, withdrew from the public debate for about a decade, without however giving up his principles. On the contrary, during his last remaining years, from 1827 on, he coined and developed his idea of *Weltliteratur* as a counterthrust to the religious universalism of backward-looking Romantics both in the political and the aesthetic realm. As he remarked to Eckermann: 'National literature does not mean anything these days, the epoch of world literature is about to arrive and each one of us must act in order to accelerate this era' (31 January 1827).

Yet this was not as innovative an idea as he may have thought. To be sure, he clearly went beyond his previous polemics, but it was to embrace a synthesis of Romantic and classical programmes that Friedrich Schlegel had developed a generation earlier when he pointed out the need for increased cooperation among European nations and promoted the idea of a universal poetry.[5] In his cosmopolitan sketch of 1825, his brother August Wilhelm had also already referred to 'literary traffic among nations'.[6] Goethe differed from their approach, however, in his insistence that art alone cannot renew society and that the model of the Christian Middle Ages as prescribed by the Romantics was, in its blend of religious zeal, emotional patriotism and outright subjectivism, nothing but a cause for concern. At the same time he maintained his belief that 'pathologisch, oder auch romantisch', in the sense of 'excessive and absurd', were exchangeable terms (Eckermann, 5 September 1829), a notion applied to the works of Wackenroder (*Herzensergießungen*), Brentano, E. T. A. Hoffmann, and Kleist (*Das Käthchen von Heilbronn*) and which crystallized into the famous statement: 'Classical art I call sound, Romantic art sick' (Eckermann, 2 April 1829).

This categorical statement expressed his frustration with all excesses of Romanticism and amounted to a rejection of the younger generation, a position that, after the death of his friend and collaborator Schiller in 1805, increased his isolation. His awkward situation was further exacerbated by a rising chorus of voices that had first admired him and his works, and then, experiencing a change of heart, attacked the classical poet. The effect was all the more disconcerting to him, since an enthusiastic Goethe cult had already formed in the famous intellectual gathering in Jena (the 'Early Romantic School' of 1796) and in the intellectual circles of Berlin (the Romantic 'salons' led, among others, by Rahel Levin-Varnhagen). Many young people – poets, artists and critics alike, of both genders – associated with each other in Jena, Berlin, Heidelberg, Göttingen and Weimar, met at universities, in private homes or in Romantic 'salons' and worshipped Goethe. 'May I mention what united us all? One poet had aroused us all; the spirit of his works had become the centre of self-recognition and association with others', wrote Clemens Brentano in *Godwi*.[7] Yet the Jena Romantics went far beyond this initial 'unconditional worship' of the master; they also supplied the necessary theoretical underpinnings to their assertion of his merits. In their reviews, their lectures, and their poetic system in fragmentary shape (aphorisms), both the Schlegel brothers and Novalis considered Goethe the ideal synthesis of antiquity and modernity and therefore granted him, as the initiator of a new school of poetry, the position of 'steward of poetry on earth',[8] a view that would be shared by later critics such as Madame de Staël. *Wilhelm Meister* became the bible of Romanticism and thanks to it, novel-writing and Romanticism neatly fused for a while.

However, once these theoreticians realized that they had to go beyond Goethe's towering achievements in order to reach their own goal of a progressive 'Transzendentalpoesie', at the very height of their admiration a more critical stance emerged, first in private notebooks (F. Schlegel, Novalis), thereafter in lectures and publications. A case in point is Novalis, who shortly before his death in 1801 changed his positive assessment of *Wilhelm Meister* and began to regard it as an expression of artistic atheism,[9] because Romantic characters such as Mignon were doomed in the overall plan of Wilhelm's education. Friedrich Schlegel agreed and kept elaborating his own Romantic, anti-Goethean agenda in his periodical *Europa* (especially in the essay 'Literatur' of 1803), criticizing the Reformation and the Enlightenment in the wake of Wackenroder's *Herzensergießungen* and focussing on medieval Christian poetry even before his conversion to Catholicism in 1808. From his new vantage point it was easy for him to label Goethe 'a German Voltaire'.[10] Earlier, August Wilhelm Schlegel had blasted *Faust I* and *Iphigenie auf Tauris* as not stageworthy,[11] so that Goethe felt excluded from the ruling spirit of the period. Indeed, he would later claim: 'The Schlegel brothers barely left me standing in the great revolution that they accomplished, to the dismay of Hardenberg who had also wanted to delete me' (HAB IV, 455). Goethe's massive presence on the literary scene, like that of a boulder standing in an otherwise changing landscape, had its tragic consequences for young poets, painters and musicians. For they constantly approached him in search of a word of encouragement, but found the master unresponsive. Hölderlin, Kleist, E. T. A. Hoffmann and other German Romantics all had this experience.

One of these young men who had grown up under the spell of Goethe was Heinrich Heine. Driven by a strong sense of rivalry[12] and a radical view of the function of literature, after a disappointing visit to Weimar he called Goethe a 'servant of princes' who as a classical author seemed to have betrayed his youthful promise, a reproach that was to reverberate into the twentieth century. According to Heine, Goethe had become an old robber baron living the life of a philistine indifferent to the problems in society.[13] Yet in the very same year, Heine, apparently torn in his ambivalent perception of Goethe, depicted him as an Olympian, 'with his clear Greek eye' and with his 'sculptor's gaze';[14] he celebrates him as the great pagan,[15] the incarnation of the bygone 'Kunstperiode' (period of art),[16] and looks up to him as a model both for his struggle to settle accounts with the Catholic brand of Romanticism, and for his desire to establish the autonomy of the arts in the face of all types of 'Tendenzdichtung' (tendentious poetry; see his *Atta Troll*). In *Die romantische Schule* Heine followed his Berlin professor Hegel by using a dialectical method, scolding Goethe from a political angle for his indifferentism, but praising him from a poetic perspective as a perfect artist on the scale of Homer and Shakespeare.[17]

As mentioned above, Goethe had been the intellectual focus of the Jena Romantics, who developed the notion of *Universalpoesie* anticipation of Goethe's *Weltliteratur* and disseminated his fame beyond Germany's borders (Schlegel brothers). Even more important was Goethe's exchange of ideas with the philosophers of nature in Jena, for whose *Idealismus* Goethe was a source of inspiration. In his turn, Goethe acknowledged the intellectual debt he owed to Fichte, Schelling, Hegel, the von Humboldt brothers and Schlegel, for example in his essay 'Einwirkung der neueren Philosophie'(Effect of Modern Philosophy, 1820). To what extent the Age of Romanticism, the Age of Goethe and idealistic philosophy overlapped in Germany, can be assessed by studying Schelling, professor at Jena University and member of the early 'School of Romanticism'; generally regarded as more poet than philosopher, Schelling was a friend of Hegel and Hölderlin, and in touch with Goethe. The Weimar poet saw in Schelling an ally in his attempt in *Zur Farbenlehre* (Theory of Colour, 1810) to overthrow Sir Isaac Newton's mechanical conception of Nature. He could not agree more with Schelling's definition: 'To philosophize about nature means to create nature . . . to elevate her from the dead mechanism in which she seems to be caught, to animate her with freedom, as it were, and to set her free to embark on her own development.'[18] Essentially, Schelling, Goethe, and above all Novalis would see a definite congruence in the philosopher's and the poet's task, namely to recognize the spirit in nature, hitherto frozen yet in need of redemption through a second creative act in the mind, in philosophy as well as in fiction. Goethe felt attracted to this 'Identitätsschule' (letter to Zelter, 15 January 1813, HAB III, 222), because it confirmed his organic view of nature as guided by a 'Weltseele' (world spirit). In addition, he appreciated Hegel's support of his dialectic approach to nature and aesthetics. In his *Aesthetics* the philosopher interpreted *Faust* as the paradigm of an 'absolute philosophical tragedy' and defined classical poetry as harmony of form and content, using Goethe's masterpieces as counter-examples to the failings of subjective and fragmentary Romantic art. Thus it appears that Goethe was indeed not quite as isolated in Germany as he sometimes gave people to understand.

Yet after his death, the ambivalence of Goethe's position in Germany and abroad did not diminish. While *Jungdeutsche* (Young Germans) of the 1830s tried to distance themselves from his work as being too 'Romantic' or 'idealistic', and also many foreign writers liked to think of Goethe as a prototypical Romantic, the subsequent generation of realists discovered a fundamental continuity between the master and their own prose works. They saw in him a forerunner of their movement. But how was this turn-around possible?

In their correspondence (1794–1805) Goethe and Schiller discussed poetic genres and styles. Goethe even used his own 'realistic tic' to defend his *Wilhelm Meisters Lehrjahre* against Schiller's criticism of its weakly delineated philosophical ideas (9 July 1796, HAB II, 229–30). But it was Schiller who established his friend as the 'naive' poet who tends towards realism on account of his oneness with nature (*Über naive und sentimentalische Dichtung*, 1795–6). In *Wilhelm Meisters Lehrjahre* he praised the faithful depiction of the world of theatre and Wilhelm, the protagonist, as the incarnation of 'realism' (letter to Goethe, 5 July 1796, MA VIII/1, 196–7). To the amazement of both camps, Goethe's novels, above all the Wilhelm Meister trilogy, inspired all novel-writing in Goethe's wake, as evidenced by the Romantics' *Künstlerroman* (artist's novel) as well as the Realists' *Bildungsroman* (novel of education). For the Realists (1830s–1880s) Goethe had not only drawn psychologically convincing character portraits, but also focussed on social and cultural problems of his age, for example the question of a national theatre, the role of Pietism and emigration to America, thereby creating a paradigm for the poetic reproduction of reality in writers from Karl Immermann (*Die Epigonen*, 1836), Gottfried Keller (*Der Grüne Heinrich*, 1854–5) and Adalbert Stifter (*Der Nachsommer*, 1857) to later Goethe admirers such as Wilhelm Raabe and Theodor Fontane. All these novelists addressed the inherent dissociation between society and the individual, the clash between man and the harsh realities of life, without jeopardizing the traditional order. Often they found a compromise solution with an emphasis on duty and humane behaviour. Like Goethe, they chose both a symbolic style that hovers between the universal and the specific, and a humorous tone. Stifter for instance knew that although he was not a second Goethe he was one of his kinsmen (letter to Heckenast, 13 May 1854), because he vied with his forerunner for an undogmatic and objective approach to this world. Thus it appears that the contemporary German Romantics had tried to go beyond Goethe, transforming the impulses emanating from his works for their own purposes, but essentially leaving him alone, whereas the Realists turned to Goethe's prose for inspiration after his death.

Goethe's role in European Romanticism

Ostensibly 'marginalized' at home, Goethe succeeded in finding allies abroad. Simultaneously, important translators and intermediaries acquainted foreign readers with his work and ideas.

Mention has already been made of the 'Helena' reviews, for Goethe a signal of *Weltliteratur* on the move (letter to Carlyle, 15 June 1828, HAB IV, 281). However, as Goethe's changing perception proves, its approach was fraught with ambivalences, ironies and setbacks. In a sketch of 1826 he acknowledges the recent impact of his works in France: 'Clearly the anticlassicists welcome my aesthetic maxim and use the works fashioned according to it as examples' (FA I, vol. XXII, 766). Here he refers to J.-J. Ampère's review of F.-A. Stapfer's edition of translations, *Œuvres dramatiques de Goethe*, that had appeared in *Le Globe* (1826), a liberal-progressive periodical in Paris. In his overview of Goethe's development, Ampère draws a parallel between the literary stagnation in France in the 1820s and that of the threshold to the Storm and Stress movement, crediting the subsequent regeneration of German literature to Goethe's principle of replacing the classicist rule of imitation with a creative process that draws its strength from looking inside, 'den Stoff seiner Produktionen in sich selbst zu finden' (finding the subject matter within oneself) (Goethe's translation of Ampère, 'Die Zeitschrift Le Globe', FA I, vol. XXII, 262). That a young Frenchman had discovered his insistence on originality and confession as the only way to unhinge the system of neoclassicism delighted Goethe, because such an unbiased assessment of his art seemed to him out of the question in Germany (Eckermann, 4 May 1827); unfortunately, his enthusiasm was dampened when he realized the extreme and reckless political liberalism of the *Globe* contributors.

In the same periodical Goethe encountered a review of Victor Hugo's *Odes et Ballades* (1826) and praised his poetry for its reproduction of an objective reality that was anathema to the 'German fools' (of the Romantic generation; Eckermann, 4 January 1827). His enthusiasm lasted until he read Hugo's revolutionary play *Hernani* (1830), 'an absurd composition' (*Gespräche* III/2, 599), and until he learned about the battles and excesses on the Paris stage. Even worse, Romanticism in all its disgusting abominations seemed to jump at him from Hugo's novel *Notre-Dame de Paris* (1831). Confronted with the 'aesthetics of the grotesque' that revolutionized French literary conventions two generations after the Storm and Stress, Goethe in his old age did not want any part of it. What he was reading here, 'the most abominable book ever written' (Eckermann III, 27 January 1831), jeopardized everything he had striven for in his life and poetic career: clarity and order, beauty and humanity, as well as the harmonious polarity of things. Not surprisingly, Goethe relegated *Notre-Dame de Paris* to the category of 'literature of despair' (letter to Zelter, 28 June 1831, HAB IV, 435), composed in a state of pathological fever that reminded him of his own beginnings as well as of German Romanticism. In his view, the only difference was that things were getting worse: he noticed a satanic strain, 'devils, witches and vampires' (Eckermann III, 14 March 1830) in Hugo and the works of his followers that threatened to undermine his world view and his programme of 'Weltliteratur'. Apparently, he was not aware of the irony of this outcome, the reception of his works in France having been instrumental in unleashing this very satanism, as we shall see. Evidently, he needed to look for support somewhere else, and he found it in Béranger, Manzoni and Byron.

Pierre-Jean Béranger (1780–1857) was the popular author of light-hearted and sometimes satirical *chansons* that promoted the cult of Napoleon and attacked the abuses of the Church. In his songs Goethe, who also had a strong admiration for Napoleon, saw a reflection of himself, because they were not only full of grace, irony and artistic accomplishment (Eckermann III, 3 May 1827), but they also express his own heart and the voice of the people simultaneously (Eckermann III, 14 March 1830), something Goethe could only wish for in Germany. So he claimed Béranger as a possible ally in his struggle against Romantic excesses.

Personally well disposed towards Manzoni (see his 'Teilnahme Goethes an Manzoni') Goethe corresponded with the author of the plays *Il Conte di Carmagnola* and *Adelchi*, and of the novel *I promessi sposi* since 1818, and he also reviewed and translated his works. Goethe seems to have considered him both as a substitute for Schiller and as a mirror-image of himself. Reviewing his work he asks: 'Why can't I do a German contemporary a good turn like this!' (letter to Knebel, 14 December 1822, HAB IV, 55). But more than personal reasons drew him to Manzoni, namely his position between pedantic classicists and extreme Romantics. Goethe refers to his 'humane' ideas, his serious purpose and clarity of presentation, his judiciousness in maintaining a balanced form without arbitrariness, 'sentiment without sentimentality' (Eckermann, 18 July 1827), as well as religion without hypocrisy (see 'Klassiker und Romantiker in Italien', 1820). Goethe objected to the confusion of poetic truth and historical documentation in *I promessi sposi*, but Manzoni was still convinced that he owed his fame to a large extent to Goethe.

On the personal and historical level, Goethe's response to Lord Byron constituted an extraordinary event in the evolution of his concept of *Weltliteratur*. Whereas he rejected French Romantic excesses as reminders of his youthful rebellion, for Byron he made a surprising exception: 'From his first appearance I accompanied him – so steadfast, immensely productive, continually forging ahead and affectionate – in all his endeavours' (letter to G. F. Benecke, 12 November 1822, HAB IV, 53). Lord Byron was the only one among his contemporaries whom he loved like a son and admired as the greatest 'incommensurable' talent of the century (Eckermann, 24 February 1825). He even went so far as to extend an entire epoch of world history from

Homer to Byron, from Troy to Missolonghi, with the British Lord playing a central role in the inauguration of *Weltliteratur*. However, Goethe did not arrive at this happy conclusion without considerable shifts in his stance. Early on, even before 1816, he had been troubled by Byron's eccentric personality, especially his hypochondria, his self-hatred and self-torment, his constant polemics and dissoluteness. This last feature and Byron's rebelliousness he traced to the poet's aristocratic British background. Yet beyond these obvious shortcomings he perceived an outstanding characteristic: Byron was a born genius who created his works without the crutches of erudition and reflection: 'His works he begot as women beget beautiful children; they don't think about it and don't know how they did it' (Eckermann, 24 February 1825). Because Byron's genius had such an awe-inspiring quality, Goethe decided to place him in a different category from other poets, namely that of outstanding people such as Napoleon, who are driven by a 'daimon', a supernatural power, incommensurable and uncanny. Such people are engaged in a mission of their own that cannot be judged within the constraints of normal social and moral conventions, but who nonetheless need to be appreciated as world-historical individuals (Eckermann, 8 March 1831).

Before and after Byron's death, Goethe worked with surprising devotion on translations and commentaries of *Manfred* (1817), *Don Juan* (1819–24) and *Cain* (1821). As was to be expected, he did not reject *Manfred* as a possible plagiarism of *Faust I*, but praised it as a creative recasting that projects the same mood of despair but not the same outcome, since Faust struggles with metaphysical problems, Manfred with his self-consciousness and desire for oblivion. What is more important than these translations is Goethe's poetic monument to Byron in the mythical figure of Euphorion, the son of Faust and Helena, who as the representative of modern poetry rises like Icarus to great heights before he plunges to earth without having obtained his goal, his mission in Greece. Did Goethe impress Lord Byron as well? Byron expressed a certain affinity to the German poet and his work, although he had only read *Werther* in translation and heard 'Monk' Lewis translate from *Faust I* at Madame de Staël's home, Coppet, in 1816. Both poets seemed to believe that they understood each other, but beyond *Manfred* and the Goethe dedication to *Werner* (1823), there are few tangible traces in Byron.

European translators and mediators of Goethe

As a rule, mediators of the works and ideas of European Romanticism did not proceed in an intellectual vacuum. Shelley in the preface to *The Revolt of Islam* (1818) made the pertinent observation on this score: 'there must be a resemblance which does not depend upon their own will, between all the writers of any particular age. They cannot escape from subjection to a common influence which arises out of an infinite combination of circumstances belonging to the times in which they live.' Inspired by the intellectual temper of the age, they used their predecessors as starting points for their innovative ideas, before they influenced contemporary artists and critics or those of the next generation. That Goethe became well-known in all of Europe around 1800 was mainly due to the efforts of the Schlegel brothers, who analyzed and praised his work in their notes, essays and lectures. In spite of his ambivalence to Goethe, August Wilhelm Schlegel became a vital mediator.

With his *Vorlesungen über dramatische Kunst und Literatur*, especially in their French version, *Cours de littérature dramatique* (1809; part II: 1814), Schlegel's ideas spread to France (de Staël, Constant, Lemercier, Nerval, Hugo, Sismondi, Sainte-Beuve), Britain (*Lectures on Dramatic Art and Literature*, trans. John Black, 1815; Wordsworth and Coleridge, Hazlitt), Russia (Pushkin, V. Zukovsky), Italy (Gherardini, Manzoni) and Spain (Böhl de Faber, Alcalá Galiano). What had such a tremendous effect was his contrast of classical and Romantic-medieval literature, including Dante, Petrarch, Shakespeare and Calderón, the dichotomy between the northern and the southern tradition as well as the concept of literature as an expression of society. With these precepts he challenged the young generation to throw overboard the mechanical rules of neoclassicism and to compose plays that combine organic form with patriotic content, such as Goethe and Schiller had conceived them from the Storm and Stress to the classical period. To make his point even stronger, Schlegel translated five plays of Calderón (in 1803–9) and, most importantly, seventeen plays of Shakespeare (in 1797–1810). Sir James Mackintosh, the Scottish historian, spoke for many Europeans when he wrote to Schlegel: 'You are become our National Critic.'[19]

An English student at Jena University, Henry Crabb Robinson, introduced Schlegel to Madame de Staël, who made him her companion and children's tutor. Her book *De l'Allemagne* (Germany, 1813) became perhaps even more important than Schlegel's lectures in the transmission of Romantic ideas and their prime example, Goethe's works. By turning Germany into a shining example for France to follow, she inaugurated a new era inverting France's age-old cultural dominance over Germany. Undermining the main tenets of neoclassicism by advocating new literary models, she made German literature known all over the world as 'Romantic' art, with Weimar as its centre. Apart from presenting Goethe as an exemplary figure, she provided an analysis of *Faust* that was to inspire a series of playwrights and composers. Basing her reading on the 1790 *Fragment* and as a consequence disregarding the prologues, the pact, and the dungeon scene with the salvation of Gretchen, she offered a notorious moralistic misreading. She interprets the drama erroneously as presided over by Mephistopheles, the Prince of Evil, who according to her view is its hero, and thus as an example of Satanism. Whereas Faust is seen as an ineffectual libertine, Mephisto seizes pure Gretchen and 'renders her culpable, without depriving her of that rectitude of heart which can find repose only in virtue' (373).[20] 'Though presumption and vice are cruelly punished, the hand of beneficence is not perceived in the administration of the punishment' (390). To make matters worse, even the dreamlike quality of this spectacle hovering between tragedy and novel is 'an offspring of the delirium of the mind, or of the satiety of reason' (391) beyond the bounds of true art. Therefore, she concludes, such productions should not be repeated. Jane Brown has formulated thus the impact of these judgements: 'Such proximity to the Gothic, such satanism, the insatiable debauched hero, the simple opposition between evil and the angelic beauty . . . – all these clichés imposed upon Goethe's play are a burden from which it has yet fully to free itself.'[21]

Yet something extraordinary happened: what de Staël strongly criticized in form and content was taken up with fervour, first by French and thereafter by English and other European Romantics in order to emancipate themselves from the fetters of neoclassicism. Not that they worshipped the evil principle in Satan. The 'Satanic school' of Romanticism (the term used by Robert Southey in A Vision of Judgement, 1821) – as represented by Blake, Shelley, Keats and Byron; Goethe, Jean Paul Richter and E. T. A. Hoffmann; Nodier, Gautier, Musset, Baudelaire and Berlioz – exalted their own creative pride in Satan, brother of Prometheus, while Zeus or the conventional God represented the hated counter-principle of intellectual stagnation.

With the publication of De l'Allemagne, de Staël's views, particularly on Werther and Faust, increased the preexisting divide between the admirers and detractors of Goethe. A case in point are the Lake Poets Wordsworth and Coleridge, who were unable to overcome their moral objections to Goethe, despite Crabb Robinson's enthusiastic advocacy. Coleridge rejected even the latter's proposal to translate Faust, because to him this play seemed poorly motivated, loosely constructed and morally reprehensible. To get away from this blasphemous piece, he drafted his own, never completed Faust project, 'Michael Scott' (Table Talk, 16 February 1833).[22] By contrast, both Byron and Shelley saw Faust in a positive light. After some intensive language studies in Germany (1816), Shelley embarked on his Faust scenes, first haltingly in mostly literal versions ('Erdgeist'; 'Vor dem Tor'; 'Passages from Faust'), thereafter more successfully ('Raphaels Gesang'; 'Brocken-Szene'). How much he valued Faust is expressed in this remark: 'Perhaps . . . we admirers of Faust are in the right road to Paradise' (letter to John Gisborne,

10 April 1822),[23] an observation that in its boundless admiration paved the way for later Goethe admirers such as Scott and Carlyle.

Scott had an early interest in Scottish 'Reliques', and in addition his decisive turn to the Middle Ages seems to have come from German poets such as G. A. Bürger ('Lenore', trans. 1797) and the young Goethe ('Erlkönig', trans. 1796). His translation of Goethe's *Götz von Berlichingen* was not a great achievement in itself; he made quite a few mistakes, suppressed important scenes and added others so that he transformed the original play into a historical-gothic product. When Goethe conceived of the notion of *Weltliteratur*, the two poets started a brief correspondence in which Scott admitted his youthful errors (Eckermann III, 25 July 1827). Whether Scott ever gained a genuine understanding of Goethe's views and intentions is doubtful, because in his *Journal* he refers to him as a blend of Ariosto and Voltaire (15 February 1827), a remark considered an insult in the age of Romanticism. Nonetheless, Scott used a variety of motifs from Goethe's works in his own poems and novels. The vehmic court features in *Anne of Geierstein* (1829). In his novel *Peveril of the Peak* (1823), Mignon reappears as Fenella, a deaf-mute daughter of a Moorish woman. The meeting between the Earl of Leicester and Countess Amy in *Kenilworth* (1821; chapter 7) bears some resemblance to the scene 'Klärchens Wohnung' from *Egmont*, Act III. Although Scott's historical novels were imitated with gusto in Germany as they were in all of Europe, judgements on Scott's merits vary. Goethe in particular praised his unmatched poetic talent as well as his gift for realistic detail (Eckermann, 8/9 March 1831); yet his facility of narration for Goethe sometimes verged on 'Fabrikarbeiten' (factory output; conversation with Fürst von Pückler, 15 October 1826, *Gespräche* III/2, 72).

When Goethe received a package of books, poems and letters first from French admirers (1830), then from Britain (1831), his efforts to help inaugurate *Weltliteratur* seemed to have come to a crowning achievement. Thomas Carlyle had joined up with fifteen British Goethe admirers. Although not a Romantic himself but a Scottish Calvinist in his outlook, it was mainly due to him that the hitherto prevailing negative assessment of Goethe in Britain underwent a significant change towards a more judicious appreciation, a feat that in scale and impact can only be compared to Madame de Stäel's for France. Corresponding with Goethe since 1824, when he translated *Wilhelm Meisters Lehrjahre*, Carlyle saw in Goethe's career a reflection of his own spiritual development that led from gloomy despair (Goethe's *Werther*; Carlyle's Byronic youth) to the recognition of community service (Goethe's *Faust II*, *Wilhelm Meisters Wanderjahre*; Carlyle's essays 'Goethe's Works', 1832). Studying, translating and commenting on Goethe helped Carlyle to overcome a religious and moral crisis and thus enabled him to lead a *vita nova* according to the basic principle: 'Close thy *Byron*, open thy *Goethe*' (*Sartor Resartus. The Life and Opinions of Herr Teufelsdröckh*, 1833–4). What Carlyle admired particularly in *Wilhelm Meister's Travels* (trans. 1827) was the idea of renunciation, moral behaviour, and activity in the service of others. For him, Goethe had transformed darkness into light, both as a strong character and as author. Having been rejected as an immoral pagan by the Lake Poets, but now approached from an equally moralistic, yet positive viewpoint, the author of the *Wilhelm Meister* novels became a true hero, a saviour and prophet: 'a great heroic ancient man ... in the guise of a most modern, highbred, high-cultured Man of Letters!'[24] This implies that Carlyle short-changed Goethe's artistic achievements in favour of a moralistic interpretation that Goethe himself recognized –'Carlyle is a moral force of great significance' (Eckermann, III, 25 July 1827) – and accepted; Goethe indeed appreciated Carlyle as a great intermediary in Anglo-German literary relations (Eckermann, 11 October 1828) and even beyond in the realm of *Weltliteratur* (letter to Carlyle, 20 July 1824, HAB IV, 236–7). But above all, in contrast to de Staël's negative assessment of *Wilhelm Meister* (*Germany* II, chapter 28), Carlyle's positive interpretation gave rise to a surprising sequence of British 'apprenticeship novels': Edward Bulwer published *The Disowned* (1829) and *Ernest Maltravers* (1837); similarly, Disraeli portrayed the development of a poetic character in *Contarini Fleming* (1832). George Eliot also admired *Wilhelm Meister* and knew Goethe's work well when she embarked on *Middlemarch* (see her essay 'The Morality of Wilhelm Meister', 1855).

In France, Gérard de Nerval (1808–55) played a mediating role second in importance only to Madame de Staël's and similar to Scott's in Britain. Strongly influenced by German Romanticism in his youth and a translator of *Faust I* (1828) and parts of *Faust II* (1840), he inspired Delacroix (paintings and etchings), Berlioz (*La Damnation de Faust*, 1846) and Gounod (*Faust*, 1859). Blending verse and prose translations with paraphrases (especially in his translations of *Faust II*), Nerval succeeded in presenting a 'French Faust' that Goethe favoured over his original: 'I don't like reading *Faust* in German any more; yet in this French translation everything makes a refreshing, novel, and spirited impression' (Eckermann, 3 January 1830).

The exemplary Goethe

That Goethe turned into an incarnation of world literature was the result both of his own lively interest in European letters and of the disseminators I have already mentioned. Although as a young man he had been a strong believer in the ethnic roots of art he did not become a political chauvinist;

on the contrary, he was afraid of Germany's unification and much attacked for his non-partisan admiration of Napoleon. His answer to the question 'Deutschland, aber wo liegt es?' (Germany, but where is it located?) in *Xenien* (no. 95: 'Das deutsche Reich') was not that it was to be found in German national unity, but in Germany's cultural mission, at the very point where the *Kulturnation* – a people united through its cultural heritage and achievements – arises from a constant exchange with its neighbours. The role of the German was 'to become the representative of all cosmopolitans' (letter to J. L. Büchler, 14 June 1820, WA IV, vol. XXXIII, 67). This lofty idea of a *Kulturnation* could easily be misused by later German nationalists who would consider the German nation as the means to salvation of the world. Schiller, the poet of national freedom and patriotic action, was a less ambivalent mouthpiece for nationalistic ideas than Goethe and was more easily exploited by later German chauvinists.

Equally, the growth of the Goethe cult, extolling the master's merits in poetic, religious or nationalistic terms, would play into the hands of nationalists before the serious academic study of Goethe could reverse the trend. Romantic women had been in the forefront of an incipient Goethe-worship (Rahel Levin-Varnhagen, Henriette Herz, Bettina von Arnim, Johanna Schopenhauer). Beyond the world of their salons, a hero-worship took hold that frequently combined the names of three geniuses: Napoleon, Byron and Goethe (for example with Mazzini in Italy, Mickiewicz in Poland, Carlyle in Scotland), Goethe being in the forefront, because he had transformed his life into a work of art. Within Germany, a decisive turn towards the mythologization of Goethe took place in the very year of his death, when Johannes Falk raised his stature to the divine and holy in *Goethe aus näherem persönlichen Umgang dargestellt* (Goethe portrayed on the basis of close personal association, 1832). Goethe's companion and assistant Eckermann followed suit in his *Gespräche mit Goethe* (Conversations with Goethe, 1836–48), glorifying him as a hero: 'Denn ich hatte es mit einem Helden zu tun, den ich nicht durfte sinken lassen' (for I was dealing with a hero, whom I dared not diminish; preface to volume III).

All too often, Goethe seemed to rule impassively like an Olympian god over every artistic activity, a genius either to be hated in his grandeur or to be admired and taken as a signal for constant renewal. However, the impassive god was easily appropriated for ulterior pseudo-religious or nationalistic purposes. According to the Hegel disciple Karl Rosenkranz in 1847, Faust proclaimed the gospel of a new Christianity, since the protagonist had defeated Satan and redeemed himself.[25] That is the reason why some people regarded Goethe as a religious leader and his works as their bible. In retrospect, Konrad Burdach, professor of German literature at Halle university, summarized Goethe's role in the latter half of the nineteenth century in these words: 'Indeed, the author of *Faust*... was propelled by fate to take over the role of Moses; like him he gradually became a leader, priest, prophet of his people, the founder of a new covenant with God, and of a new national culture.'[26] After Bismarck's unification of Germany in 1871, religious overtones increasingly blended with nationalistic fervour, as for instance in Albert Bielschowsky's *Goethe, sein Leben und seine Werke* (1895): 'Without Goethe no Bismarck! without Goethe no German Reich!... our poets and thinkers created a united people, next to Schiller above all Goethe, the superb representative of German art and life.'[27]

Above all others it was this biography that shifted the focus from his works to Goethe as the creator of his life as a work of art, surrounding him with a divine aura. In addition, Herman Grimm's Goethe studies elevated the Weimar poet to Bismarckian stature as the embodiment of German freedom: 'The first successor to Goethe is Bismarck as author of his own life, a work that may be called the first German work of art written in Goethe's language.'[28] Accordingly, Faust the colonizer could easily become a national hero with a cultural-imperialistic mission that anticipated the Third Reich. Nietzsche had tried in vain to put a stop to this chauvinistic trend by declaring Goethe an exceptional German and by stating: 'Let's look at the best of our statesmen and artists: Goethe has not been their educator – he could not have been.'[29]

The academic study of Goethe, or *Goethephilologie*, goes back to the 1830s, when G. G. Gervinus published his *Geschichte der poetischen National-Literatur der Deutschen* (1835–42), which canonized Goethe's and Schiller's decade-long collaboration as an absolute standard of artistic achievement, at the expense of Goethe's early and late works. During the *Gründerjahre* (years of foundation of the Second Empire) Gervinus's canonical approach was still influential, but it was securely anchored in the positivistic editorial work of *Goethephilologie* by the Scherer School. Wilhelm Scherer's text-critical editions as well as his causal-genetic interpretations were modelled on the natural sciences; they coincided with the opening of the Weimarer Archiv (1885) and with the beginning of the Weimar edition of Goethe's collected works (1887–1919), the first historical and critical edition in 143 volumes, and of the *Goethe-Jahrbuch* (1880) and the *Schriften der Goethe-Gesellschaft* (1885). The genetic-biographical method of positivism carried the day until the end of the First World War, but was repeatedly challenged before then and thereafter replaced by *Geistesgeschichte* (the history of ideas), as represented by H. A. Korff's *Geist der Goethezeit* (1923–54), a monumental work in four volumes that is based on the idea of the congruence of literature and idealistic philosophy (Hegel) in the age of Goethe and recreates the nineteenth-century image of Goethe as a Christ-like figure.

Similar attempts would be made until the 1950s, but during the Third Reich Nazi politicians as well as scholars who followed the party line tried to exploit Goethe and his works for their ideological purposes. In the light of Nietzsche, who had declared Goethe an exceptional, non-nationalistic German of European stature, this was a rather difficult task. It was much easier to appropriate Schiller and Richard Wagner for the party, yet from 1932 onwards eager voices could be heard that inverted Nietzsche's judgement, referring to Goethe as 'the towering figure of the eternal German'. Only a small step was needed for someone to draw an analogy between Hitler's Nazi dictatorship with its 'Gleichschaltung' (bringing all the institutions and individuals into line), and Goethe's 'pedagogic province' (*Wilhelm Meisters Wanderjahre*), and also to turn Faust into the incarnation of the new man, the Faustian leader who colonizes recently conquered living space (*Lebensraum*). In the long run, however, to invoke Goethe in order to support Nazi propaganda would backfire, because along with Schiller, it was he and his work that provided an important spiritual refuge for the opposition to the Nazi system.

In the immediate postwar era, two distinct developments took place: first, the underground revival of Goethe came out into the open and even gained in strength as a result of the appreciation of him as the great humanist, representative of the other, better Germany, and beyond that of the Christian West, a bulwark against the loss of traditional values. Thus a new Goethe cult was forming around 1950, which culminated in studies that either saw in Goethe a 'homo religiosus' in the wake of Dante (for example Ernst Beutler and Wilhelm Flitner, both in 1947) or a second Shakespeare who creates order out of chaos (Fritz-Joachim von Rintelen, *Der Rang des Geistes* (1955)).[30] Second, an awareness of how scholars had yielded to political pressure under the Nazis gradually led to a reversal of bankrupt scholarly methods. In general, the tendency among professional Goethe interpreters was to reject *Geistesgeschichte* with its ideological ramifications and instead to focus on pure *Werkinterpretation*, as best illustrated by the Hamburg edition of Goethe's works and Emil Staiger's three-volume study *Goethe* (1952–9). Published in 1943, but exerting a significant impact in the postwar era, was Wilhelm Emrich's *Die Symbolik von Faust II*, a study that also excludes the socio-historical conditions of the work's creation in analyzing its symbolism.

Despite the continuity of the Goethe-Gesellschaft in Weimar as the only pan-German institution in a divided Germany, Goethe reception during the Cold War developed a two-pronged approach. In West Germany, a variation of New Criticism prevailed, whereas in the German Democratic Republic a new image of Goethe emerged after 1949, based on the prewar studies of the Marxist scholar Georg Lukács. The classical Goethe, writing in the age of the

French Revolution, was integrated into the canon of Socialist Realism as an antidote to all brands of irrational Romanticisms. In the Federal Republic, things started to move from *Werkimmanenz* – the analysis of literary works as autonomous wholes without regard to their authors and readers – to a decisively socio-historical approach in the 1960s, first in response to Marxist studies and then propelled by the student rebellion of 1968. This development involved not only Goethe, but Weimar Classicism and traditional German literature studies as a whole: 'Reevaluating the Enlightenment and the French Revolution as political norms of judgement about Weimar Classicism, the New Left in the FRG started from where GDR literary studies had set out in the Fifties in the wake of Georg Lukács.'[31] In other words, Goethe studies had to accept the presence of the Nazi concentration camp Buchenwald right next to Weimar[32] and to attempt to gain some meaningful perspective on the darkest period in German history, although to hold Classical Weimar accountable for the Holocaust wrongfully equates the realm of art with the physical world of cause and effect. The way the New Left treated Goethe seemed to be a revival of the anti-classical polemics of the *Jungdeutschen* (Young Germans, e.g. Börne, Laube, Heine) in the 1830s. In the wake of the Napoleonic Wars they had denounced Goethe as an aristocrat and 'servant of princes' who had hindered the emancipation of the German people. In a similar vein, the political opposition in West Germany as well as East German scholars of the 1960s accused Goethe of treachery, referring to the antirevolutionary stance that he had developed at the court of Weimar and projected onto *Wilhelm Meisters Lehrjahre*, a novel that in Novalis's assessment was already 'a pilgrimage to the certificate of nobility'.[33] One result of this 'Klassikschelte' (scolding of the classical authors) was *Die Klassik-Legende* (1971), a collection of essays edited by R. Grimm and J. Hermand, who advocated an innovative approach to German classicism, intending to replace its 'mummification' as a canonical ideal of perfection with an undogmatic search for its significance in relation to our time.

Since then, socio-historically oriented literary histories have abounded[34] and reception aesthetics and discourse analysis have become popular, without however derailing the 'Klassik-Boom' of the 1980s and 90s. Dethroning the Olympian Goethe did not entail his demise, on the contrary, it increased his popularity. As Goethe was pulled down from his marble pedestal he turned into a more human figure and by the same token a more approachable one. The more Goethe was worshipped, the more he and his works were played upon, parodied and caricatured. This phenomenon has been a significant trend since his *Werther* was parodied by Friedrich Nicolai (*The Joys of Young Werther*, 1775) and his *Faust* by Friedrich Th. Vischer (1862), a trend that escalated after the days of the student rebellion of the 1960s and manifested itself on several levels simultaneously: in irreverent theatre productions of his classical plays (for example Peter Stein's *Tasso*, Bremen 1968), in modern-day adaptations of his prose works (for instance when Ulrich Plenzdorf's GDR protagonist Edgar Wibeau encounters the *Werther* text as toilet paper in *Die neuen Leiden des jungen W.*, 1972), and in imitations and exaggerated parodies of his most famous poems. Many disrespectful versions of 'Über allen Gipfeln ist Ruh', 'Sah ein Knab ein Röslein stehn' and 'Erlkönig' have been published in addition to *Faust* parodies and plays dealing with Goethe's relationship to Eckermann.[35] Mention should also be made of Goethe in pop culture, from Goethe T-shirts, comic books and a Goethe rap CD down to paper towels. An additional indication of Goethe's viability at the end of the second millenium is the frequent reportraiture of the famous J. H. Tischbein painting 'Goethe in der Campagna' (1788), whether for environmentalist or tourist-oriented uses, or as computer imagery. Thus even in twentieth-century Germany, Goethe remained a central reference point for both critics and admirers. The crowning achievement of all these exertions, particularly during the last two decades, is probably the completion of the multi-volume Munich and Frankfurt editions of Goethe's works in 1999.

Goethe reception outside Germany

In the twentieth century, the debate over Goethe's exemplary stature continued unabated. Three critics from different countries had a major international impact: Benedetto Croce, Ortega y Gasset and T. S. Eliot. At the dawn of New Criticism, Croce (1866–1952) distinguished poetry from literature such as historiography, philosophy and scientific prose. As an example, in *Goethe* (1923) he set out to describe Goethe without any 'historical-ideal structure' (202),[36] coming down from the 'fine idol' as 'a play of the imagination' to 'what he was', 'just himself, Goethe' (200). After all the exaggerated views of Goethe, Croce's insistence on purely 'artistic considerations' (16) created a new standard, a search for the classical 'perfect fusion of matter and form' (20) that Croce found both in the early and the mature works, in *Werther* as well as in *Faust I*: 'In the Gretchen tragedy... there is not a trace of a social thesis or a legislative demand' (67), but in the 'scholar's tragedy' Goethe committed the artistic error of answering 'with a poetical work the question as to the value... of human life' (83). Despite Croce's critical stance, the image of Goethe as the wise person who coined the concept of *Weltliteratur* from his conviction of 'the supernationality of poetry' (11) and acted as 'a liberator, who had taught men to cultivate art "von innen heraus", from the heart' (9), would remain a powerful influence on Ortega and T. S. Eliot.

Tired of Goethe the marble statue, like Sainte-Beuve (*Causeries du lundi*, 1858) and Nietzsche before him, Ortega attempted to bring Goethe down from his pedestal and back to life by confronting him, as it were, with people drowning in a shipwreck. Starting from the premise that life is not harmony but constant strife, as opposed to culture and security, Ortega's view of Goethe took on a Janus face. In 'Pidiendo un Goethe de adentro' (Seeking a Goethe from within, 1932) Goethe appeared on the one hand as a useless legend, 'the most questionable of all classics'(398),[37] who worse still had betrayed his destiny by having fallen for Weimar, this sterilized glasshouse and 'ridiculous Liliputian court' (412) that had immobilized him. On the other hand, he appreciated Goethe as a liberating force for Ortega as well as a paradigm for young people who want to emancipate themselves (421–7). A few years later in Hamburg he constructed a 'Goethe sin Weimar' (Goethe Without Weimar, 1949) and discovered under his serene surface an insecure Goethe who had suffered much, a dissatisfied, restless, and fearful genius at odds with himself and the conventions of his time who created 'hellenistic' masterpieces despite all the obstacles.

Whereas Ortega y Gasset interpreted Goethe from the perspective of *Geistesgeschichte*, T. S. Eliot appears to be a follower of Croce's New Criticism in that early on he focussed on 'emotion which has its life in the poem and not in the history of the poet. The emotion of art is impersonal.'[38] However, like Sainte-Beuve before him he completely reversed his opinion of Goethe. In the 1920s he did not count him among the great classical poets of *Weltliteratur*, seeing him as a rather provincial writer and a sage of worldly wisdom à la Voltaire: 'Of Goethe perhaps it is truer to say that he dabbled in both philosophy and poetry and made no great success of either.'[39] The proof of this for Eliot was in *Faust*, a play that in his view does not match Dante's *Divine Comedy* because here Goethe subordinated art to philosophy.[40] This short-changing of Goethe's achievements is all the more surprising since it was Eliot who had applied the phrase 'dissociation of sensibility' (*The Metaphysical Poets*, 1921) to characterize poets after the seventeenth century, without realizing at this stage in his career that Goethe provided an ideal model in his attempt to recapture that lost fusion of thought and feeling. It is to Eliot's credit, however, that early on he admitted his 'inability [to enjoy Goethe] as an unfortunate limitation and prejudice' on his part, claiming 'that we cannot understand that century [the nineteenth] until we are able to understand Goethe' (*Faust* review in *The Nation and Athenaeum*, 12 Jan. 1929, p. 527). Coming to terms with Goethe thus presented itself as a challenge to Eliot, just as it did to any intellectual of the twentieth century.

In an address delivered at Hamburg University in 1955, Eliot was ready to acknowledge both traditional British obstacles to a proper appreciation of

Goethe and the reasons for his own antipathy: 'For anyone like myself, who combines a Catholic cast of mind, a Calvinistic heritage, and a Puritanical temperament, Goethe does indeed present some obstacles to be surmounted' ('Goethe as the Sage' (1955), 243).[41] What this statement implies is a fundamental clash between two world views, Eliot's belief in the Christian dogma of man's wickedness and sin, and Goethe's Renaissance optimism and belief in man's essential goodness and continual progress. Yet in accounting for 'the evolution of my own mind' Eliot finally came to realize the fusion of wisdom and poetry in Goethe and set out to prove that, next to Dante and Shakespeare, Goethe is 'one of the Great Europeans'(244), more significant than Cervantes and Wordsworth because Goethe met the criteria of permanence and universality, abundance, amplitude, unity and wisdom. What had struck Eliot as provincial in his first encounters with Goethe was essentially based on a misunderstanding. Now he establishes the poet as 'representative man' (see also Emerson in his essay, 'Goethe, or, the Writer', 1850), not in the sense of a mere mouthpiece of his people, but on a much grander scale: Goethe, 'sometimes in complete opposition to his age', 'lived more fully and consciously on several levels than most other men' and asserted 'a different type of consciousness' (244) from conventional beliefs of his time, so that he was in a position 'to help his fellow-countrymen to understand themselves, and help other people to understand, and to accept them' (252). This is what Goethe intended to do with his project of *Weltliteratur* and what makes him a great European, 'the common countryman of all of us' (258). Matchless are T. S. Eliot's own words of wisdom that appreciate Goethe as an exemplary figure, a 'European event' with ramifications for our and future generations: 'And perhaps the time has come when we can say that there is something in favour of being able to see the universe as Goethe saw it, rather than as the scientists have seen it: now that the "living garment of God" has become somewhat tattered from the results of scientific manipulation' (255).

'To see the universe as Goethe saw it', is, however, a challenging undertaking in our times of rampant 'dissociations' in all areas of life. To be sure, Goethe signalled the rise of modernity in several ways. On the one hand, in *Faust* he diagnosed the essence of modern times, man's quest for ever increasing 'velocity', as the greatest disaster looming to destroy all order and continuity in society. On the other hand, Goethe did everything in his power to restrain and to reverse this chaotic course. Even after T. S. Eliot, this Goethean approach to the 'universe' has received keen interest inside as well as outside Germany; one of the key questions being asked is whether Goethe can even be seen as the precursor of modern chaos theory. Based on his reading of the essay 'Die Natur' (1782/3),[42] Walter Benjamin claimed that 'Goethe's worldview is chaotic',[43] in the sense that he sees 'Nature' as an amorphic, destructive, and ugly force. But Goethe fought a lifelong battle to control chaos both in society and nature. To show him in a devil-like pose on the front cover of *Der Spiegel* (no. 33, 16 August 1999) does not do justice to Goethe, because for him, out of the confusion of chaos emerges a world of structured beauty.

As a natural scientist, Goethe always looked for these very structures or principles of unity hidden beneath the chaotic surface of nature. Thus it comes as no surprise to realize that he anticipated some of the tenets of natural science (see, for example, morphological studies such as D'Arcy Thompson's *On Growth and Form*, 1917) and even exerted some influence on modern chaos theorists, among them Mitchell Feigenbaum and Albert Libchaber. In their work, chaos theory proceeds 'specifically from the recognition . . . that systems exhibiting chaotic behavior on the surface at the same time reveal deep-lying structure, indeed, that chaos and order arise together systematically'.[44] As in Goethe's case, the search is still on for archetypal principles holding a seemingly disorderly 'universe' together. In addition to Goethe's universal appeal as a world-class author, this is one more tangible reason why, as Nicholas Boyle wrote in the same issue of *Der Spiegel*, 'his time has perhaps just arrived'.

NOTES

1 Madame de Staël, 'Goethe', in *Germany*, trans. O. W. Wight, 2 vols. (Boston: Houghton, Mifflin & Co., 1887), I, p. 178.
2 See for example Dieter Borchmeyer's *Die Weimarer Klassik. Porträt einer Epoche* (1980) (Weinheim: Beltz, Athenäum, 1994).
3 Virgil Nemoianu, *The Taming of Romanticism: European Literature and the Age of the Biedermeier* (Cambridge, MA: Harvard University Press, 1984).
4 On 'Reproduktion der Welt' see Goethe's letter to Jacobi, 21 August 1774, HAB I, 166. On the 'Romantic' Goethe see for instance Schiller's remarks about his *Iphigenie auf Tauris*, quoted in Eckermann, 21 March 1830; also de Staël, *Germany*, I, p. 18.
5 *Geschichte der europäischen Literatur* (1803–4); *Kritische Friedrich-Schlegel-Ausgabe*, ed. E. Behler, 35 vols. (Paderborn etc.: Schöningh, 1958–), XI, p. 10.
6 'Abriß von den europäischen Verhältnissen der deutschen Literatur', in *Sämtliche Werke*, ed. E. Böcking, 16 vols. (Leipzig 1846; Reprint Hildesheim: Olms, 1971–2), VIII, p. 217.
7 Clemens Brentano, *Sämtliche Werke*, ed. C. Schüddekopf, 14 vols. (Munich: Müller, 1909–13), V, pp. 465–6.
8 See chapter 2, note 3.
9 Novalis, *Schriften*, ed. P. Kluckhohn, R. Samuel and others (Stuttgart: Kohlhammer, 1960–), III, p. 639.

10 *Kritische Friedrich-Schlegel-Ausgabe*, VI, p. 403.

11 *Sämtliche Werke*, VI, pp. 416–17.

12 See his 'Ich und Goethe' letter to H. Moser, 1 July 1825, in *Heinrich Heine Säkularausgabe, Werke, Briefwechsel, Lebenszeugnisse*, 27 vols. (Berlin: Akademie-Verlag and Paris: CNRS, 1978).

13 Düsseldorfer Heine-Ausgabe, ed. M. Windfuhr (Hamburg: Hoffmann & Campe, 1975–97), X, p. 248.

14 Düsseldorfer Heine-Ausgabe, VI, 147.

15 Düsseldorfer Heine-Ausgabe, XV, 112.

16 Düsseldorfer Heine-Ausgabe, VIII/1, 154.

17 Düsseldorfer Heine-Ausgabe, VIII/1, 158.

18 *W. Schellings Sämmtliche Werke*, ed. K. T. A. Schelling, 14 vols. (Stuttgart and Augsburg: Cotta, 1856–61), III, p. 13.

19 Quoted in Schlegel's letter to Riemer, December 1838, *Sämtliche Werke*, VII, p. 286.

20 Page references are to the translation by O. W. Wight; see note 1.

21 'Faust', in Gerhart Hoffmeister (ed.), *European Romanticism. Literary Cross-Currents, Modes, and Models* (Detroit, MI: Wayne State University Press, 1990), p. 189.

22 *Table Talk*, ed. Carl Wooding, 2 vols., in *The Collected Works of Samuel Taylor Coleridge*, general editor Kathleen Coburn, 16 vols. (London and Princeton: Routledge and Princeton University Press, 1976–), I, pp. 342–3.

23 *The Letters of Percy Bysshe Shelley*, ed. Frederick L. Jones, 2 vols. (Oxford: Oxford University Press, 1964), II, p. 406.

24 Carlyle, *On Heroes, Hero-Worship, and the Heroic in History* (1841); *The Works of Thomas Carlyle*, 30 vols. (New York: Scribner's Sons, 1898–1905), V, p. 158.

25 See H.-W. Kelling, *Idolatry of Poetic Genius in German Goethe Criticism* (Berne: Lang, 1970), pp. 64–5; see also Karl Robert Mandelkow, *Goethe in Deutschland. Rezeptionsgeschichte eines Klassikers*, 2 vols. (Munich: Beck, 1980), I, pp. 201–2: 'Der Olympier Goethe'.

26 'Faust und Moses' (1912), quoted in Kelling, *Idolatry of Poetic Genius*, p. 158.

27 2 vols. (Munich: Beck, 1922), II, p. 683.

28 Quoted in Karl Robert Mandelkow (ed.), *Goethe im Urteil seiner Kritiker. Dokumente zur Wirkungsgeschichte Goethes in Deutschland*, 4 vols. (Munich: Beck, 1975–84), III, p. 302.

29 Ibid., III, p. 28.

30 Mandelkow, *Goethe in Deutschland*, III, pp. 78–152.

31 Ibid., II, p. 225.

32 Ibid., II, p. 221.

33 Mandelkow, *Goethe im Urteil seiner Kritiker*, I, p. 175.

34 For example, Gerhard Schulz, *Die deutsche Literatur zwischen Französischer Revolution und Restauration*, vol. VII of *Geschichte der deutschen Literatur von den Anfängen bis zur Gegenwart*, ed. Helmut de Boor and Richard Newald, 2 tomes (Munich: Beck, 1983–9).

35 See *Unser Goethe... Ein Lesebuch*, ed. E. Henscheid and F. W. Bernstein (Zurich: zweitausendeins, 1982).

36 References are to *Goethe* (London: Methuen, 1923).

37 Page references are to 'Pidiendo un Goethe de adentro' (1932), in *Obras completas*, 2nd edn, 9 vols. (Madrid: Revista de Occidente, 1950), IV.

38 'Tradition and the Individual Talent' (1919), in *The Sacred Wood* (London: Methuen, 1964), p. 59.

39 *The Use of Poetry and the Use of Criticism* (London: Faber & Faber, 1933), p. 99.

40 'Dante' (1929), in *Selected Essays* (London: Faber, 1932), p. 258.

41 In *On Poetry and Poets* (New York: Farrar, 1957).

42 In fact written by G. Chr. Tobler, not by Goethe; see HA XIII, 571–2.

43 *Gesammelte Schriften*, ed. by R. Tiedemann (Frankfurt am Main: Suhrkamp, 1974), I/1, p. 149.

44 Herbert Rowland, 'Chaos and Art in Goethe's *Novelle*', *Goethe Yearbook* 8 (1996), 93–119, p. 97.

A GUIDE TO FURTHER READING

GENERAL REFERENCE

Goethe-Handbuch. Ed. by Bernd Witte and others. 4 vols. Stuttgart: Metzler, 1996–8.
Goethe-Lexikon. Ed. by Gero von Wilpert. Stuttgart: Kröner, 1998.

SOCIAL, CULTURAL AND POLITICAL BACKGROUND

Anderson, M. S. [Matthew Smith]. *War and Society in Europe of the Old Regime 1618–1789.* Leicester: Leicester University Press, 1988.
The War of the Austrian Succession, 1740–1748. London, New York: Longman, 1995.
Aretin, Karl Otmar von. *Das alte Reich: 1648–1806.* Vol. III: *Das Reich und der österreichisch-preußische Dualismus (1745–1806).* Stuttgart: Klett-Cotta, 1997.
Black, Jeremy (ed.). *European Warfare 1453–1815.* New York: St. Martin's Press, 1999.
Blanning, T. C. W. *The French Revolution in Germany. Occupation and Resistance in the Rhineland 1792–1802.* Oxford and New York: Oxford University Press, 1983.
The Origins of the French Revolutionary Wars. London and New York: Longman, 1986.
Joseph II. London and New York: Longman, 1994.
The French Revolutionary Wars 1787–1802. London and New York: Arnold, 1996.
Bruford, W. H. *Germany in the Eighteenth Century. The Social Background of the Literary Revival.* Cambridge: Cambridge University Press, 1935.
Culture and Society in Classical Weimar 1775–1806. Cambridge: Cambridge University Press, 1962.
Childs, John. *Armies and Warfare in Europe 1648–1789.* Manchester: Manchester University Press, 1982.
Ebersbach, Volker. *Carl August von Sachsen-Weimar-Eisenach: Goethes Herzog und Freund.* Cologne, Weimar and Vienna: Böhlau, 1998.
Gagliardo, John G. *Reich and Nation: The Holy Roman Empire as Idea and Reality, 1763–1806.* Bloomington and London: Indiana University Press, 1980.
Germany under the Old Regime, 1600–1790. London and New York: Longman, 1991.

Ingrao, Charles. *The Habsburg Monarchy 1618–1815*. Cambridge and New York: Cambridge University Press, 1994.

Kiesel, H. and P. Münch. *Gesellschaft und Literatur im 18. Jahrhundert: Voraussetzungen und Entstehung des literarischen Markts in Deutschland*. Munich: Beck, 1977.

Krippendorff, Ekkehart. *'Wie die Großen mit den Menschen spielen': Versuch über Goethes Politik*. Frankfurt am Main: Suhrkamp, 1988.

Lefebvre, Georges. *The French Revolution*. Vol. I: *From Its Origins to 1793*. Vol. II: *From 1793 to 1799*. New York and London: Columbia University Press and Routledge & Kegan Paul, 1962.

Napoleon. Vol. I: *From 18 Brumaire to Tilsit 1799–1807*. Vol. II: *From Tilsit to Waterloo*. New York: Columbia University Press, 1969 (first published 1936).

Mommsen, Wilhelm. *Die politischen Anschauungen Goethes*. Stuttgart: Deutsche Verlags-Anstalt, 1948.

Rothe, Wolfgang. *Der politische Goethe: Dichter und Staatsdiener im deutschen Spätabsolutismus*. Göttingen: Vandenhoeck & Ruprecht, 1998.

Saine, Thomas P. *Black Bread – White Bread: German Intellectuals and the French Revolution*. Columbia, SC: Camden House, 1988.

Sengle, Friedrich. *Das Genie und sein Fürst. Die Geschichte der Lebensgemeinschaft Goethes mit dem Herzog Carl August von Sachsen-Weimar-Eisenach: Ein Beitrag zum Spätfeudalismus und zu einem vernachlässigten Thema der Goetheforschung*. Stuttgart: Metzler, 1993.

Sheehan, James J. *German History, 1770–1866*. Oxford and New York: Clarendon Press, 1989.

Tümmler, Hans. *Goethe in Staat und Politik. Gesammelte Aufsätze*. Cologne and Graz: Böhlau, 1964.

Carl August von Weimar, Goethes Freund. Eine vorwiegend politische Biographie. Stuttgart: Klett-Cotta, 1978.

Walker, Mack. *German Home Towns: Community, State, and General Estate 1648–1871*. Ithaca and London: Cornell University Press, 1971.

Wilson, W. Daniel. *Das Goethe-Tabu: Protest und Menschenrechte im klassischen Weimar*. Munich: DTV, 1999.

BIOGRAPHY AND STUDIES OF GOETHE AND WEIMAR CLASSICISM

There is much biographical information and detail on Goethe's times and associates in *Goethe-Handbuch*, vol. IV (in 2 vols): *Personen, Sachen, Begriffe*, ed. by Hans-Dietrich Dahnke and Regine Otto.

Borchmeyer, Dieter. *Die Weimarer Klassik. Porträt einer Epoche*. Weinheim: Beltz, Athenäum, 1994.

Boyle, Nicholas. *Goethe: The Poet and the Age*. Vol. I: *The Poetry of Desire (1749–1790)*. Oxford: Oxford University Press, 1990. Vol. II: *Revolution and Renunciation (1790–1803)*. Oxford: Oxford University Press, 1999.

Chiarini, Paolo (ed.). *Bausteine zu einem neuen Goethe*. Frankfurt am Main: Athenäum, 1984.

Conrady, Karl Otto. *Goethe. Leben und Werk.* 2 vols. Königstein im Taunus: Athenäum, 1982–5.

Croce, Benedetto. *Goethe.* London: Methuen, 1923.

Eissler, Kurt Robert. *Goethe: A Psychoanalytic Study.* Detroit: Wayne State University Press, 1963.

Fairley, Barker. *A Study of Goethe.* Oxford: Oxford University Press, 1947.

Friedenthal, Richard. *Goethe. Sein Leben und sein Werk.* Munich: Piper, 1963. Translated by Richard Friedenthal and John Nowell as: *Goethe, his Life and Times.* London: Weidenfeld and Nicholson, 1965.

Gray, Ronald. *Goethe: A Critical Introduction.* Cambridge: Cambridge University Press, 1967.

Gundolf, Friedrich. *Goethe.* Berlin: Bondi, 1916.

Jessing, Benedikt. *Johann Wolfgang Goethe.* (Sammlung Metzler) Stuttgart: Metzler, 1995.

Korff, Hermann August. *Geist der Goethezeit. Versuch einer ideellen Entwicklung der klassisch-romantischen Literaturgeschichte,* 4 vols. Leipzig: Weber and Koehler & Amelang, 1923–53.

Körner, Josef. *Romantiker und Klassiker. Die Brüder Schlegel in ihren Beziehungen zu Schiller und Goethe.* Darmstadt: Wissenschaftliche Buchgesellschaft, 1971 (first published 1924).

Lamport, F. J. *A Student's Guide to Goethe.* London: Heinemann, 1971.

Lewes, George Henry. *The Life and Works of Goethe.* London: Routledge, 1855.

Lukács, Georg. *Goethe and his Age.* Trans. by Robert Anchor. London: Merlin Press, 1968.

Matussek, Peter. *Goethe zur Einführung.* Hamburg: Junius, 1998.

Reed, T. J. *The Classical Centre: Goethe and Weimar 1775–1832.* London: Croom Helm, 1980.

Goethe. (Past Masters) Oxford: Oxford University Press, 1984 (new edn 1998).

Staiger, Emil. *Goethe.* 3 vols. Zurich and Freiburg im Breisgau: Artemis, 1952–9.

Steiger, Robert and Angelika Reimann (eds.). *Goethes Leben von Tag zu Tag. Eine dokumentarische Chronik.* 8 vols. Zurich and Düsseldorf: Artemis, 1982–6.

Voßkamp, Wilhelm (ed.). *Klassik im Vergleich. Normativität und Historizität europäischer Klassiken. DFG Symposion 1990.* Stuttgart: Metzler, 1993.

Williams, John R. *The Life of Goethe. A Critical Biography.* Oxford: Blackwell, 1998.

POETRY

Detailed bibliographies for individual poems, cycles and collections can be found in HA, vols. I–II, *Goethe-Handbuch,* vol. I, and FA, vols. I–III. Commentaries and notes on individual poems can be found in HA, MA, FA and the Berliner Ausgabe: *Goethe. Poetische Werke. Kunsthistorische Schriften und Übersetzungen,* 22 vols. (Berlin and Weimar: Aufbau Verlag, 1960–78). The *Goethe-Handbuch,* vol. I (ed. by Regine Otto and Bernd Witte) is devoted to poetry. See also *German Life and Letters* 36 (1982–3) and *Oxford German Studies* 15 (1984) for articles on poetry and on individual poems.

Translations

Goethe. *Erotic Poems.* Trans. by David Luke, introduced by Hans Rudolf Vaget. Oxford: Oxford University Press, 1997.

Goethe. *Poems of the West and East. West-Eastern Divan – West-östlicher Divan.* Trans. by John Whaley, introduced by Katharina Mommsen. Berne: Lang, 1998.

Goethe. *Selected Poems.* Ed. by Christopher Middleton. Vol 1 of *Goethe. The Collected Works in 12 Volumes.* Cambridge, MA: Suhrkamp, 1983; paperback edn, Princeton, NJ: Princeton University Press, 1994.

Goethe. *Selected Poems.* Trans. by John Whaley, introduced by Matthew Bell. London: Dent, 1998.

Goethe. *Selected Poetry.* Trans. and introduced by David Luke. London: Libris, 1999.

Studies

Behrmann, Alfred. *Einführung in den neueren deutschen Vers von Luther bis zur Gegenwart.* Stuttgart: Metzler, 1989.

Blackall, Eric A. *The Emergence of German as a Literary Language 1700–1775.* Cambridge: Cambridge University Press, 1959.

Kaiser, Gerhard. *Geschichte der deutschen Lyrik von Goethe bis Heine. Ein Grundriß in Interpretationen.* 3 vols. Frankfurt am Main: Suhrkamp, 1988.

Kommerell, Max. *Gedanken über Gedichte.* Frankfurt am Main: Klostermann, 1943.

Lee, Meredith. *Studies in Goethe's Lyric Cycles.* Chapel Hill: University of North Carolina Press, 1978.

Displacing Authority. Goethe's Poetic Reception of Klopstock. Heidelberg: Winter, 1999.

Reed, T. J. (ed. and intro.). *Goethe. Selected Poems.* Bristol: Bristol Classical Press, 1999.

Sauder, Gerhard (ed.). *Goethe-Gedichte. Zweiunddreißig Interpretationen. Karl Richter zum 60. Geburtstag.* Munich: Hanser, 1996.

Wagenknecht, Christian. *Deutsche Metrik. Eine historische Einführung.* Munich: Beck, 1981.

Wilkinson, Elizabeth M. and L. A. Willoughby. *Goethe: Poet and Thinker.* London: Arnold, 1962.

DRAMA AND THEATRE

Bruford, W. H. *Theatre, Drama and Audience in Goethe's Germany.* London: Routledge, 1950.

Buck, Theo (ed.). *Goethe-Handbuch*, vol. II: *Dramen.* Stuttgart: Metzler, 1996.

Carlson, Marvin. *Goethe and the Weimar Theatre.* Ithaca and London: Cornell University Press, 1978.

Fischer-Lichte, Erika. *Kurze Geschichte des deutschen Theaters* (UTB, 1667). Tübingen and Basel: Francke, 1993.

Graham, Ilse Appelbaum. 'Götz von Berlichingen's Right Hand'. *German Life and Letters* NS 16 (1962/3), 212–28.

Heller, Erich. 'Goethe and the Avoidance of Tragedy'. In Heller, *The Disinherited Mind: Essays in Modern German Literature and Thought*, 4th edn (London: Bowes & Bowes, 1975), pp. 35–63.

Hinderer, Walter (ed.). *Goethes Dramen: Neue Interpretationen.* Stuttgart: Reclam, 1980.

Keller, Werner. 'Das Drama Goethes'. In Walter Hinck (ed.), *Handbuch des deutschen Dramas* (Düsseldorf: Bagel, 1980), pp. 133–56.

Lamport, Francis J. *German Classical Drama: Theatre, Humanity and Nation, 1750–1870.* Cambridge: Cambridge University Press, 1990.

Michelsen, Peter. 'Egmonts Freiheit'. *Euphorion* 65 (1971), 274–97.

Peacock, Ronald. *Goethe's Major Plays.* Manchester: Manchester University Press, 1959.

'Tasso und die Besserwisser'. In John L. Hibberd and H. B. Nisbet (eds.), *Texte, Motive und Gestalten der Goethezeit: Festschrift für Hans Reiss* (Tübingen: Niemeyer, 1989), pp. 95–112.

Politzer, Heinz. 'No Man is an Island. A Note on Image and Thought in Goethe's *Iphigenie*'. *Germanic Review* 37 (1962), 285–311.

Swales, Martin. 'A Questionable Politician. A Discussion of the Ending to Goethe's *Egmont*'. *Modern Language Review* 66 (1971), 832–40.

Wagner, Irmgard. *Critical Approaches to Goethe's Classical Dramas: Iphigenie, Torquato Tasso, and Die natürliche Tochter.* Columbia, SC: Camden House, 1995.

Wilkinson, E. M. 'Goethe's Tasso: The Tragedy of a Creative Artist'. *Proceedings of the English Goethe Society* NS 15 (1946), 96–127.

'The Relation of Form and Meaning in *Egmont*'. *Publications of the English Goethe Society* NS 18 (1947), 149–82.

Williams, J. J. 'Reflections on Tasso's Final Speech'. *Publications of the English Goethe Society* NS 47 (1977), 47–67.

FAUST

Adorno, Theodor W. 'On the Final Scene of Faust'. In Adorno, *Notes to Literature*, ed. by Rolf Tiedemann, trans. by Shierry Weber Nicholsen (New York: Columbia University Press, 1991), vol. I, pp. 111–20.

Arens, Hans. *Kommentar zu Goethes 'Faust I'.* Heidelberg: Winter, 1982.
Kommentar zu Goethes 'Faust II'. Heidelberg: Winter, 1989.

Atkins, Stuart P. *Goethe's Faust: A Literary Analysis.* Cambridge, MA: Harvard University Press, 1958.

Bennett, Benjamin. *Goethe's Theory of Poetry: Faust and the Regeneration of Language.* Ithaca, NY: Cornell University Press, 1986.

Boyle, Nicholas. *Goethe: Faust. Part One.* Cambridge: Cambridge University Press, 1987.

Brown, Jane K. *Goethe's Faust: The German Tragedy.* Ithaca, NY: Cornell University Press, 1986.
Goethe's Faust: Theater of the World. New York: Twayne, 1992.

Cottrell, Alan P. *Goethe's Faust: Seven Essays.* Chapel Hill, NC: University of North Carolina Press, 1976.

Durrani, Osman. *Faust and the Bible: A Study of Goethe's Use of Scriptural Allusions and Christian Religious Motifs in Faust I and II.* Berne: Lang, 1977.

Emrich, Wilhelm. *Die Symbolik von 'Faust II': Sinn und Vorformen.* Frankfurt am Main and Bonn: Athenäum, 1957.

Haile, H. G. *Invitation to Goethe's Faust.* University, AL: University of Alabama Press, 1978.

Hamlin, Cyrus (ed.). *Faust: A Tragedy*, trans. by Walter Arndt, commentary by Cyrus Hamlin. 2nd edn, New York: Norton, 2000.

HölscherLohmeyer, Dorothea. *Faust und die Welt: Der zweite Teil der Dichtung: Eine Anleitung zum Lesen des Textes.* Munich: Beck, 1975.

Keller, Werner (ed.). *Aufsätze zu Goethes 'Faust I'.* 3rd edn, Darmstadt: Wissenschaftliche Buchgesellschaft, 1991.

Aufsätze zu Goethes 'Faust II'. Darmstadt: Wissenschaftliche Buchgesellschaft, 1992.

Kittler, Friedrich. 'The Scholar's Tragedy: Prelude in the Theater'. In *Discourse Networks 1800/1900* (Stanford: Stanford University Press, 1990), pp. 3–24.

Mason, Eudo C. *Goethe's Faust: Its Genesis and Purport.* Berkeley: University of California Press, 1967.

Moretti, Franco. 'Faust and the Nineteenth Century'. In *Modern Epic: The World-System from Goethe to Garcia Marquez* (London: Verso, 1996), pp. 9–98.

Requadt, Paul. *Goethes Faust I: Leitmotivik und Architektur.* Munich: Fink, 1972.

Weinrich, Harald. 'Faust's Forgetting'. *Modern Language Quarterly* 55 (1994), 281–95.

PROSE FICTION

Adler, Jeremy. *'Eine fast magische Anziehungskraft': Goethes 'Wahlverwandt-schaften' und die Chemie seiner Zeit.* Munich: Beck, 1987.

Bahr, Ehrhard. *The Novel as Archive: the Genesis, Reception, and Criticism of Goethe's 'Wilhelm Meisters Wanderjahre'.* Columbia, SC: Camden House, 1998.

Barnes, H. G. *Goethe's 'Die Wahlverwandtschaften': a Literary Interpretation.* Oxford: Oxford University Press, 1976.

Blackall, Eric. *Goethe and the Novel.* Ithaca and New York: Cornell University Press, 1976.

Blair, John. *Tracing Subversive Currents in Goethe's 'Wilhelm Meister's Apprenticeship'.* Columbia, SC: Camden House, 1997.

Blessin, Stefan. *Erzählstruktur und Leserhandlung: Zur Theorie der literarischen Kommunikation am Beispiel von Goethes 'Wahlverwandtschaften'.* Heidelberg: Winter, 1974.

Die Romane Goethes. Königstein im Taunus: Athenäum, 1979.

Brown, Jane K. *Goethe's Cyclical Narratives: 'Die Unterhaltungen deutscher Ausgewanderten' and 'Wilhelm Meisters Wanderjahre'.* Chapel Hill, NC: University of North Carolina Press, 1975.

Gille, Klaus F. *Wilhelm Meister im Urteil seiner Zeitgenossen.* Assen: Van Gorcum, 1971.

Herrmann, Hans Peter (ed.). *Goethes 'Werther': Kritik und Forschung.* Darmstadt: Wissenschaftliche Buchgesellschaft, 1994.

Jäger, Georg. *Die Leiden des alten und neuen Werther.* Munich: Hanser, 1984.

Lillyman, W. J. (ed.). *Goethe's Narrative Fiction. The Irvine Symposium.* Berlin and New York: de Gruyter, 1983.

Muenzer, Clark. *Figures of Identity: Goethe's Novels and the Enigmatic Self.* University Park, PA and London: Pennsylvania State University Press, 1984.

Reiss, Hans. *Goethe's Novels*. London: Macmillan, 1969.
Rösch, Ewald (ed.). *Goethes Roman 'Die Wahlverwandtschaften'*. Darmstadt: Wissenschaftliche Buchgesellschaft, 1975.
Scherpe, Klaus. *Werther und Wertherwirkung*. Bad Homburg: Gehlen, 1970.
Schlechta, Karl. *Goethes Wilhelm Meister*. Frankfurt am Main: Suhrkamp, 1985.
Steiner, Jacob. *Goethes 'Wilhelm Meister': Sprache und Stilwandel*. Stuttgart: Kohlhammer, 1966.
Swales, Martin. *Goethe: 'The Sorrows of Young Werther'*. Cambridge: Cambridge University Press, 1987.
Witte, Bernd (ed.). *Goethe-Handbuch*, vol. III: *Prosaschriften*. Stuttgart: Metzler, 1997.

AUTOBIOGRAPHY

Boerner, Peter. *'Italienische Reise'*. In Paul Michael Lützeler and James E. McLeod (eds.), *Goethes Erzählwerk: Interpretationen* (Stuttgart: Reclam, 1985), pp. 344–62.
Boeschenstein, Hermann. *'Tag- und Jahreshefte*: A New Type of Autobiography'. *German Life and Letters* 10 (1956–7), 169–76.
Bowman, Derek. *Life into Autobiography: A Study of Goethe's 'Dichtung und Wahrheit'*. Berne: Lang, 1971.
Boyle, Nicholas (with additional material by John Kington). 'Goethe in Paestum: a Higher-Critical Look at the *Italienische Reise*'. *Oxford German Studies* 20/21 (1991–2), 18–31.
Brown, Robert H. 'The "Demonic" Earthquake: Goethe's Myth of the Lisbon Earthquake and Fear of Modern Change'. *German Studies Review* 15 (1992), 475–91.
Brude-Firnau, Gisela. *'Aus meinem Leben: Dichtung und Wahrheit'*. In Paul Michael Lützeler and James E. McLeod (eds.), *Goethes Erzählwerk: Interpretationen* (Stuttgart: Reclam, 1985), pp. 319–43.
Cardinal, Roger. 'The Passionate Traveller: Goethe in Italy'. *Publications of the English Goethe Society* 67 (1997), 17–32.
Fisher, Richard. ' "Dichter" and "Geschichte": Goethe's *Campagne in Frankreich*'. *Goethe Yearbook* 4 (1988), 235–74.
Gould, Robert. 'The Functions of the Non-Literary Quotations in Part 4 of *Dichtung und Wahrheit*'. *German Life and Letters* 44 (1991), 291–305.
Larkin, Edward T. *War in Goethe's Writings: Representation and Assessment*. Lewiston, Queenston and Lampeter: Mellen, 1992.
Pascal, Roy. *Design and Truth in Autobiography*. London: Routledge & Kegan Paul, 1960.
Plenderleith, H. Jane. 'An Approach to Goethe's Treatment of Religion in *Dichtung und Wahrheit*'. *German Life and Letters* 46 (1993), 297–310.
Reiss, Hans. 'Goethe on War: Some Reflections on *Campagne in Frankreich*'. *Publications of the English Goethe Society* 53 (1982–3), 98–123.
Ronell, Avital. *Dictations: On Haunted Writing*. Bloomington, IN: Indiana University Press, 1986.
Rüdiger, Horst. 'Zur Komposition von Goethes *Zweitem römischen Aufenthalt*: Das melodramatische Finale und die Novelle von der "schönen Mailänderin"'. In Stanley A. Corngold, Michael Curschmann, and Theodore J. Ziolkowski

(eds.), *Aspekte der Goethezeit* (Göttingen: Vandenhoeck & Ruprecht, 1977), pp. 97–114.

Saine, Thomas P. 'Goethe's Novel: Campagne in Frankreich'. In William J. Lillyman (ed.), *Goethe's Narrative Fiction: The Irvine Goethe Symposium* (Berlin: de Gruyter, 1983), pp. 193–223.

Wackerl, Georg. *Goethes 'Tag- und Jahres-Hefte'*. Berlin: de Gruyter, 1970.

Weisinger, Kenneth D. 'Fathering the Canon: The Correspondence between Goethe and Schiller'. In Gerhart Hoffmeister (ed.), *A Reassessment of Weimar Classicism* (Lewiston, Queenston and Lampeter: Mellen, 1996), pp. 77–95.

Zapperi, Robert. *Das Inkognito: Goethes ganz andere Existenz in Rom*. Trans. Ingeborg Walter. Munich: Beck, 1999.

GOETHE AND THE NATURAL SCIENCES

Amrine, F., F. J. Zucker and H. Wheeler (eds.). *Goethe and the Sciences: A Reappraisal*. Dordrecht: Reidel, 1987.

Böhme, G. *Am Ende des Baconischen Zeitalters. Studien zur Wissenschaftsentwicklung*. Frankfurt am Main: Suhrkamp, 1993.

Böhme, H. *Natur und Subjekt*. Frankfurt am Main: Suhrkamp, 1988.

Bortoft, H. *Goethe's Scientific Consciousness*. Tunbridge Wells: ICR, 1986.

Feyerabend, P. *Against Method*. London: Verso, 1988.

Fink, K. J. *Goethe's History of Science*. Cambridge: Cambridge University Press, 1991.

Gould, Stephen Jay. 'More Light on Leaves'. *Natural History* 2 (1991), 16–23.

Hanson, N. R. *Patterns of Discovery. An Inquiry into the Conceptual Foundations of Science*. Cambridge: Cambridge University Press, 1958.

Henderson, F. 'Goethe's Naturphilosophie' (review essay on R. H. Stephenson, *Goethe's Conception of Knowledge and Science*, Edinburgh: Edinburgh University Press, 1995). *Studies in the History and Philosophy of Science* 29/1 (1998), 143–53.

Kuhn, T. S. *The Structure of Scientific Revolutions*. Chicago: Chicago University Press, 1970.

Lenoir, T. 'The Göttingen School and the Development of Transcendental Naturphilosophie in the Romantic Era'. *Studies in the History of Biology* 5 (1981), 111–205.

Miller, D. (ed.). *Scientific Studies*. Vol. XII of *Goethe: The Collected Works in 12 Volumes*. Princeton University Press, 1995.

Nisbet, H. B. *Goethe and the Scientific Tradition*. London: Institute of Germanic Studies, 1972.

Nyhart, Lynn K. *Biology Takes Form. Animal Morphology and the German Universities, 1800–1900*. Chicago and London: University of Chicago Press, 1995.

Rehbock, T. *Goethe und die 'Rettung der Phänomene'. Philosophische Kritik des naturwissenschaftlichen Weltbilds am Beispiel der Farbenlehre*. Konstanz: Verlag am Hockgraben, 1995.

Ribe, N. M. 'Goethe's Critique of Newton. A Reconsideration'. *Studies in the History and Philosophy of Science* 16/4 (1985), 315–35.

Russell, E. S. *Form and Function. A Contribution to the History of Animal Morphology*. London: John Murray, 1916.

Schmidt, A. *Goethes herrlich leuchtende Natur. Philosophische Studien zur deutschen Spätaufklärung.* Munich and Vienna: Hanser, 1984.

Seamon, D. and A. Zajonc (eds.). *Goethe's Way of Science. A Phenomenology of Nature.* Albany, NY: State University of New York Press, 1998.

Sepper, D. L. *Goethe contra Newton. Polemics and the Project for a New Science of Colour.* Cambridge: Cambridge University Press, 1988.

Sherrington, C. *Goethe on Nature and on Science.* Cambridge: Cambridge University Press, 1949.

Steuer, D. *Die stillen Grenzen der Theorie. Übergänge zwischen Sprache und Erfahrung bei Goethe und Wittgenstein.* Cologne, Weimar and Vienna: Böhlau, 1999.

GOETHE AND GENDER

Becker-Cantarino, Barbara. 'Goethe as a Critic of Literary Women'. In Karl Fink (ed.), *Goethe as a Literary Critic* (Washington: University Press of America, 1984), pp. 160–81.

'The Discourse of Patriarchy in Goethe's *Wilhelm Meister*'. *Neohelicon* 20 (1993), 137–53.

'Witch and Infanticide: Imaging the Female in Goethe's *Faust I*'. *Goethe Yearbook* 7 (1994), 152–75.

Bovenschen, Silvia. *Die imaginierte Weiblichkeit. Exemplarische Untersuchungen zu kulturgeschichtlichen und literarischen Präsentationsformen des Weiblichen.* Frankfurt am Main: Suhrkamp, 1979.

Crawford, Mary Caroline. *Goethe and His Women* (1911). Reprint: New York: Haskell House, 1973.

Damm, Sigrid. *Christiane und Goethe. Eine Recherche.* Frankfurt am Main: Insel, 1998.

Eissler, Kurt Robert. *Goethe: A Psychoanalytic Study.* Detroit: Wayne State University Press, 1963.

Elsaghe, Yahya A. 'Wilhelm Meisters letzter Brief. Homosexualität und Nekrophilie bei Goethe'. *Forum Homosexualität und Literatur* 24 (1995), 5–36.

Graham, Ilse A. 'Von Eva zu Ave. Über die Würde des Verworfenen in Goethe's *Faust*'. In Hans-Joachim Mähl and E. Mannack (eds.), *Studien zur Goethezeit. Erich Trunz zum 75. Geburtstag* (Heidelberg: Winter, 1981), pp. 63–89.

Hart, Gail. *Tragedy in Paradise. Family and Gender Politics in German Bourgeois Tragedy 1750–1850.* Columbia, SC: Camden House, 1996.

Herwig, Henriette. *Das ewig Männliche zieht uns hinab: 'Wilhelm Meisters Wanderjahre'. Geschlechterdifferenz, sozialer Wandel, historische Anthropologie.* Tübingen and Basel: Francke, 1997.

Kuzniar, Alice (ed.). *Outing Goethe and His Age.* Stanford: Stanford University Press, 1996.

Lange Sigrid. *Die Utopie des Weiblichen im Drama Goethes, Schillers und Kleists.* Frankfurt am Main: Lang, 1993.

Mahlendorf, Ursula. 'The Mystery of Mignon: Object Relations, Abandonment, Child Abuse, and Narrative Structure'. *Goethe Yearbook* 7 (1994), 23–39.

Rigby, Catherine E. *Transgressions of the Feminine. Tragedy, Enlightenment and the Figure of Woman in Classical German Drama.* Heidelberg: Winter, 1996.

Schlaffer, Hannelore. 'Goethe als Muse. Der Autor und die Schriftstellerinnen seiner Zeit'. *Goethe-Jahrbuch* 112 (1995), 183–95.

Seele, Astrid. *Frauen um Goethe*. Reinbek: Rowohlt, 1997.

Simpson, James. *Goethe and Patriarchy. Faust and the Fates of Desire*. Oxford: European Humanities Research Centre, 1998.

Willim, Petra. *So frei geboren wie ein Mann? Frauengestalten im Werk Goethes*. Frankfurt am Main: Ulrike Helmer Verlag, 1997.

GOETHE AND THE VISUAL ARTS

Alewyn, Richard. 'Goethe und die Antike'. In *Probleme und Gestalten. Essays* (Frankfurt am Main: Suhrkamp, 1982), pp. 255–70.

Allert, Beate. 'Text-Image-Relations: Seeing and Antiocular Discourse in Berkeley, Jean Paul, and Goethe'. In Werner Schneiders, Jane Godden et al. (eds.), *Transactions of the Ninth International Congress on the Enlightenment: Actes du Neuvième congrès international des Lumières* (Studies on Voltaire and the Eighteenth Century 346–8) (Oxford: Voltaire Foundation, 1996), vol. II, pp. 789–92.

'Hidden Aspects of Goethe's Writings on Color, Seeing, and Motion and their Significance for a Cultural Vision Theory'. In Laura Doyle (ed.), *Bodies of Resistance: Phenomenology, Agency, Culture*, Evanston: Northwestern University Press, 2001 (forthcoming).

Beckmann, Peter. 'Zur Semiotik der Straßburger Münsterfassade und der beiden Goethe-Aufsätze "Von deutscher Baukunst" (1772; 1823)'. *Kodikas* 13: 3/4 (1990), 151–75.

Bergmann, Günther. *Goethe – Der Zeichner und Maler. Ein Porträt*. Munich: Callwey, 1999.

Geary, John (ed.). *Goethe: Essays on Art and Literature*. Translated by Ellen von Nardroff and Ernest H. von Nardoff. Vol. III of *Goethe. The Collected Works in 12 volumes*. Princeton, NJ: Princeton University Press, 1986.

Goethe on Art. Selected, edited, and translated by John Gage. Berkeley, CA: University of California Press, 1980.

Kovalevski, Bärbel. *Zwischen Ideal und Wirklichkeit: Künstlerinnen der Goethe-Zeit zwischen 1750 und 1850*. Ostfildern-Ruit: Hatje, 1999.

Lichtenstern, Christa. *Die Wirkungsgeschichte der Metamorphosenlehre Goethes. Von Philipp Otto Runge bis Joseph Beuys*. Weinheim: VCH, Acta Humaniora, 1990.

Maisak, Petra. *Johann Wolfgang Goethe: Zeichnungen*. Stuttgart: Reclam, 1996.

Muenzer, Clark. ' "Ihr ältesten, würdigsten Denkmäler der Zeit." Goethe's "Über den Granit" and his Aesthetics of Monuments'. In Richard Fisher (ed.), *Ethik und Ästhetik: Werke und Werte in der Literatur vom 18. bis zum 20. Jahrhundert. Festschrift für Wolfgang Wittkowski zum 70 Geburtstag* (Frankfurt am Main: Lang, 1995), pp. 181–98.

Osterkamp, Ernst. *Im Buchstabenbilde: Studien zum Verfahren Goethescher Bildbeschreibungen*. Stuttgart: Metzler, 1991.

Pörksen, Uwe. *Raumzeit: Goethes Zeitbegriff, abgelesen an seinen sprachlichen und zeichnerischen Naturstudien*. Mainz: Akademie der Wissenschaften und der Literatur / Stuttgart: Steiner, 1999.

Robson-Scott, W. D. *The Younger Goethe and the Visual Arts*. Cambridge: Cambridge University Press, 1965.

Schulze, Sabine (ed.). *Goethe und die Kunst*. Stuttgart: Hatje, 1994.

Strohschneider-Kohrs, Ingrid. 'Bilder und Gegenbilder der Antike-Rezeption'. In *Poesie und Reflexion: Aufsätze zur Literatur* (Tübingen: Niemeyer, 1999), pp. 249–76.

Trevelyan, Humphry, *Goethe and the Greeks* (1941). Foreword by Hugh Lloyd-Jones. 1st paperback edn, Cambridge: Cambridge University Press, 1981.

Zajonc, Arthur. *Catching the Light: The Entwined History of Light and Mind*. New York and Toronto: Bantam Books, 1993.

RELIGION AND PHILOSOPHY

Bell, David. *Spinoza in Germany from 1670 to the Age of Goethe*. London: Institute of Germanic Studies, 1984.

Bollacher, Martin. *Der junge Goethe und Spinoza*. Tübingen: Niemeyer, 1969.

Cassirer, Ernst. 'Goethe and the Kantian Philosophy'. In *Rousseau, Kant, Goethe. Two Essays* (Princeton, NJ: Princeton University Press, 1970), pp. 61–98.

Gray, Ronald Douglas. *Goethe the Alchemist*. Cambridge: Cambridge University Press, 1952.

Grützmacher, Richard Heinrich. *Die Religionen in der Anschauung Goethes*. Baden-Baden: P. Keppler, 1950.

Mason, Eudo C. 'Goethe's sense of evil'. *Publications of the English Goethe Society* 34 (1964), 1–53.

Molnár, Géza von. *Goethes Kantstudien*. Weimar: Böhlau, 1994.

Schmitz, Hermann. *Goethes Altersdenken im problemgeschichtlichen Zusammenhang*. Bonn: Bouvier, 1959.

Schrimpf, Hans Joachim. *Das Weltbild des späten Goethe*. Stuttgart: Kohlhammer, 1956.

Thielicke, Helmut. *Goethe und das Christentum*. Munich: Piper, 1982.

Vietor, Karl. *Goethe the Thinker*. Cambridge, MA: Harvard University Press, 1950.

Zimmermann, Rolf Christian. *Das Weltbild des jungen Goethe*. 2 vols. Munich: Fink, 1969–79.

RECEPTION IN GERMANY AND ABROAD

Atkins, Stuart P. *The Testament of Werther in Poetry and Drama*. Cambridge, MA: Harvard University Press, 1949.

Boyd, James. *Goethe's Knowledge of English Literature*. Oxford: Oxford University Press, 1932.

Dédeyan, Charles. *Le Thème de Faust dans la littérature européenne*. 4 vols. Paris: Lettres modernes, 1954–67.

Eliot, T. S. 'Goethe as the Sage'. In *On Poetry and Poets* (1935; New York: Farrar, 1957), pp. 240–64.

Furst, Lilian. *Romanticism in Perspective. A Comparative Study of Aspects of the Romantic Movements in England, France and Germany*. London and Melbourne: Macmillan, 1969.

Heitmann, Klaus (ed.). *Europäische Romantik II*. Vol. xv of *Neues Handbuch der Literaturwissenschaft*. Wiesbaden: Athenaion, 1982.

Hoffmeister, Gerhart. 'Goethe's Faust and the theatrum mundi-tradition in European Romanticism'. *Journal of European Studies* 13 (special edn: *Perspectives on Faust*, ed. by Michael Palencia-Roth, 1983), 42–55.

Goethe und die europäische Romantik (1295). Tübingen and Basel: Francke, 1984.

Deutsche und europäische Romantik (Sammlung Metzler, 170). 2nd edn, Stuttgart: Metzler, 1990.

Hoffmeister, Gerhart (ed.). *European Romanticism. Literary Cross-Currents, Modes, and Models*. Detroit, MI: Wayne State University Press, 1990.

A Reassessment of Weimar Classicism. Lewiston, Queenston and Lampeter: Mellen, 1996.

Howe, Susanne. *'Wilhelm Meister' and his English Kinsmen* (1930). Reprint, New York: Columbia University Press, 1966.

Nemoianu, Virgil. *The Taming of Romanticism: European Literature and the Age of the Biedermeier*. Cambridge, MA: Harvard University Press, 1984.

Schanze, Helmut (ed.). *Romantik-Handbuch*. Stuttgart: Kröner, 1994.

Schulz, Gerhard. 'Chaos und Ordnung in Goethes Verständnis von Kunst und Geschichte'. *Goethe-Jahrbuch* 110 (1993), 173–83.

Stockley, V. *German Literature as Known in England 1750–1830*. London: Routledge, 1929; reprint, Port Washington and New York: Kennikat Press, 1969.

Strich, Fritz. *Goethe und die Weltliteratur*. Bern: Francke, 1946; 2nd edn 1957.

Wellek, René. *Concepts of Criticism*. New Haven, CT: Yale University Press, 1963.

Confrontations. Studies in the Intellectual and Literary Relations between Germany, England and the United States during the Nineteenth Century. Princeton, NJ: Princeton University Press, 1965.

GENERAL INDEX

INDEX OF GOETHE'S WORKS

Printed in the United Kingdom
by Lightning Source UK Ltd.
117454UKS00001B/85-90